Parenthesis

Élodie Durand

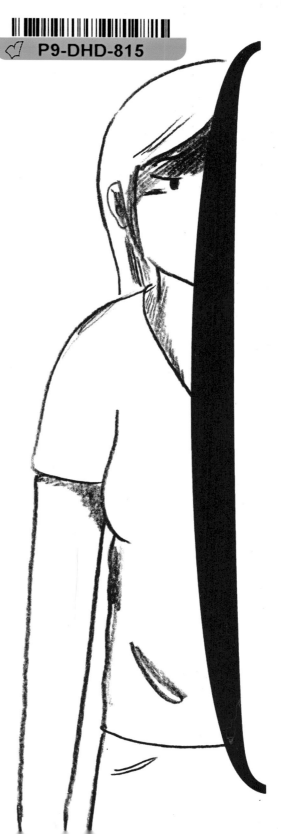

Originally published in French under the following title:
La Parenthèse by Elodie Durand © Editions Delcourt, 2010
English-language translation © 2021 Top Shelf Productions

Published by Top Shelf Productions, an imprint of IDW Publishing, a division of Idea and Design Works, LLC. Offices: Top Shelf Productions, c/o Idea & Design Works, LLC, 2765 Truxtun Road, San Diego, CA 92106. Top Shelf Productions®, the Top Shelf logo, Idea and Design Works®, and the IDW logo are registered trademarks of Idea and Design Works, LLC. All Rights Reserved. With the exception of small excerpts of artwork used for review purposes, none of the contents of this publication may be reprinted without the permission of IDW Publishing. IDW Publishing does not read or accept unsolicited submissions of ideas, stories, or artwork.

Editor-in-Chief: Chris Staros.
Design by Nathan Widick.
Translation by Edward Gauvin.

The drawings on pages 15-19, 37-39, 40-42, 86-89, 182, 184-188, 191-193, and 196-199 were done during the period from 1995 to 1998.

ISBN: 978-1-60309-481-8   25 24 23 22   5 4 3 2

Visit our online catalog at topshelfcomix.com.

Mom,

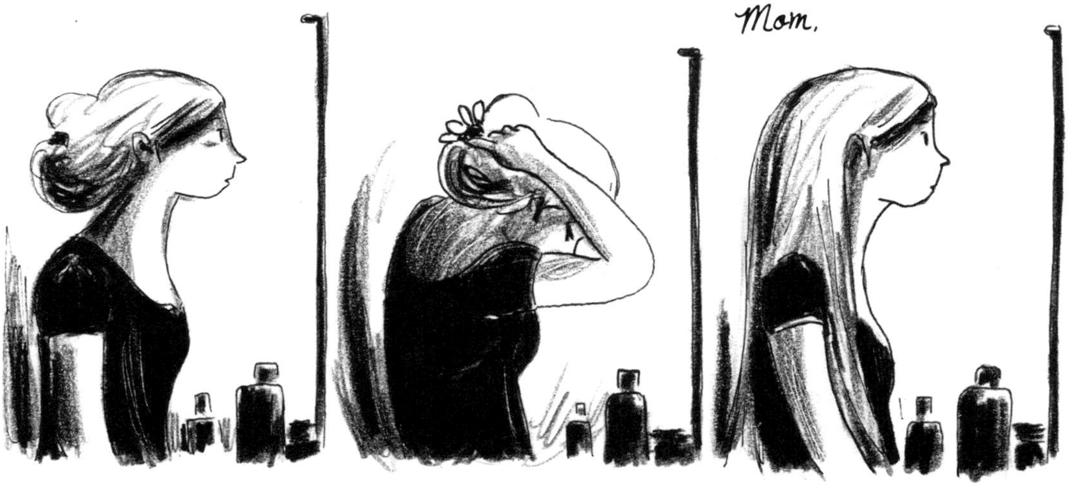

All this happened to me over a decade ago, but even now, we all still talk about it. I know it left a mark on each of us in different ways... For me, it was a brief experience that shaped and upended my first steps toward life as a grown-up...

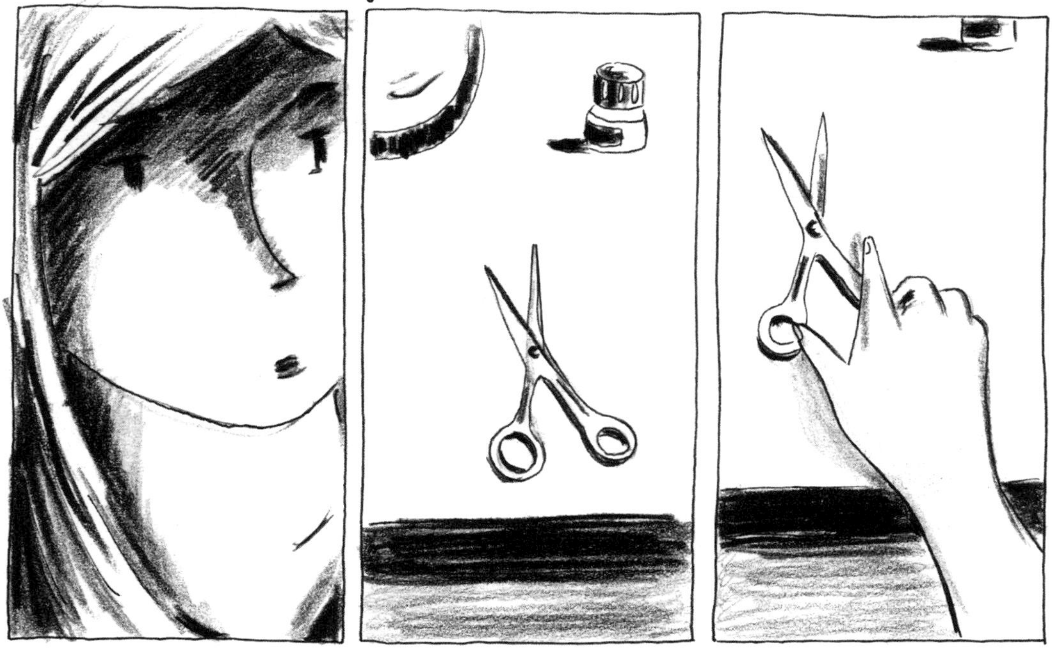

My memories shift and change with time and feelings... I'd like to sort them out, put them in order, so I can hold on to them and not have to think about them anymore.

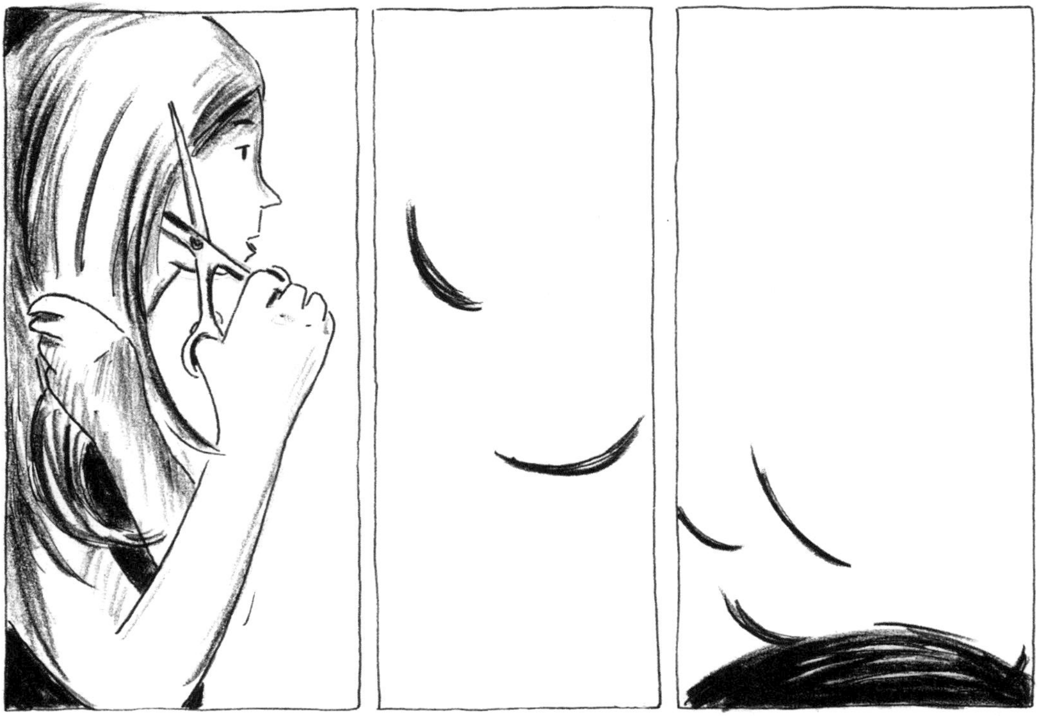

I must've been about 25 when I moved out of my parents' house.
It was a tough decision to make.

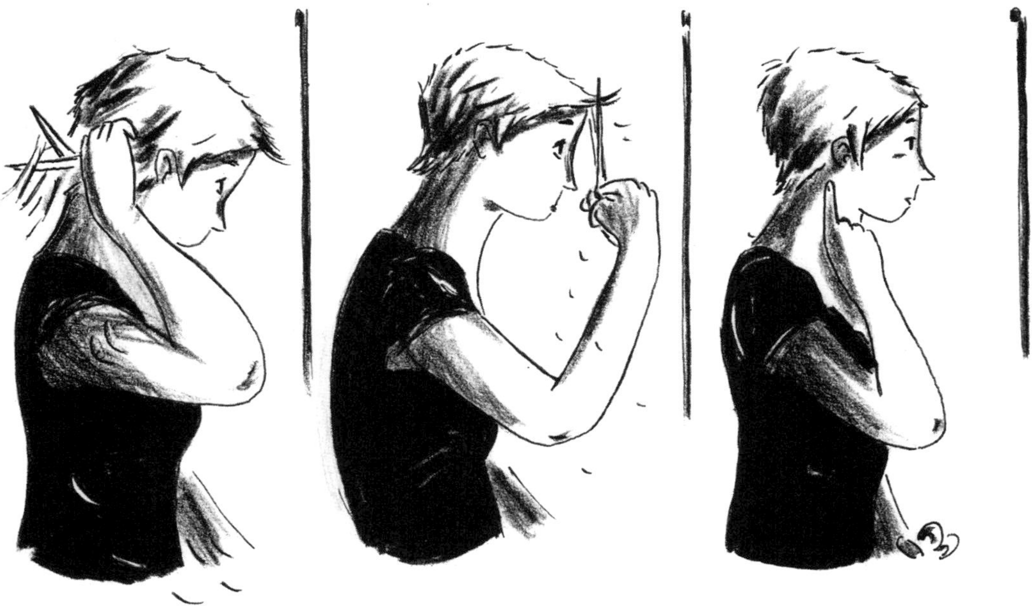

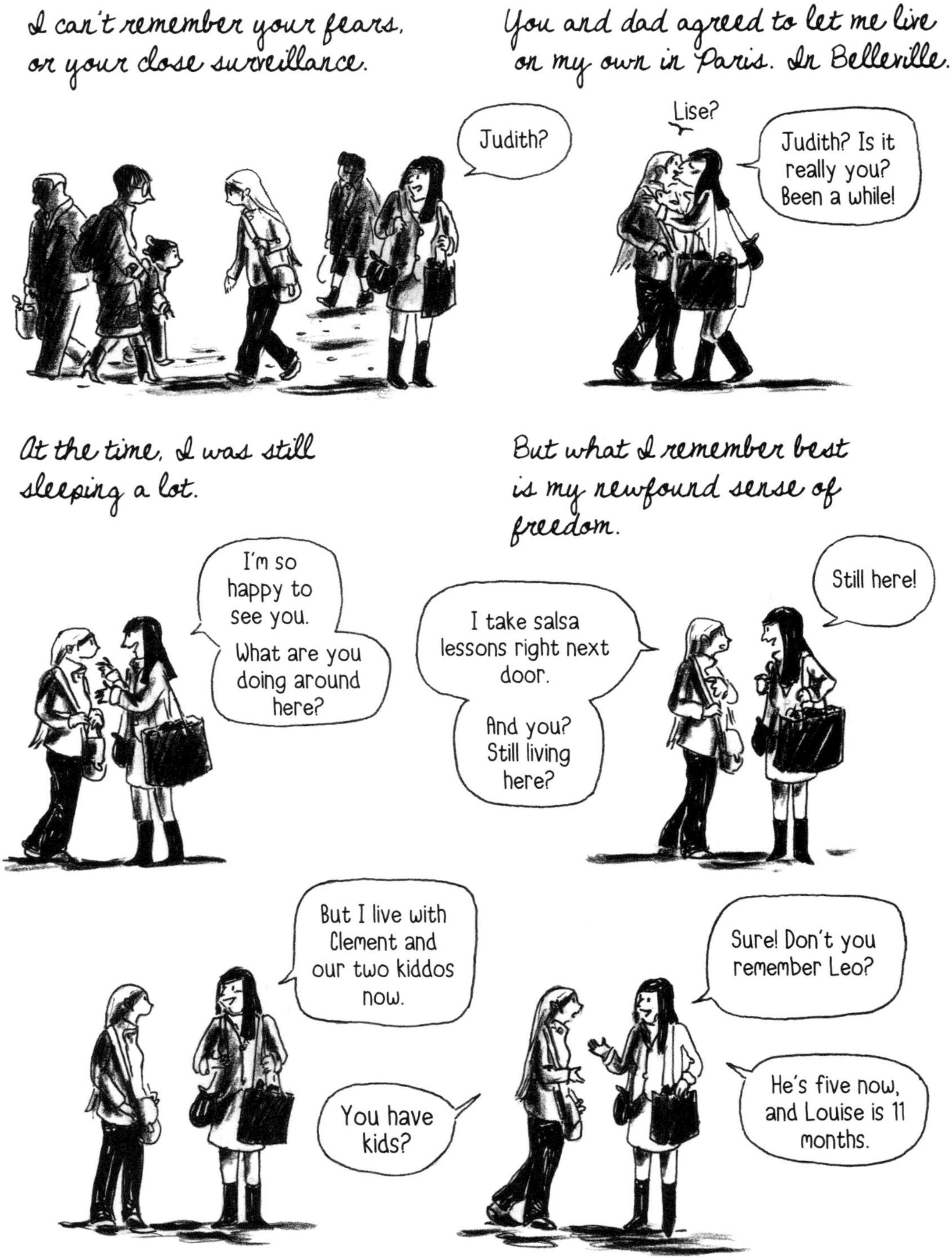
I can't remember your fears, or your close surveillance.
Judith?
You and dad agreed to let me live on my own in Paris. In Belleville.
Lise?
Judith? Is it really you? Been a while!
At the time, I was still sleeping a lot.
I'm so happy to see you.
What are you doing around here?
But what I remember best is my newfound sense of freedom.
I take salsa lessons right next door.
And you? Still living here?
Still here!
But I live with Clement and our two kiddos now.
You have kids?
Sure! Don't you remember Leo?
He's five now, and Louise is 11 months.

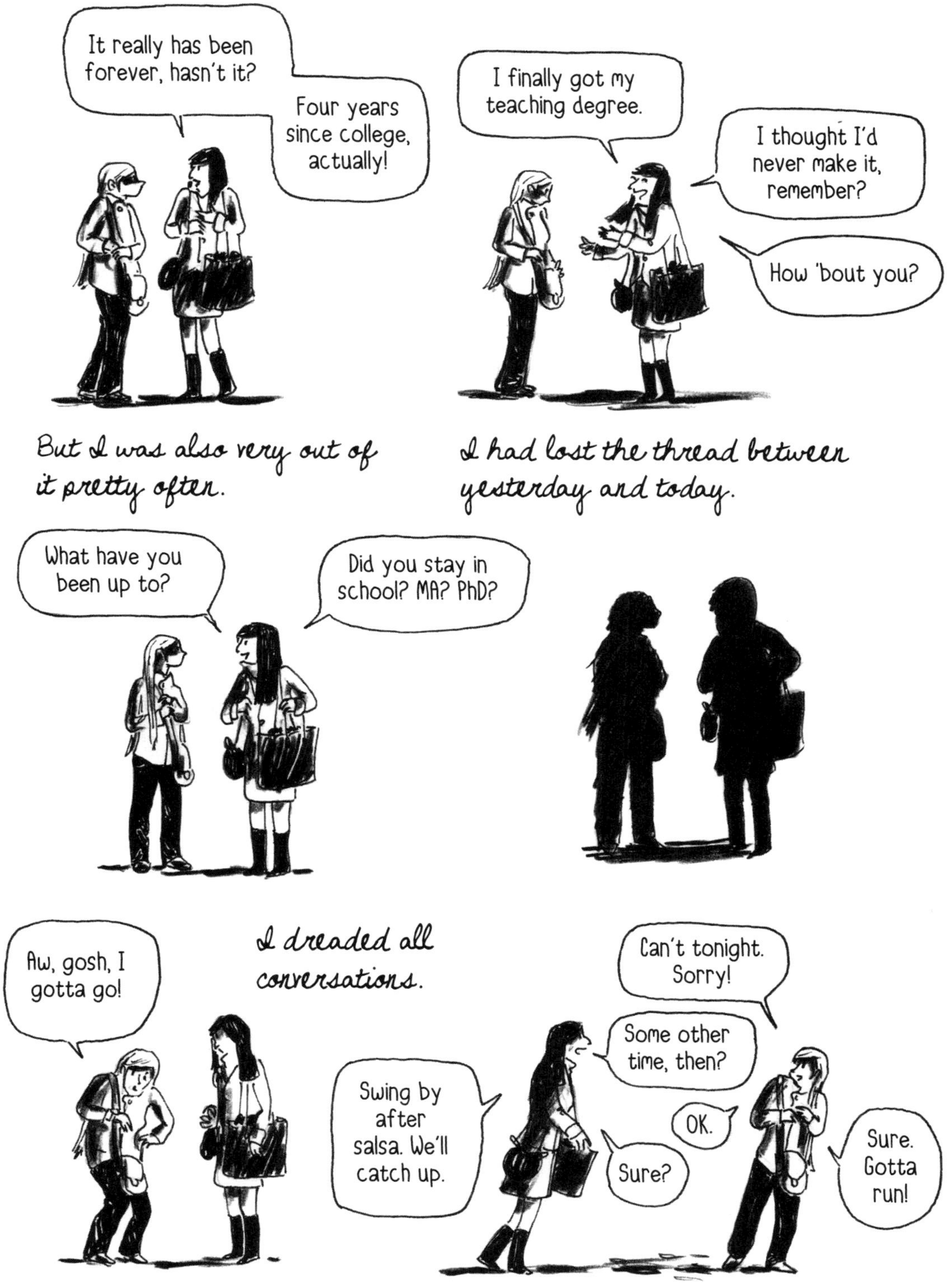
It really has been forever, hasn't it?
Four years since college, actually!
I finally got my teaching degree.
I thought I'd never make it, remember?
How 'bout you?
But I was also very out of it pretty often.
I had lost the thread between yesterday and today.
What have you been up to?
Did you stay in school? MA? PhD?
Aw, gosh, I gotta go!
I dreaded all conversations.
Swing by after salsa. We'll catch up.
Can't tonight. Sorry!
Some other time, then?
OK.
Sure?
Sure. Gotta run!

How 'bout you? What have you been up to? What have you been up to?

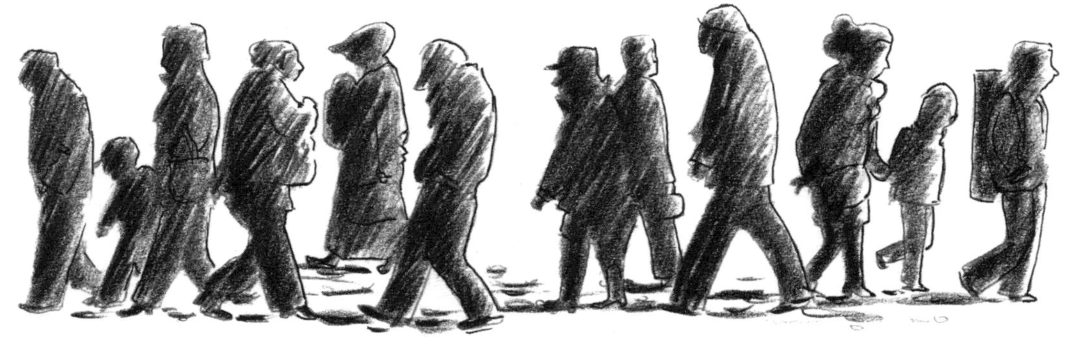

? What have you been up to? What have you been up to? How about you? What have you be

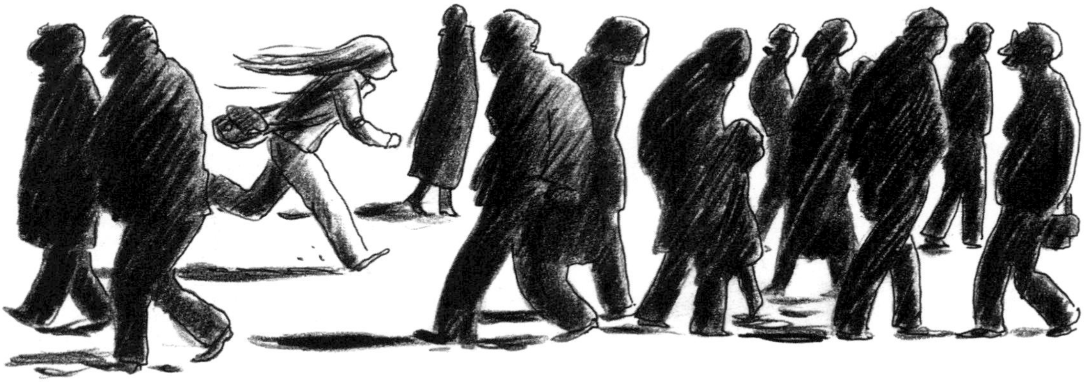

all this time?

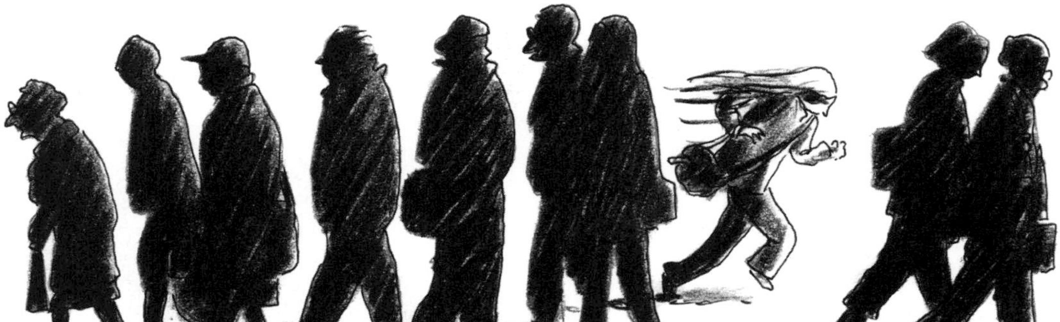

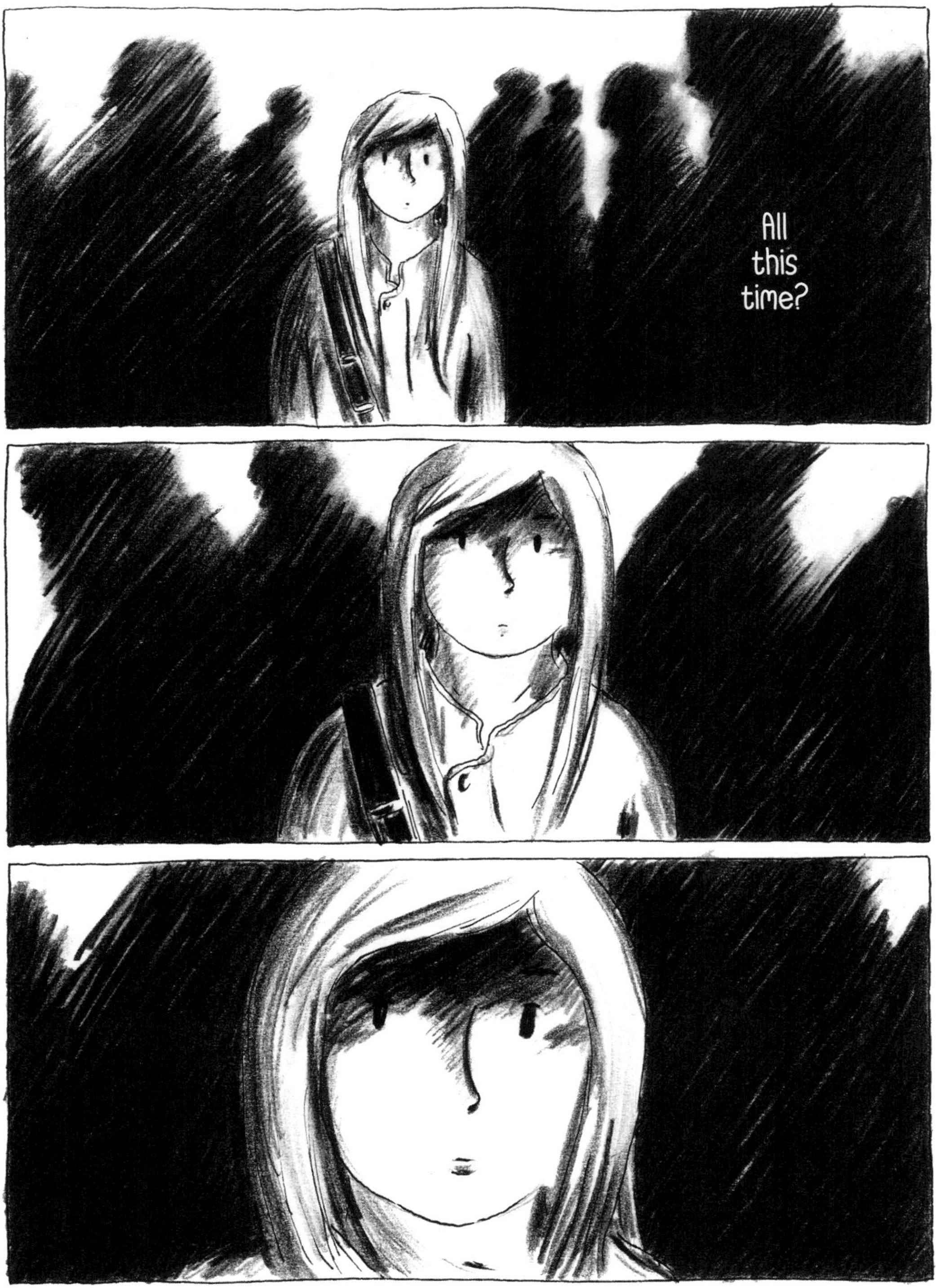
All this time?

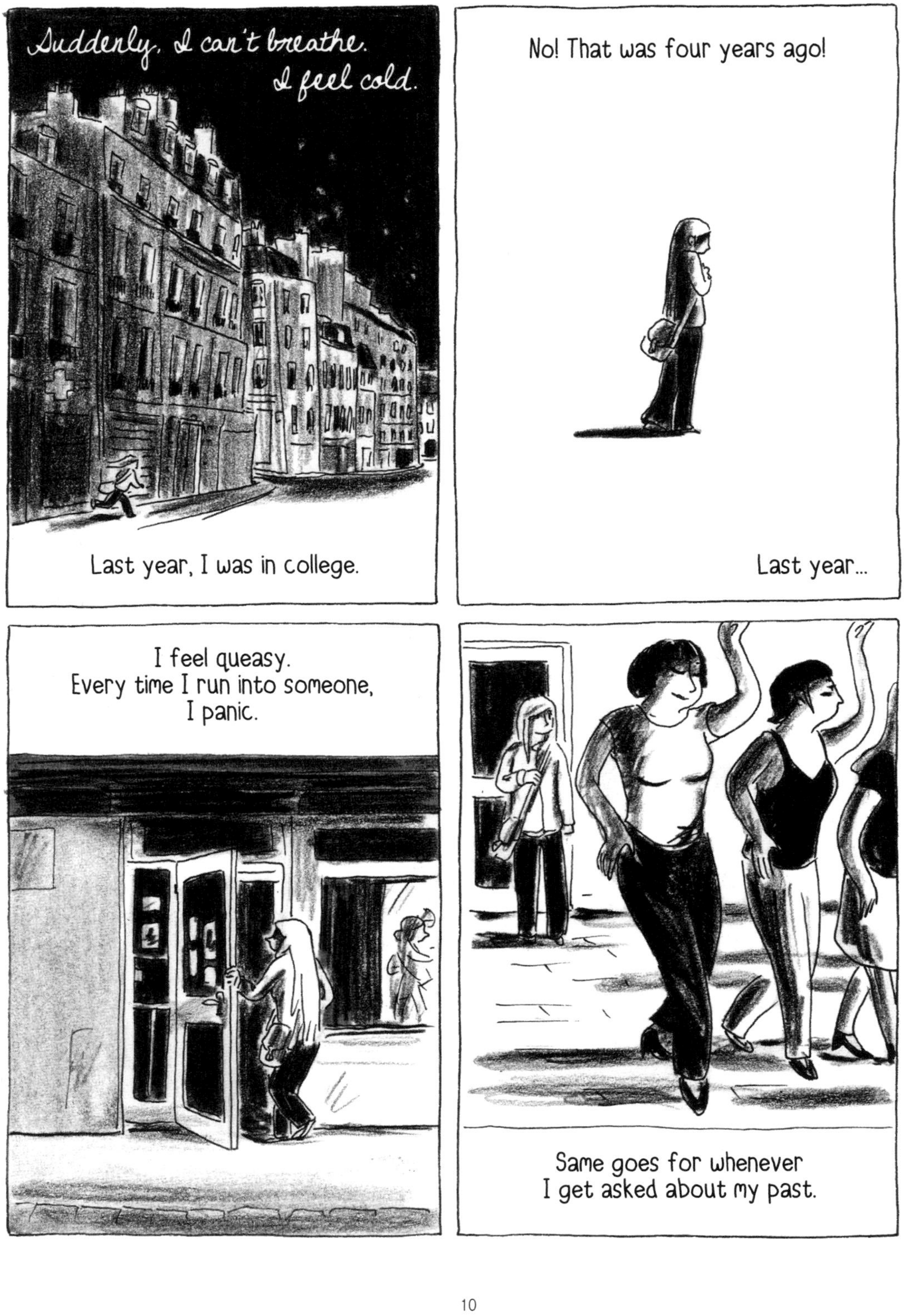
Suddenly, I can't breathe.
I feel cold.
Last year, I was in college.
No! That was four years ago!
Last year...
I feel queasy.
Every time I run into someone,
I panic.
Same goes for whenever
I get asked about my past.

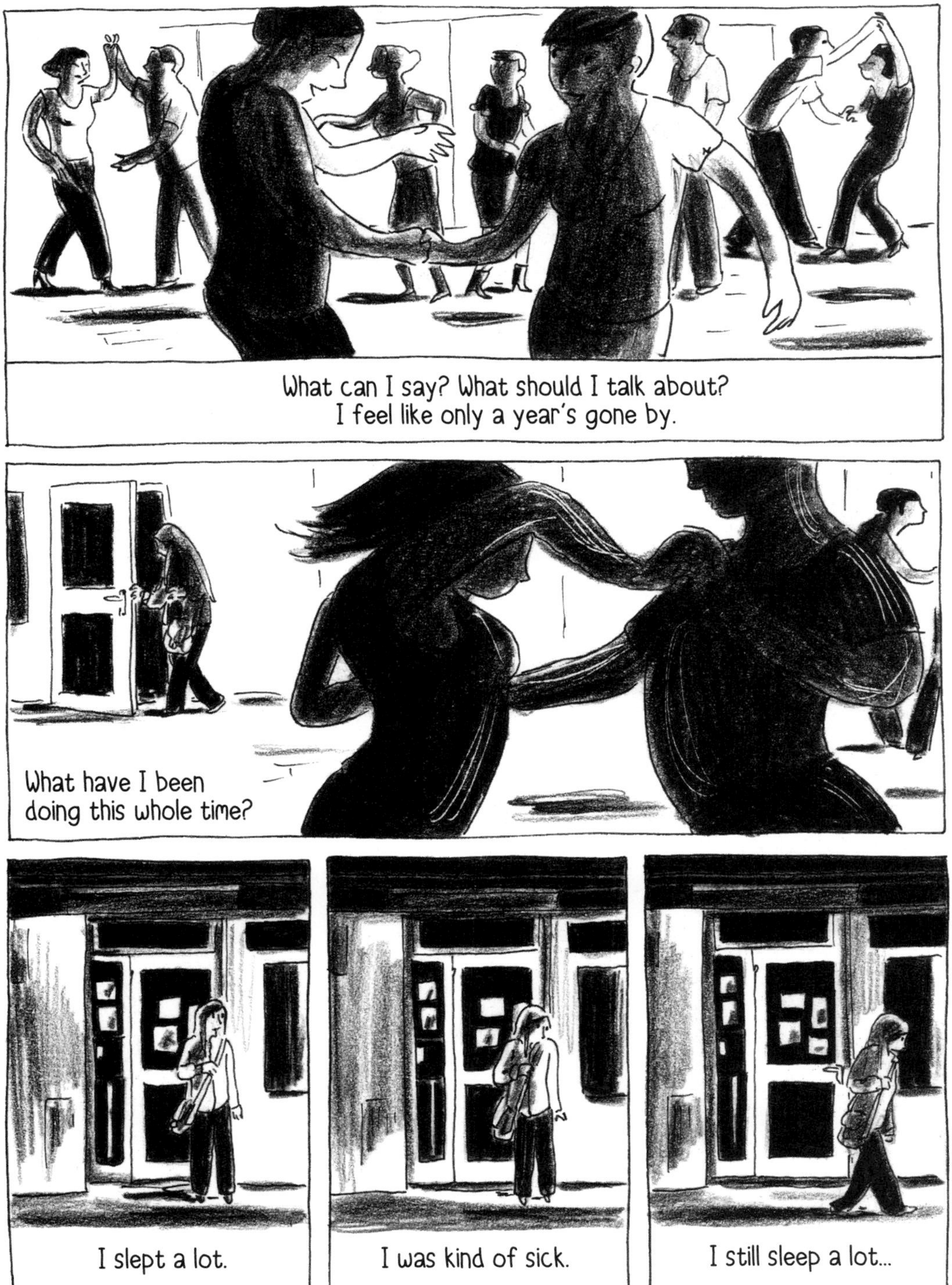
What can I say? What should I talk about?
I feel like only a year's gone by.
What have I been
doing this whole time?
I slept a lot.
I was kind of sick.
I still sleep a lot...

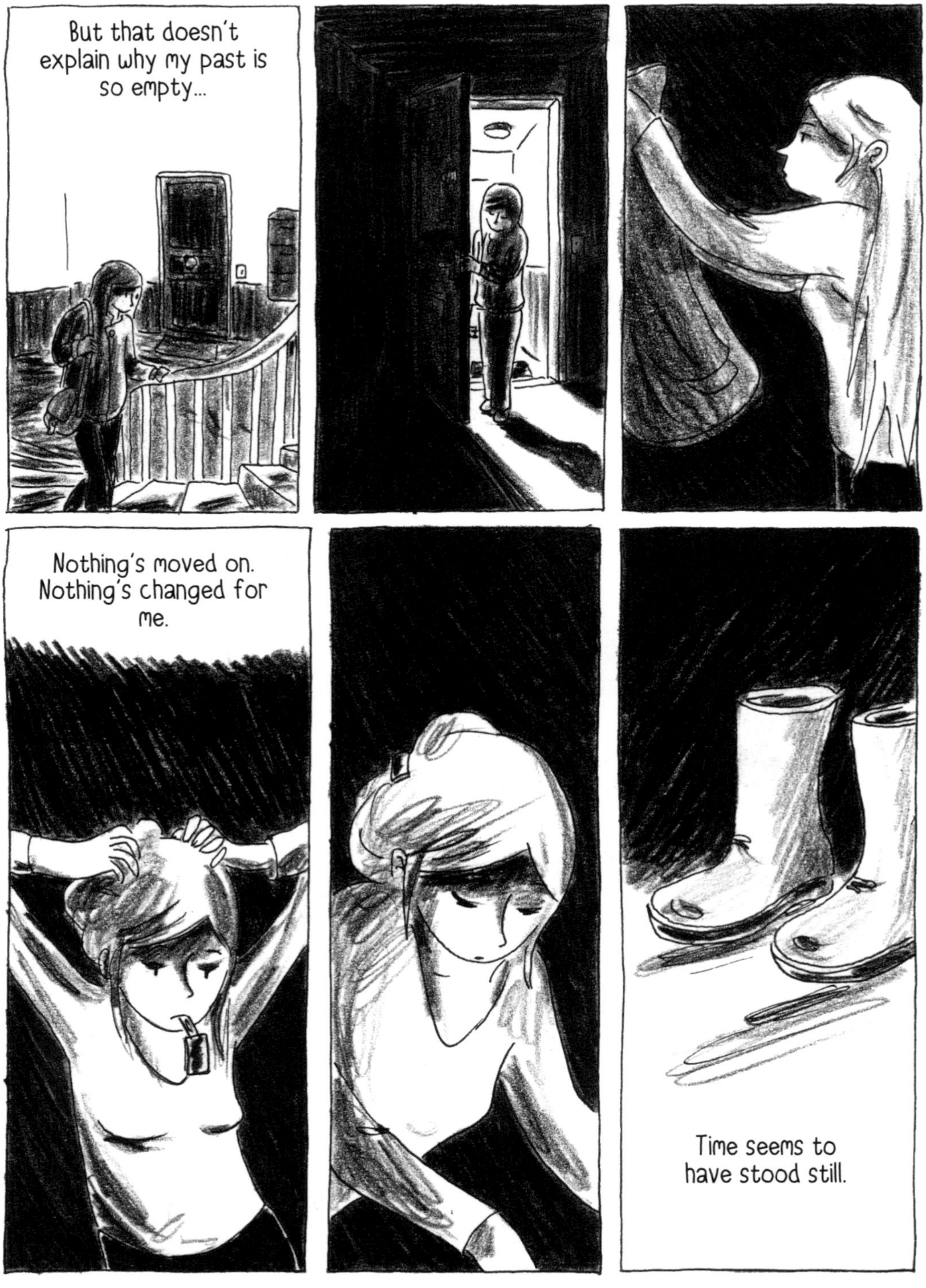
But that doesn't explain why my past is so empty...
Nothing's moved on. Nothing's changed for me.
Time seems to have stood still.

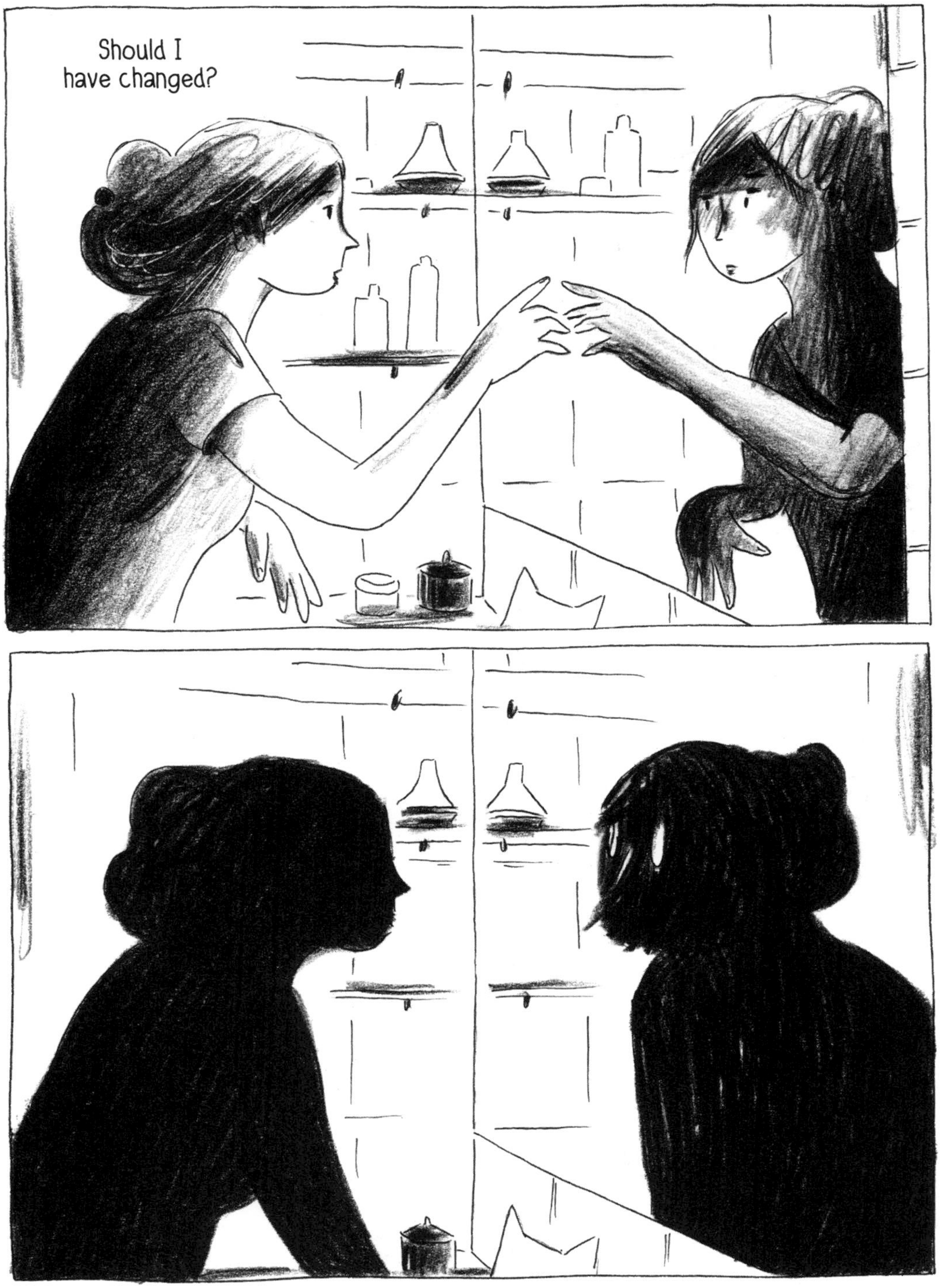
Should I
have changed?

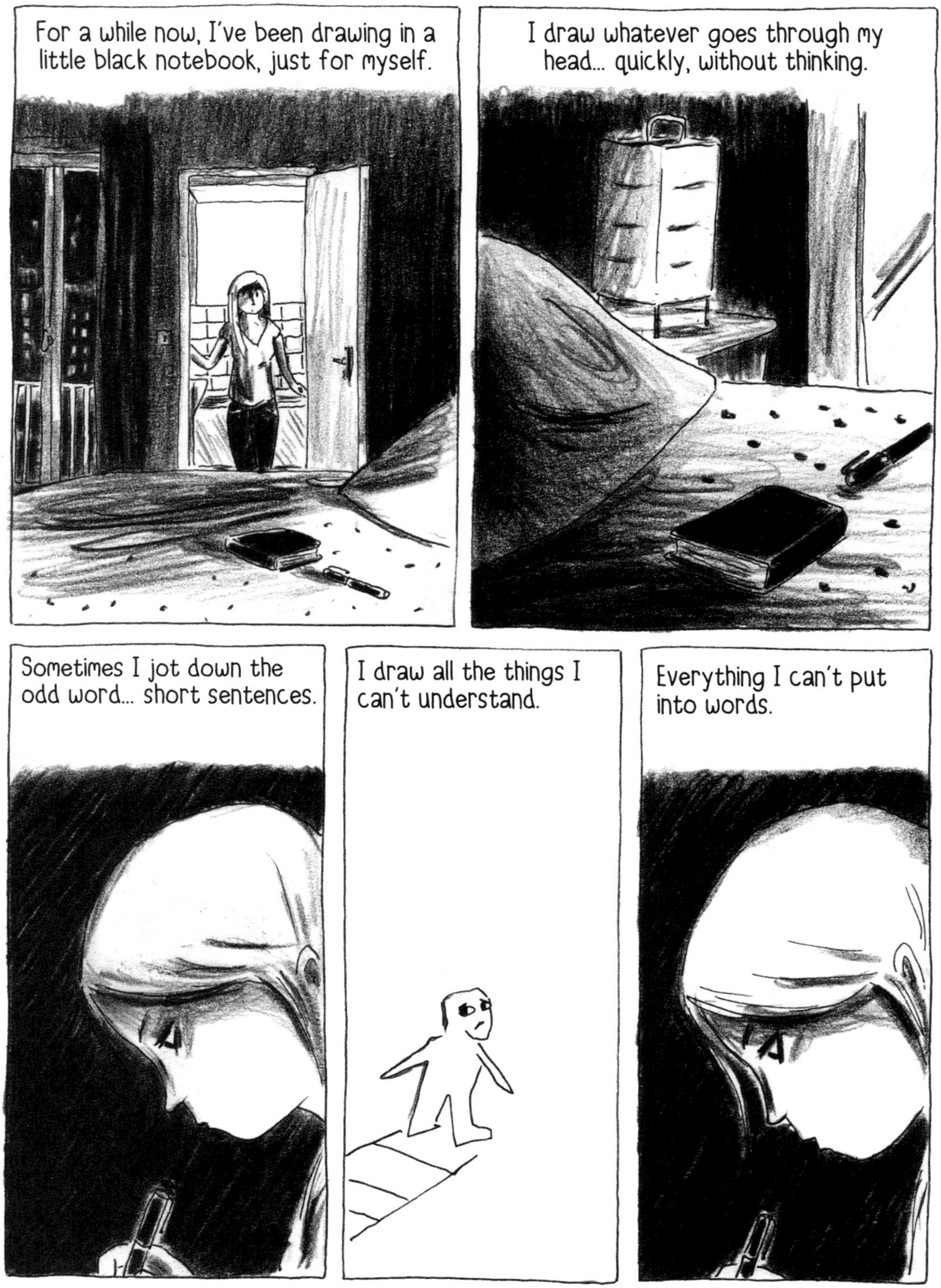
For a while now, I've been drawing in a little black notebook, just for myself.
I draw whatever goes through my head... quickly, without thinking.
Sometimes I jot down the odd word... short sentences.
I draw all the things I can't understand.
Everything I can't put into words.

I have such a hard time focusing...

I can't remember how or why I started doing these drawings anymore. But now I can't live without them.

I think they really help me understand what's happening to me. Help me find words...

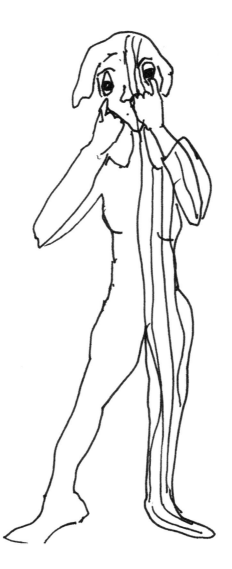

It took me several years to admit it, you know. To understand, and to recover my memories.

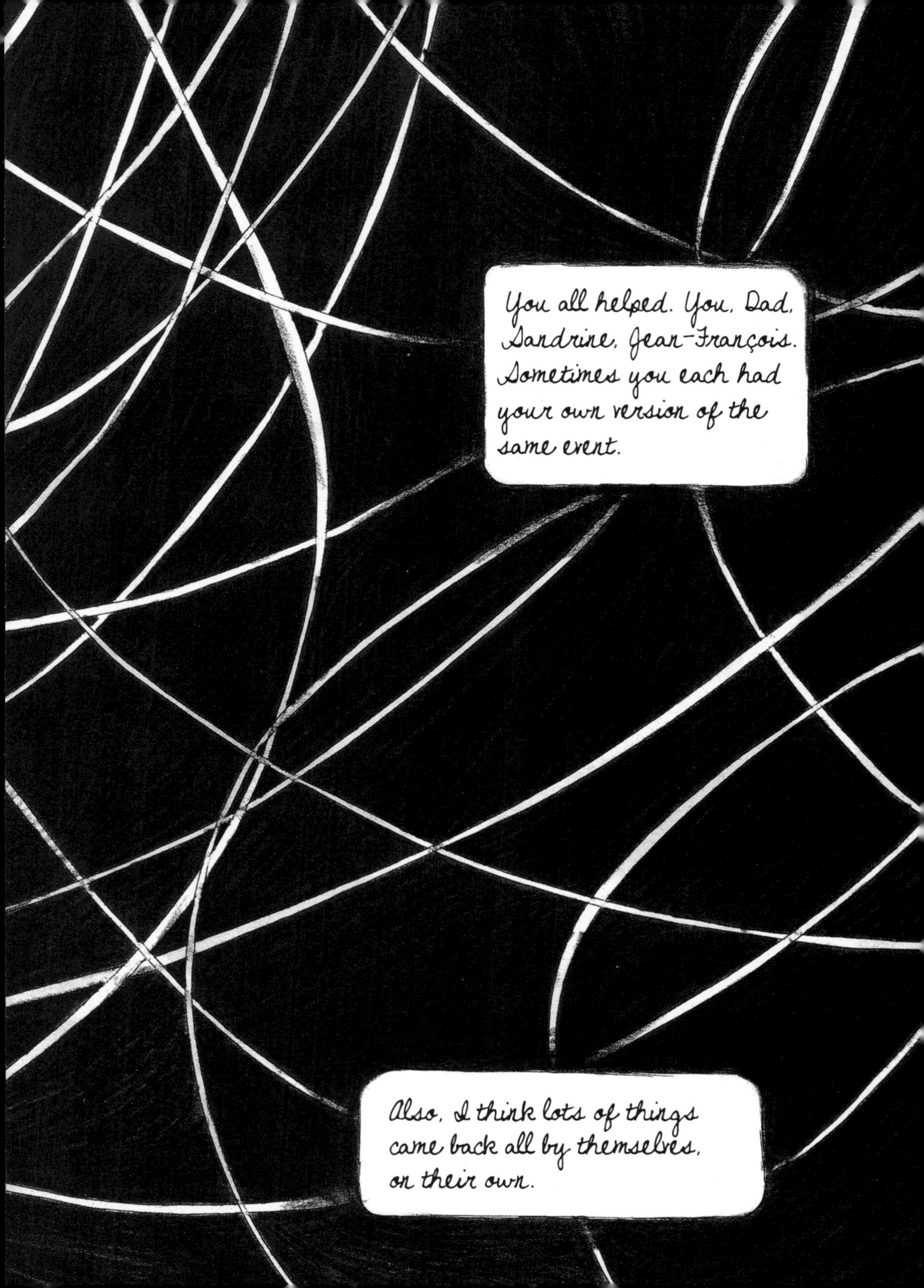
You all helped. You, Dad, Sandrine, Jean-François. Sometimes you each had your own version of the same event.
Also, I think lots of things came back all by themselves, on their own.

"Our memory is our coherence, our reason, our feeling, even our action. Without it, we are nothing."

Luis Buñuel

I must've been 24 when the first symptoms showed up. Sandrine remembers one day that stood out. Was it in 1994, or maybe 1995 already? I'd finished my bachelor's.

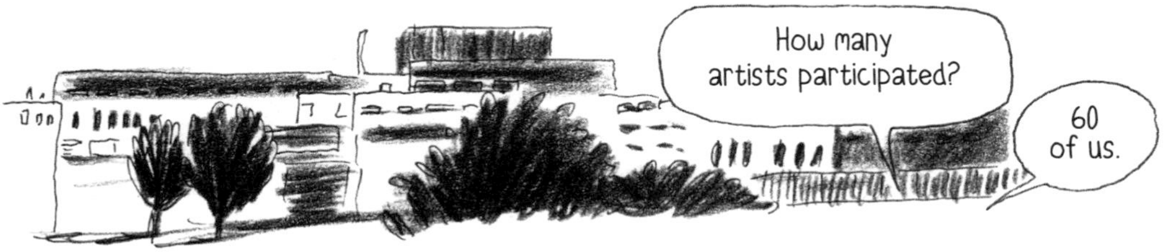
How many artists participated?
60 of us.

I was working on a big project: renovating the cellars of a hospital in Argenteuil. I'd finally finished painting my 300-foot mural.

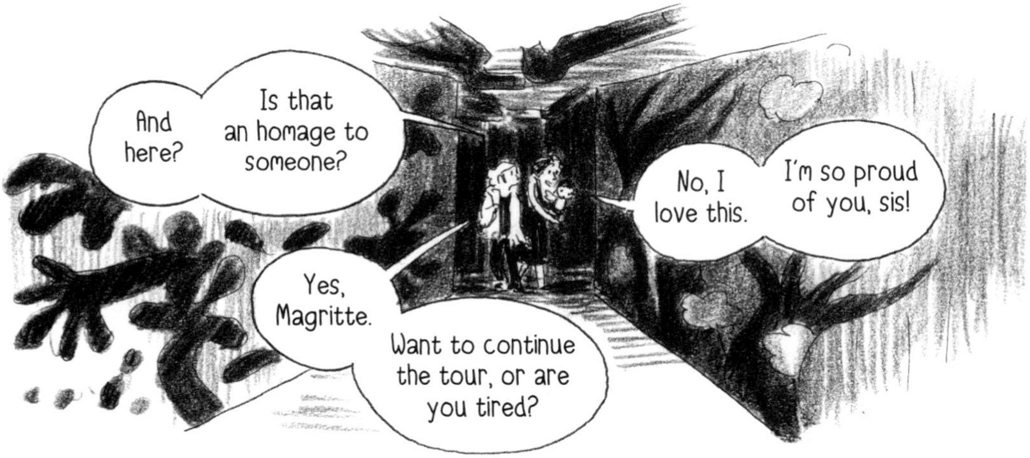
And here?
Is that an homage to someone?
Yes, Magritte.
Want to continue the tour, or are you tired?
No, I love this.
I'm so proud of you, sis!

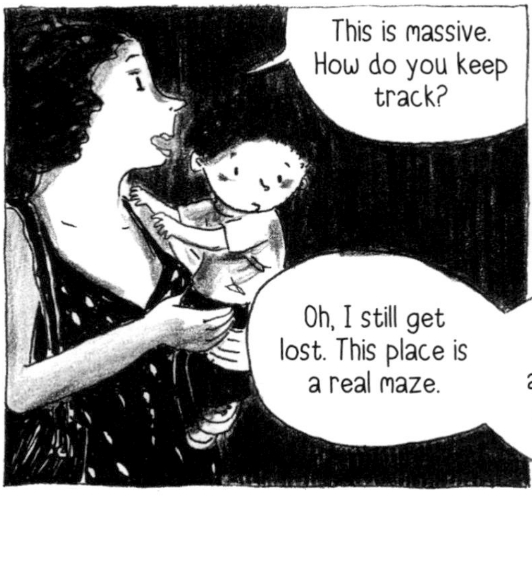
This is massive. How do you keep track?
Oh, I still get lost. This place is a real maze.

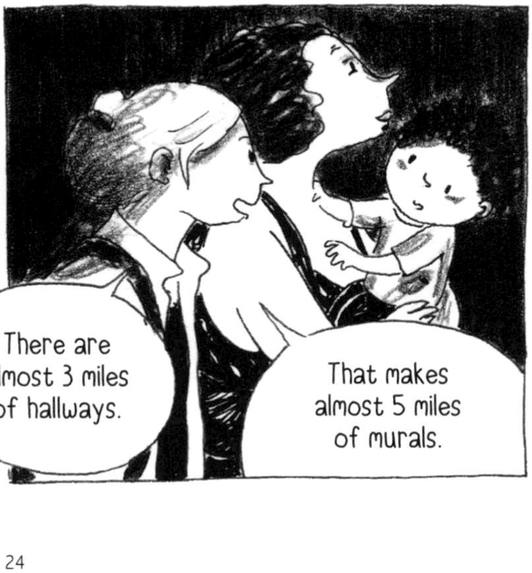
There are almost 3 miles of hallways.
That makes almost 5 miles of murals.

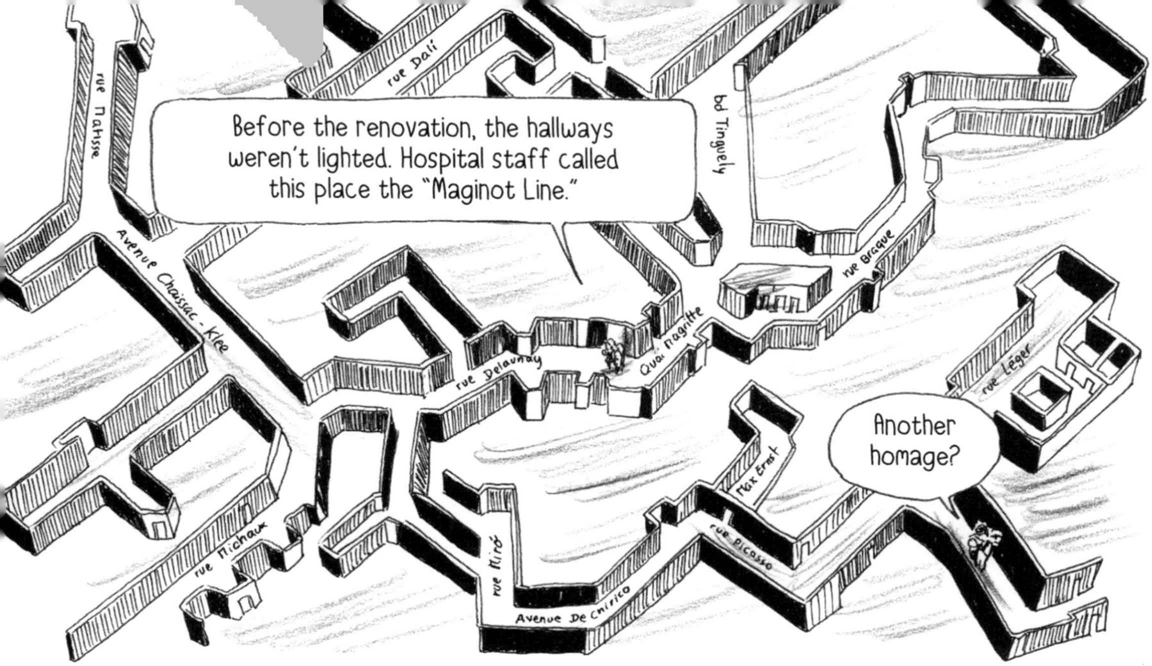
rue Dalí
rue Matisse
Before the renovation, the hallways weren't lighted. Hospital staff called this place the "Maginot Line."
bd Tinguely
Avenue Chaissac-Klee
rue Braque
Quai Magritte
rue Delaunay
rue Léger
Another homage?
Max Ernst
rue Picasso
rue Michaux
rue Miró
Avenue De Chirico

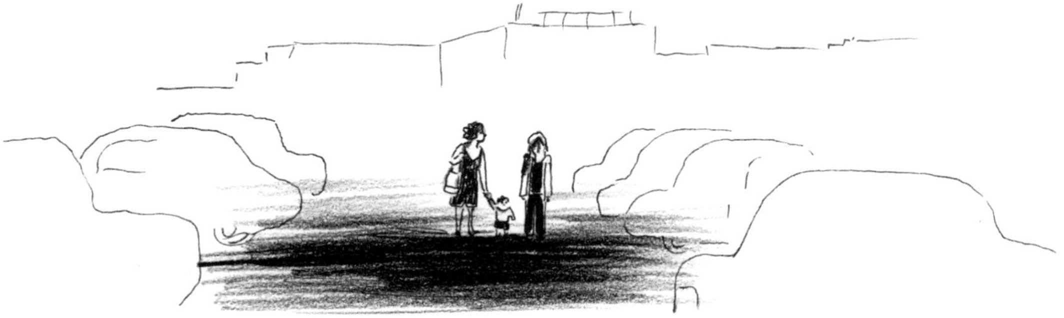

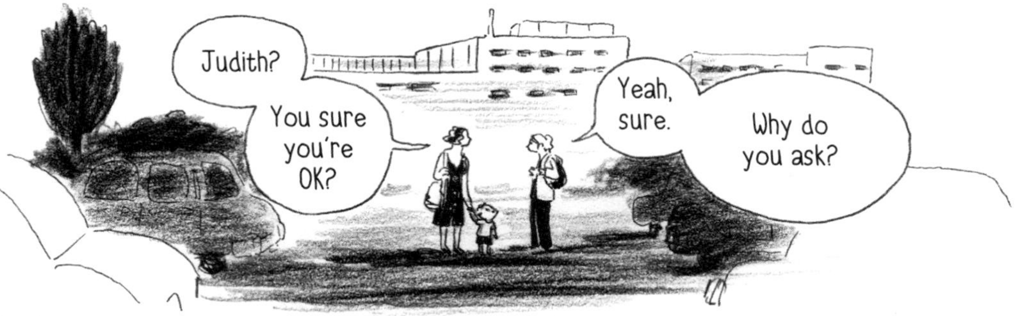
Judith?
You sure you're OK?
Yeah, sure.
Why do you ask?

I think it took the whole family a while to figure out I never remembered my "spells." That's what you called them. I thought you were all just joking...

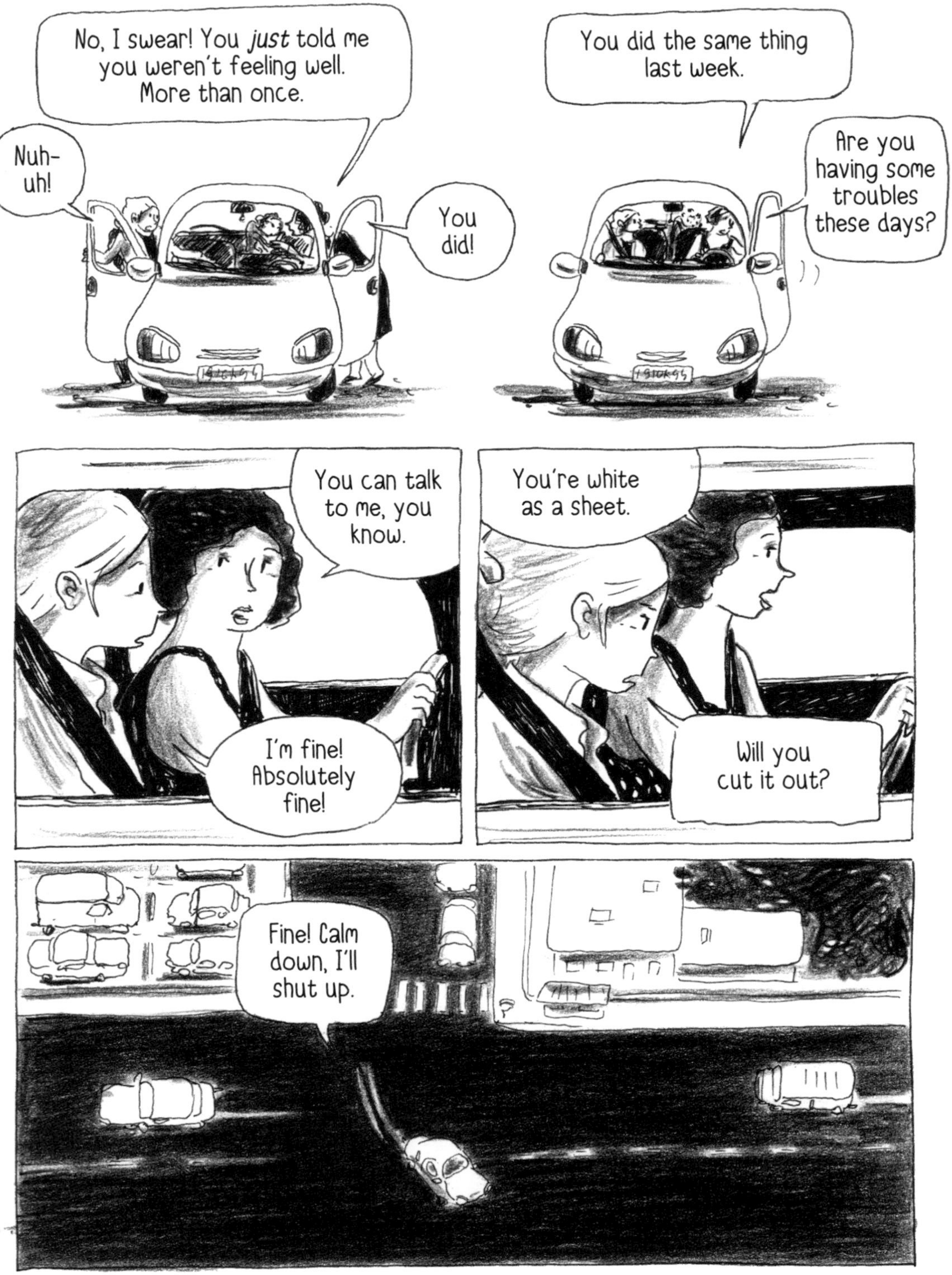
No, I swear! You *just* told me you weren't feeling well. More than once.
Nuh-uh!
You did!
You did the same thing last week.
Are you having some troubles these days?
You can talk to me, you know.
I'm fine! Absolutely fine!
You're white as a sheet.
Will you cut it out?
Fine! Calm down, I'll shut up.

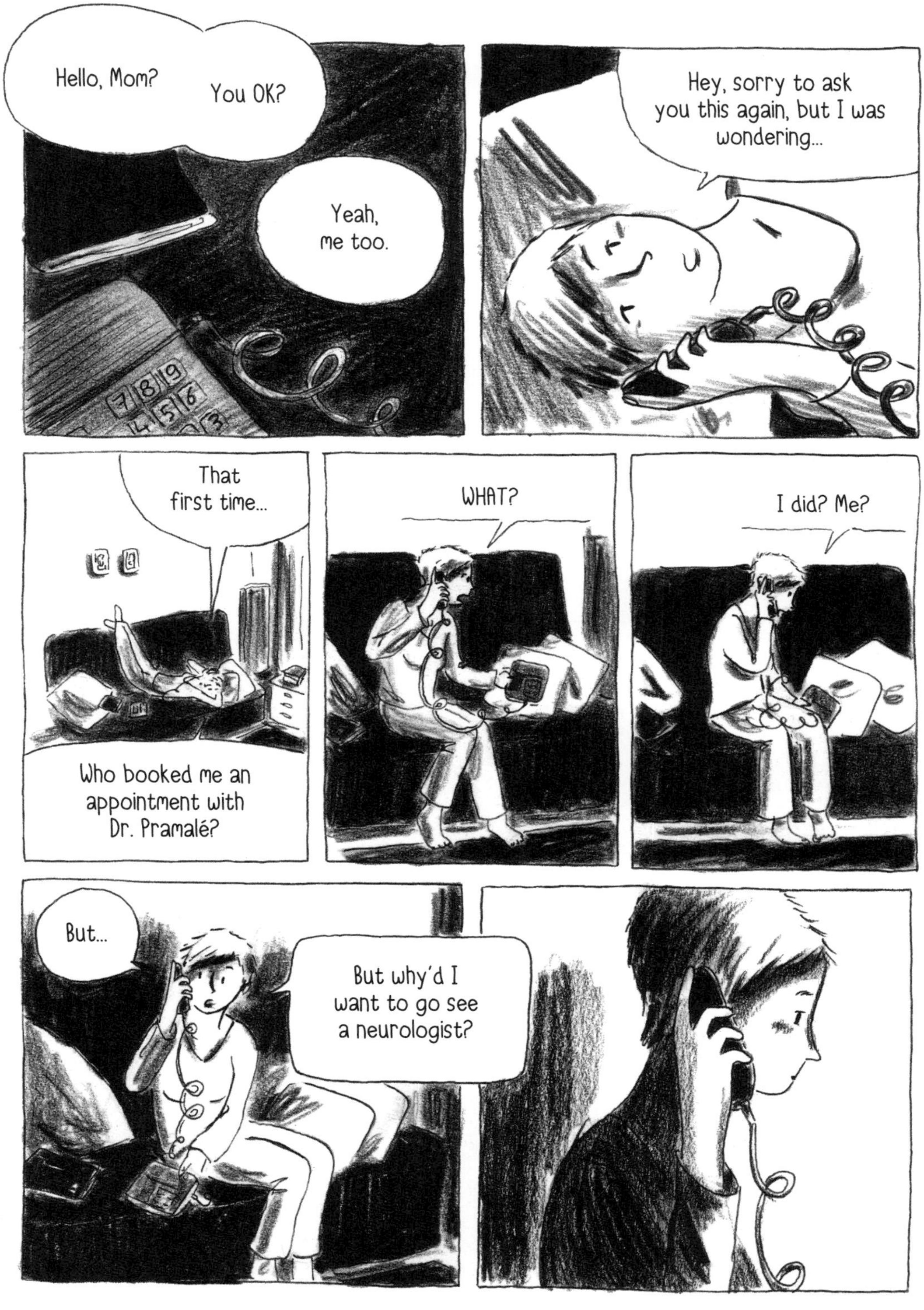
Hello, Mom?
You OK?
Yeah, me too.
Hey, sorry to ask you this again, but I was wondering...
That first time...
Who booked me an appointment with Dr. Pramalé?
WHAT?
I did? Me?
But...
But why'd I want to go see a neurologist?

Créteil. Les Choux projects.

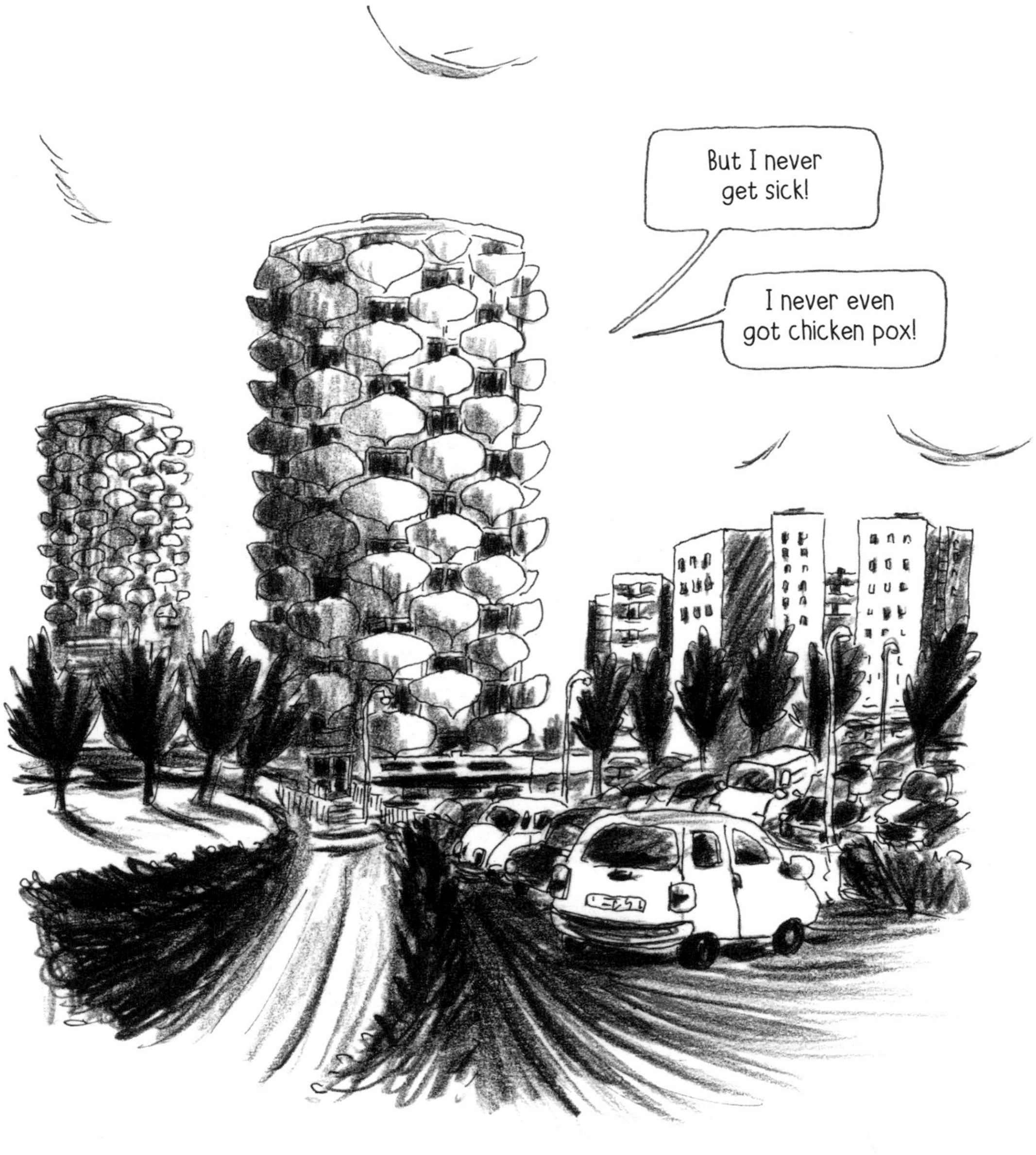
But I never get sick!
I never even got chicken pox!

The way you tell it, Mom, I went to see a G.P. for strep throat. Apparently, I mentioned my infamous "spells." He told me to go see a neurologist. This was in June 1995, I guess... As you can tell, I'm still pretty messed-up when it comes to dates and the passage of time.

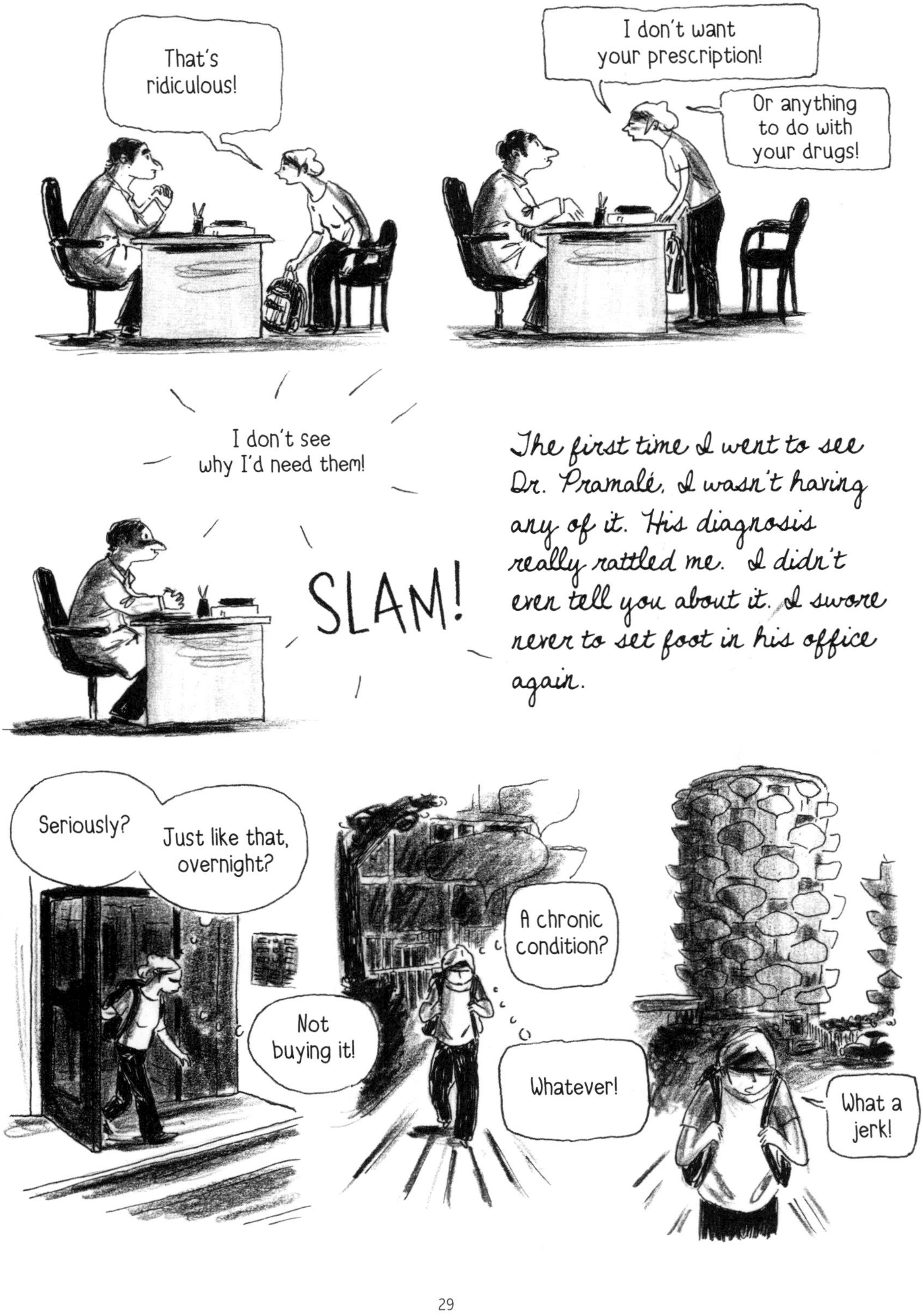
That's ridiculous!
I don't want your prescription!
Or anything to do with your drugs!
I don't see why I'd need them!
SLAM!
The first time I went to see Dr. Pramalé, I wasn't having any of it. His diagnosis really rattled me. I didn't even tell you about it. I swore never to set foot in his office again.
Seriously?
Just like that, overnight?
Not buying it!
A chronic condition?
Whatever!
What a jerk!

After that visit, my life went on normally for another few months. That summer, I worked as a camp counselor before heading off on vacation.

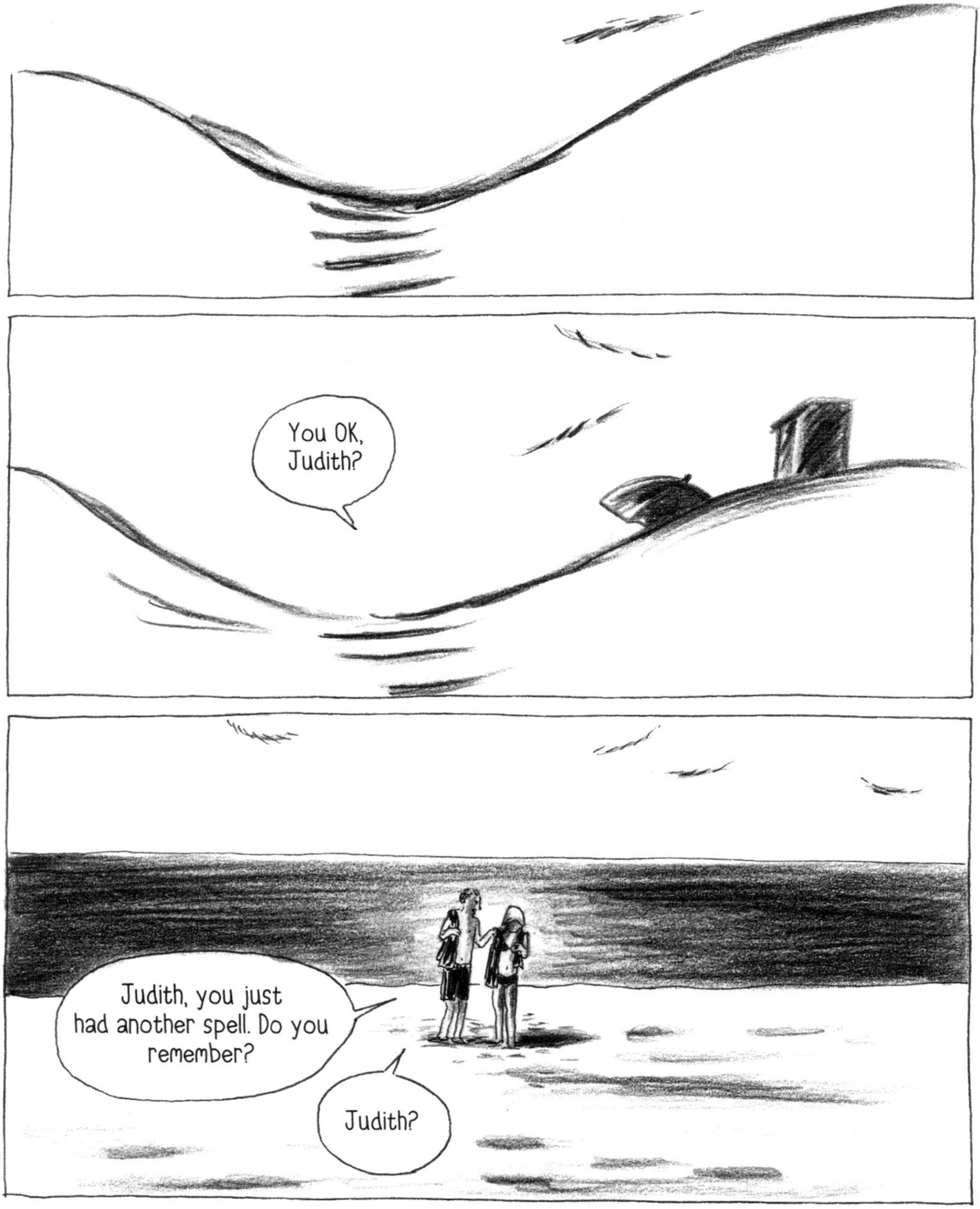
You OK, Judith?
Judith, you just had another spell. Do you remember?
Judith?

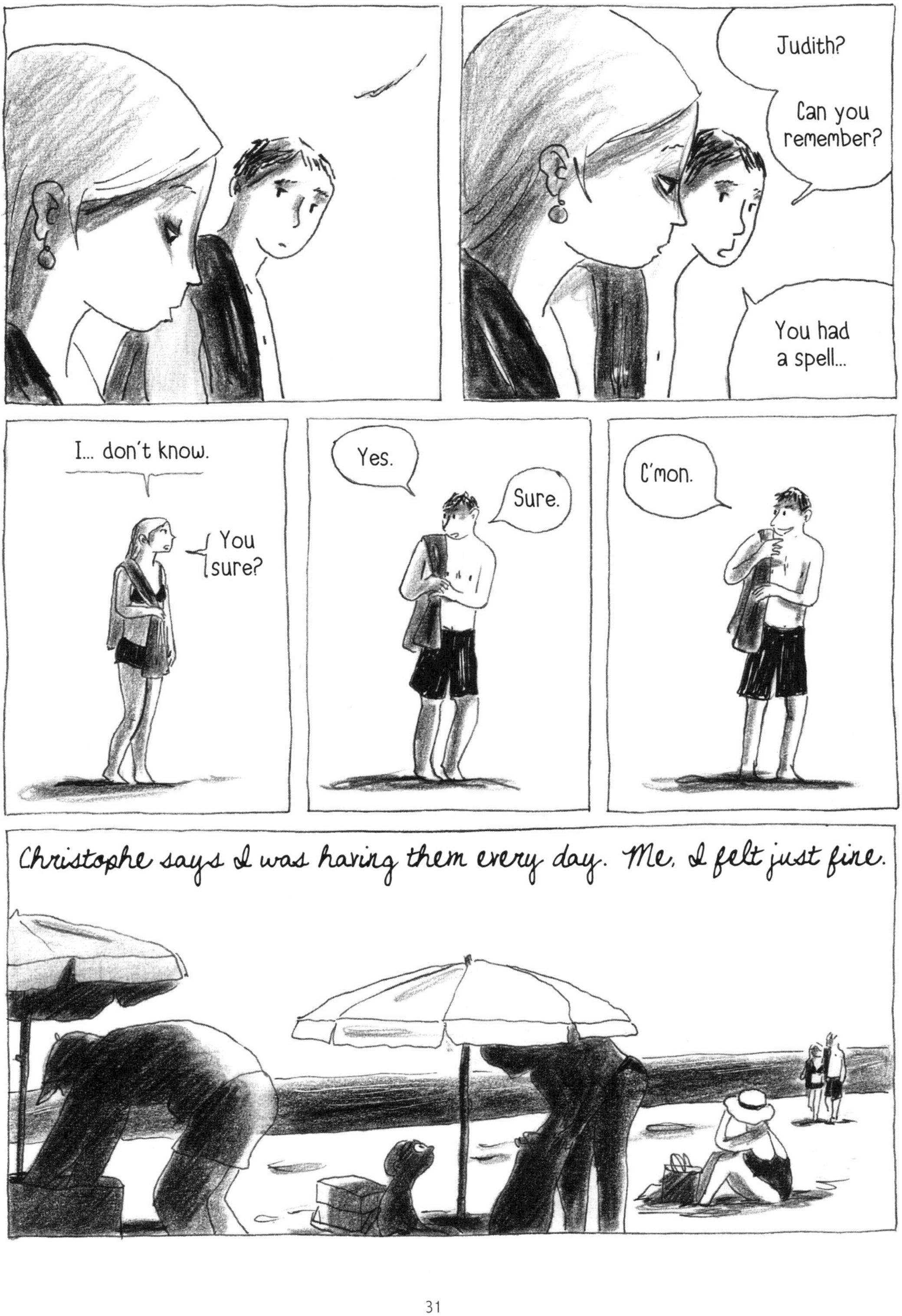
Judith?
Can you remember?
You had a spell...
I... don't know.
You sure?
Yes.
Sure.
C'mon.
Christophe says I was having them every day. Me, I felt just fine.

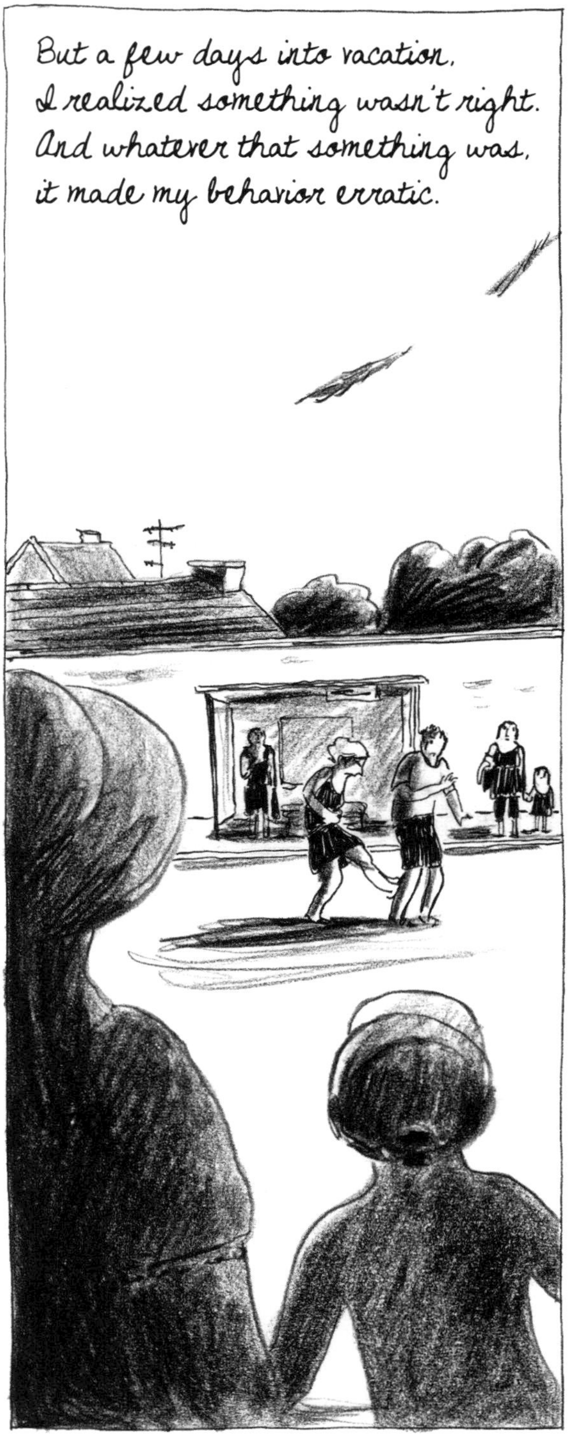
But a few days into vacation, I realized something wasn't right. And whatever that something was, it made my behavior erratic.

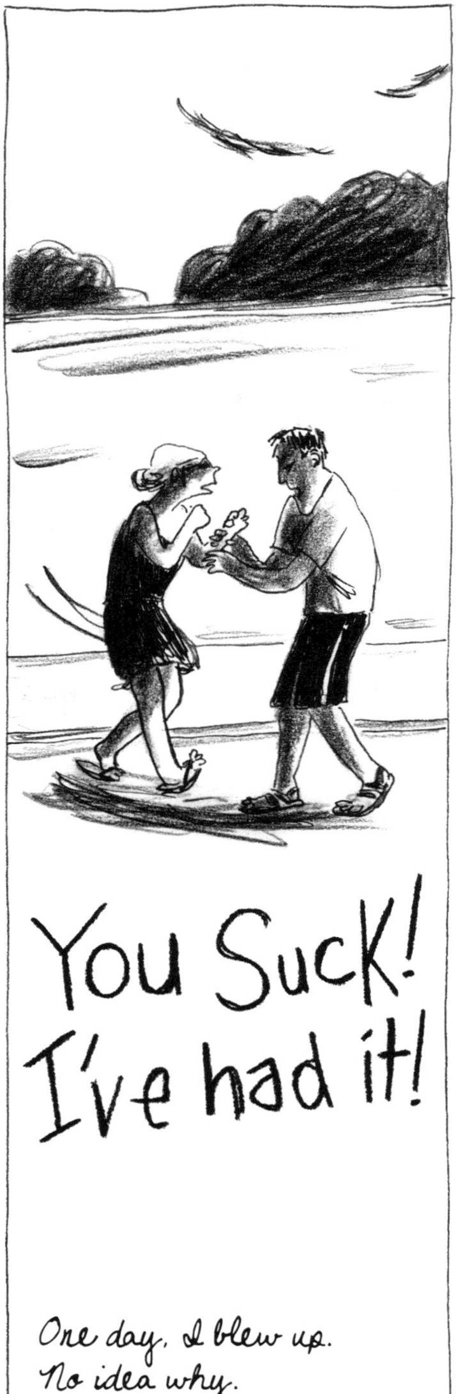
You Suck! I've had it!
One day, I blew up. No idea why.

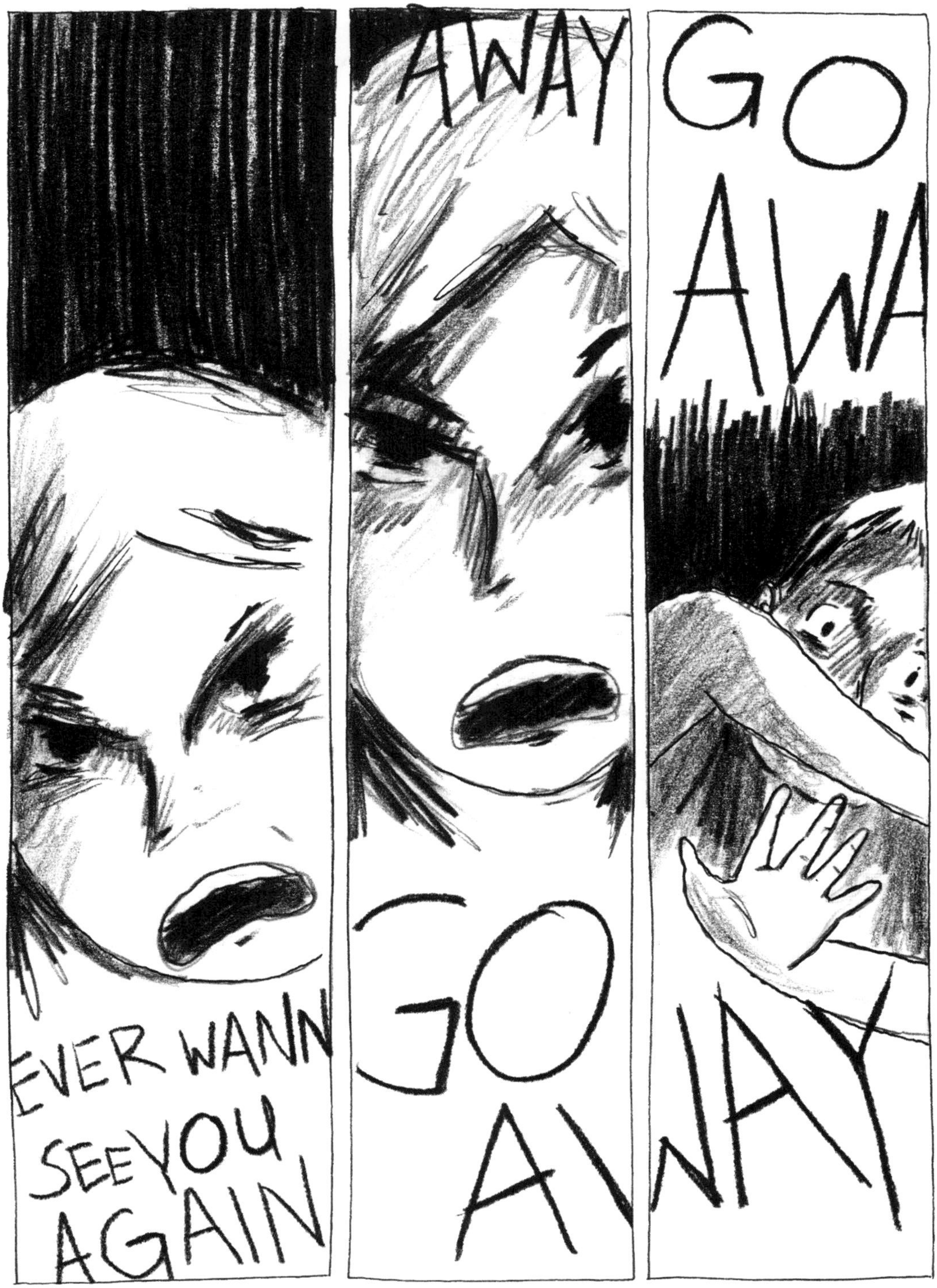
EVER WANN SEE YOU AGAIN
AWAY
GO AW
GO AWA
WAY

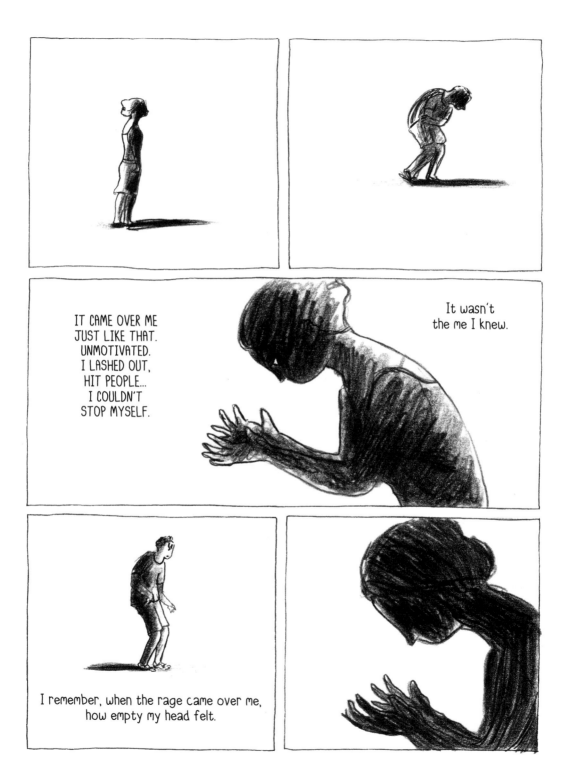

IT CAME OVER ME
JUST LIKE THAT.
UNMOTIVATED.
I LASHED OUT,
HIT PEOPLE...
I COULDN'T
STOP MYSELF.

It wasn't
the me I knew.

I remember, when the rage came over me,
how empty my head felt.

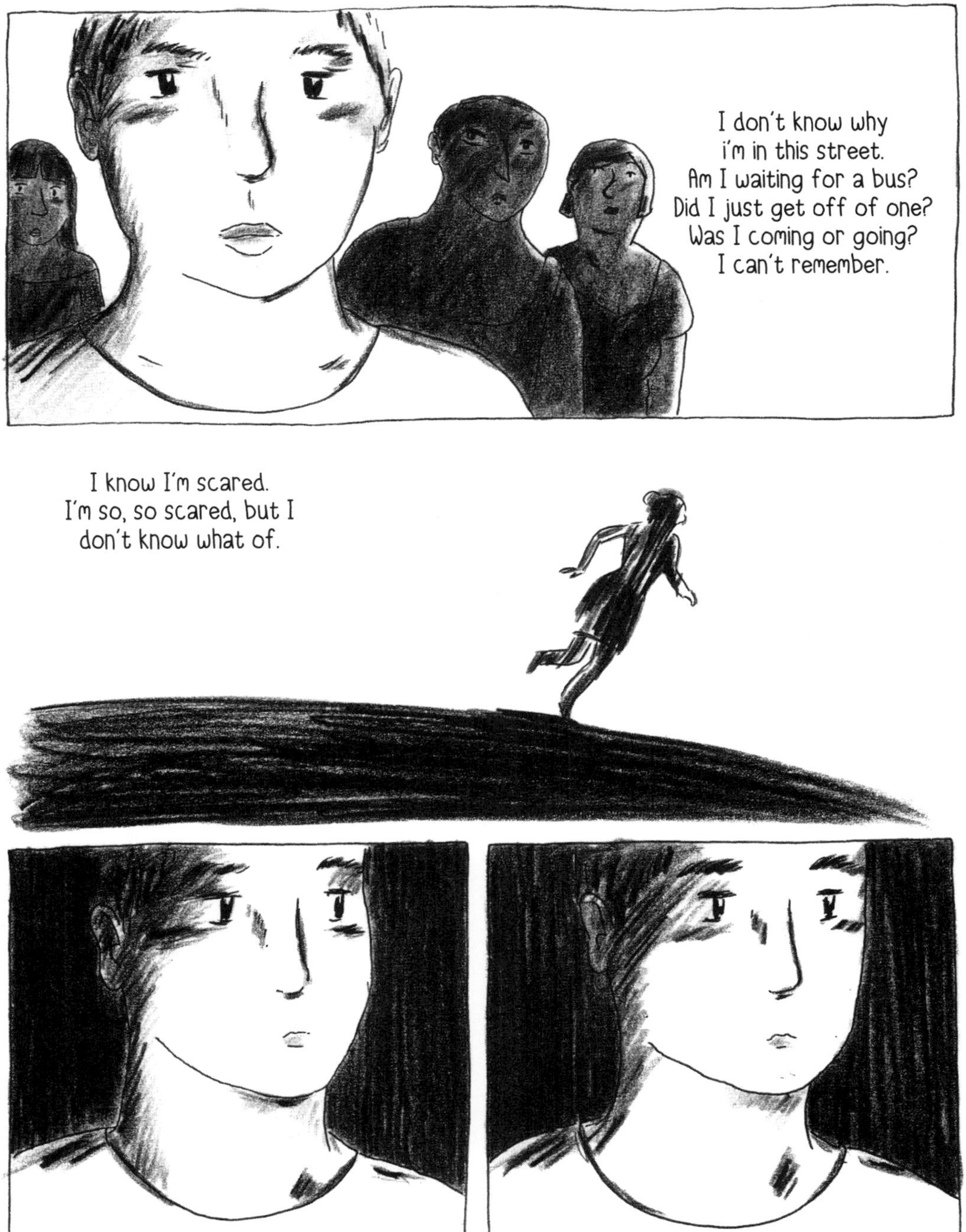
I don't know why
i'm in this street.
Am I waiting for a bus?
Did I just get off of one?
Was I coming or going?
I can't remember.
I know I'm scared.
I'm so, so scared, but I
don't know what of.
I don't know why
Christophe is here with me...
...right in front of me.

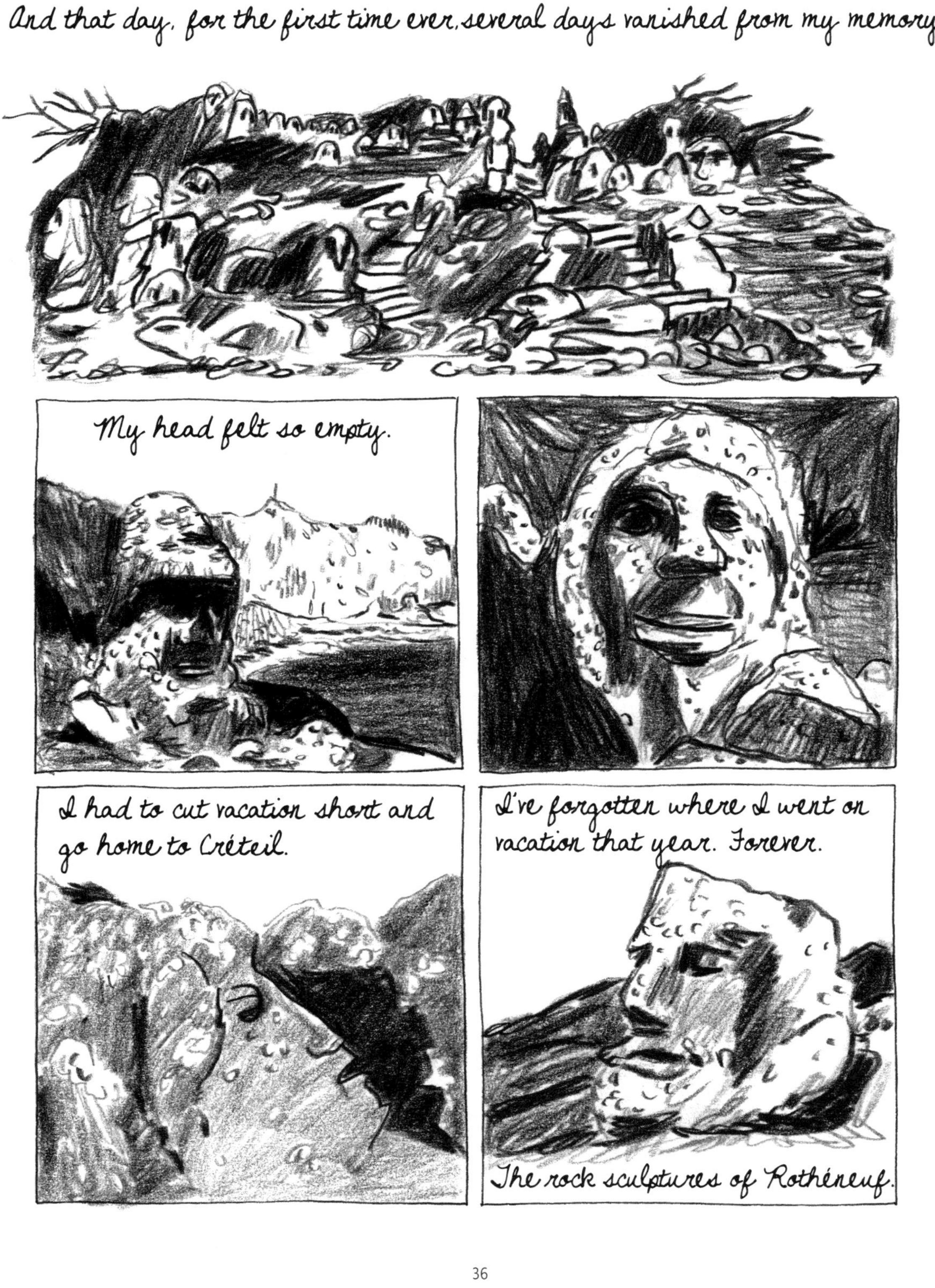
And that day, for the first time ever, several days vanished from my memory.
My head felt so empty.
I had to cut vacation short and go home to Créteil.
I've forgotten where I went on vacation that year. Forever.
The rock sculptures of Rothéneuf.

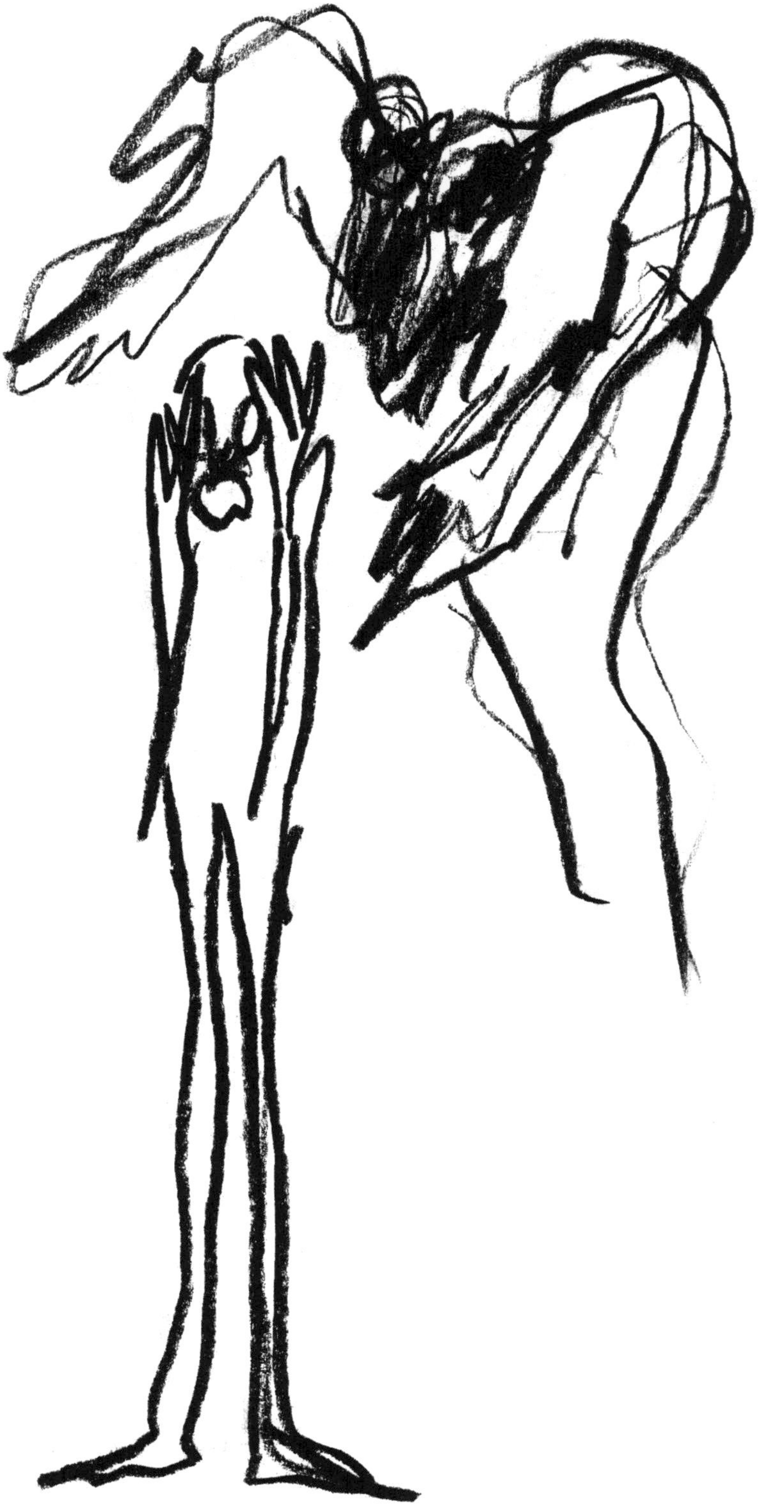

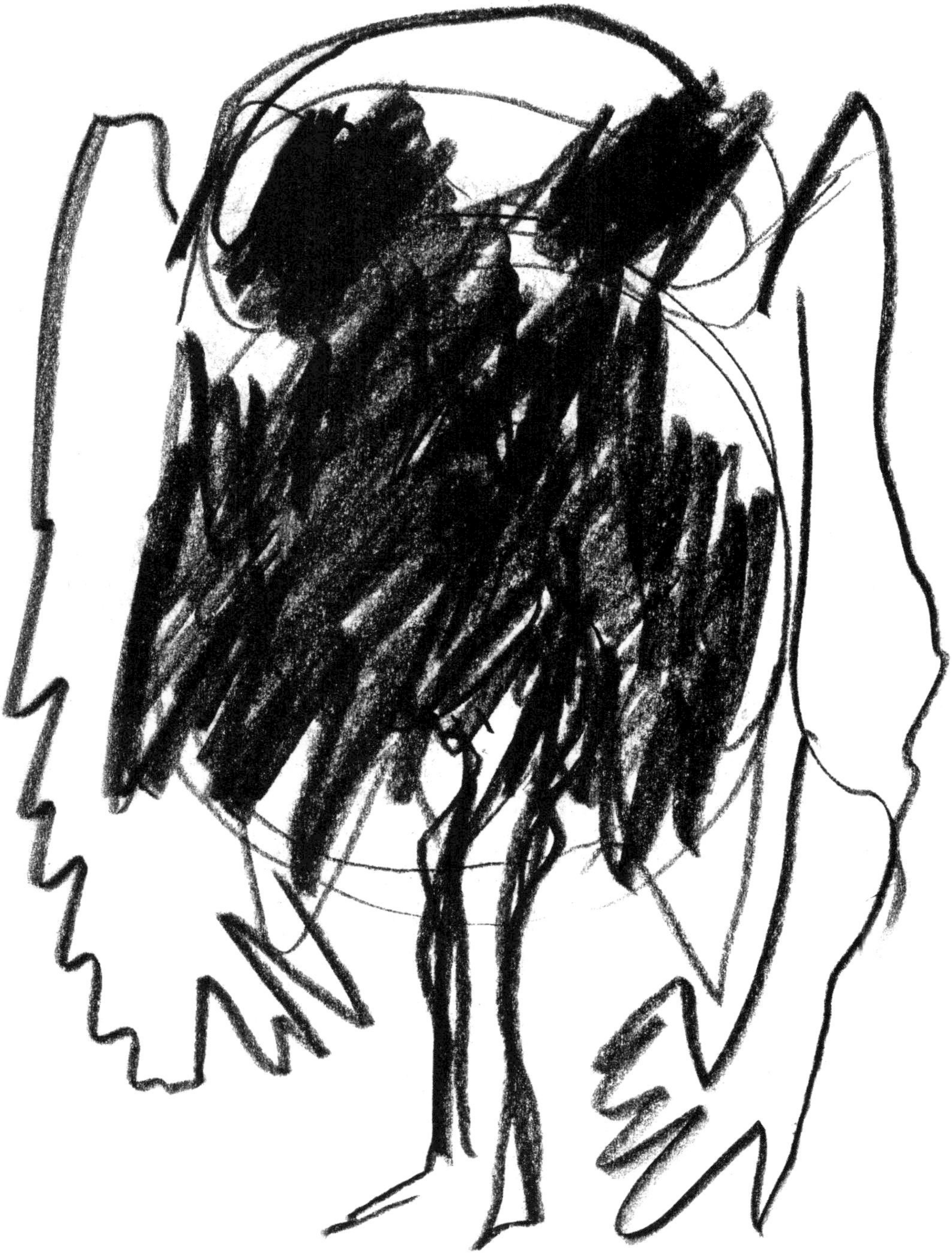

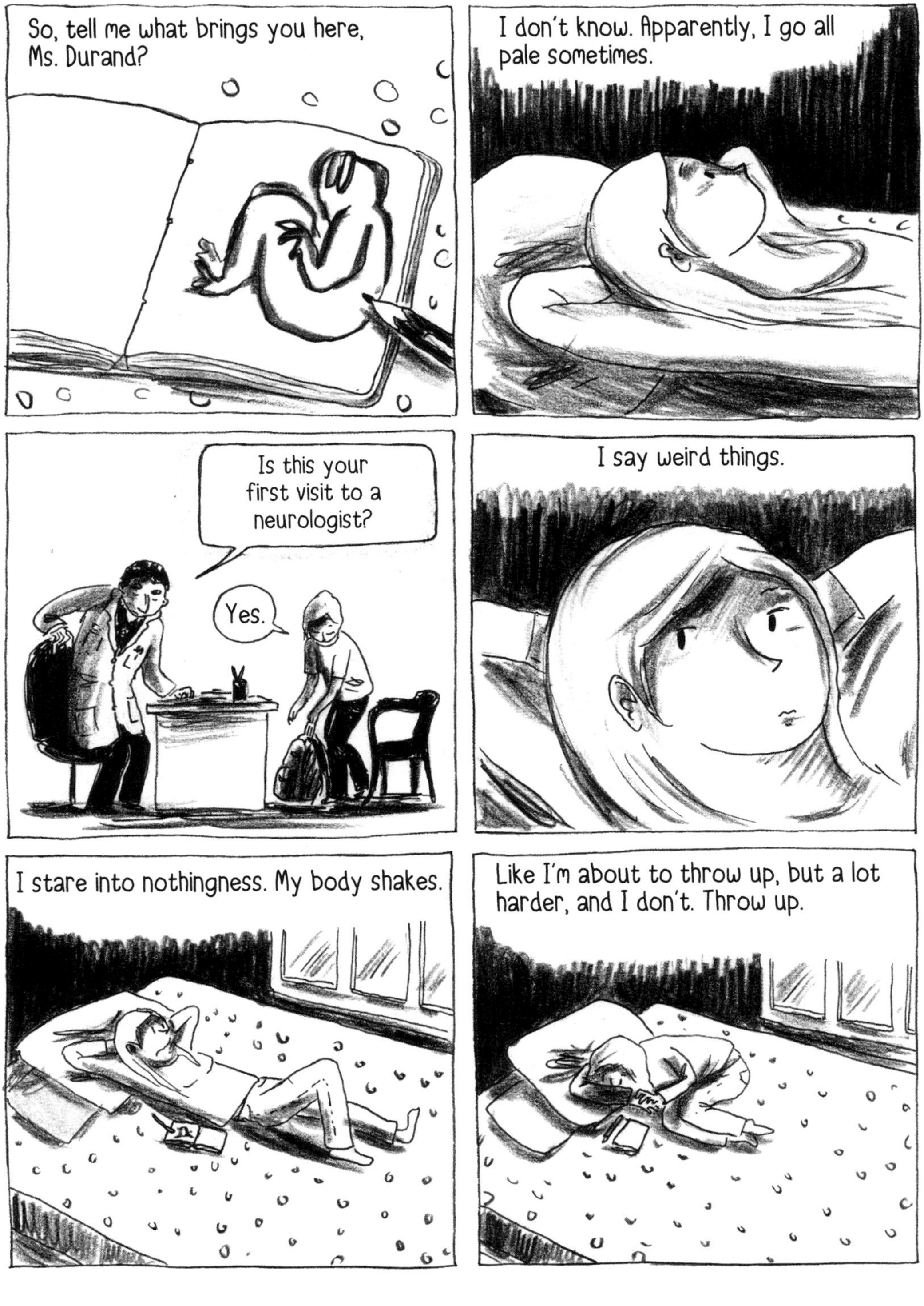
So, tell me what brings you here, Ms. Durand?
I don't know. Apparently, I go all pale sometimes.
Is this your first visit to a neurologist?
Yes.
I say weird things.
I stare into nothingness. My body shakes.
Like I'm about to throw up, but a lot harder, and I don't. Throw up.

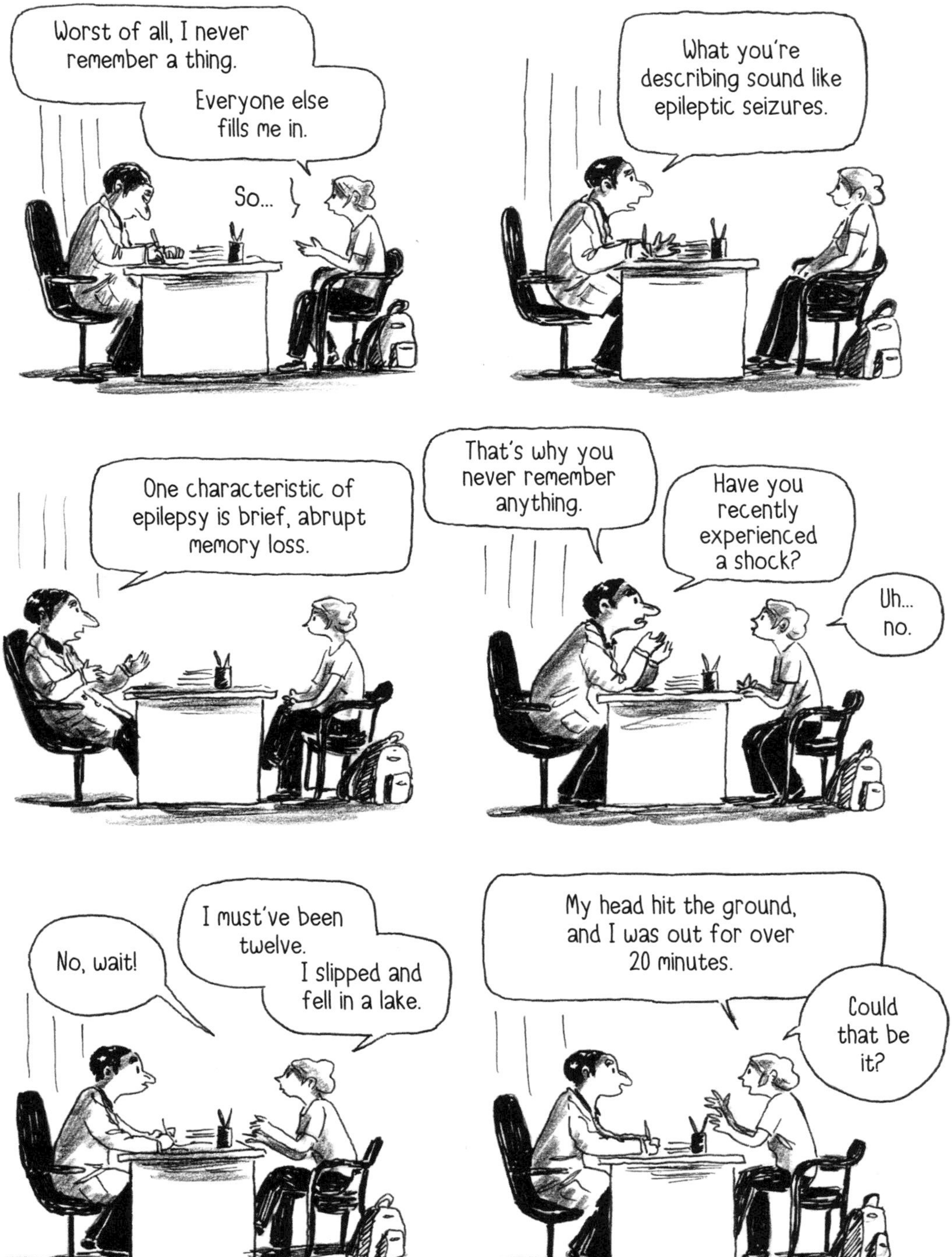
Worst of all, I never remember a thing.
Everyone else fills me in.
So...
What you're describing sound like epileptic seizures.
One characteristic of epilepsy is brief, abrupt memory loss.
That's why you never remember anything.
Have you recently experienced a shock?
Uh... no.
No, wait!
I must've been twelve.
I slipped and fell in a lake.
My head hit the ground, and I was out for over 20 minutes.
Could that be it?

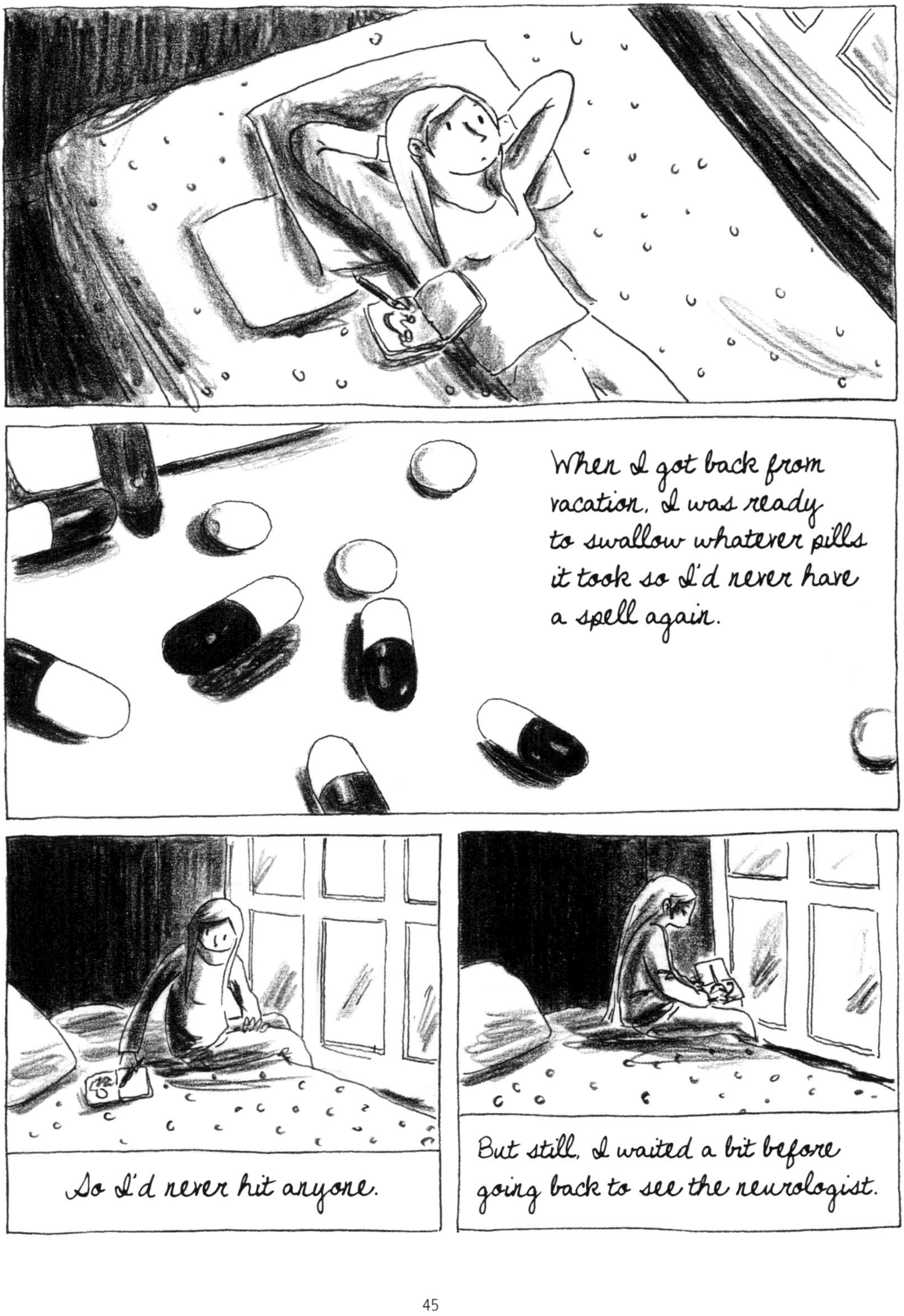
When I got back from vacation, I was ready to swallow whatever pills it took so I'd never have a spell again.
So I'd never hit anyone.
But still, I waited a bit before going back to see the neurologist.

I didn't know a thing about epilepsy. Dad has worked with epileptic children for several years, but he hadn't noticed the same illness in me.

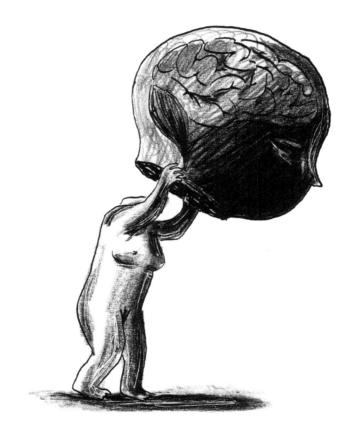

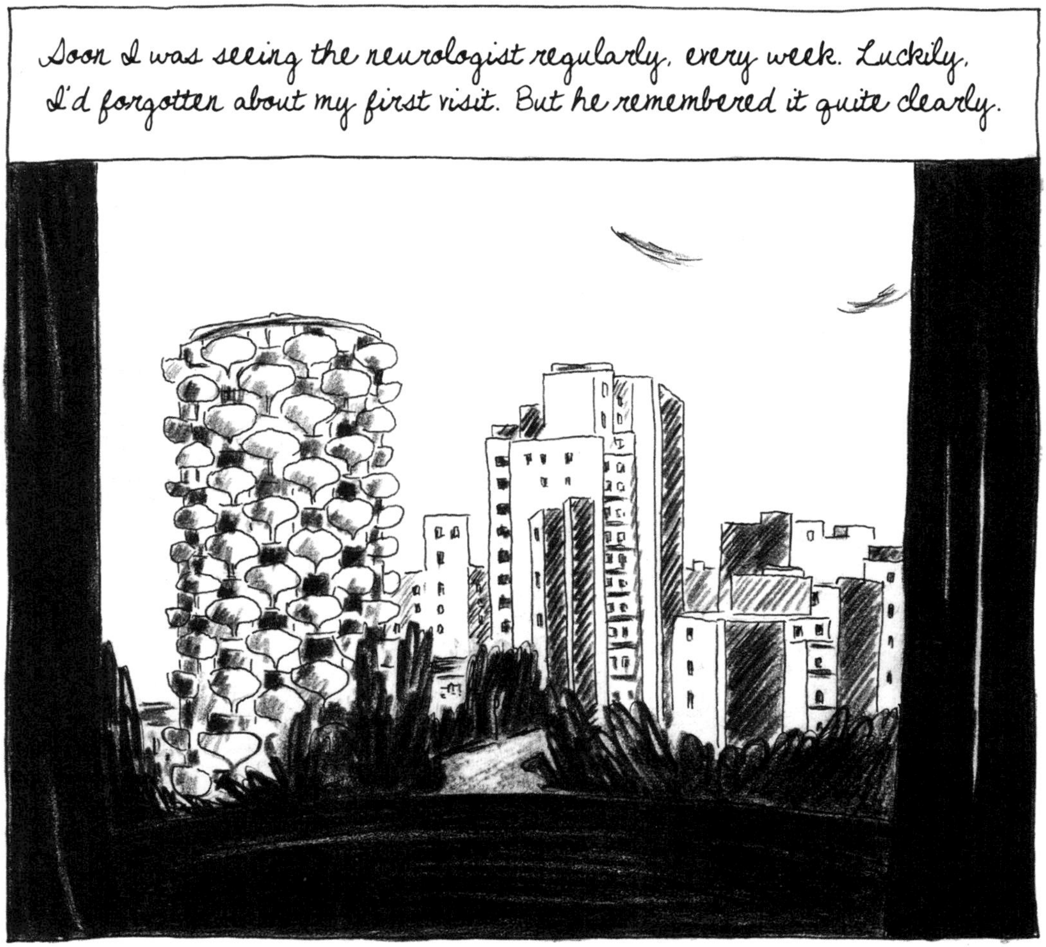
Soon I was seeing the neurologist regularly, every week. Luckily, I'd forgotten about my first visit. But he remembered it quite clearly.

After the first few treatments, I felt much calmer. Not nearly as angry. But the treatments didn't work. I kept having seizures. I wanted to switch doctors, but he was reputed to be the best.

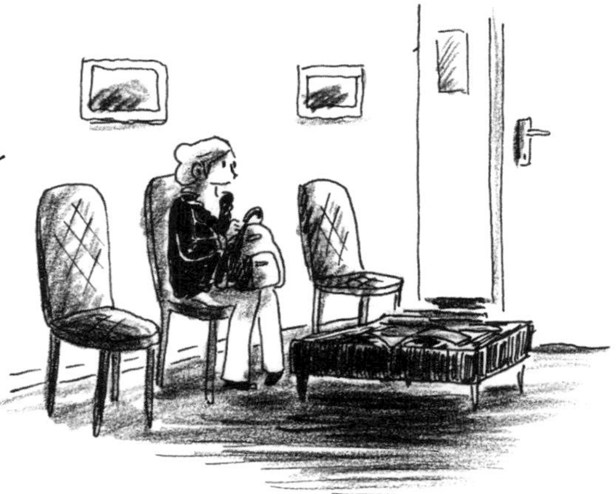

On my first visit to Dr. Pramalé, he told me:

"There are many epileptics who live quite well with their illness, you know."

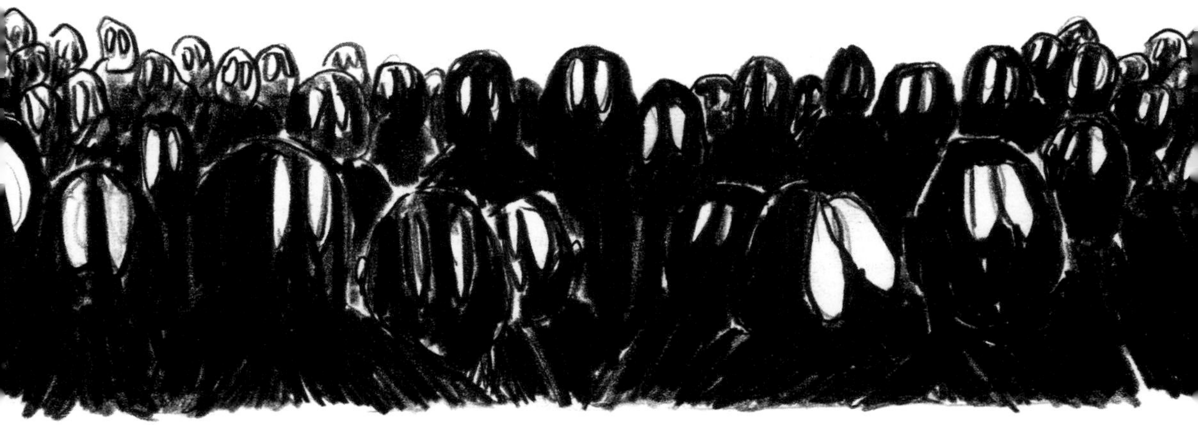

"When the seizures are under control, you can have a normal life."

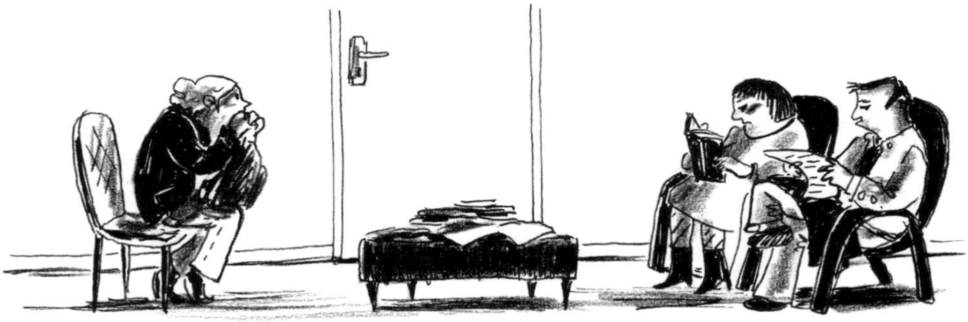

I wonder how you can live a normal life when you're chock full of drugs that knock you out. I wonder if everyone I see in his office is epileptic.

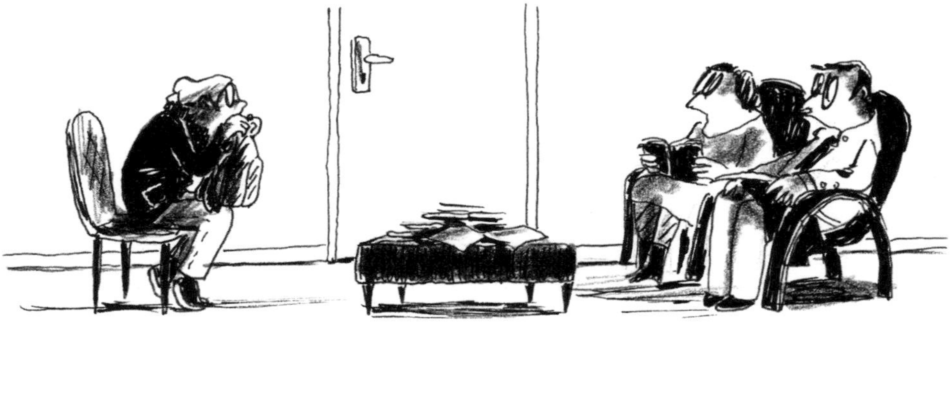

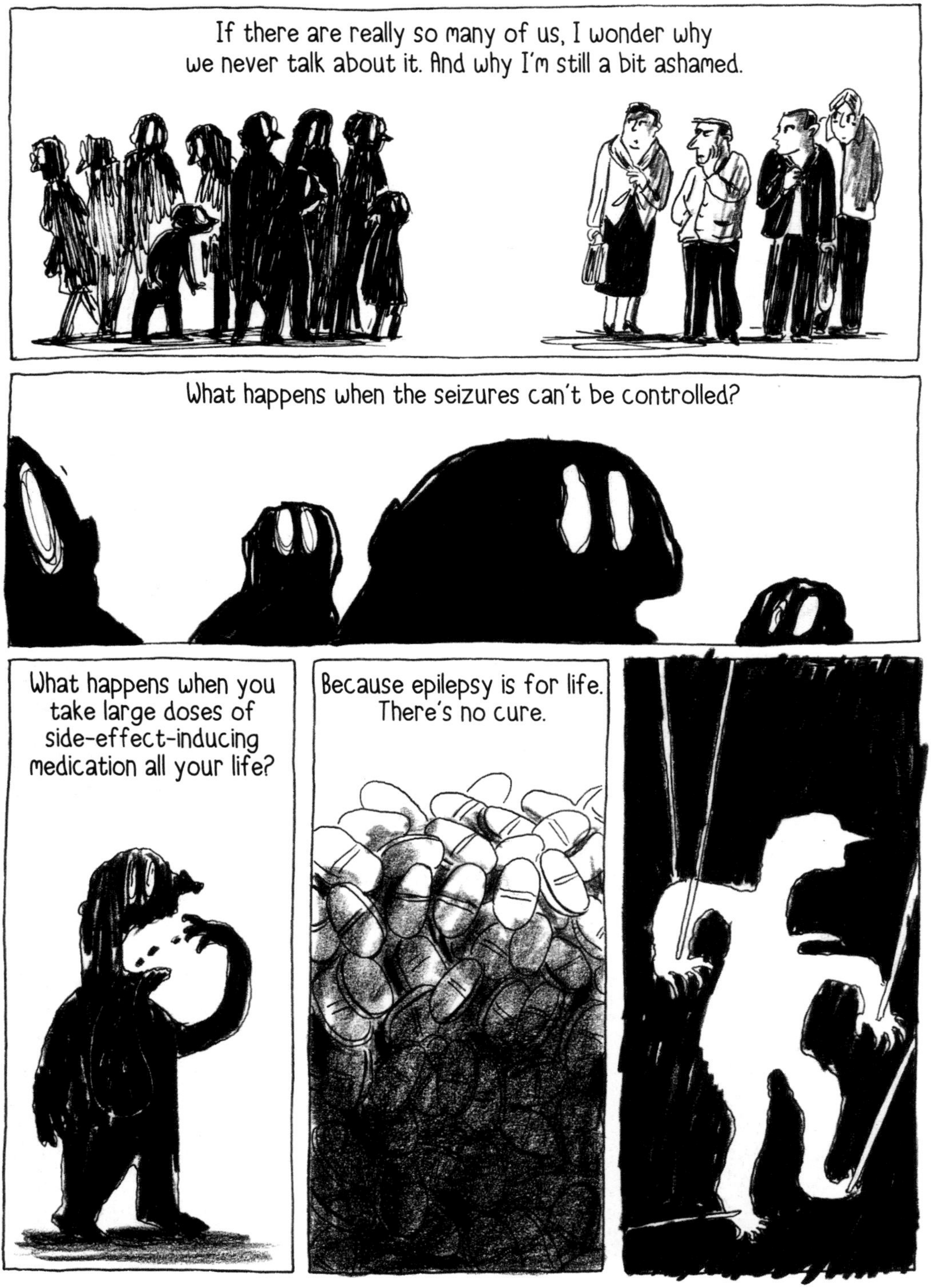
If there are really so many of us, I wonder why we never talk about it. And why I'm still a bit ashamed.
What happens when the seizures can't be controlled?
What happens when you take large doses of side-effect-inducing medication all your life?
Because epilepsy is for life. There's no cure.

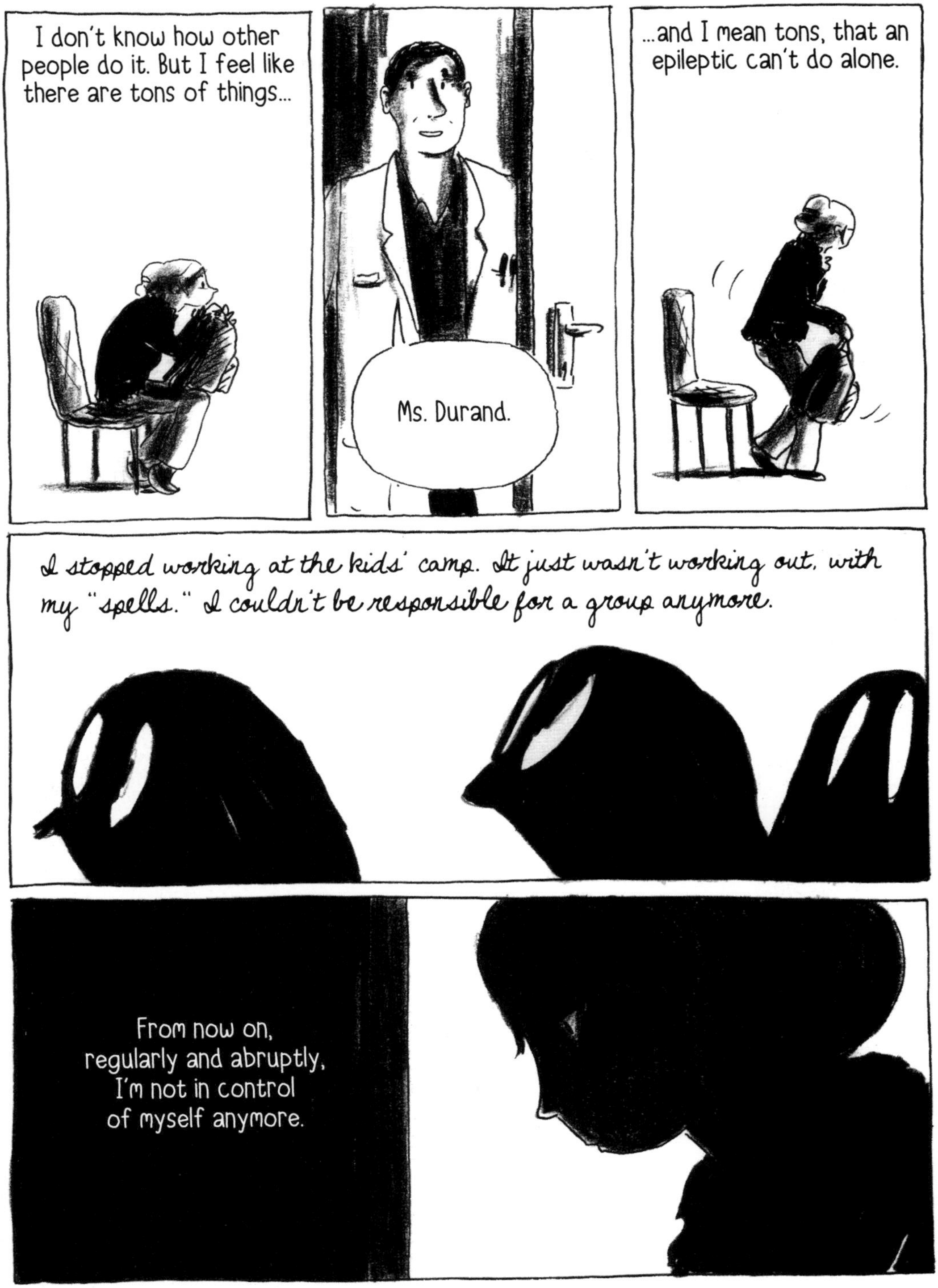
I don't know how other people do it. But I feel like there are tons of things...
Ms. Durand.
...and I mean tons, that an epileptic can't do alone.
I stopped working at the kids' camp. It just wasn't working out, with my "spells." I couldn't be responsible for a group anymore.
From now on, regularly and abruptly, I'm not in control of myself anymore.

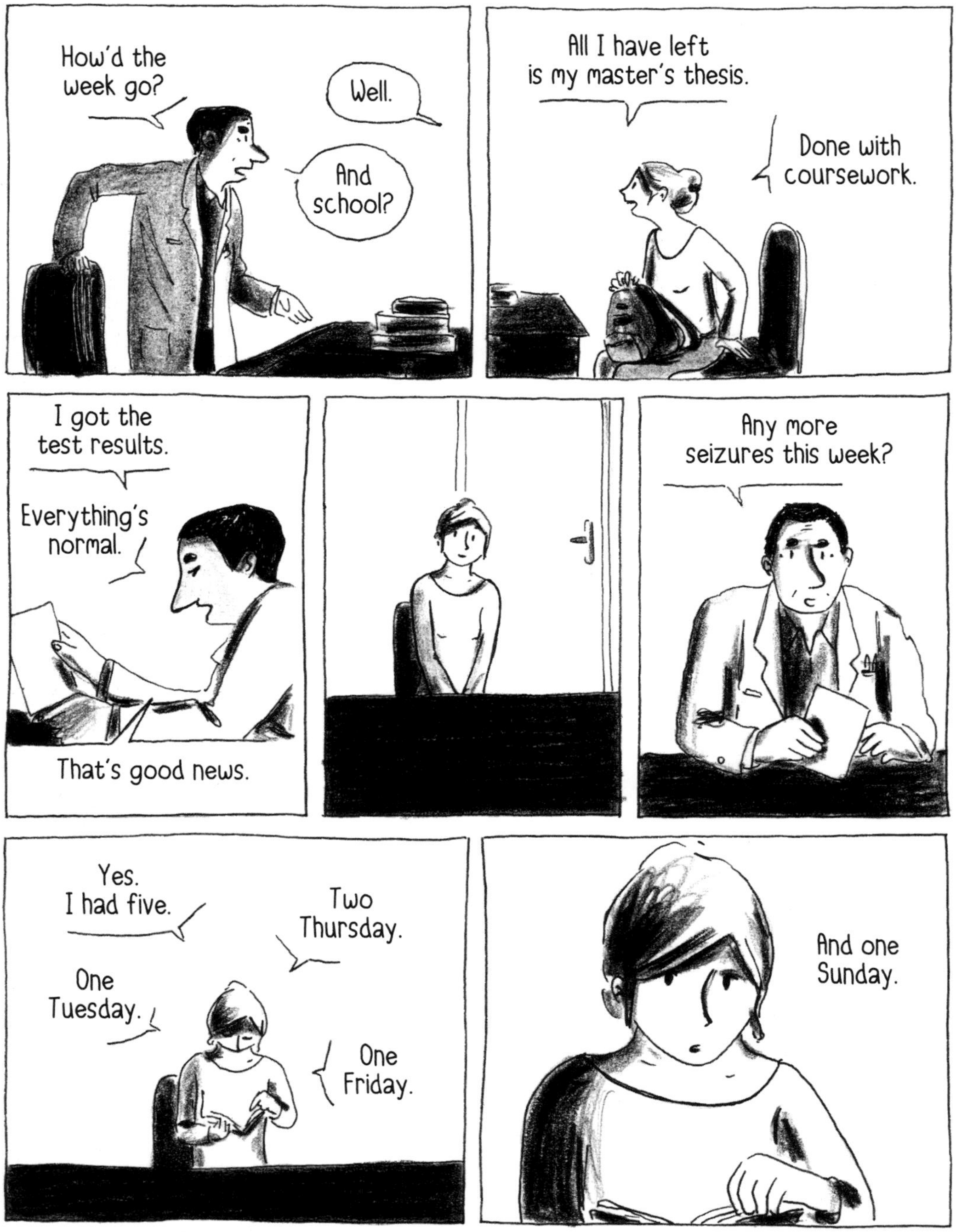
How'd the week go?
Well.
And school?
All I have left is my master's thesis.
Done with coursework.
I got the test results.
Everything's normal.
That's good news.
Any more seizures this week?
Yes. I had five.
Two Thursday.
One Tuesday.
One Friday.
And one Sunday.

I'd started writing down everything it was important to remember and say in my planner.

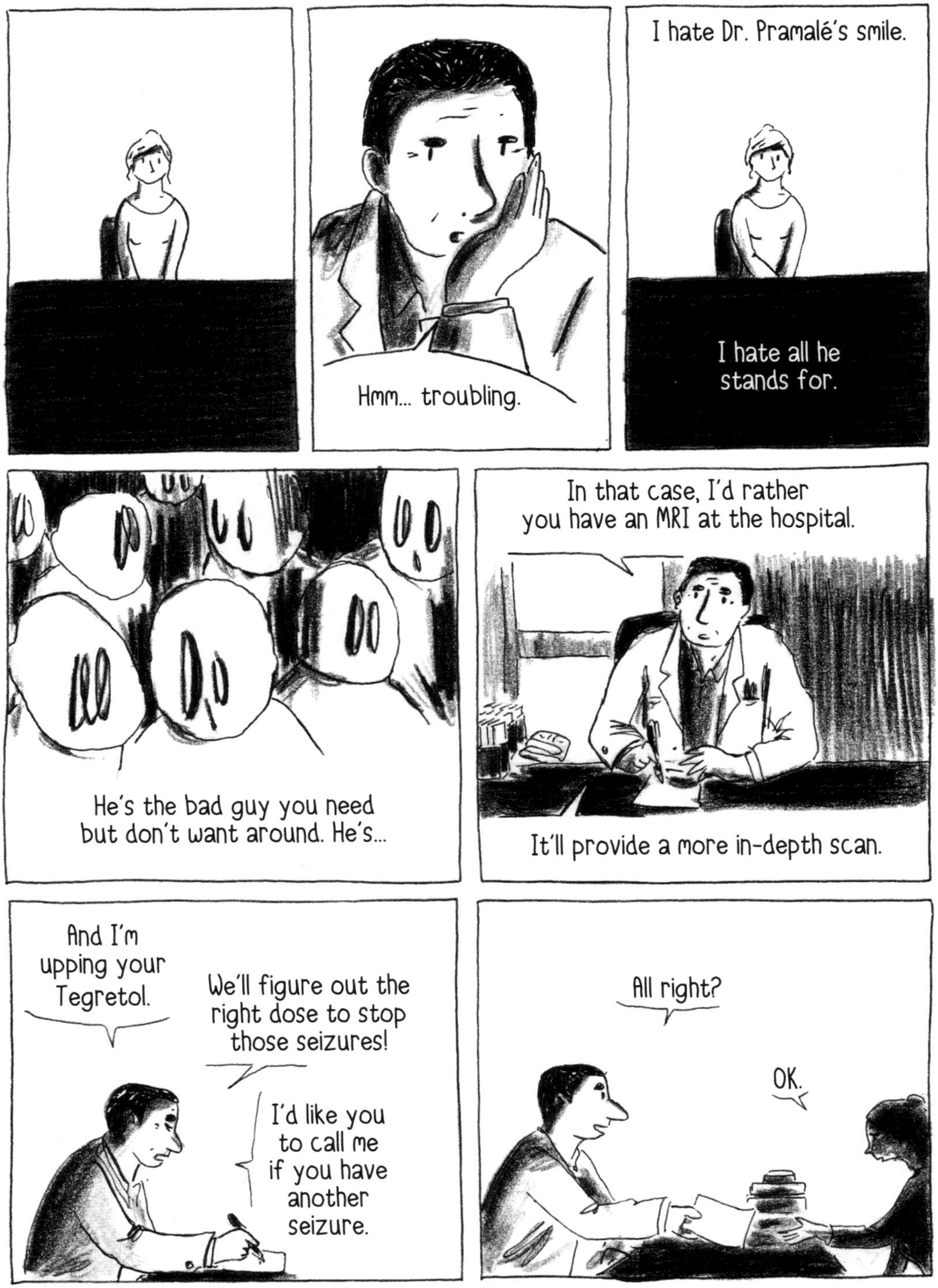
Hmm... troubling.
I hate Dr. Pramalé's smile.
I hate all he stands for.
He's the bad guy you need but don't want around. He's...
In that case, I'd rather you have an MRI at the hospital.
It'll provide a more in-depth scan.
And I'm upping your Tegretol.
We'll figure out the right dose to stop those seizures!
I'd like you to call me if you have another seizure.
All right?
OK.

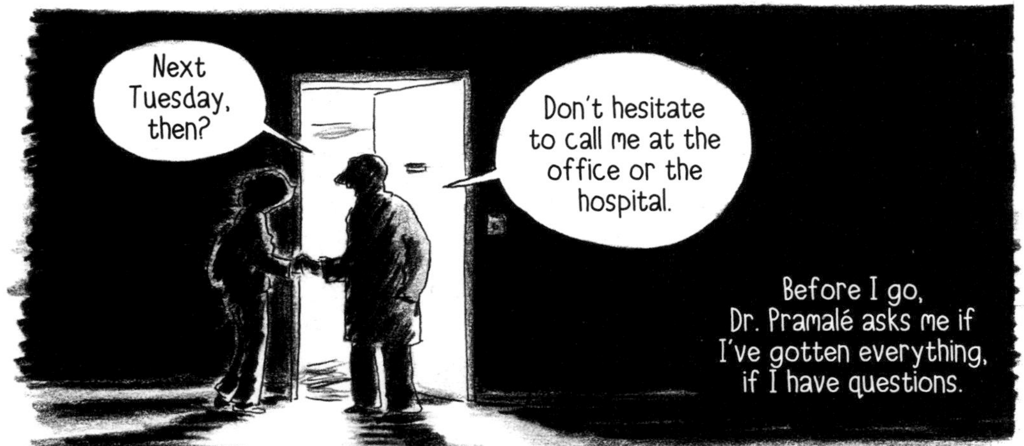
Next Tuesday, then?
Don't hesitate to call me at the office or the hospital.
Before I go, Dr. Pramalé asks me if I've gotten everything, if I have questions.

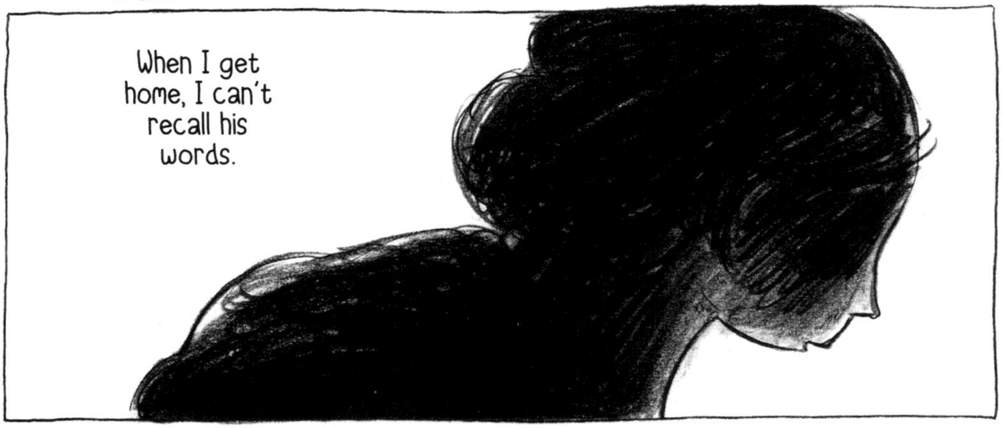
When I get home, I can't recall his words.

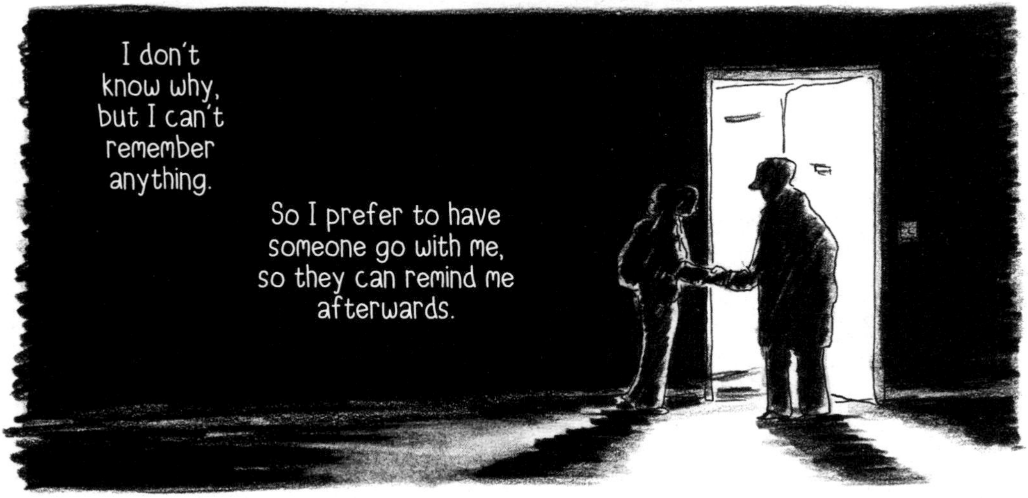
I don't know why, but I can't remember anything.
So I prefer to have someone go with me, so they can remind me afterwards.

I don't ask him lots of questions. While it's happening, I always feel like I understand. Then, later, I feel like it's the same questions always coming back to me.

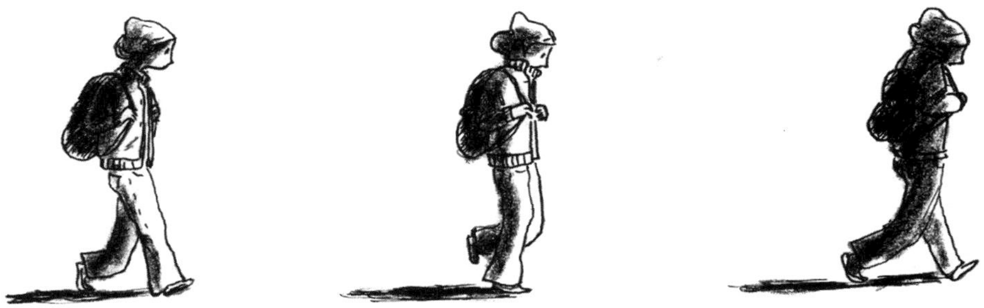

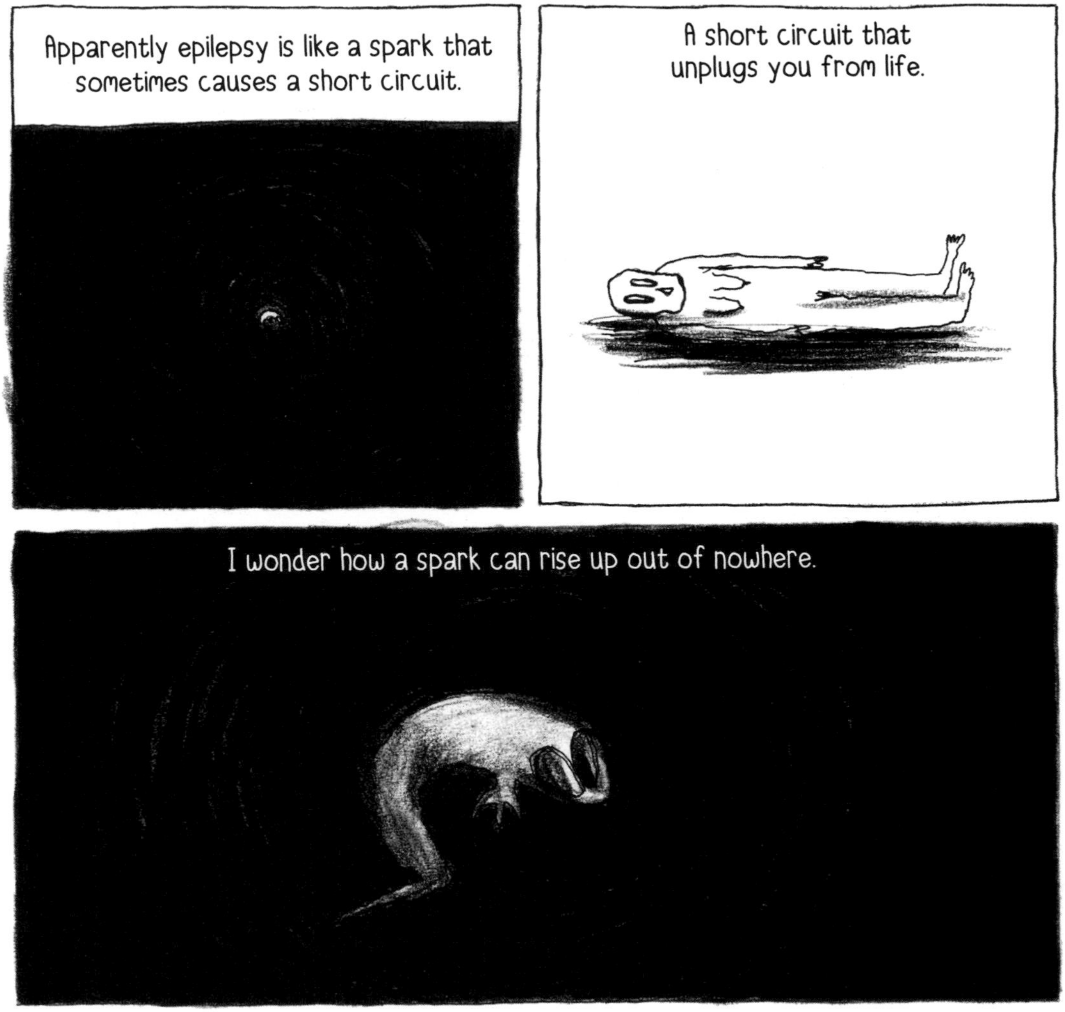
Apparently epilepsy is like a spark that sometimes causes a short circuit.
A short circuit that unplugs you from life.
I wonder how a spark can rise up out of nowhere.

I ask myself why I need so many blood tests, electroencephalograms, what MRI stands for. I tell myself that all this will go away just like it came: on its own. Even if Dr. Pramalé doesn't think so.

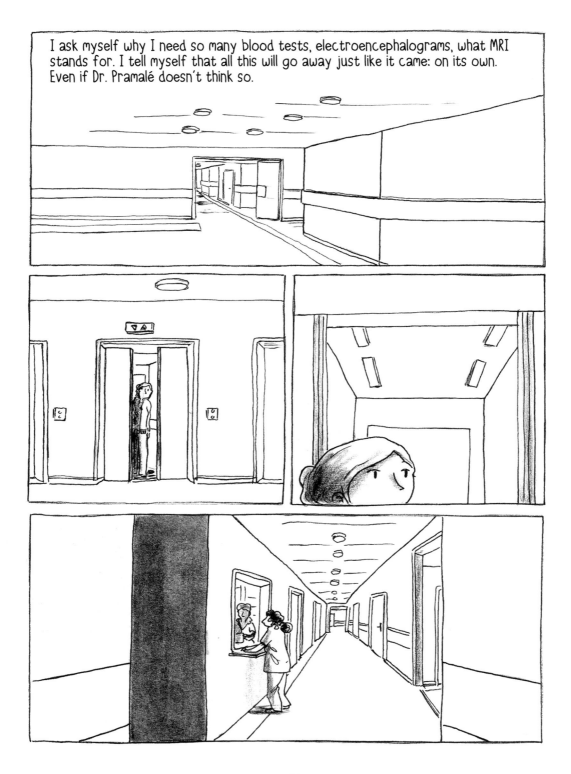

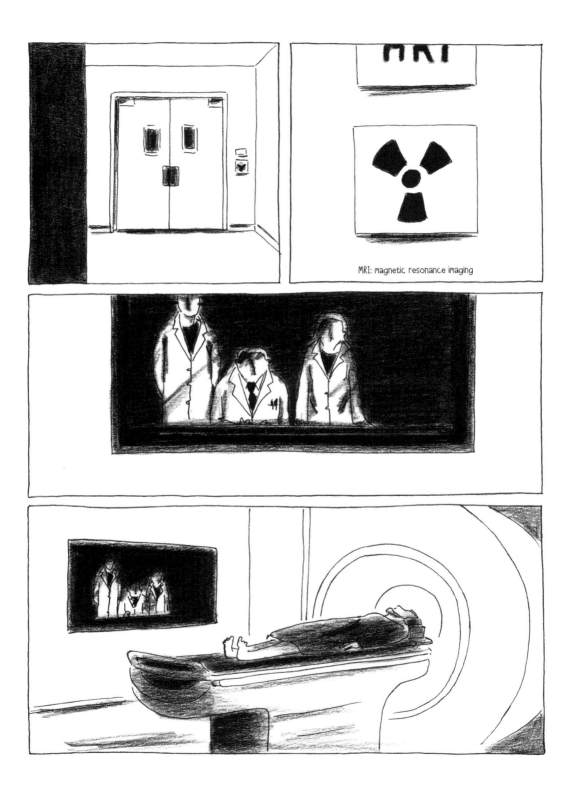

MRI: magnetic resonance imaging

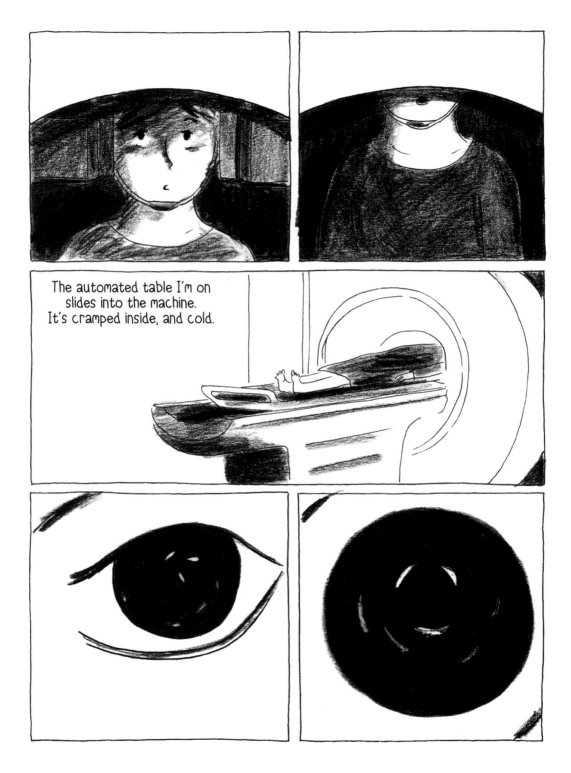

The automated table I'm on
slides into the machine.
It's cramped inside, and cold.

The doctors see nothing in the MRI scan.

Then, after the holidays, they take a second look at the same images.

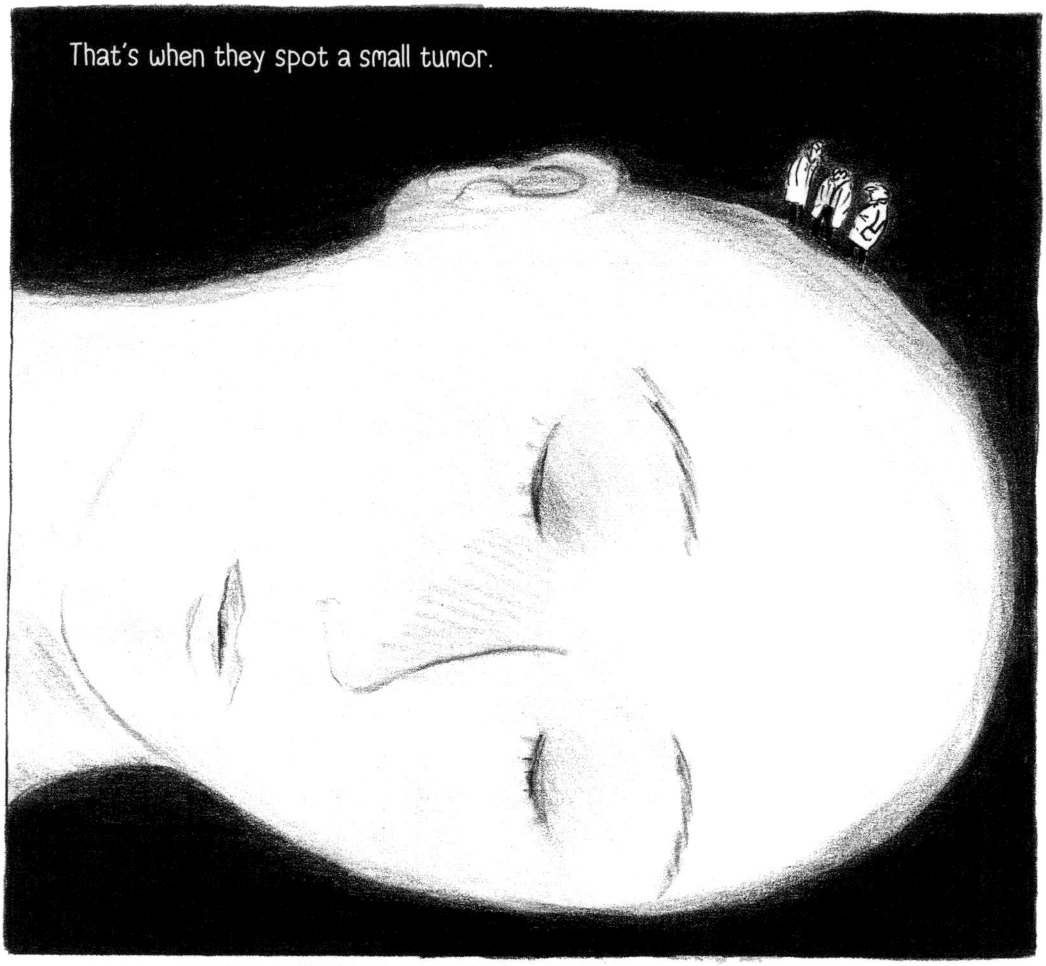
That's when they spot a small tumor.

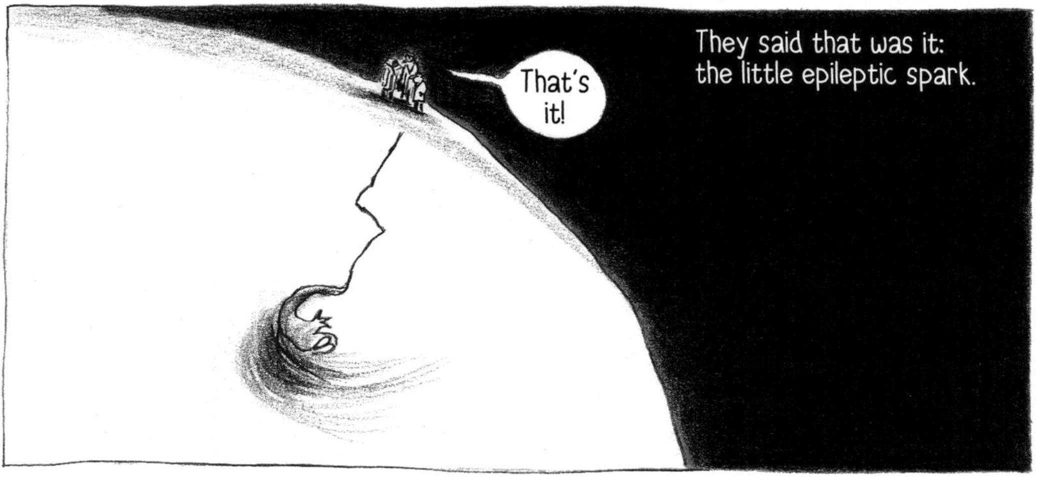
That's it!
They said that was it: the little epileptic spark.

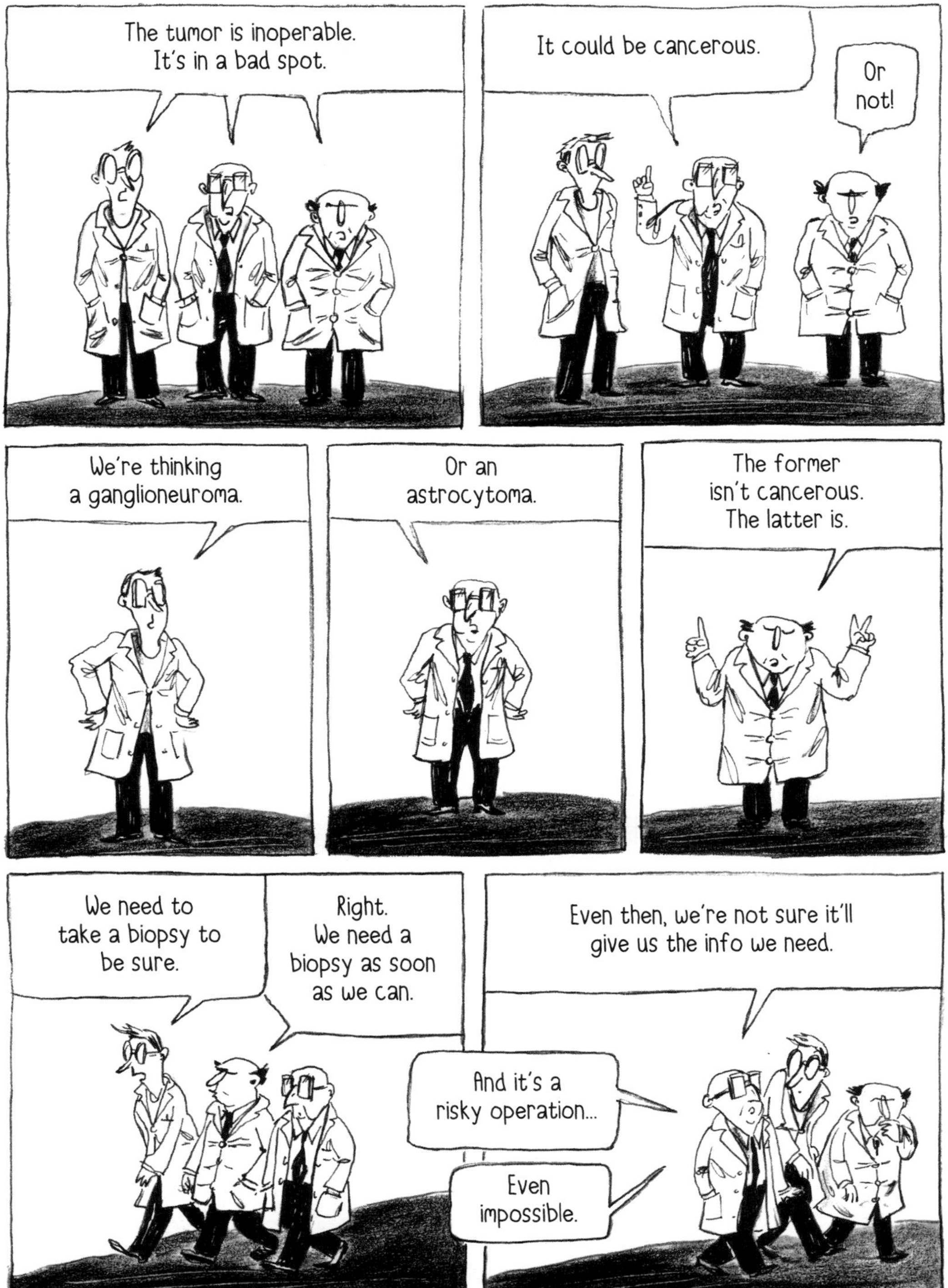
The tumor is inoperable. It's in a bad spot.
It could be cancerous.
Or not!
We're thinking a ganglioneuroma.
Or an astrocytoma.
The former isn't cancerous. The latter is.
We need to take a biopsy to be sure.
Right. We need a biopsy as soon as we can.
Even then, we're not sure it'll give us the info we need.
And it's a risky operation...
Even impossible.

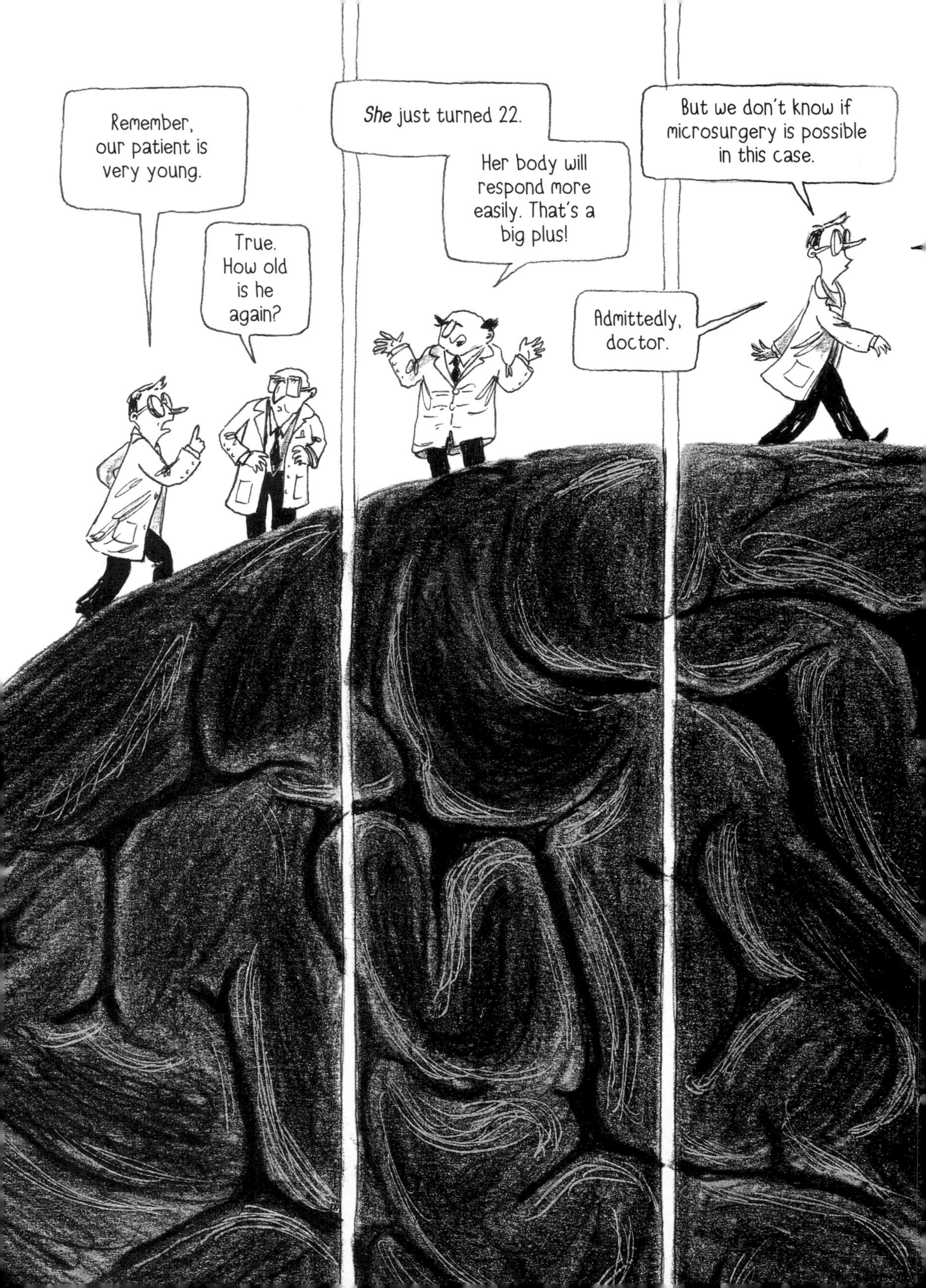
Remember, our patient is very young.
True. How old is he again?
She just turned 22.
Her body will respond more easily. That's a big plus!
Admittedly, doctor.
But we don't know if microsurgery is possible in this case.

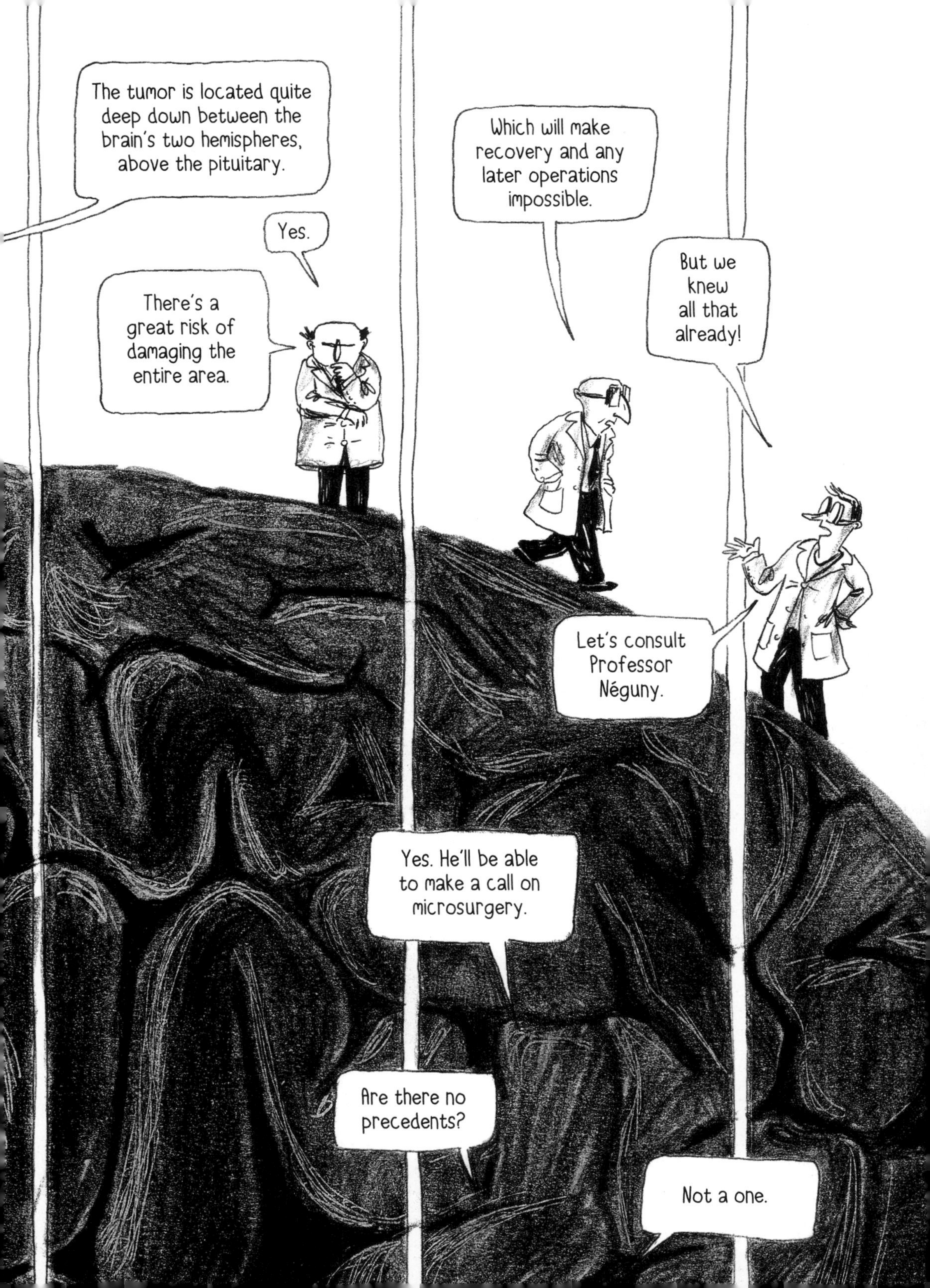
The tumor is located quite deep down between the brain's two hemispheres, above the pituitary.
Yes.
There's a great risk of damaging the entire area.
Which will make recovery and any later operations impossible.
But we knew all that already!
Let's consult Professor Néguny.
Yes. He'll be able to make a call on microsurgery.
Are there no precedents?
Not a one.

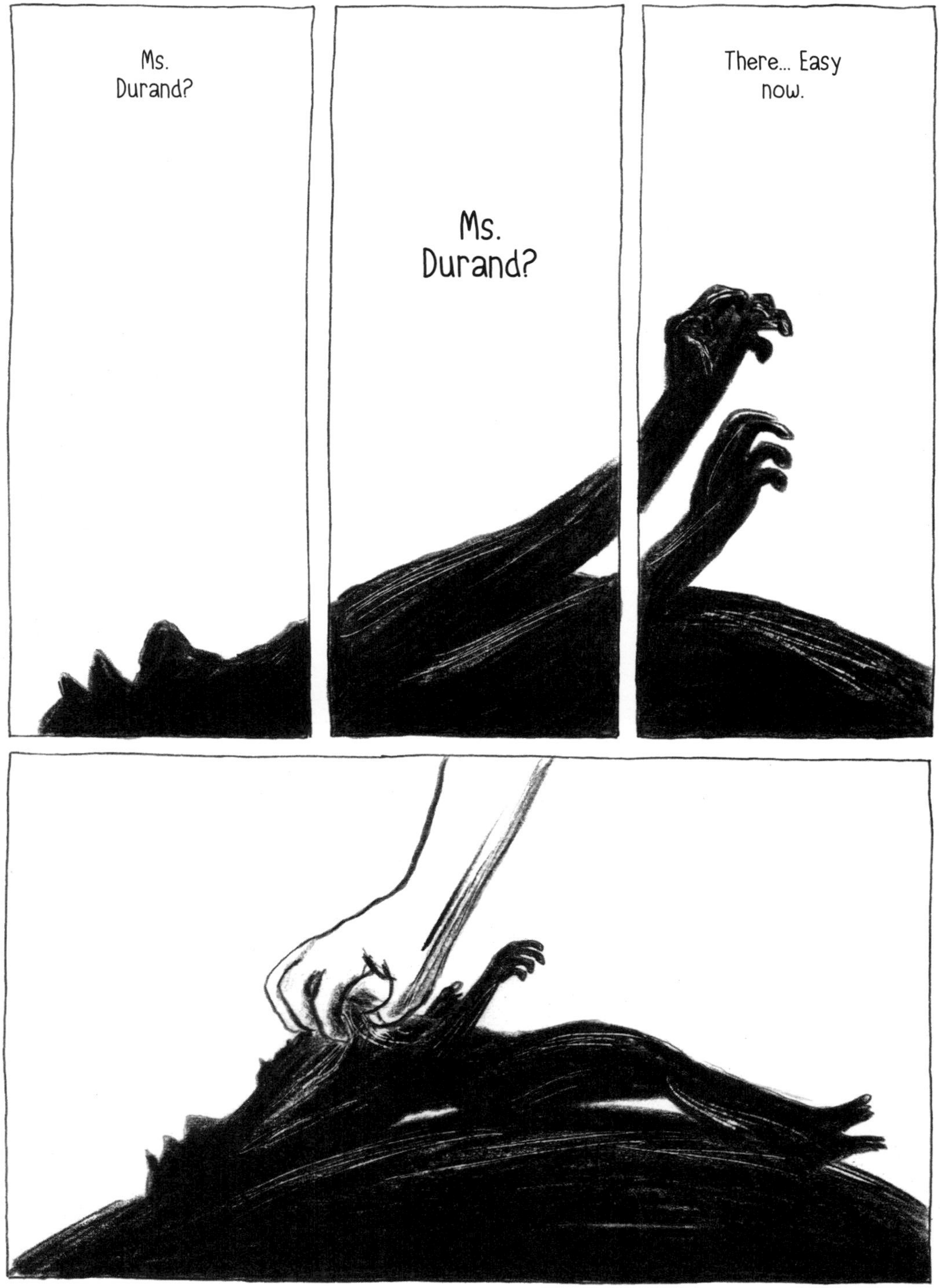
Ms.
Durand?
Ms.
Durand?
There... Easy
now.

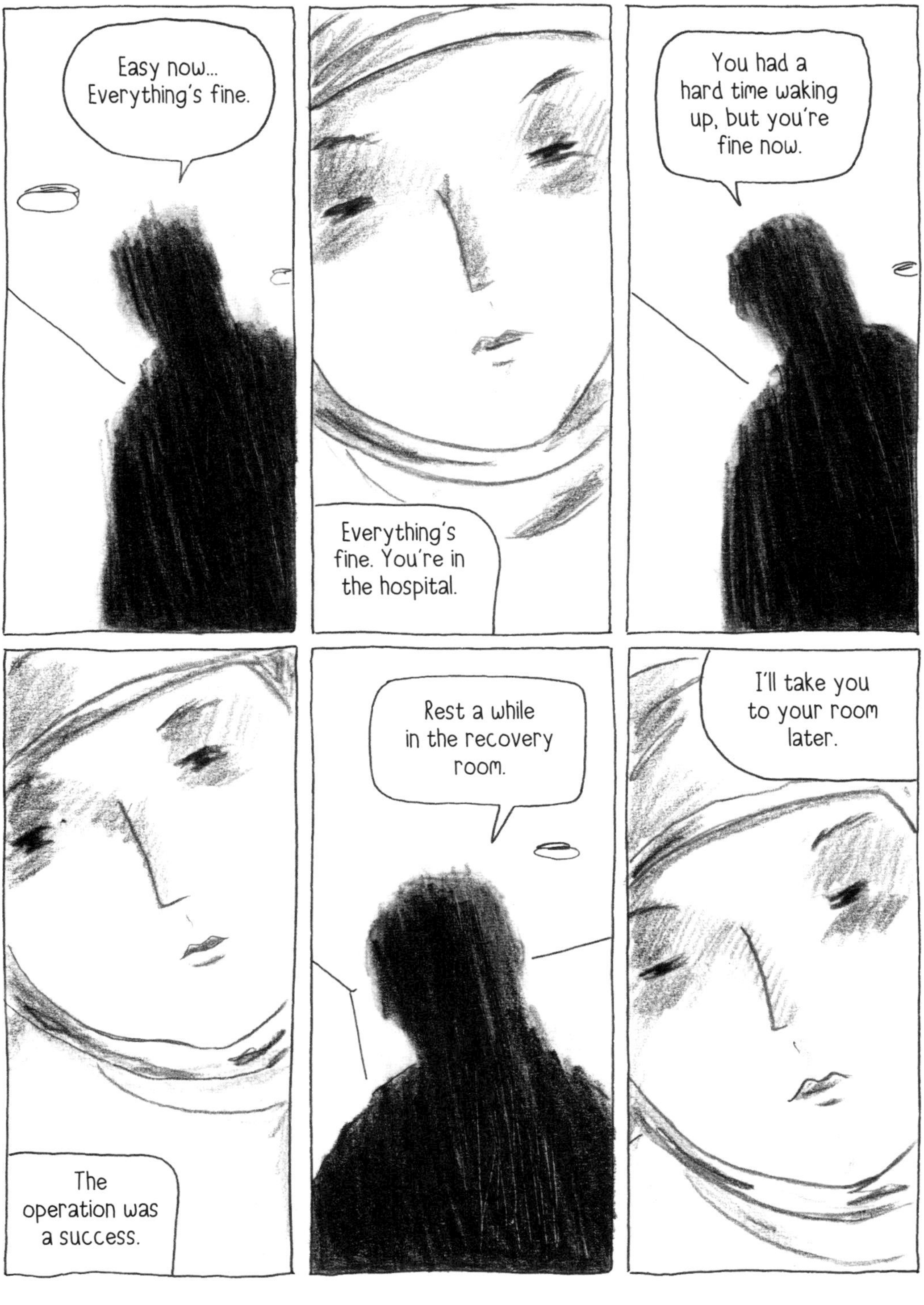
Easy now... Everything's fine.
Everything's fine. You're in the hospital.
You had a hard time waking up, but you're fine now.
The operation was a success.
Rest a while in the recovery room.
I'll take you to your room later.

Even after the tumor was discovered, even after they asked me to shave my head for the biopsy, I still wanted to go on living normally.

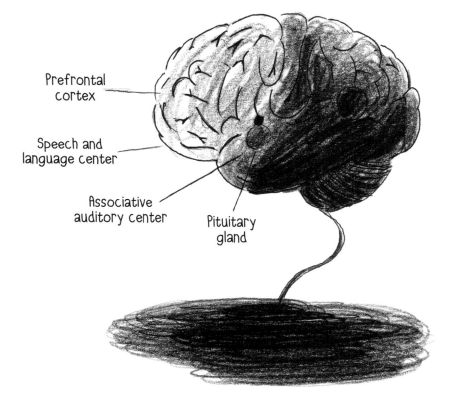

Prefrontal cortex

Speech and language center

Associative auditory center

Pituitary gland

I went to the hospital, swallowed my pills. I was already sleeping a lot, way more than normal; I wouldn't be able to go on like this... And yet, I was convinced I wasn't sick. How can I explain? I must've been someone else...

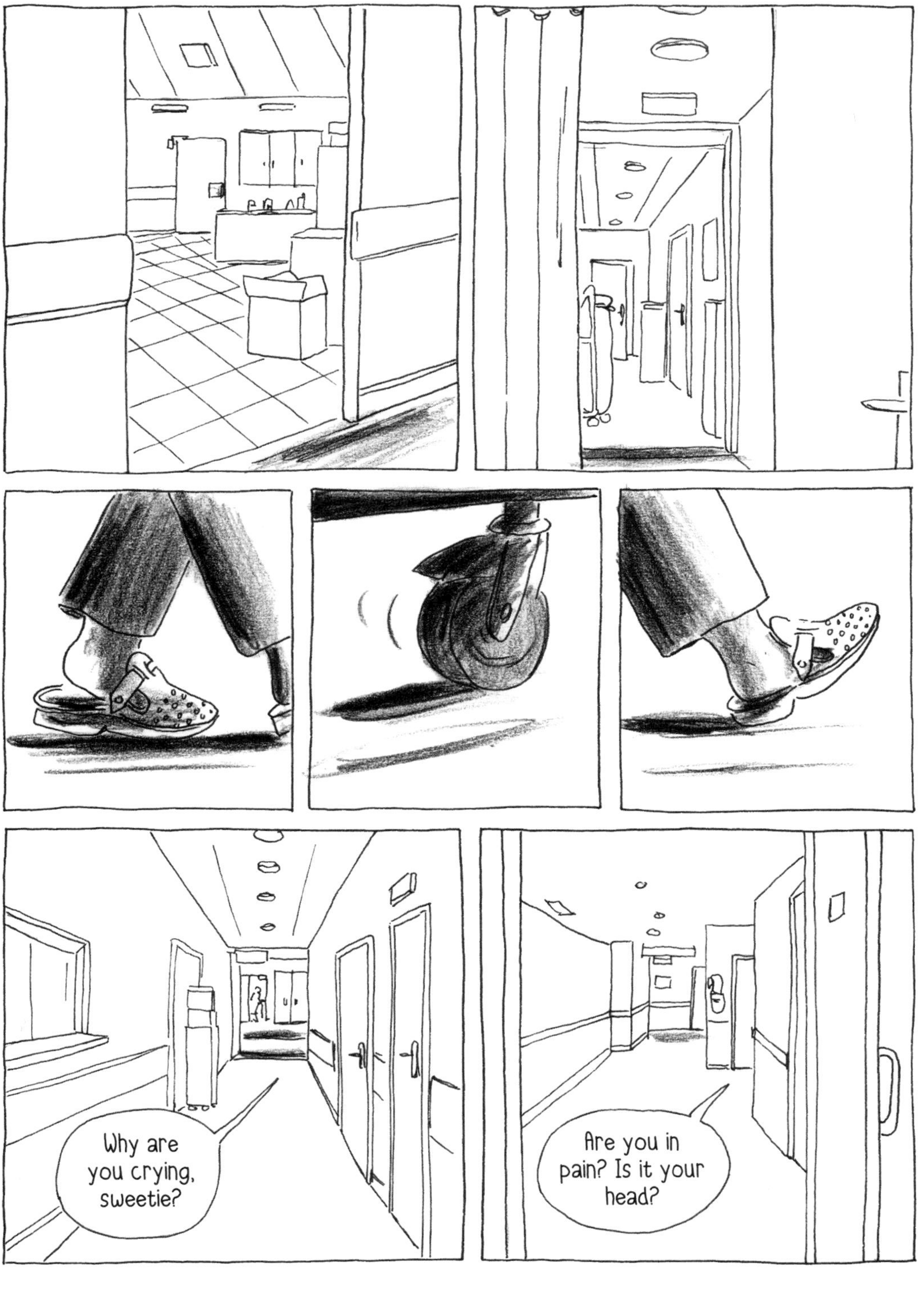
Why are you crying, sweetie?
Are you in pain? Is it your head?

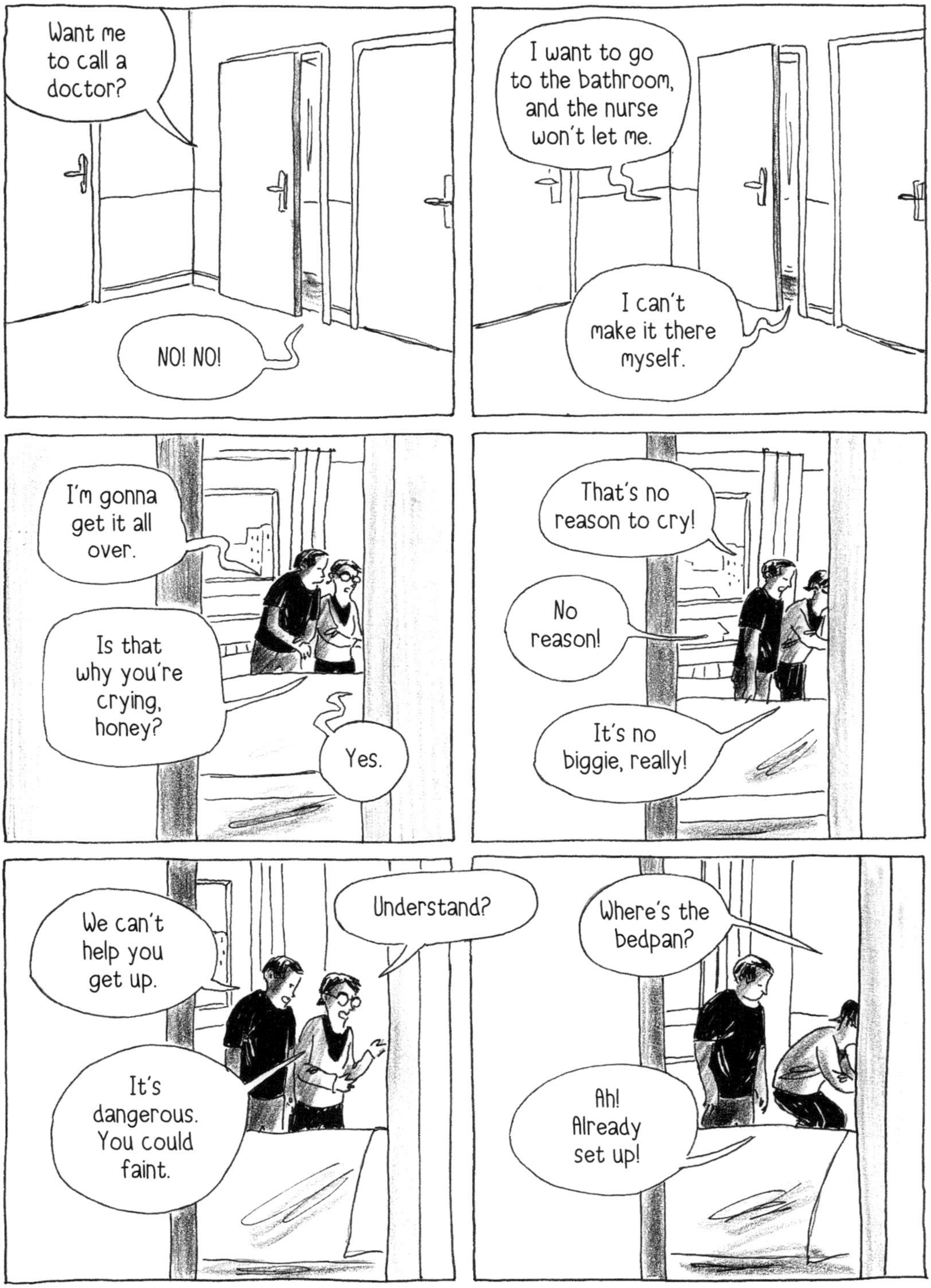
Want me to call a doctor?
NO! NO!
I want to go to the bathroom, and the nurse won't let me.
I can't make it there myself.
I'm gonna get it all over.
Is that why you're crying, honey?
Yes.
That's no reason to cry!
No reason!
It's no biggie, really!
We can't help you get up.
It's dangerous. You could faint.
Understand?
Where's the bedpan?
Ah! Already set up!

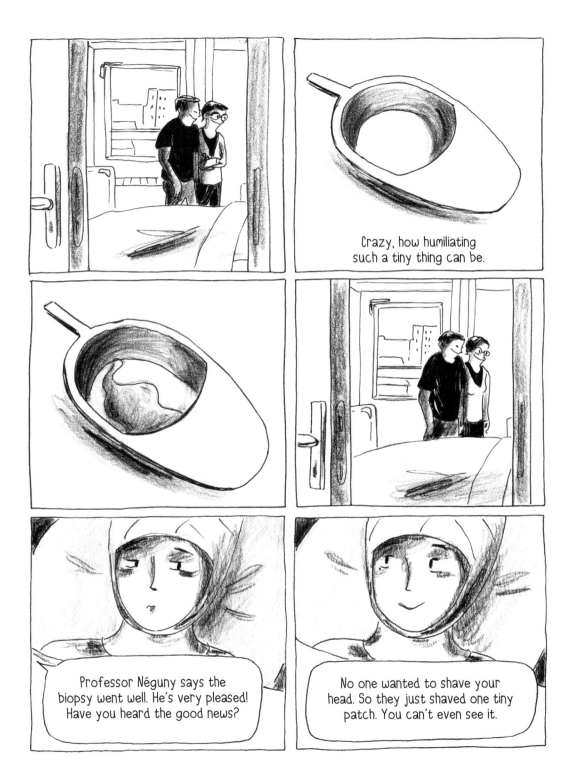

Crazy, how humiliating
such a tiny thing can be.

Professor Néguny says the
biopsy went well. He's very pleased!
Have you heard the good news?

No one wanted to shave your
head. So they just shaved one tiny
patch. You can't even see it.

Today, I still have a small divot in my skull from the operation, where they drilled through. I can feel it sometimes. I never touch it. It always feels unpleasant.

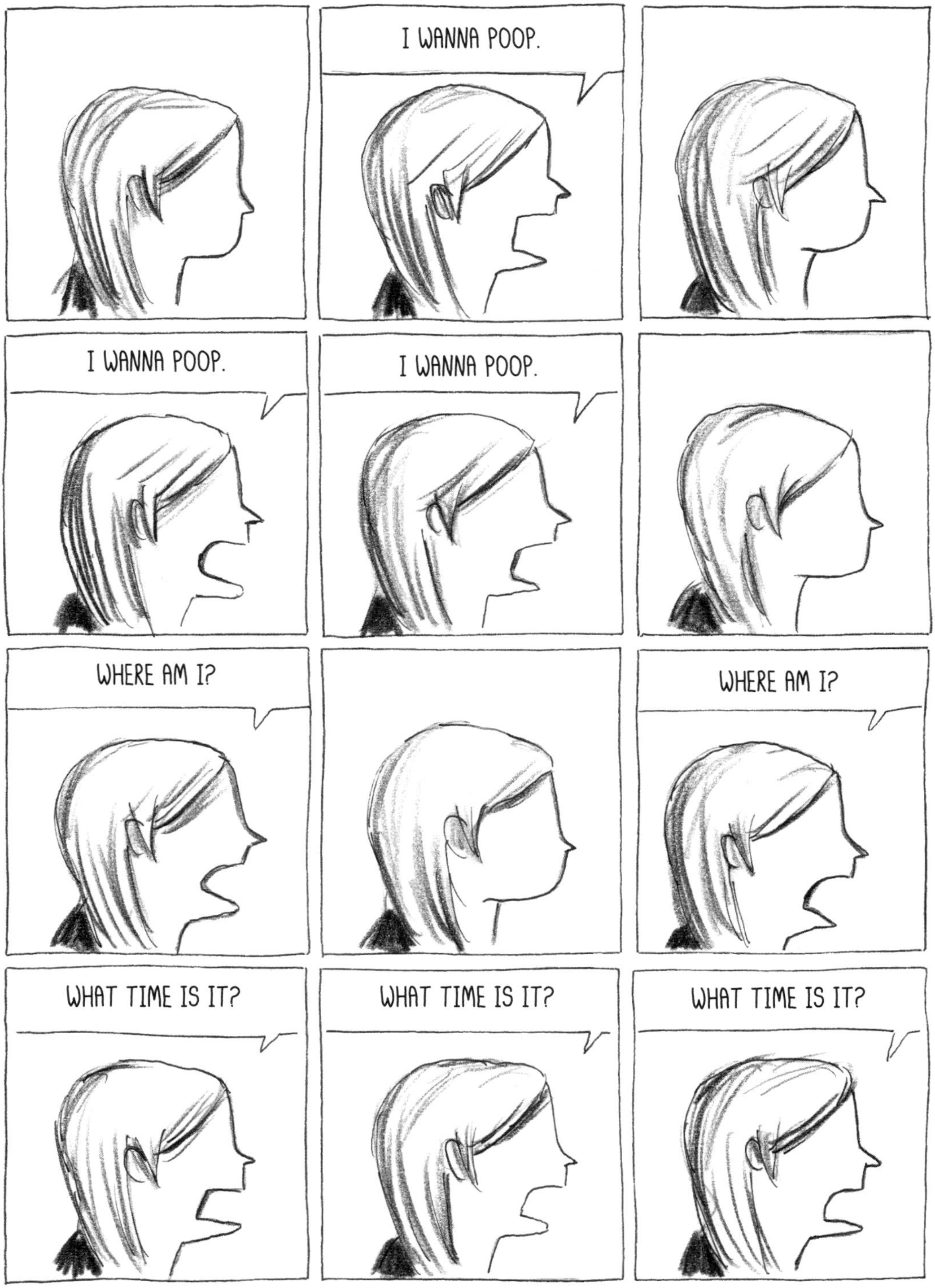
I WANNA POOP.
I WANNA POOP.
I WANNA POOP.
WHERE AM I?
WHERE AM I?
WHAT TIME IS IT?
WHAT TIME IS IT?
WHAT TIME IS IT?

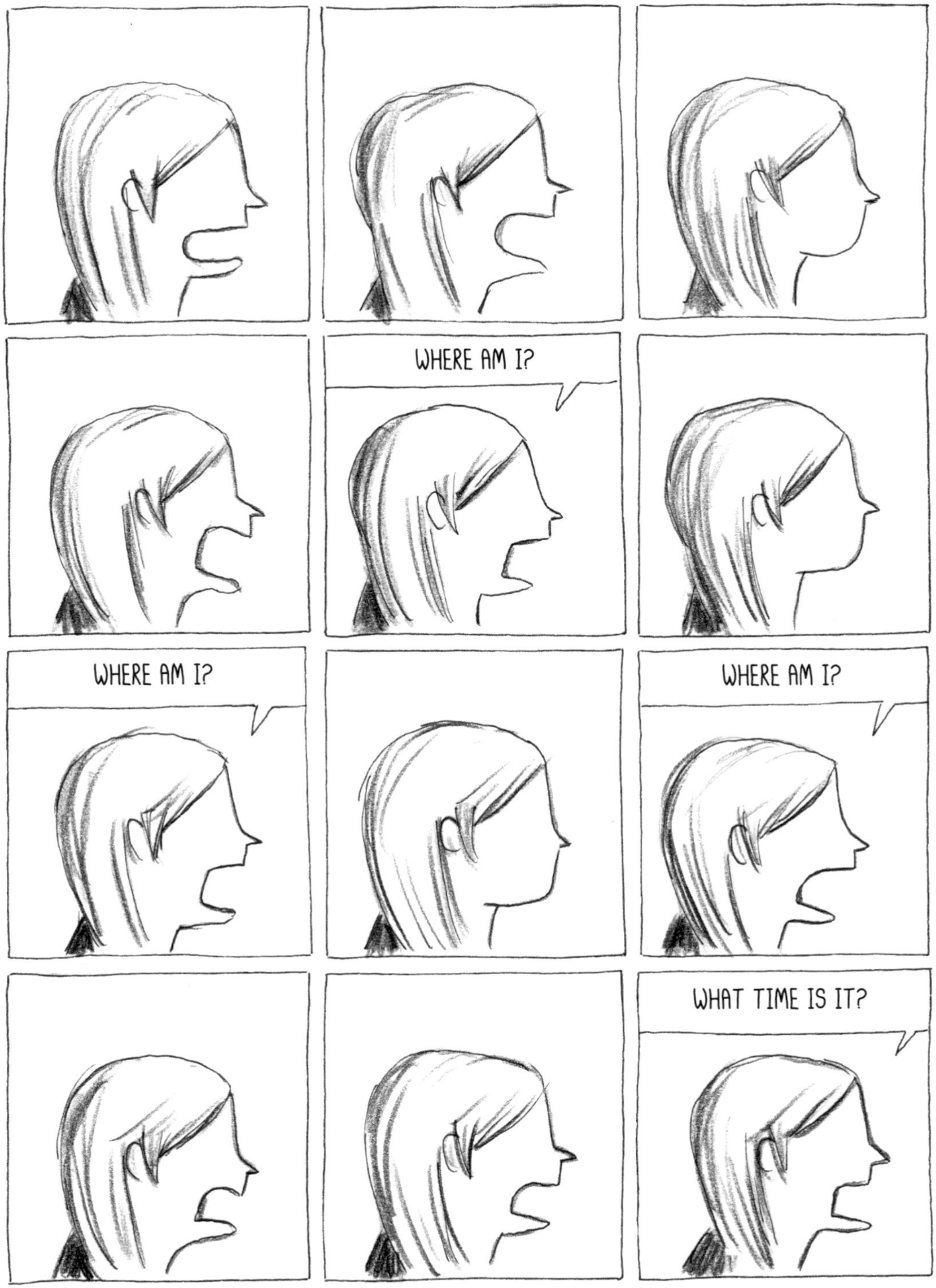
WHERE AM I?
WHERE AM I?
WHERE AM I?
WHAT TIME IS IT?

You, Dad, and Sandrine told me that I'd start talking right before a seizure.

How strange it must've been when I was still going to school, still working at that camp.

I think I often had small seizures, not necessarily noticeable if you didn't know what to look for.

You had trouble describing them. You'd say my eyes went glassy, my mouth hung open. I had these massive convulsions that intimidated you.

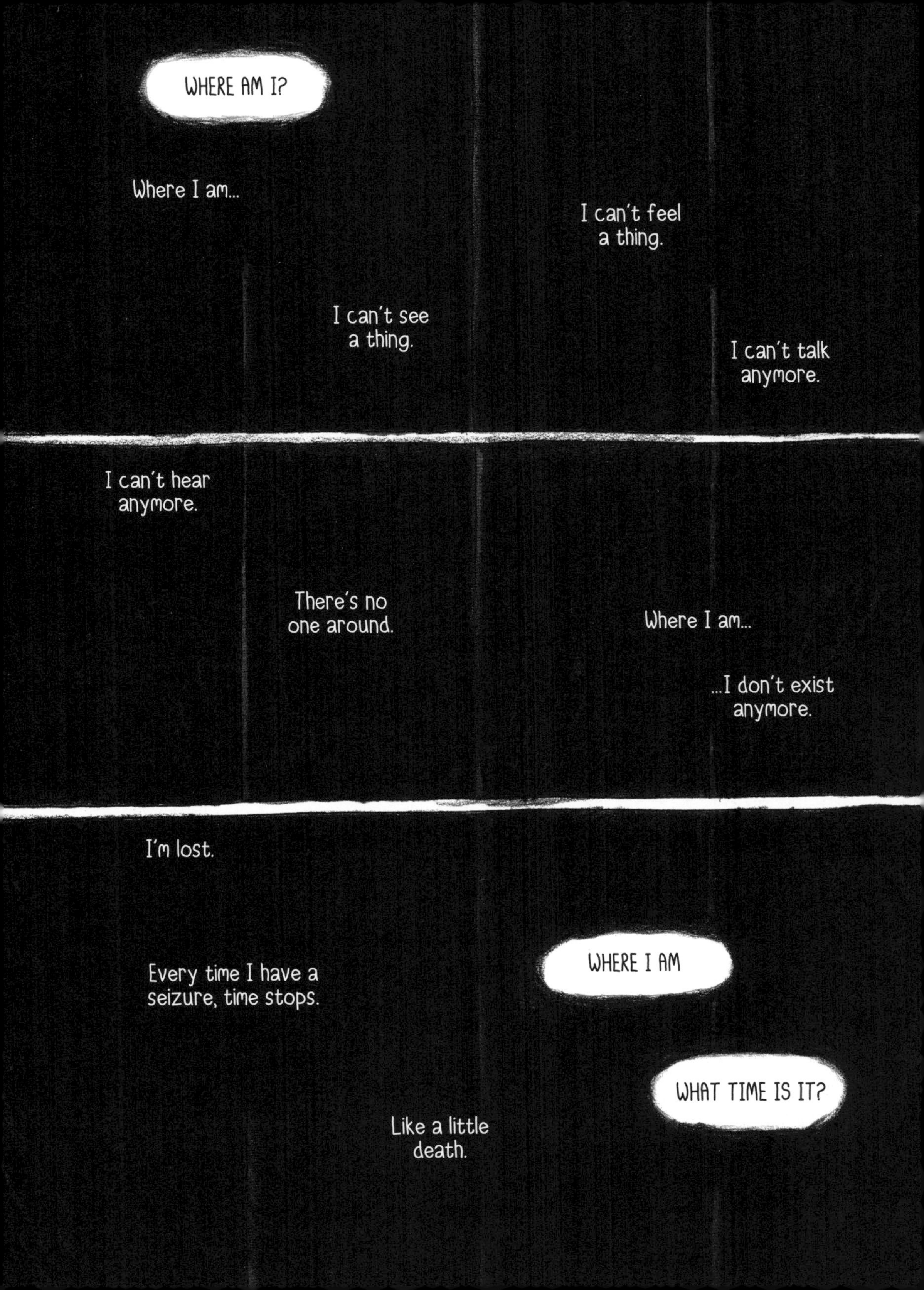
WHERE AM I?
Where I am...
I can't see a thing.
I can't feel a thing.
I can't talk anymore.
I can't hear anymore.
There's no one around.
Where I am...
...I don't exist anymore.
I'm lost.
Every time I have a seizure, time stops.
Like a little death.
WHERE I AM
WHAT TIME IS IT?

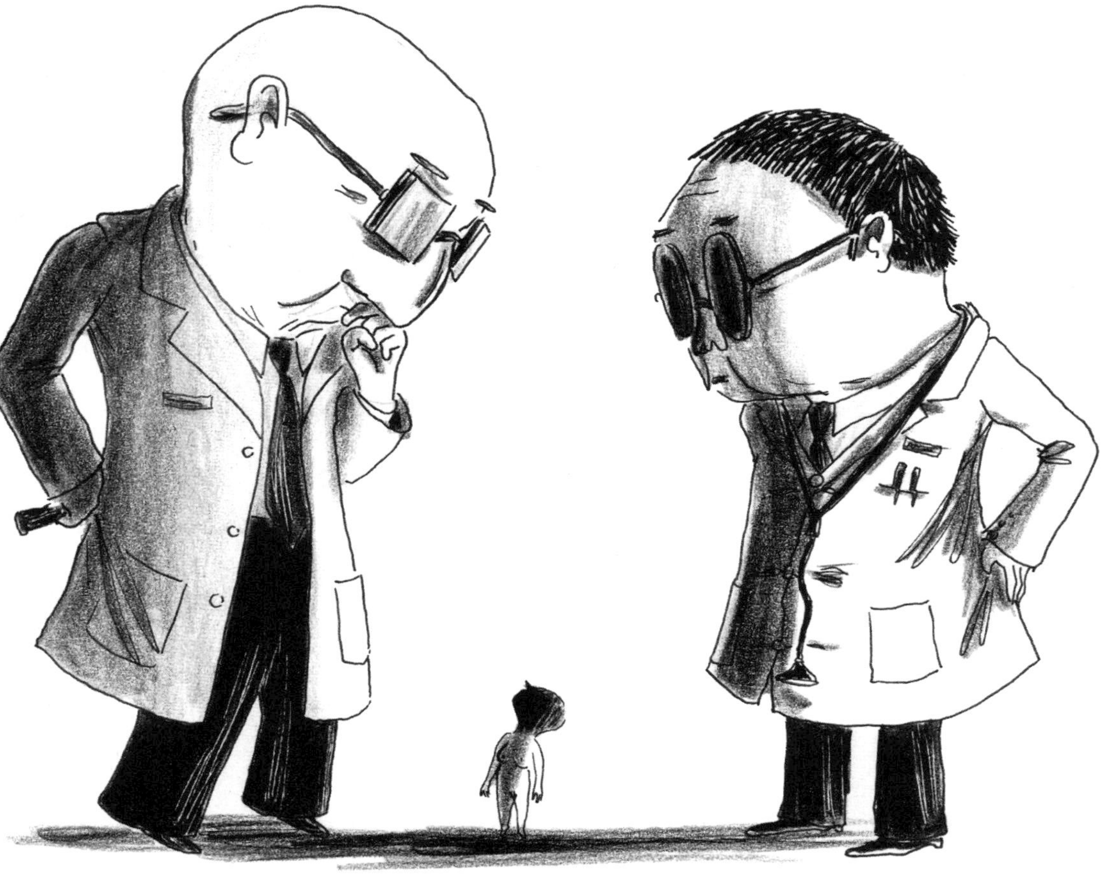

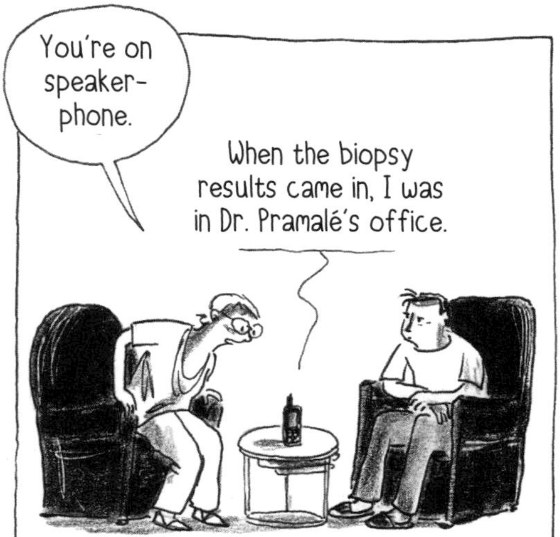
You're on speaker-phone.
When the biopsy results came in, I was in Dr. Pramalé's office.

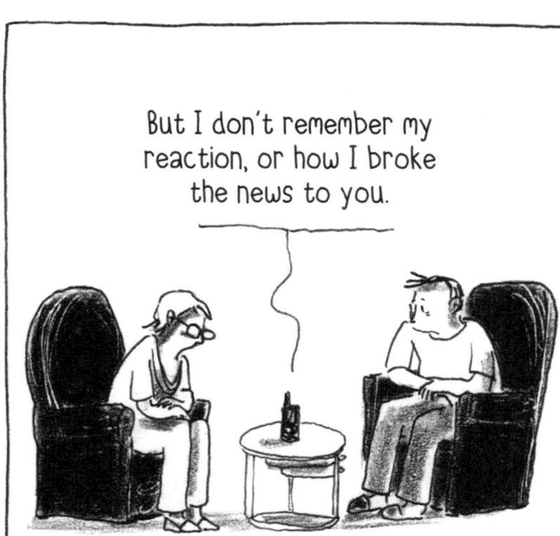
But I don't remember my reaction, or how I broke the news to you.

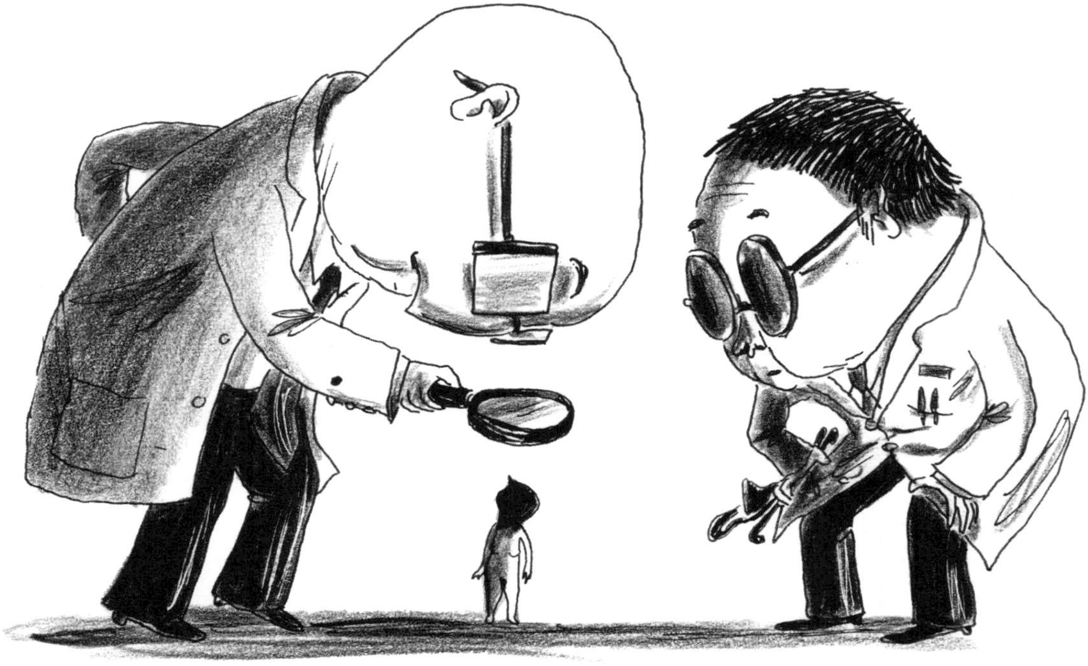

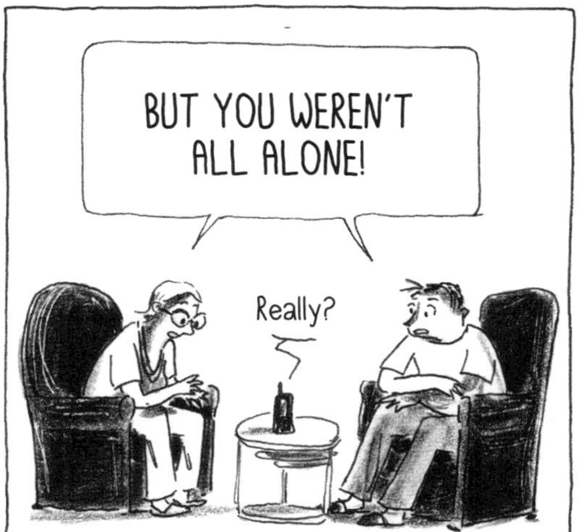
BUT YOU WEREN'T ALL ALONE!
Really?

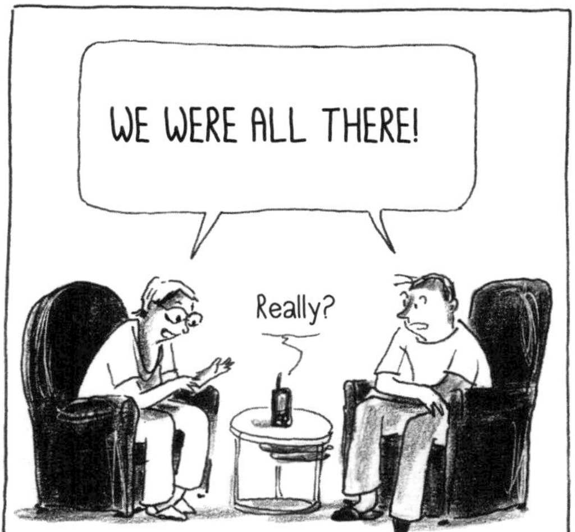
WE WERE ALL THERE!
Really?

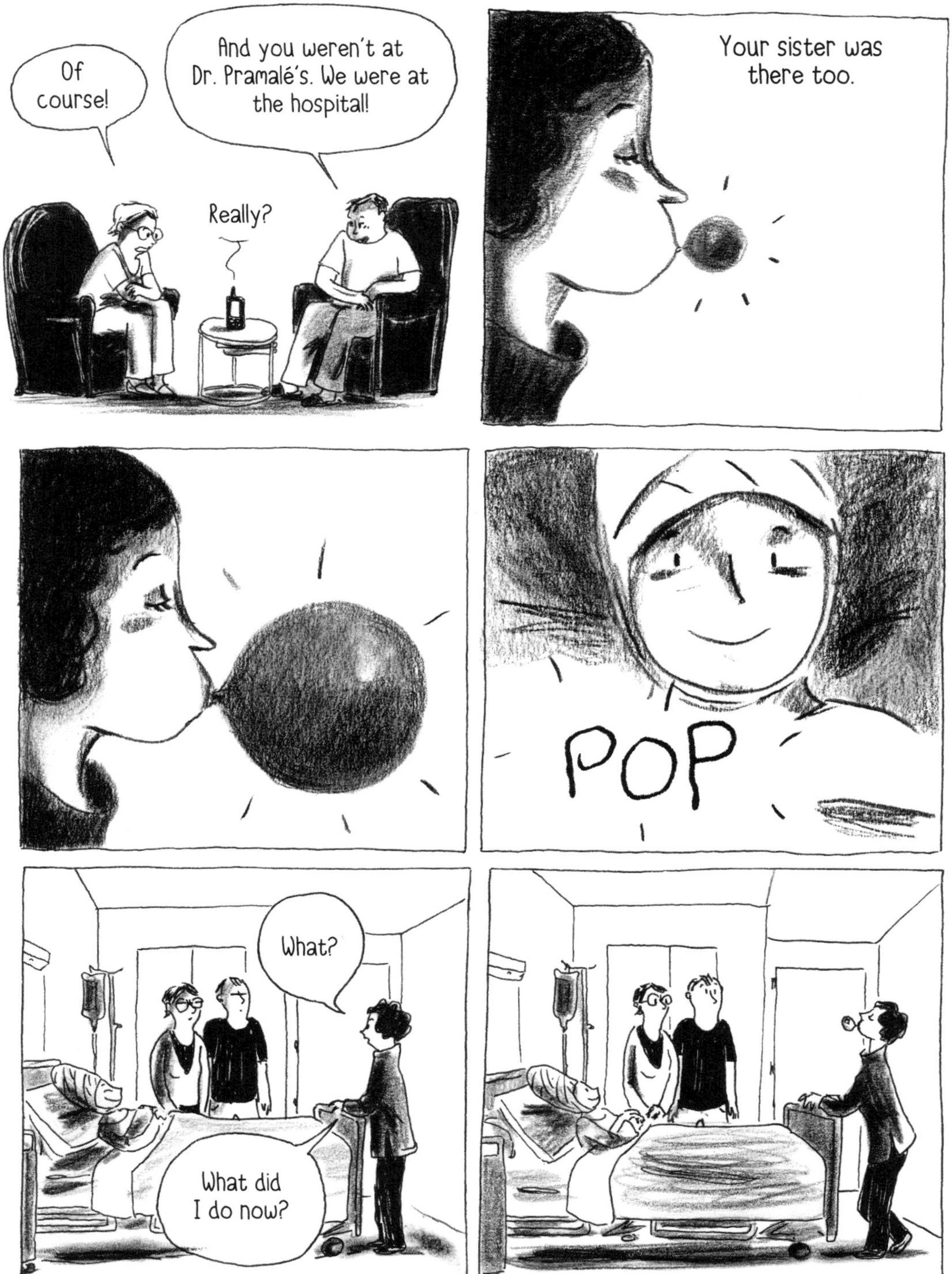
Of course!
And you weren't at Dr. Pramalé's. We were at the hospital!
Really?
Your sister was there too.
POP
What?
What did I do now?

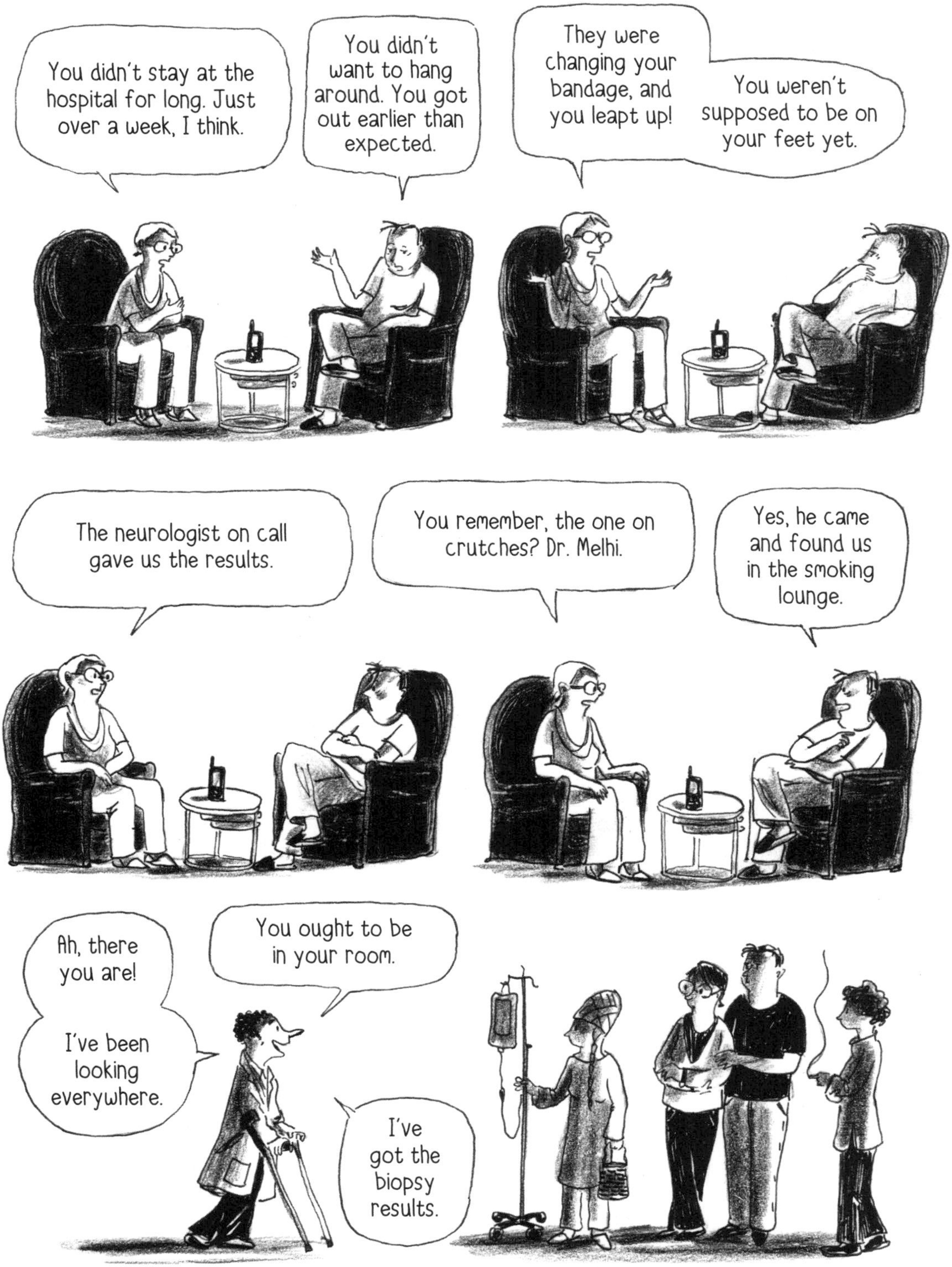

You didn't stay at the hospital for long. Just over a week, I think.
You didn't want to hang around. You got out earlier than expected.
They were changing your bandage, and you leapt up!
You weren't supposed to be on your feet yet.
The neurologist on call gave us the results.
You remember, the one on crutches? Dr. Melhi.
Yes, he came and found us in the smoking lounge.
Ah, there you are!
I've been looking everywhere.
You ought to be in your room.
I've got the biopsy results.

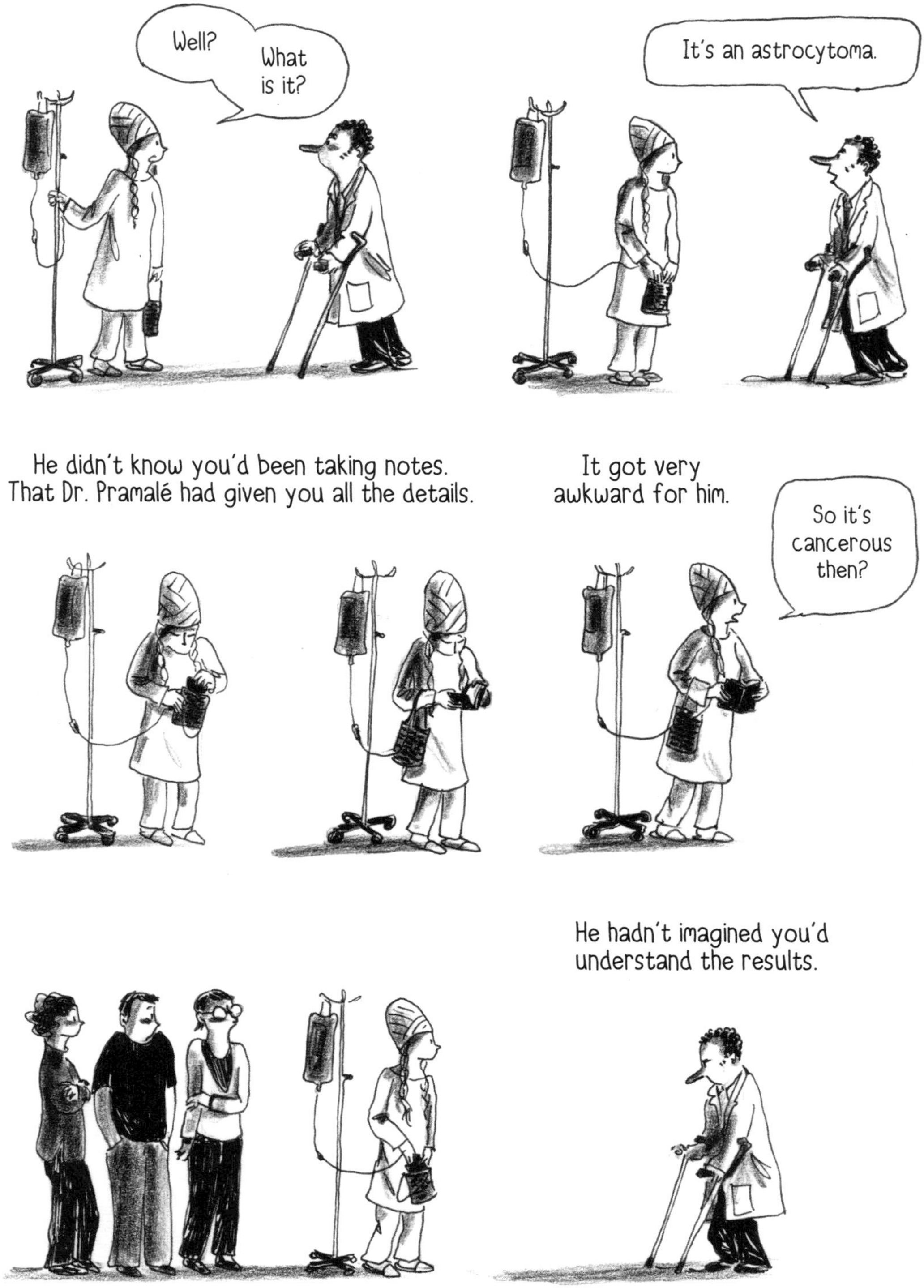
Well?
What is it?
It's an astrocytoma.
He didn't know you'd been taking notes. That Dr. Pramalé had given you all the details.
It got very awkward for him.
So it's cancerous then?
He hadn't imagined you'd understand the results.

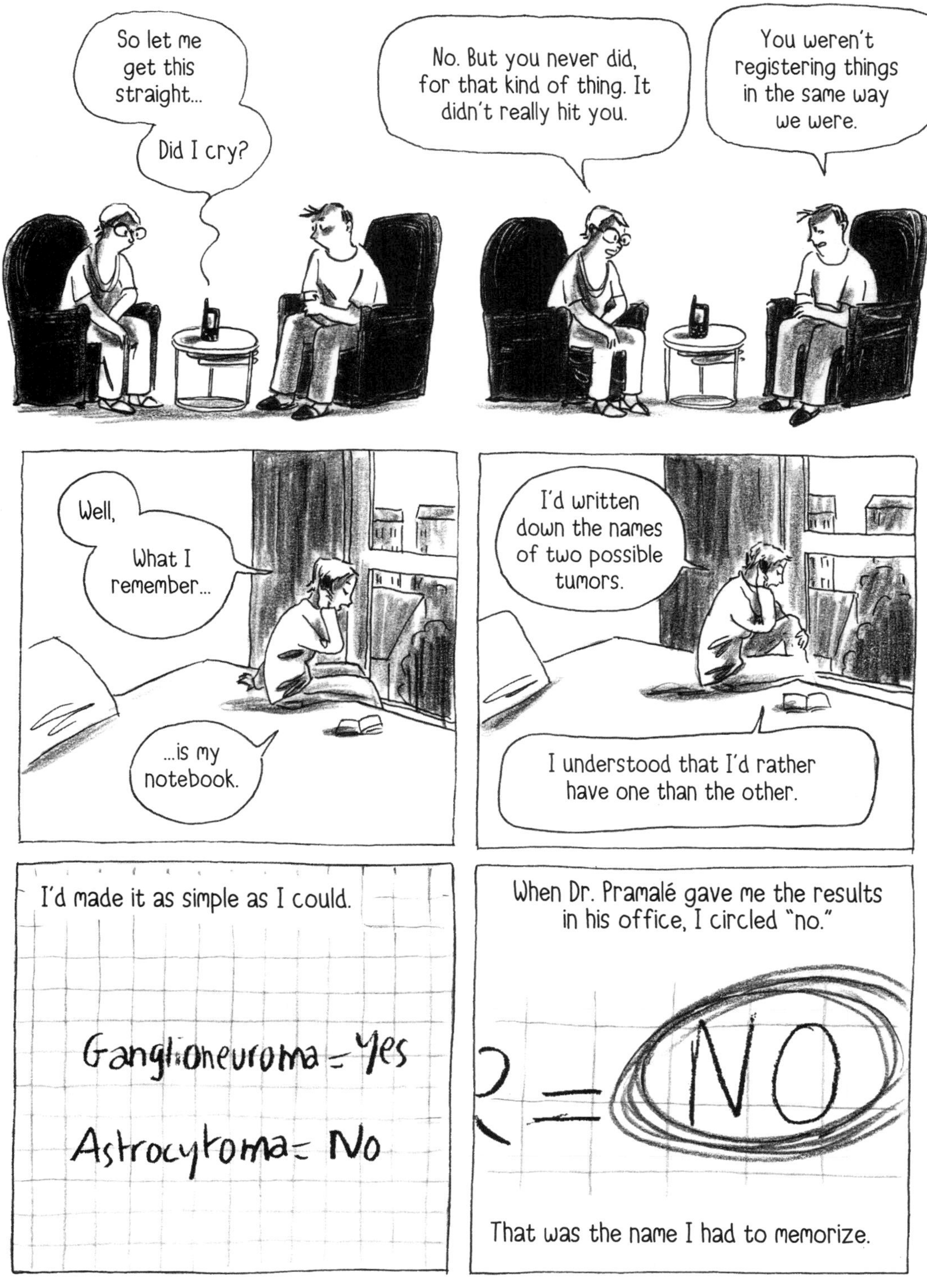
So let me get this straight...
Did I cry?
No. But you never did, for that kind of thing. It didn't really hit you.
You weren't registering things in the same way we were.
Well,
What I remember...
...is my notebook.
I'd written down the names of two possible tumors.
I understood that I'd rather have one than the other.
I'd made it as simple as I could.
Ganglioneuroma = Yes
Astrocytoma = No
When Dr. Pramalé gave me the results in his office, I circled "no."
? = NO
That was the name I had to memorize.

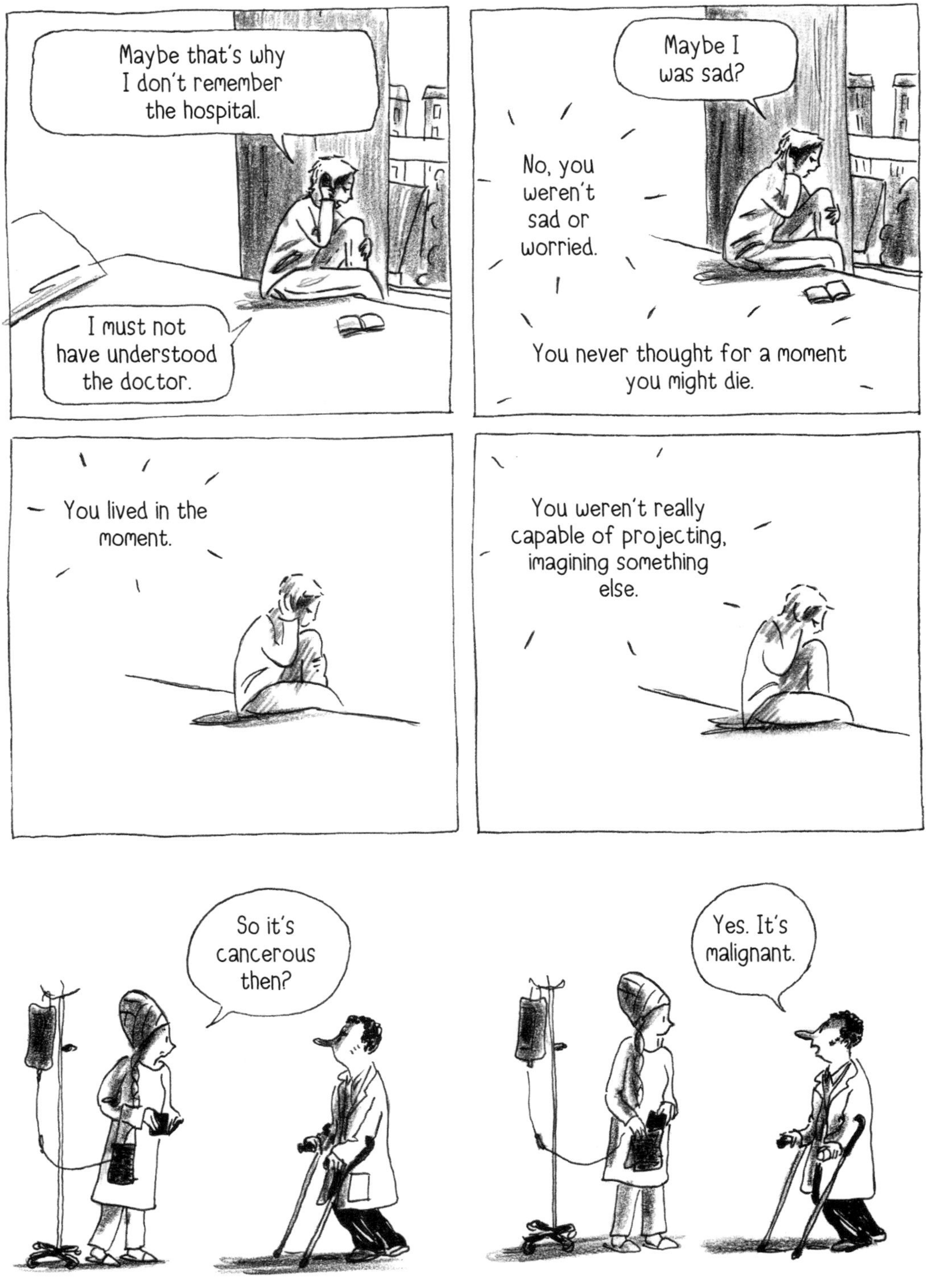
Maybe that's why I don't remember the hospital.
I must not have understood the doctor.
Maybe I was sad?
No, you weren't sad or worried.
You never thought for a moment you might die.
You lived in the moment.
You weren't really capable of projecting, imagining something else.
So it's cancerous then?
Yes. It's malignant.

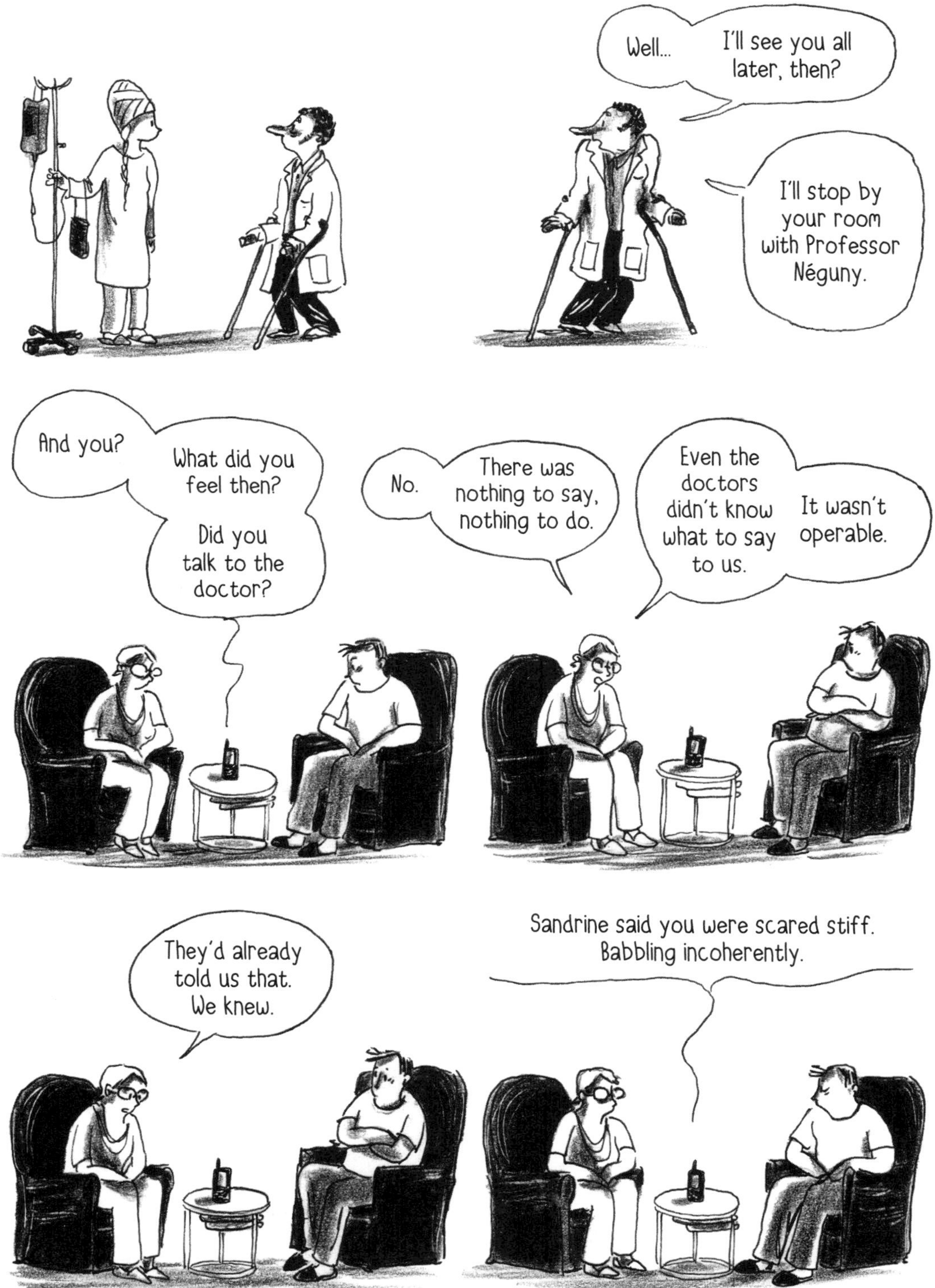
Well...
I'll see you all later, then?
I'll stop by your room with Professor Néguny.
And you?
What did you feel then?
Did you talk to the doctor?
No.
There was nothing to say, nothing to do.
Even the doctors didn't know what to say to us.
It wasn't operable.
They'd already told us that. We knew.
Sandrine said you were scared stiff. Babbling incoherently.

Thanks to the biopsy, the doctors diagnosed me with a Stage I cancerous tumor. It was a little thing, the size of the nail on my pinky finger. Maybe it had always been there... How to tell? Its growth was unpredictable. It could get really big really fast... Or take its time. It was already active. And starting to do damage.

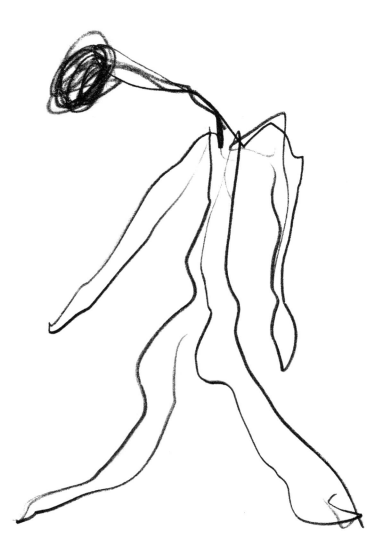

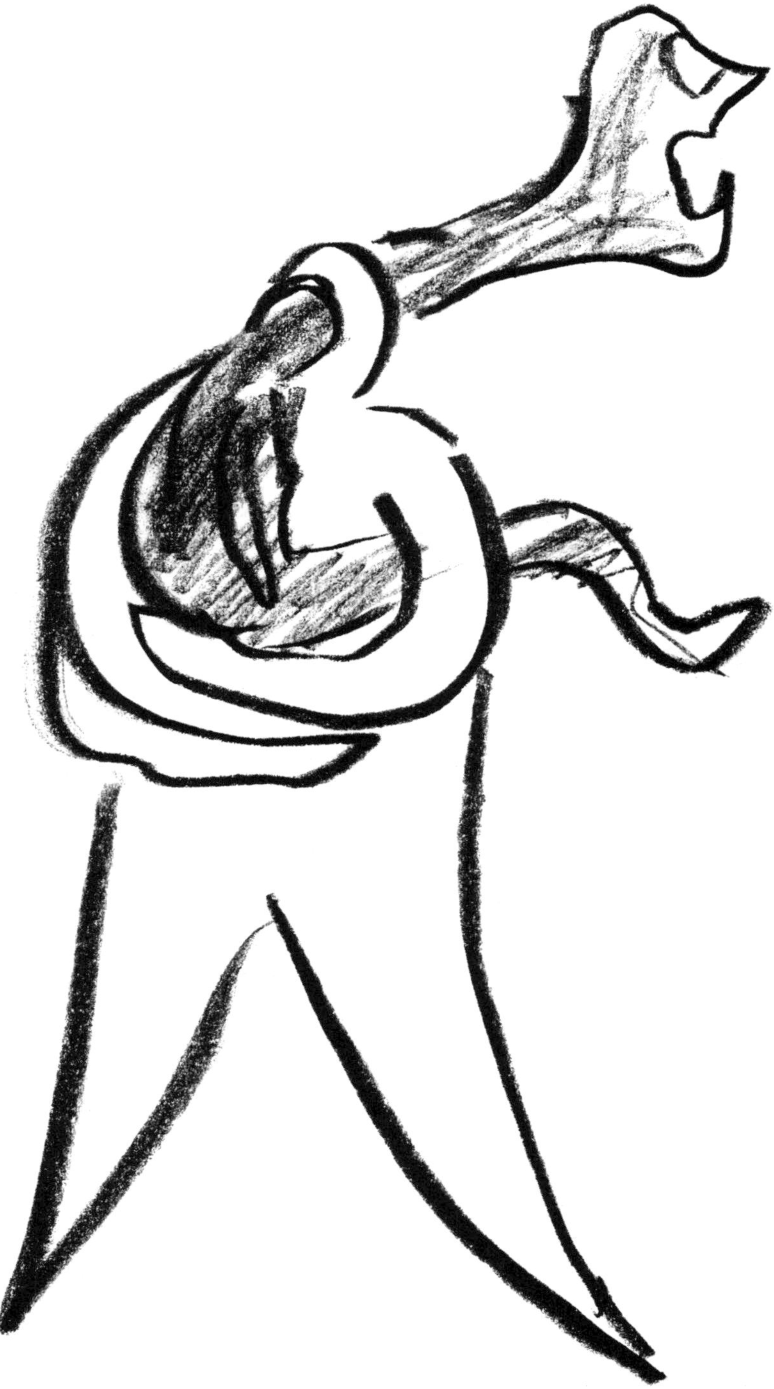

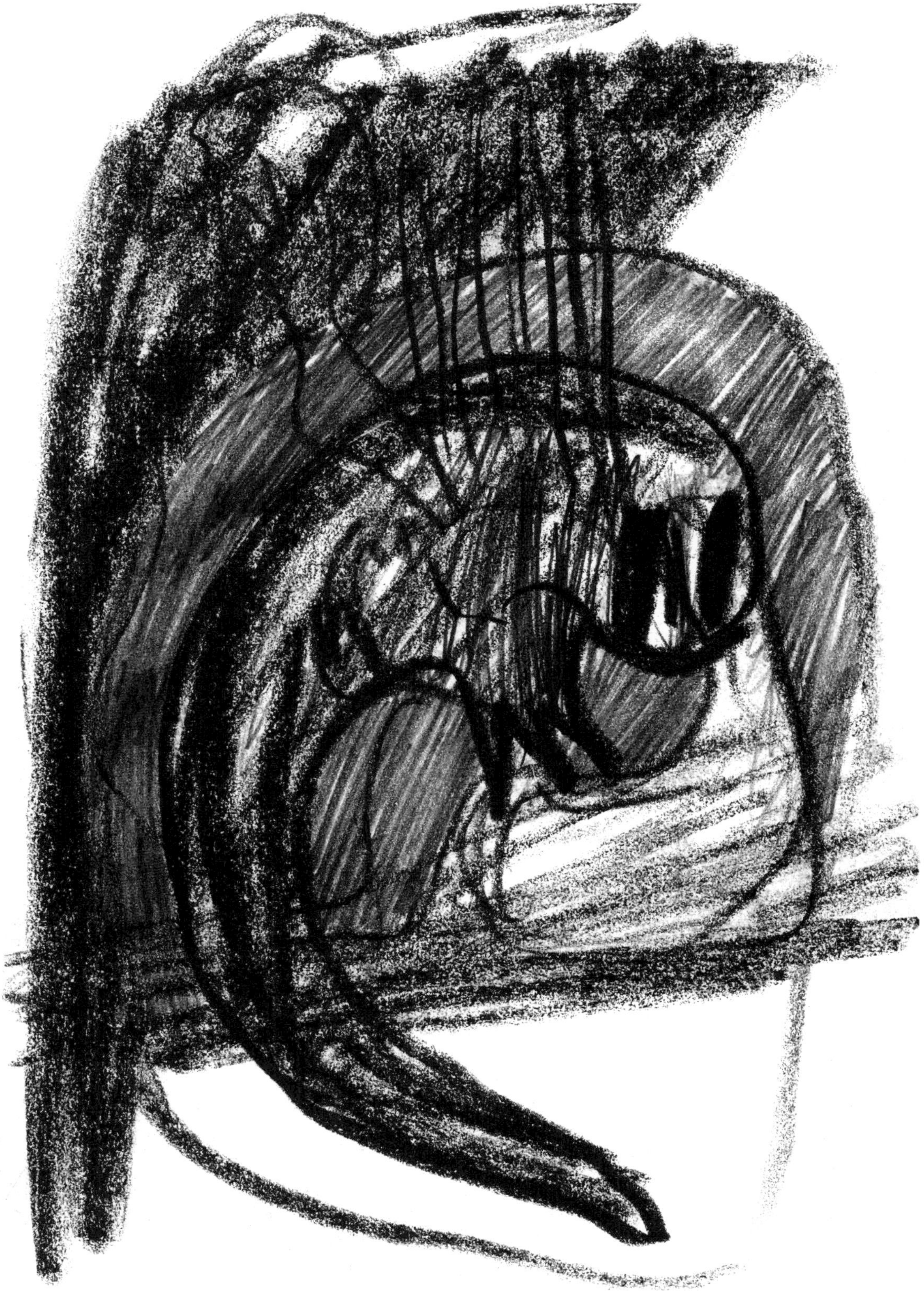

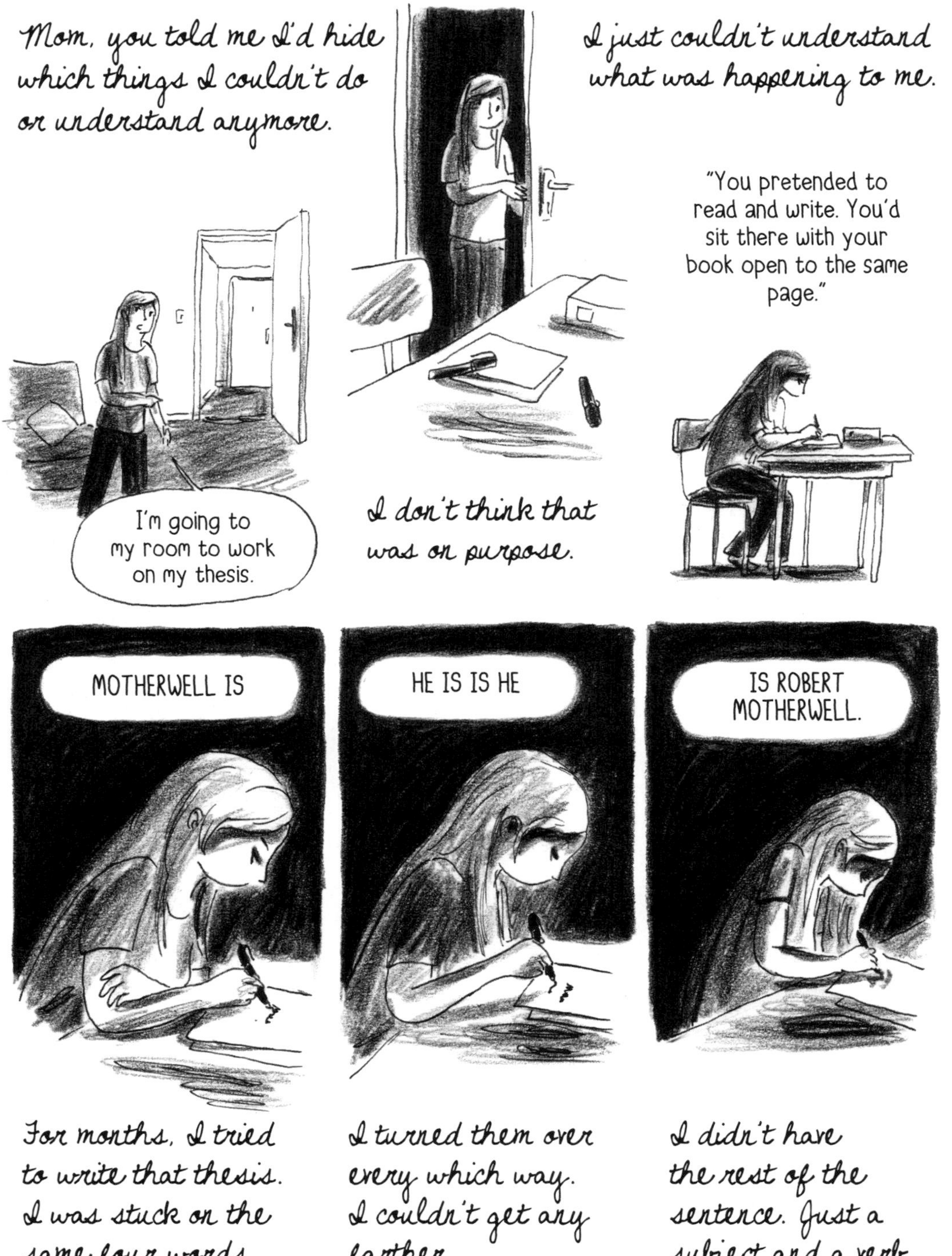
Mom, you told me I'd hide which things I couldn't do or understand anymore.
I'm going to my room to work on my thesis.
I just couldn't understand what was happening to me.
"You pretended to read and write. You'd sit there with your book open to the same page."
I don't think that was on purpose.
MOTHERWELL IS
HE IS IS HE
IS ROBERT MOTHERWELL.
For months, I tried to write that thesis. I was stuck on the same four words.
I turned them over every which way. I couldn't get any farther.
I didn't have the rest of the sentence. Just a subject and a verb.

And then one day, I told you I couldn't seem to write anymore, couldn't think.

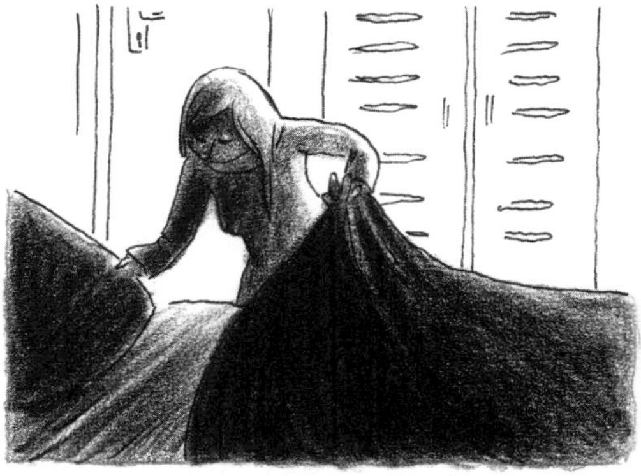

I finally stopped saying I was writing. It was a relief, giving up a little.

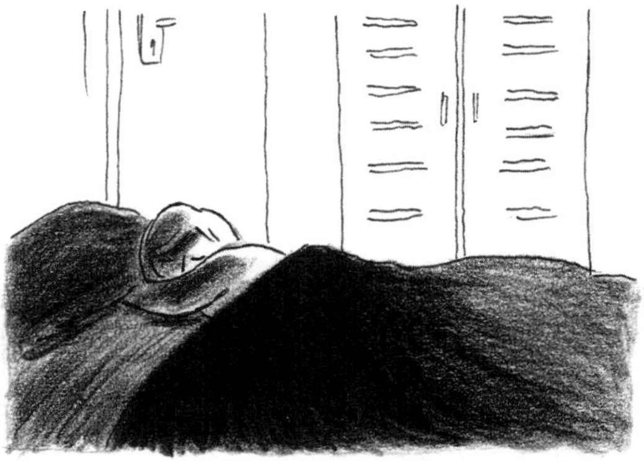

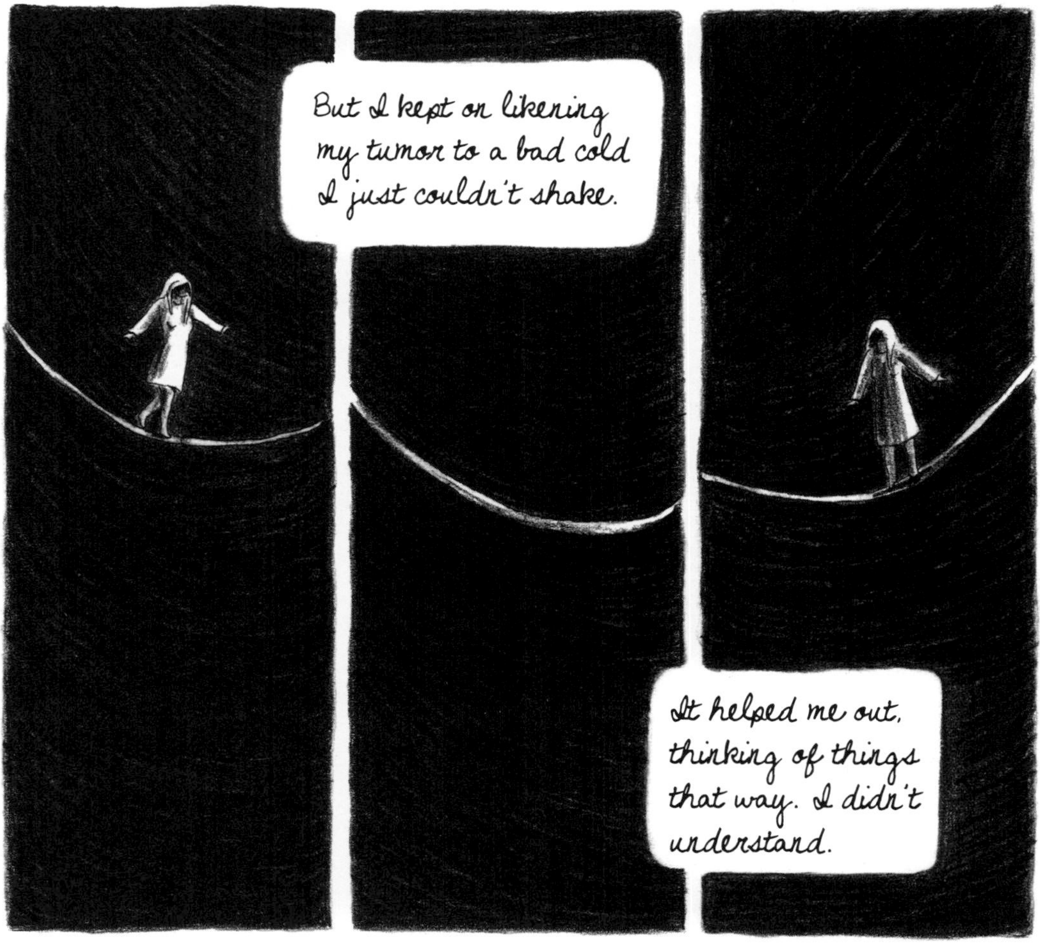
But I kept on likening my tumor to a bad cold I just couldn't shake.
It helped me out, thinking of things that way. I didn't understand.

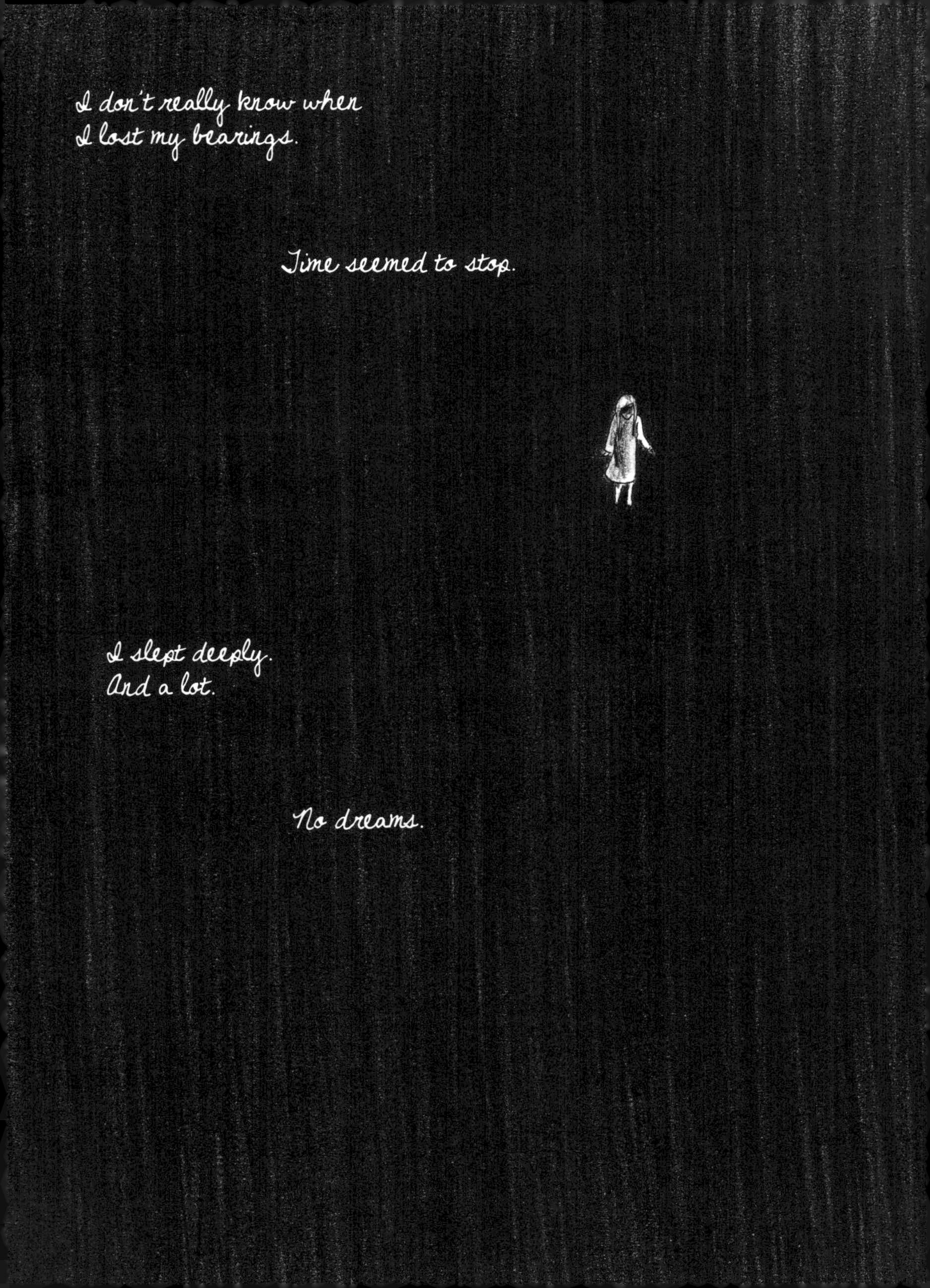
I don't really know when
I lost my bearings.
Time seemed to stop.
I slept deeply.
And a lot.
No dreams.

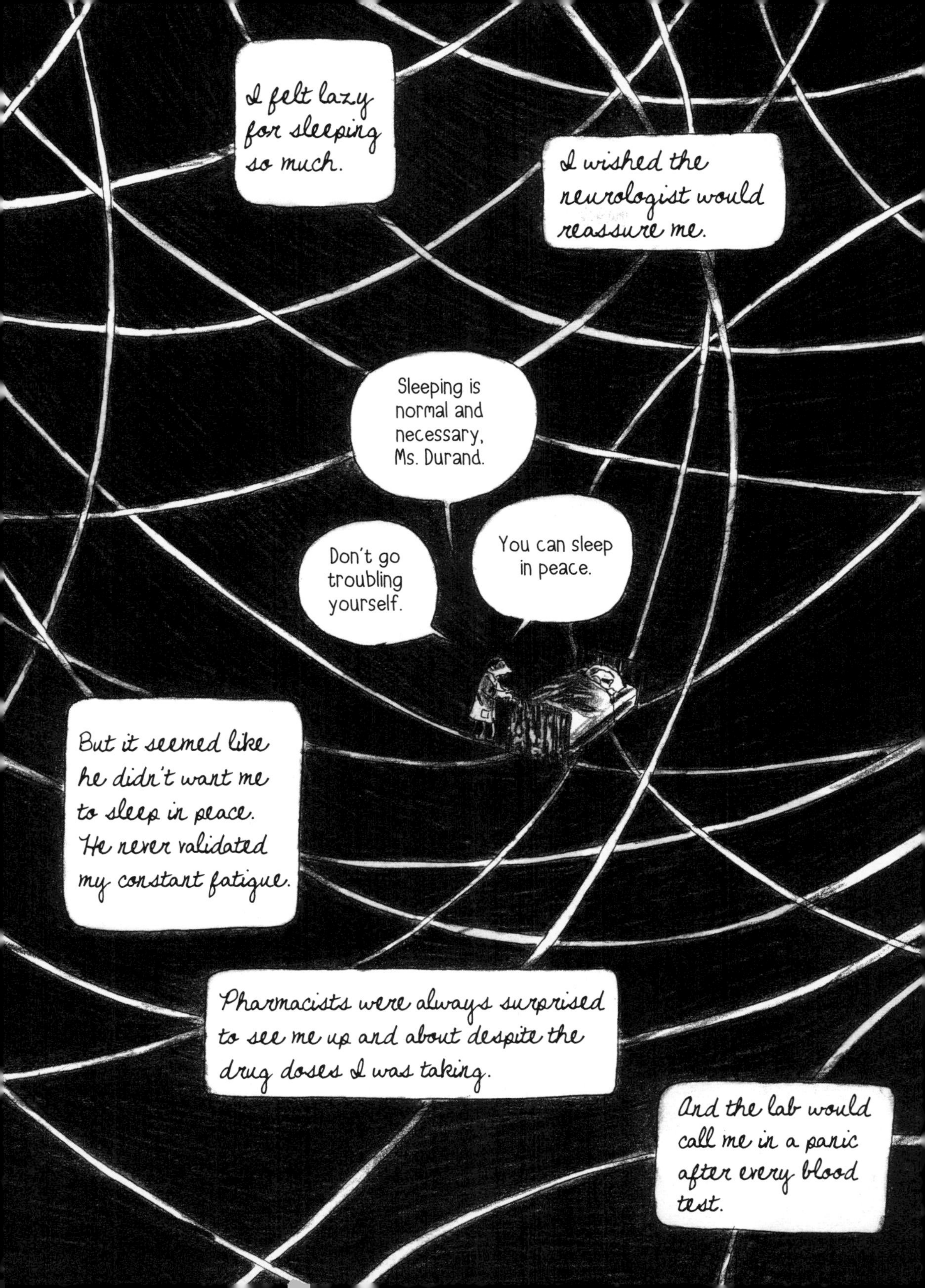
I felt lazy for sleeping so much.
I wished the neurologist would reassure me.
Sleeping is normal and necessary, Ms. Durand.
Don't go troubling yourself.
You can sleep in peace.
But it seemed like he didn't want me to sleep in peace. He never validated my constant fatigue.
Pharmacists were always surprised to see me up and about despite the drug doses I was taking.
And the lab would call me in a panic after every blood test.

So I kept on sleeping… The neurologist didn't see it as a problem. To him, the most important thing was putting an end to my seizures. My life was punctuated by treatments of ever-increasing dosage.

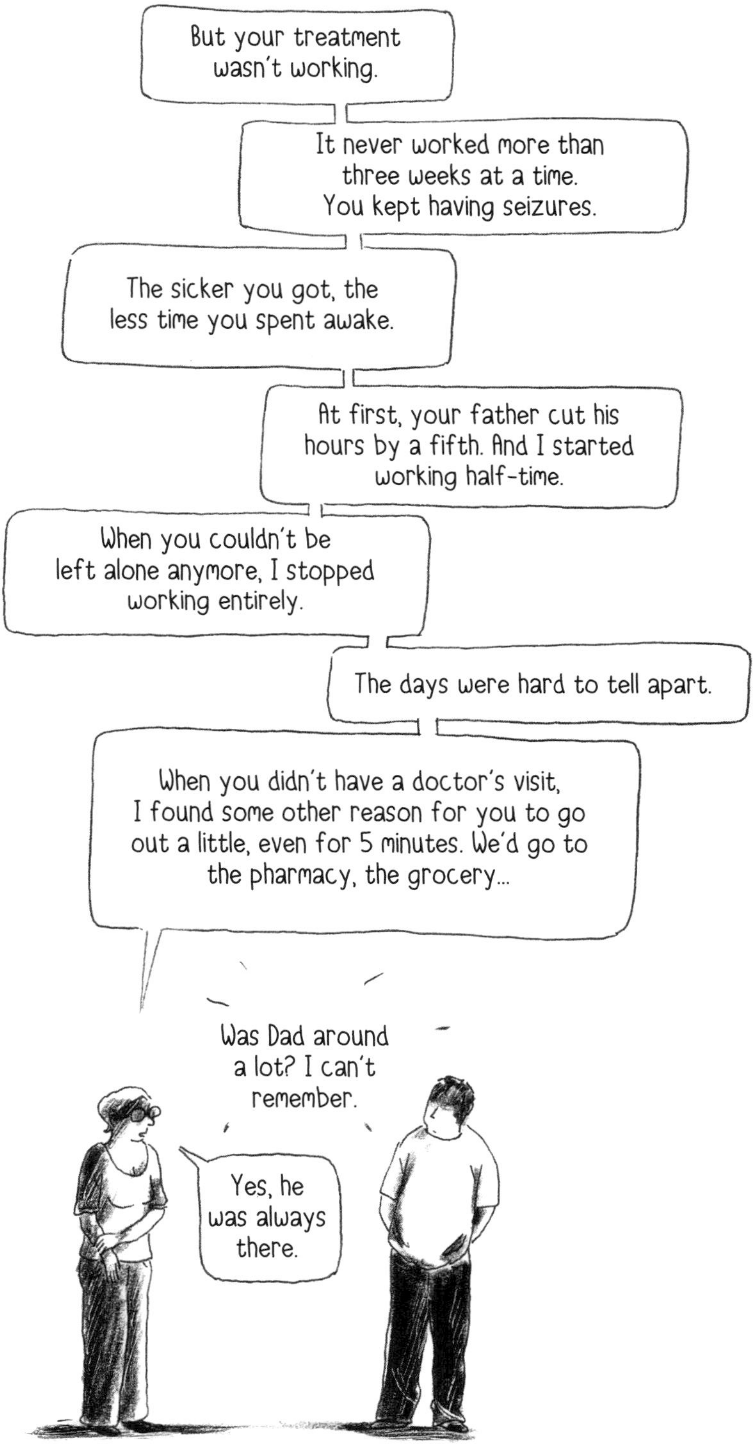

But your treatment wasn't working.
It never worked more than three weeks at a time. You kept having seizures.
The sicker you got, the less time you spent awake.
At first, your father cut his hours by a fifth. And I started working half-time.
When you couldn't be left alone anymore, I stopped working entirely.
The days were hard to tell apart.
When you didn't have a doctor's visit, I found some other reason for you to go out a little, even for 5 minutes. We'd go to the pharmacy, the grocery...
Was Dad around a lot? I can't remember.
Yes, he was always there.

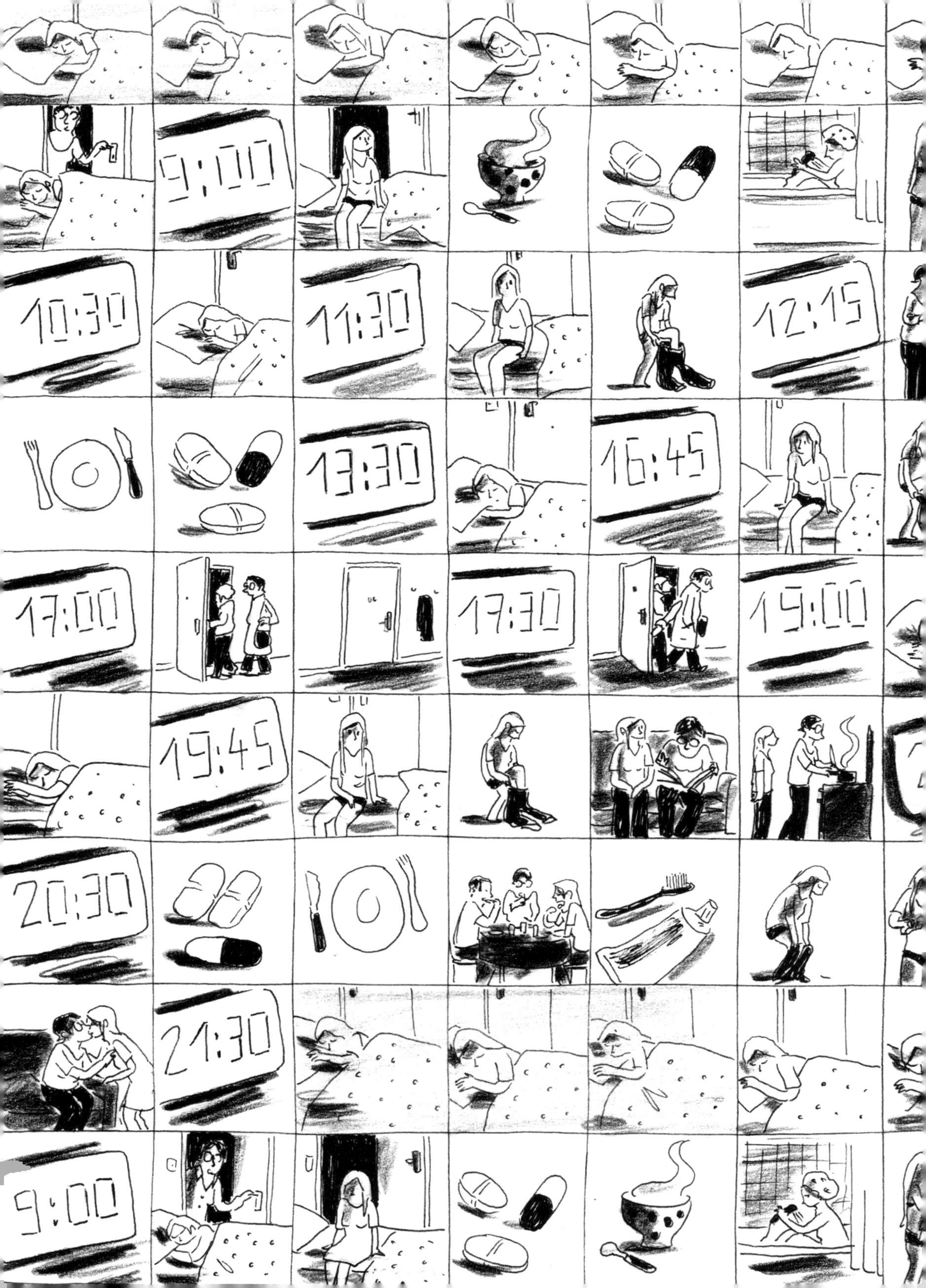
9:00
10:30
11:30
12:15
13:30
16:45
17:00
17:30
19:00
19:45
20:30
21:30
9:00

For you, Mom, our days were hard to tell apart. For me, they felt very different, because I no longer had any notion of time.

You said there were outings sometimes, special days meticulously planned and prepared for. A movie, friends... Marine and Sandra always came by to see me. But I lost all touch with school.

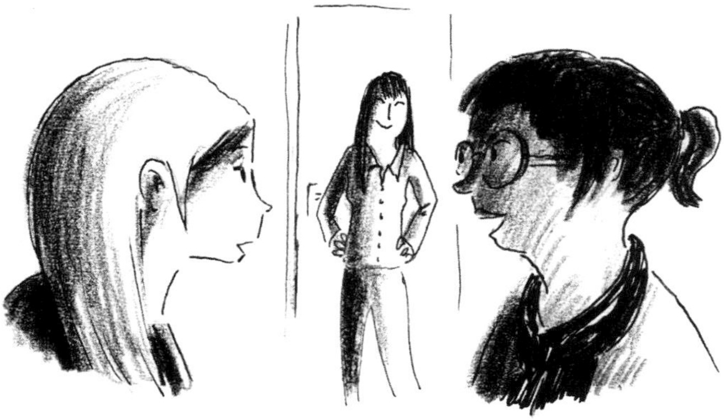

I didn't like seeing my friends. It wore me out. Everything was hard for me: having a conversation, focusing, not being tired. I had to prep before they came over, sleep and store up my strength.

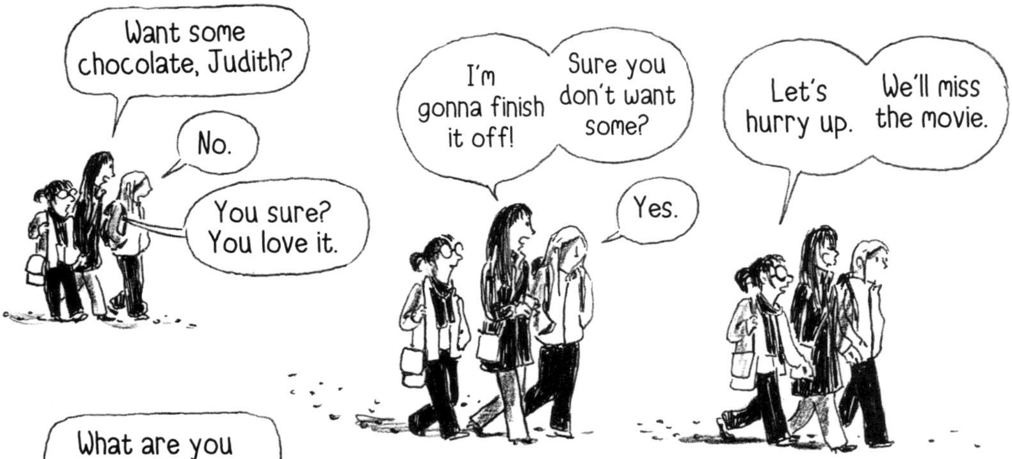
Want some chocolate, Judith?
No.
You sure? You love it.
I'm gonna finish it off!
Sure you don't want some?
Yes.
Let's hurry up.
We'll miss the movie.

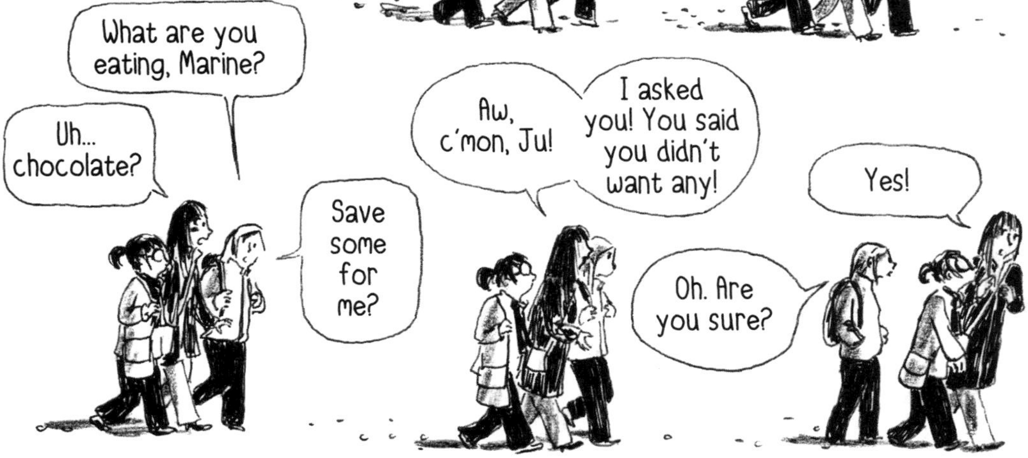
What are you eating, Marine?
Uh... chocolate?
Save some for me?
Aw, c'mon, Ju!
I asked you! You said you didn't want any!
Oh. Are you sure?
Yes!

It was disturbing. No one could tell I was ill, physically. I seemed to be in perfect health. Mood-wise, too, I think I was fine.

From the living room window in Créteil, I could see Henri-Mondor Hospital.

I felt like I'd never left. In my memory, the hospital had become my entire life.

Time didn't exist anymore, or space for anything else. And yet, I hadn't actually been there long.

My life now consisted of visits to the neurologist, for monitoring and electroencephalograms; to the hospital, for tests and MRIs; and to the pharmacy, for refills. The hospital campus housed all those things. It was a city unto itself, an actual parallel dimension with it's own rules...

The rings around your eyes worried me, your fearful looks, your questions…
No, I didn't know if I'd had a seizure, or if I was doing better.
No, I didn't know what had just happened…
All I wanted was never to be afraid ever again.

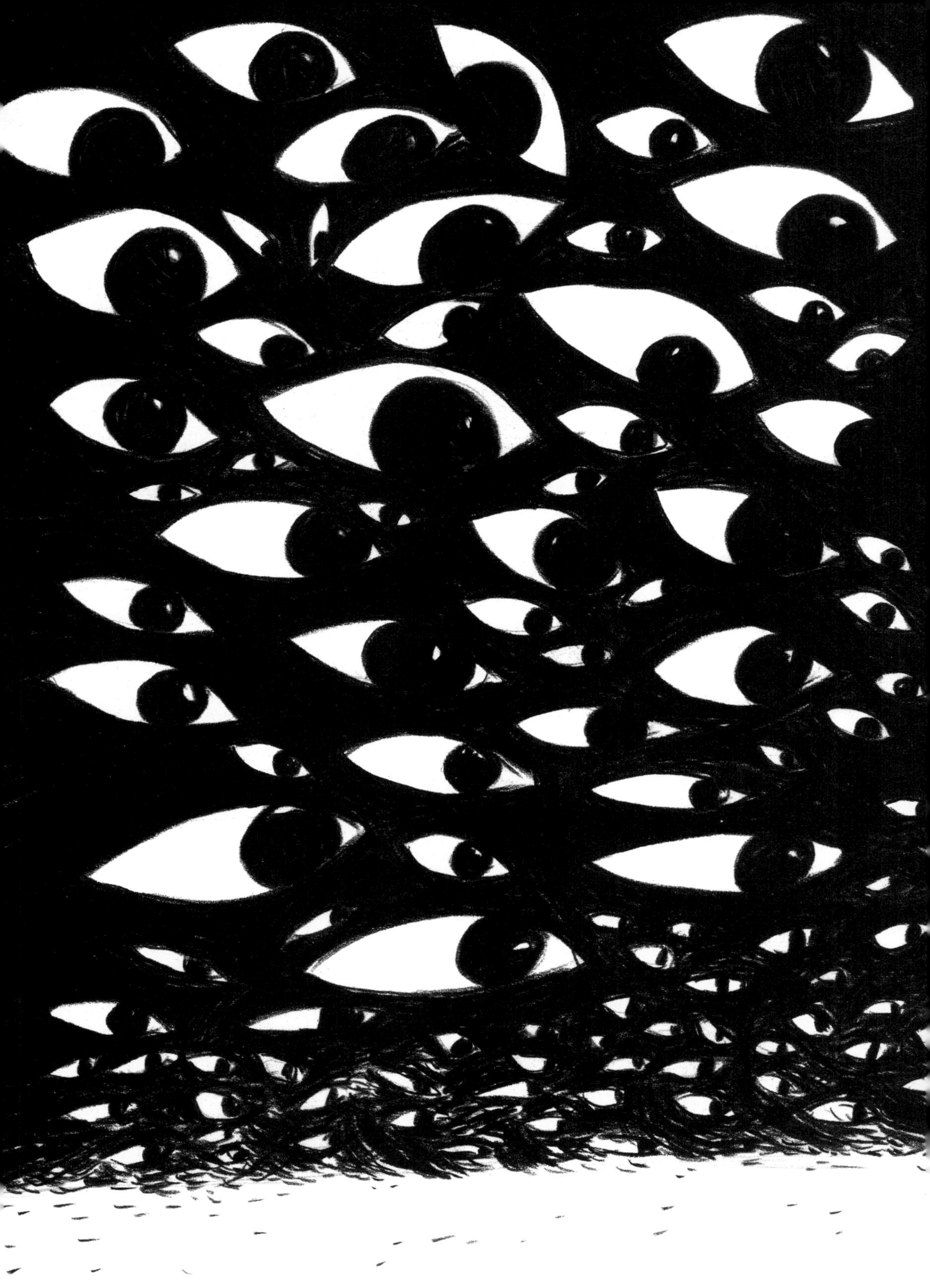

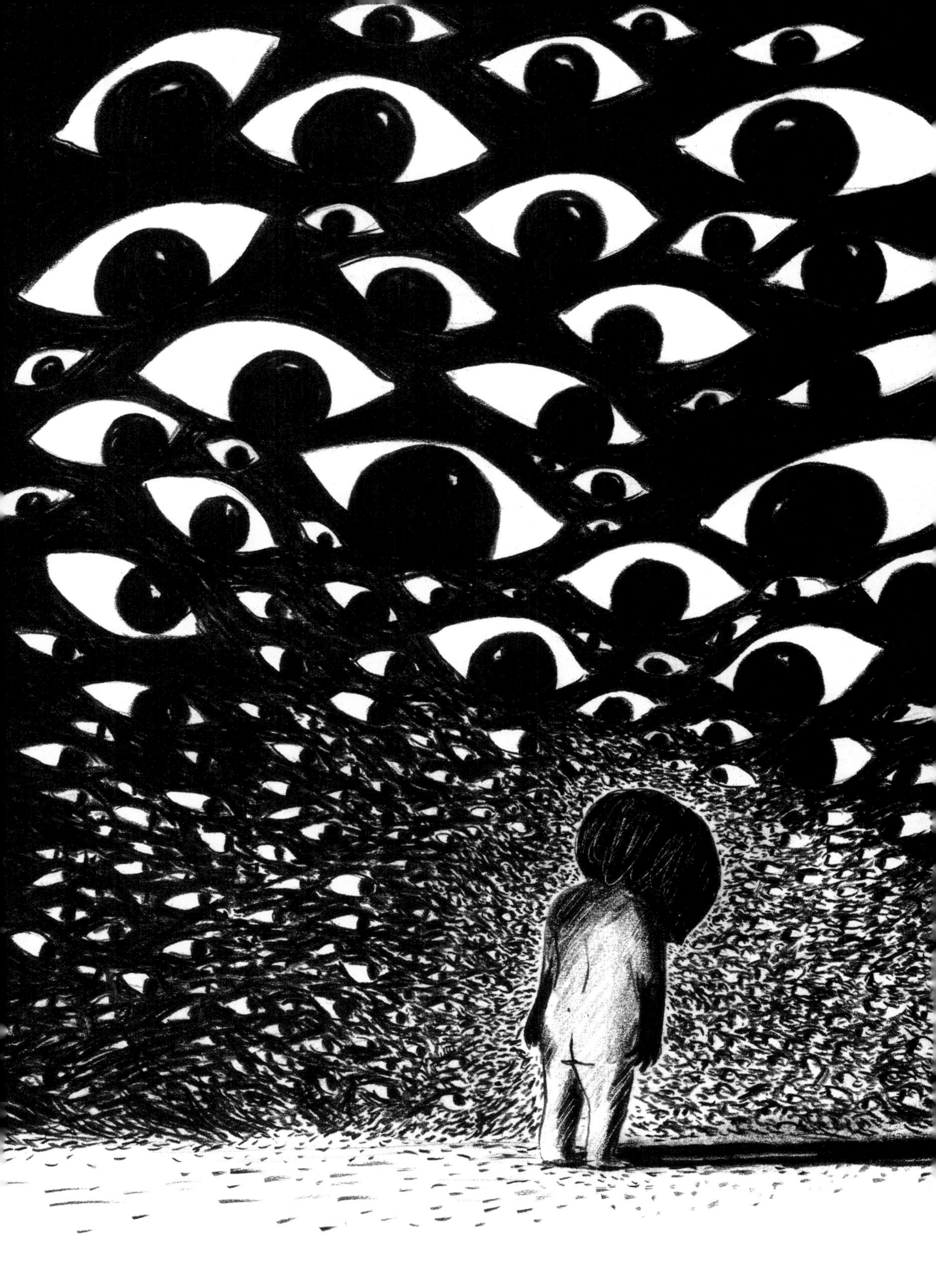

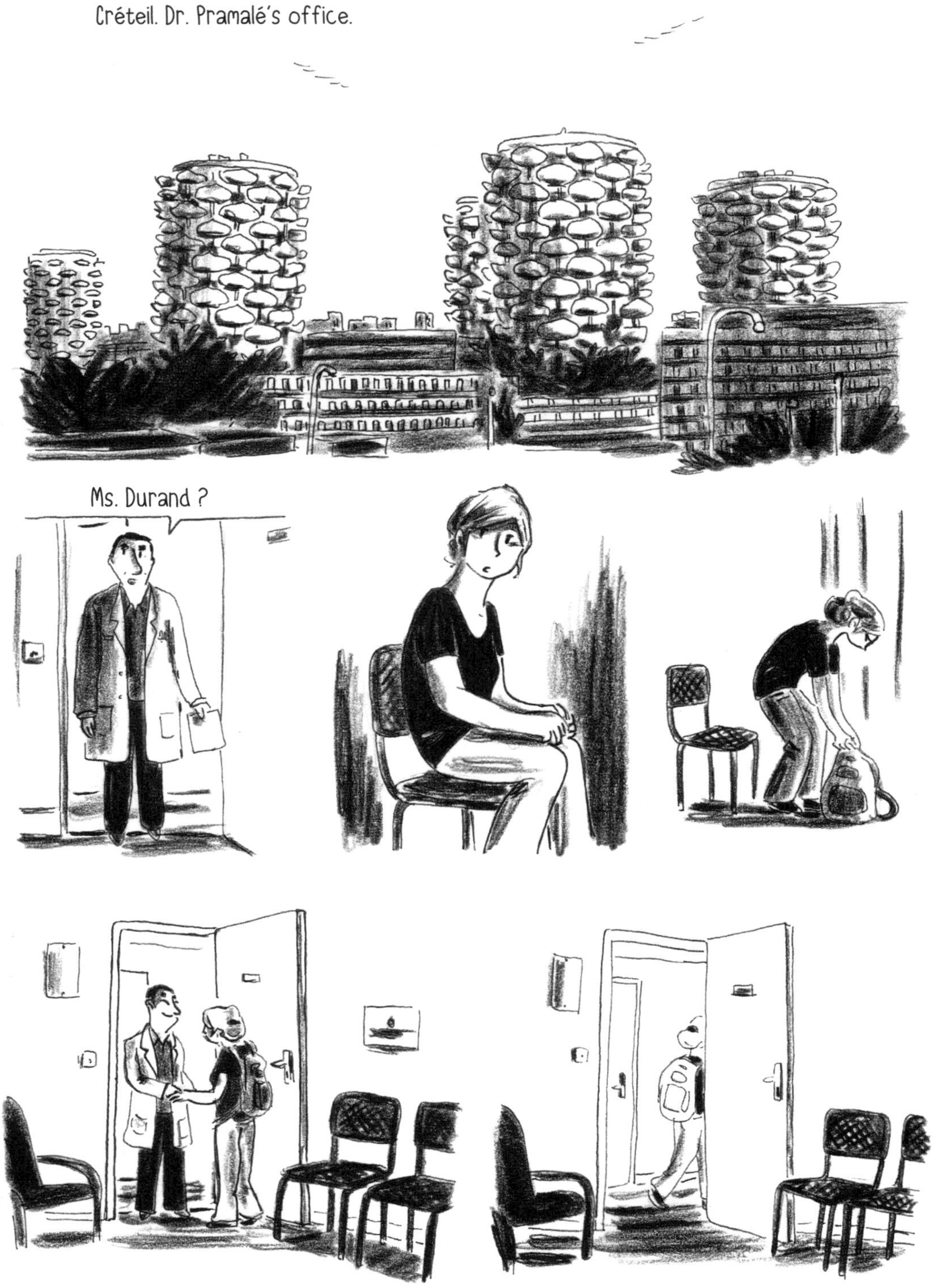
Créteil. Dr. Pramalé's office.
Ms. Durand ?

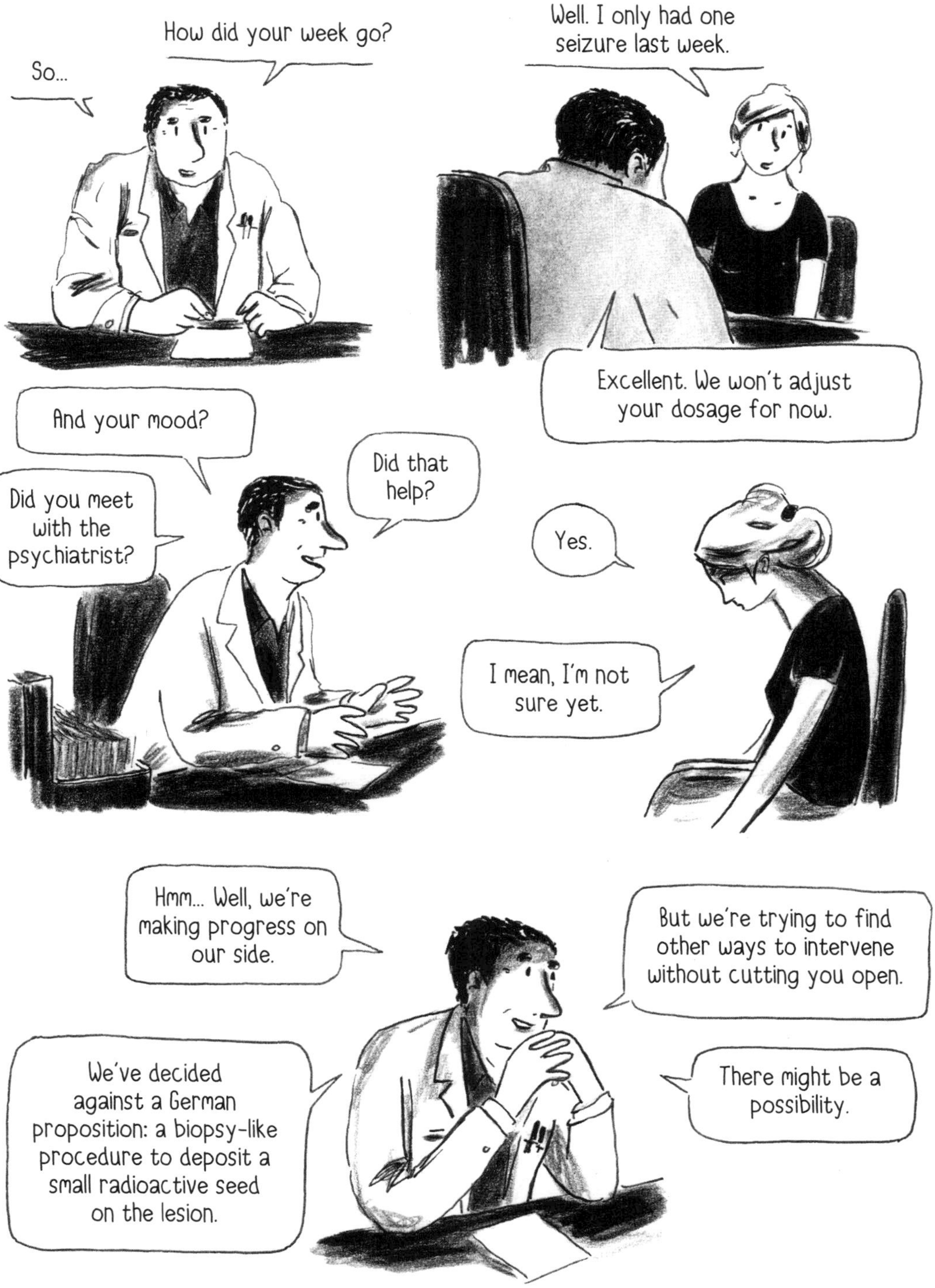
So...
How did your week go?
Well. I only had one seizure last week.
Excellent. We won't adjust your dosage for now.
And your mood?
Did you meet with the psychiatrist?
Did that help?
Yes.
I mean, I'm not sure yet.
Hmm... Well, we're making progress on our side.
We've decided against a German proposition: a biopsy-like procedure to deposit a small radioactive seed on the lesion.
But we're trying to find other ways to intervene without cutting you open.
There might be a possibility.

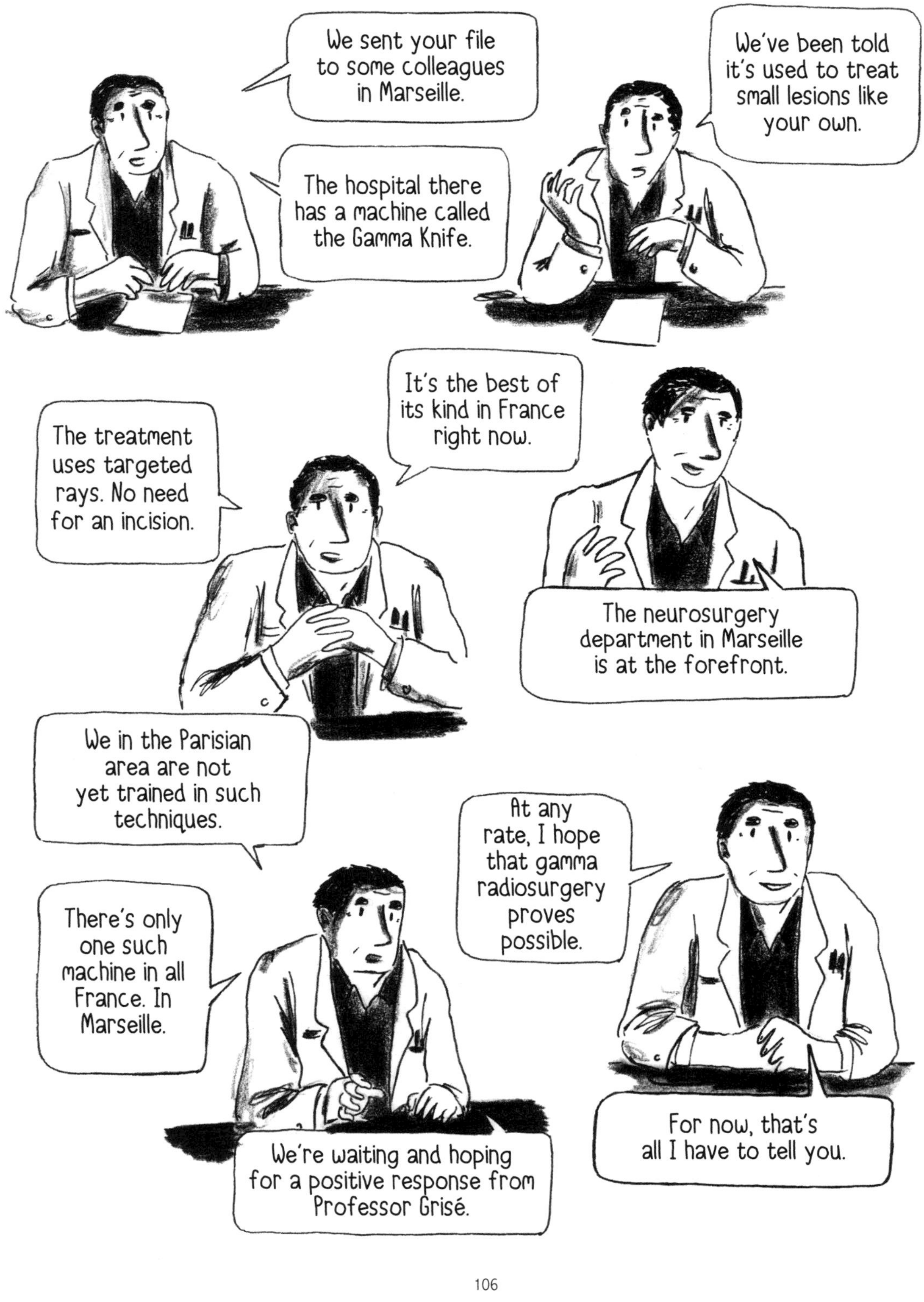
We sent your file to some colleagues in Marseille.
The hospital there has a machine called the Gamma Knife.
We've been told it's used to treat small lesions like your own.
The treatment uses targeted rays. No need for an incision.
It's the best of its kind in France right now.
The neurosurgery department in Marseille is at the forefront.
We in the Parisian area are not yet trained in such techniques.
There's only one such machine in all France. In Marseille.
We're waiting and hoping for a positive response from Professor Grisé.
At any rate, I hope that gamma radiosurgery proves possible.
For now, that's all I have to tell you.

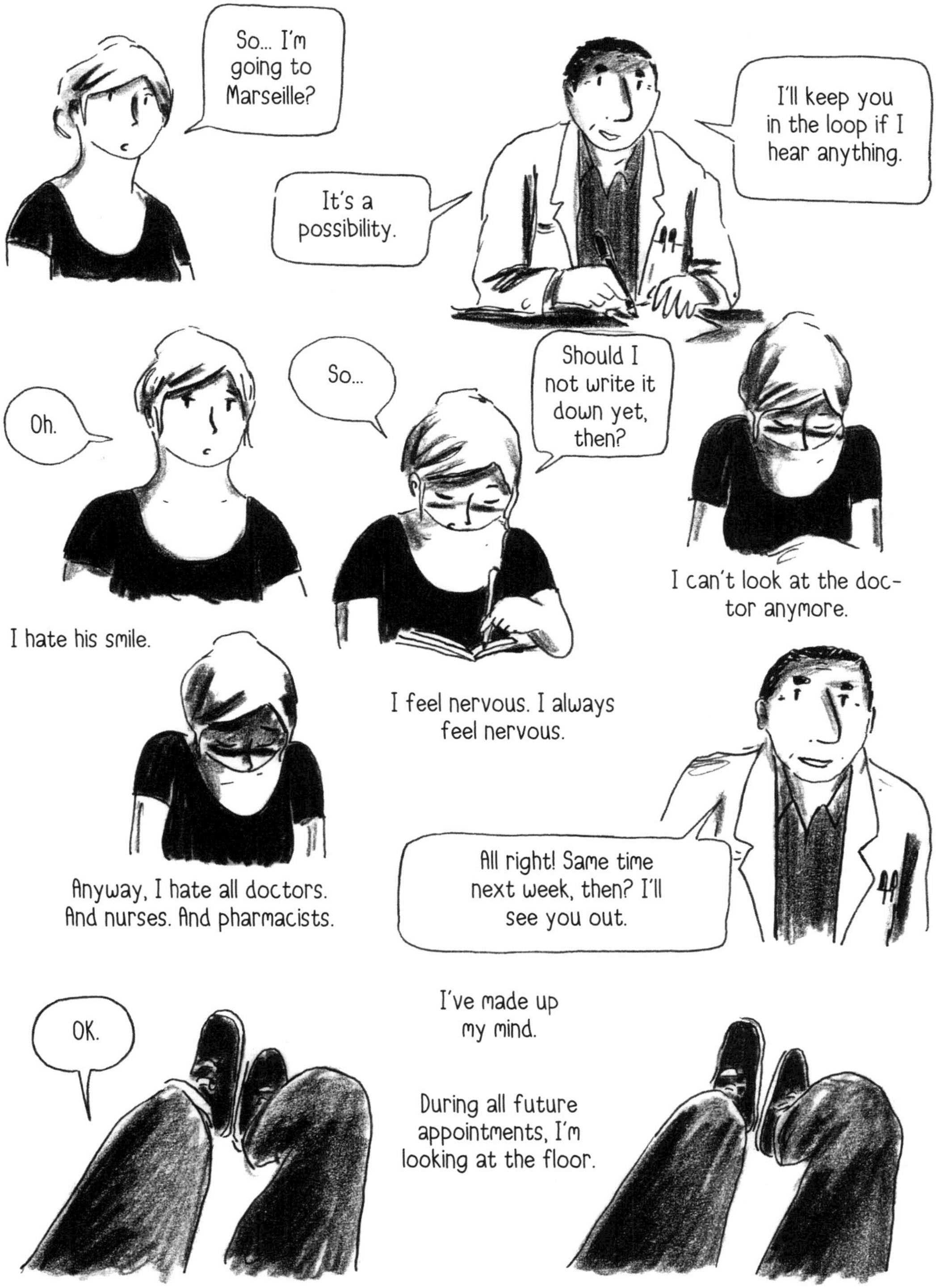

So... I'm going to Marseille?
It's a possibility.
I'll keep you in the loop if I hear anything.
Oh.
So...
Should I not write it down yet, then?
I hate his smile.
I can't look at the doctor anymore.
I feel nervous. I always feel nervous.
Anyway, I hate all doctors. And nurses. And pharmacists.
All right! Same time next week, then? I'll see you out.
OK.
I've made up my mind.
During all future appointments, I'm looking at the floor.

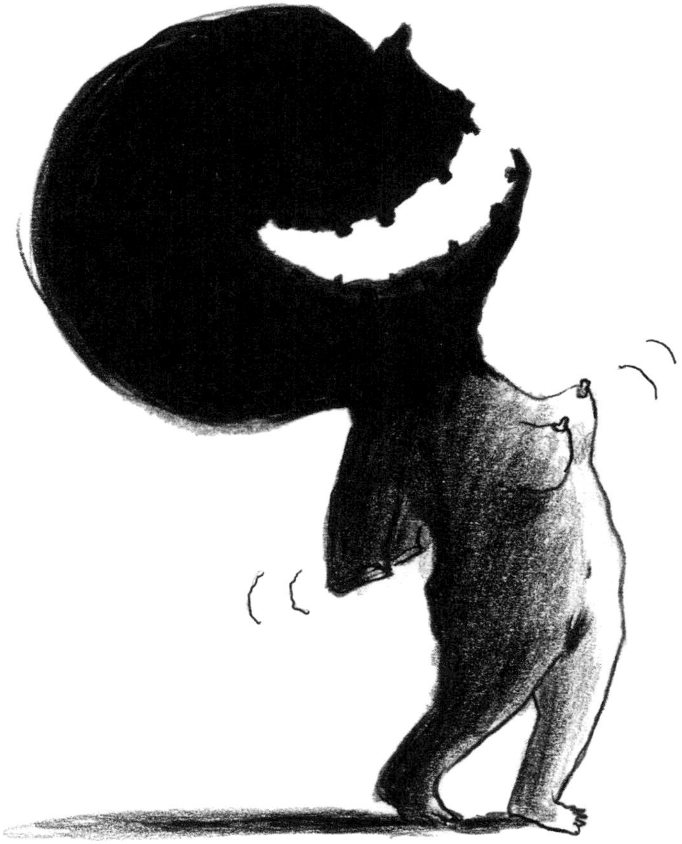

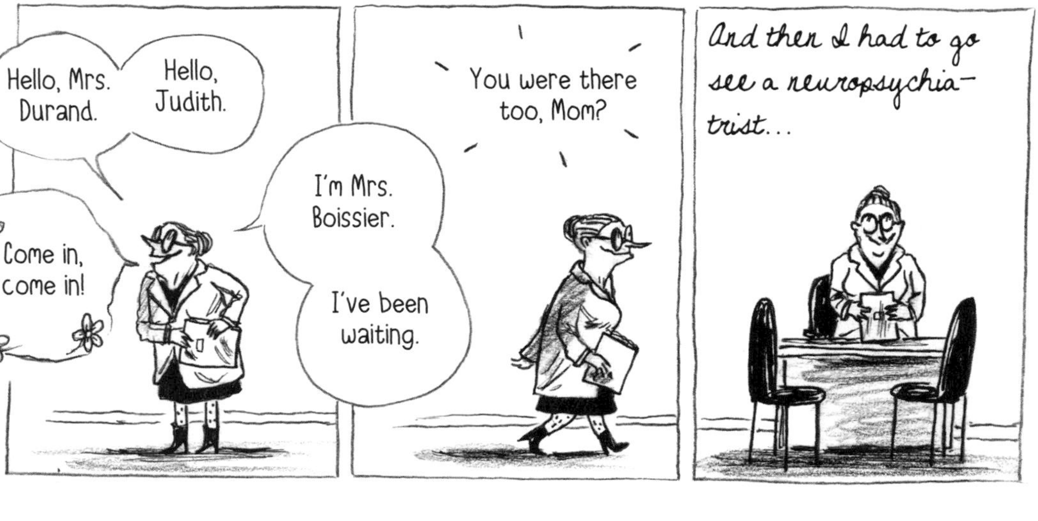
Hello, Mrs. Durand.
Hello, Judith.
Come in, come in!
I'm Mrs. Boissier.
I've been waiting.
You were there too, Mom?
And then I had to go see a neuropsychia-trist...

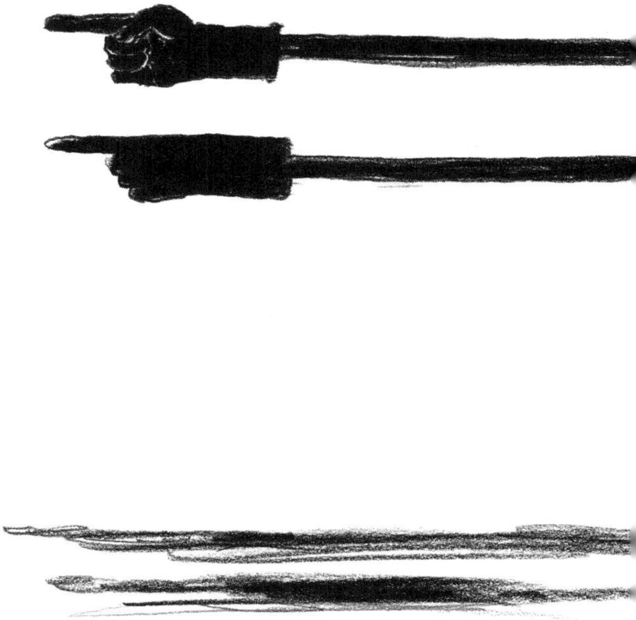

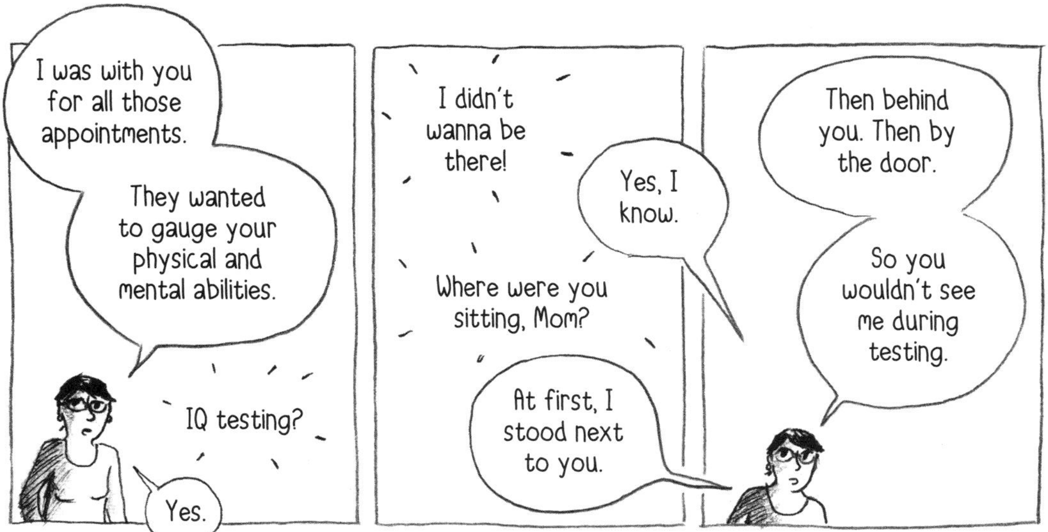
I was with you for all those appointments.
They wanted to gauge your physical and mental abilities.
IQ testing?
Yes.
I didn't wanna be there!
Yes, I know.
Where were you sitting, Mom?
At first, I stood next to you.
Then behind you. Then by the door.
So you wouldn't see me during testing.

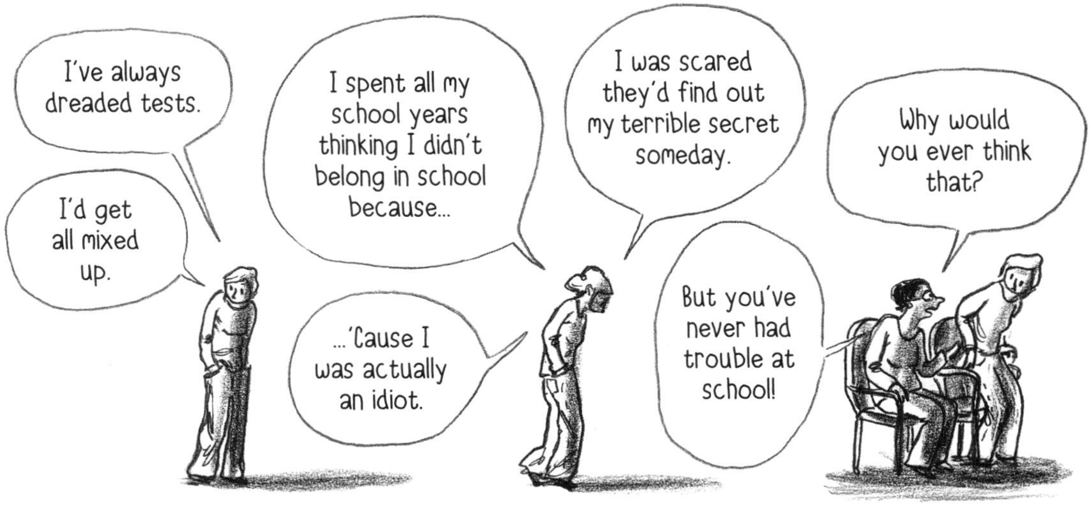
I've always dreaded tests.
I'd get all mixed up.
I spent all my school years thinking I didn't belong in school because...
...'Cause I was actually an idiot.
I was scared they'd find out my terrible secret someday.
But you've never had trouble at school!
Why would you ever think that?

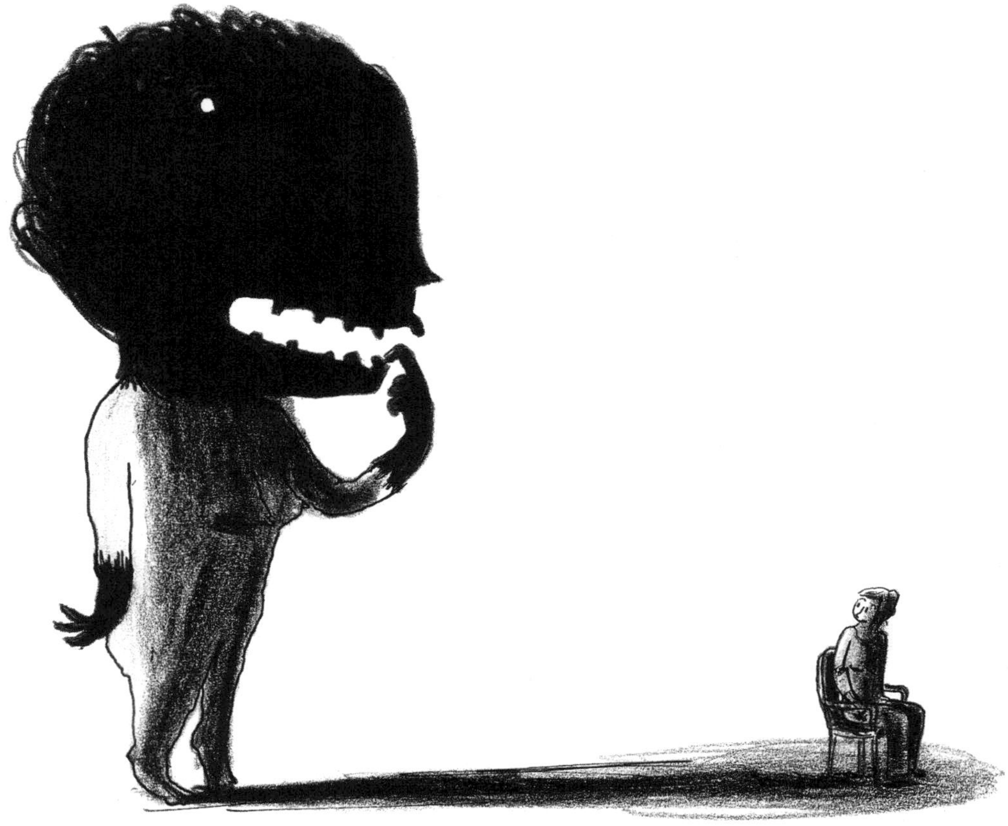

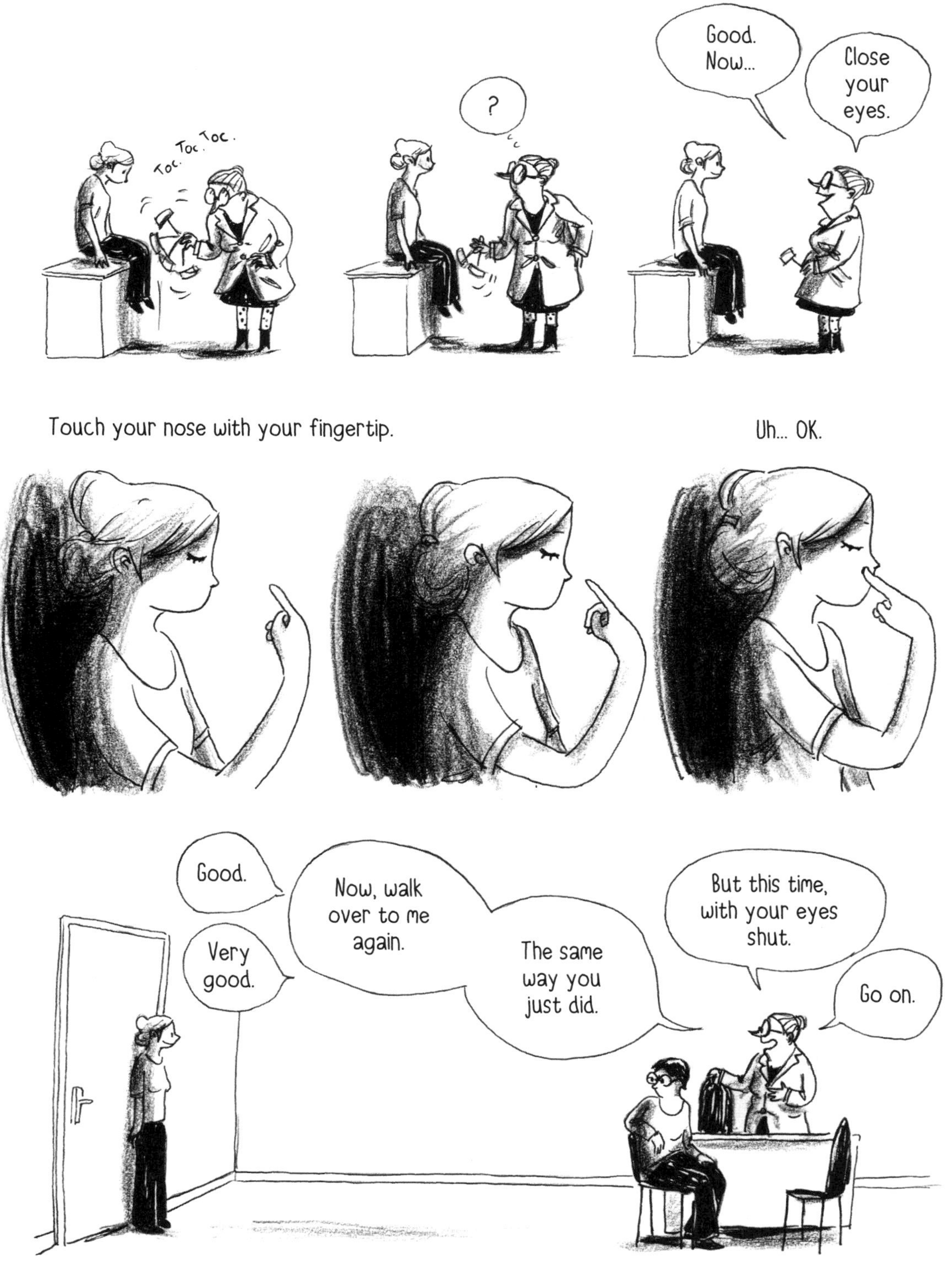
Toc. Toc. Toc.
?
Good. Now...
Close your eyes.
Touch your nose with your fingertip.
Uh... OK.
Good.
Very good.
Now, walk over to me again.
The same way you just did.
But this time, with your eyes shut.
Go on.

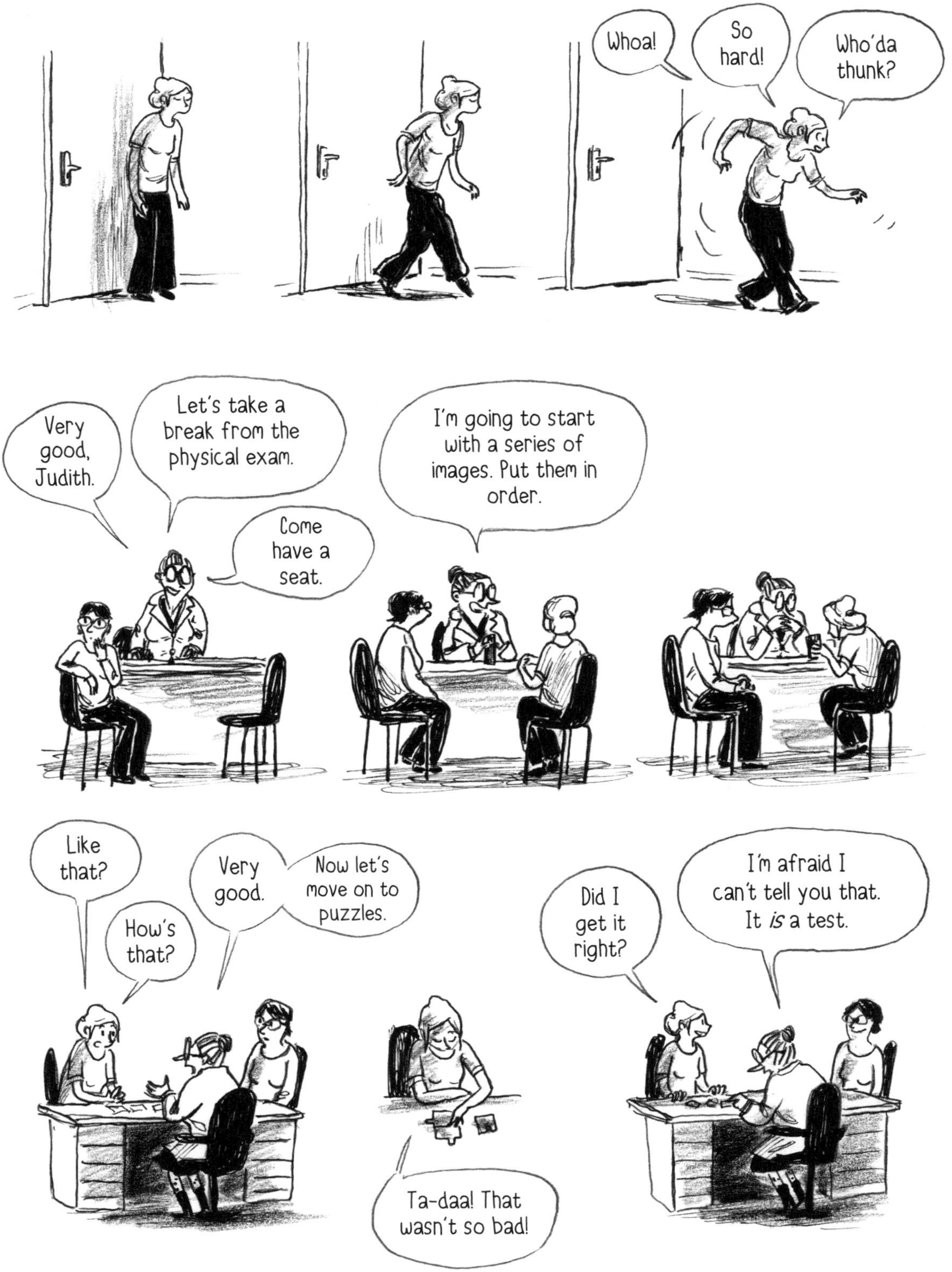
Whoa!
So hard!
Who'da thunk?
Very good, Judith.
Let's take a break from the physical exam.
Come have a seat.
I'm going to start with a series of images. Put them in order.
Like that?
How's that?
Very good.
Now let's move on to puzzles.
Ta-daa! That wasn't so bad!
Did I get it right?
I'm afraid I can't tell you that. It *is* a test.

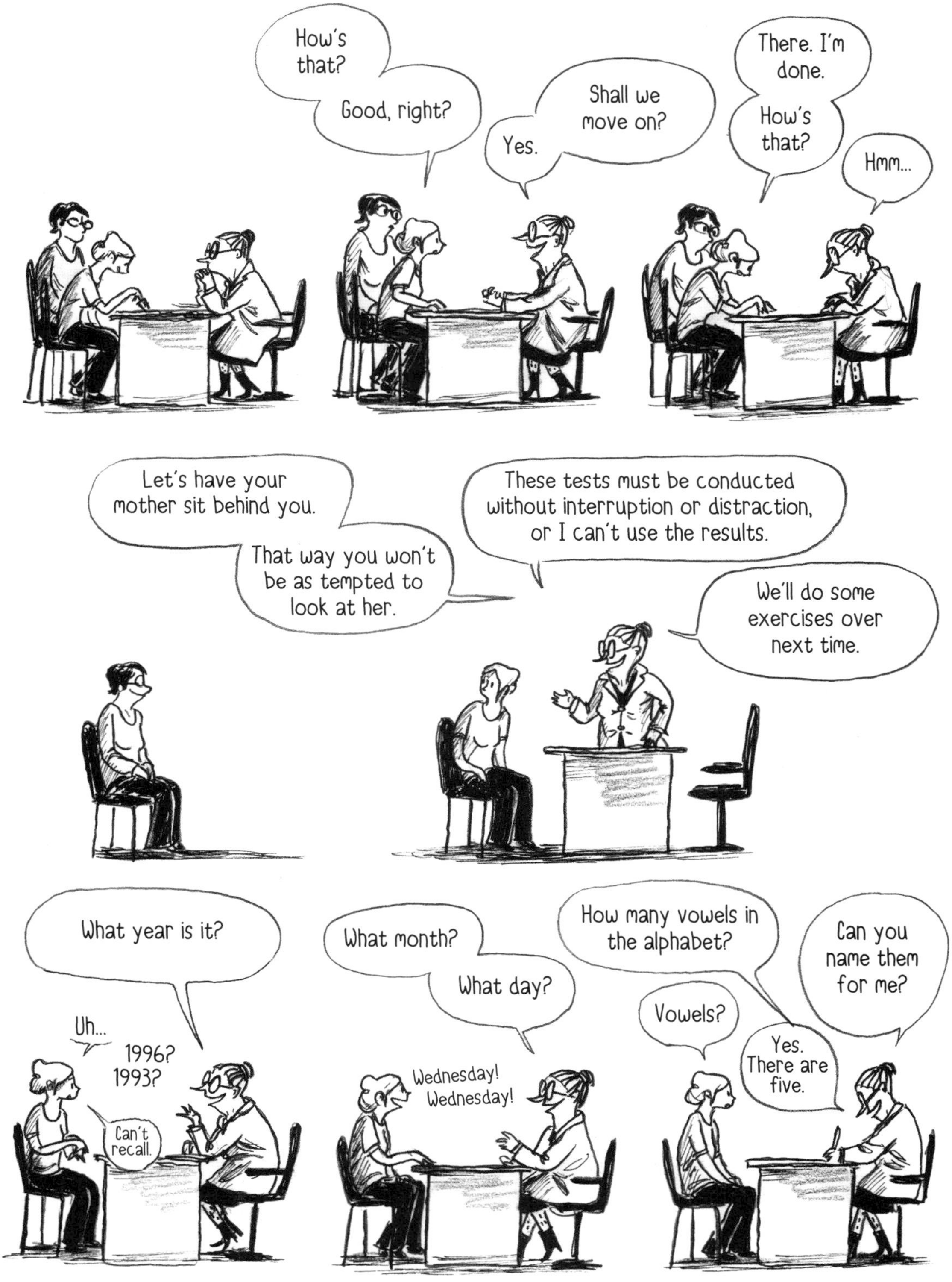
How's that?
Good, right?
Yes.
Shall we move on?
There. I'm done.
How's that?
Hmm...
Let's have your mother sit behind you.
That way you won't be as tempted to look at her.
These tests must be conducted without interruption or distraction, or I can't use the results.
We'll do some exercises over next time.
What year is it?
Uh...
1996?
1993?
Can't recall.
What month?
What day?
Wednesday! Wednesday!
How many vowels in the alphabet?
Vowels?
Yes. There are five.
Can you name them for me?

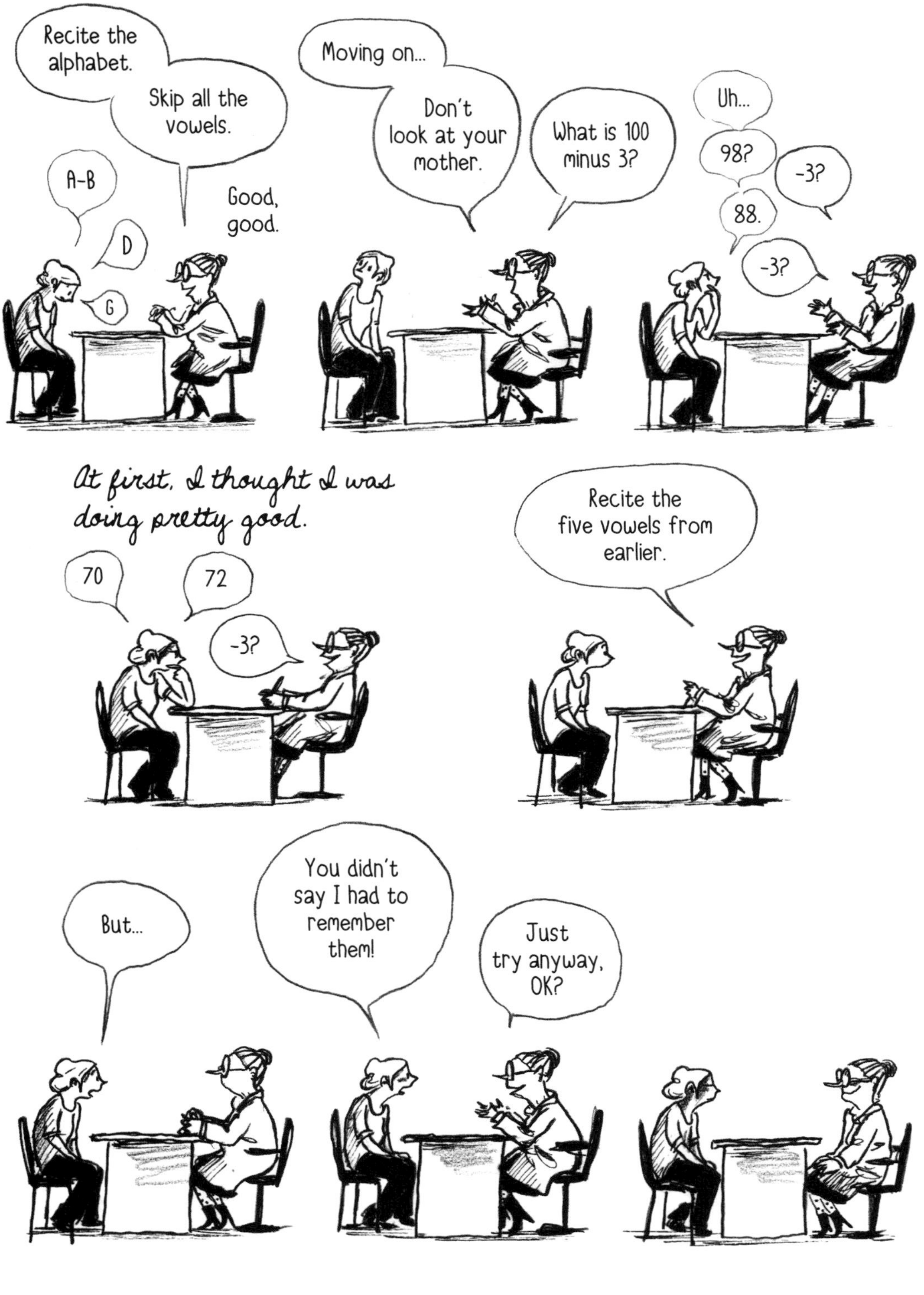
Recite the alphabet.
Skip all the vowels.
A-B
D
G
Good, good.
Moving on...
Don't look at your mother.
What is 100 minus 3?
Uh...
98?
-3?
88.
-3?
At first, I thought I was doing pretty good.
70
72
-3?
Recite the five vowels from earlier.
But...
You didn't say I had to remember them!
Just try anyway, OK?

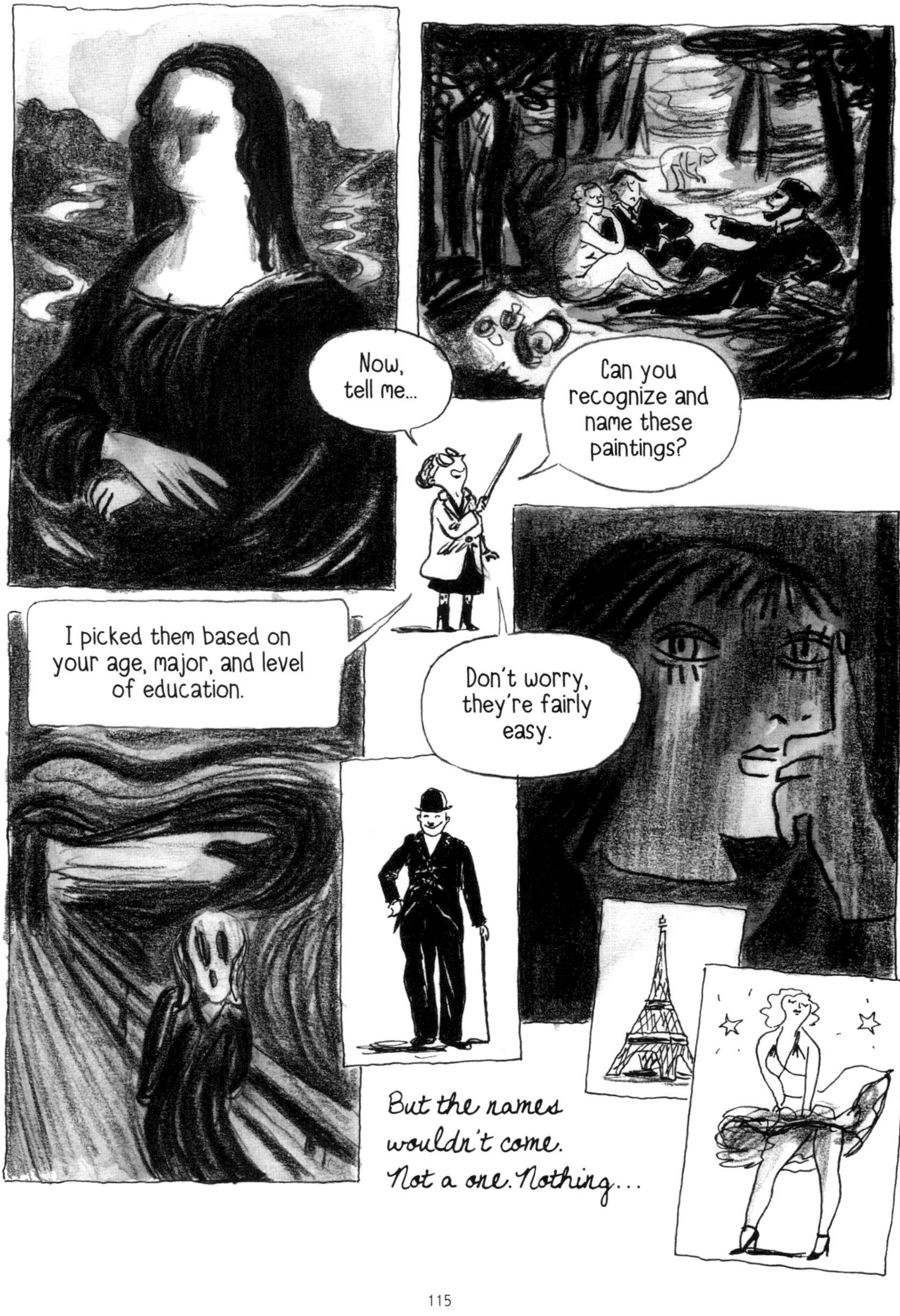
Now, tell me...
Can you recognize and name these paintings?
I picked them based on your age, major, and level of education.
Don't worry, they're fairly easy.
But the names wouldn't come. Not a one. Nothing...

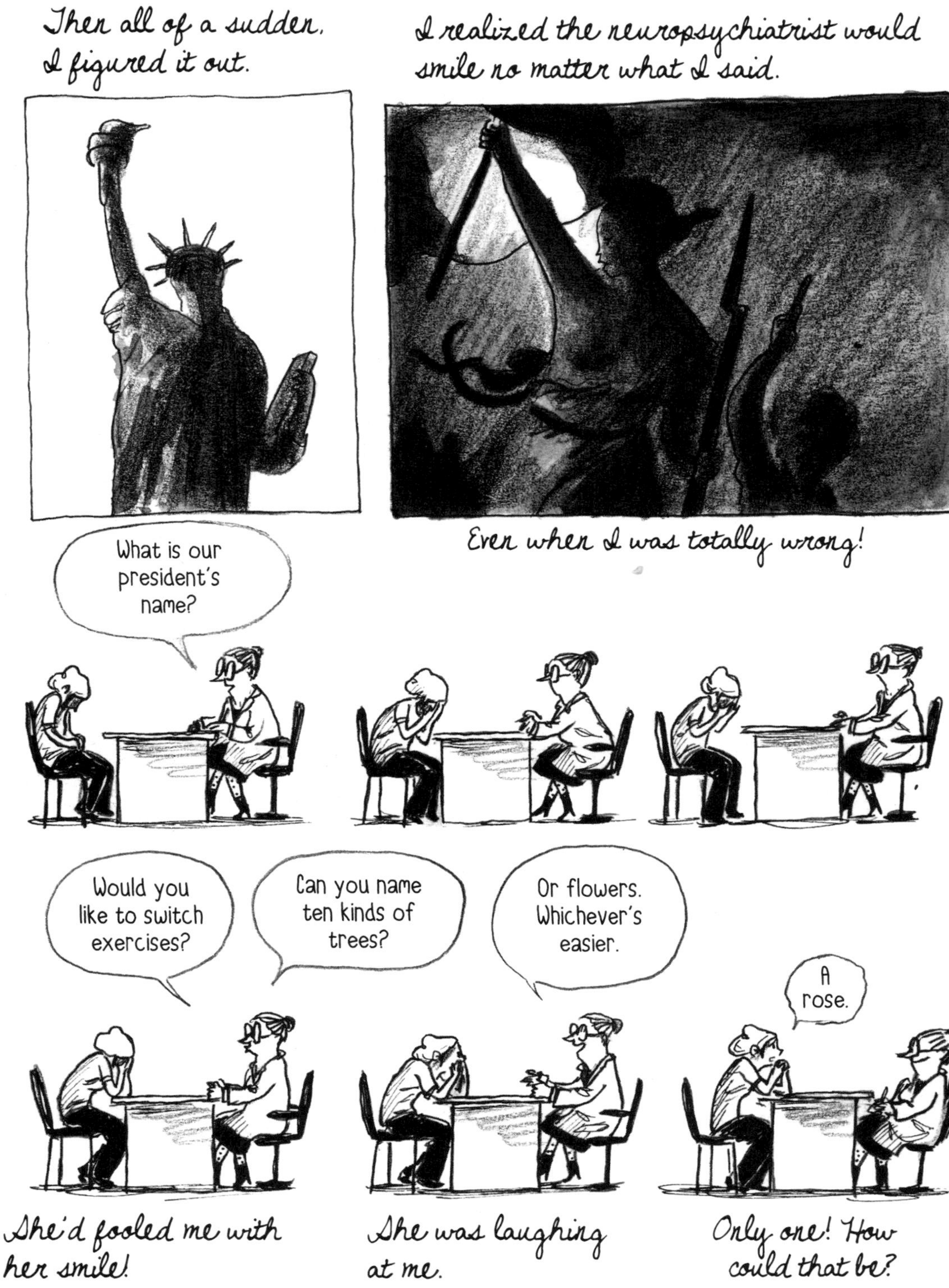

Then all of a sudden, I figured it out.
I realized the neuropsychiatrist would smile no matter what I said.
Even when I was totally wrong!
What is our president's name?
Would you like to switch exercises?
Can you name ten kinds of trees?
Or flowers. Whichever's easier.
A rose.
She'd fooled me with her smile!
She was laughing at me.
Only one! How could that be?

By the end, it wasn't going so well. But it probably never had.

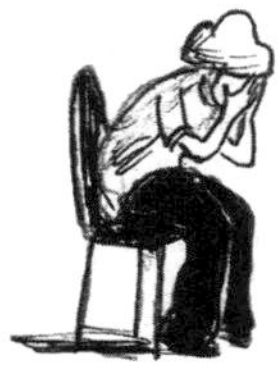

I cried a lot that day. I just couldn't stop.

I suddenly realized I didn't know anything anymore. It was brutal.

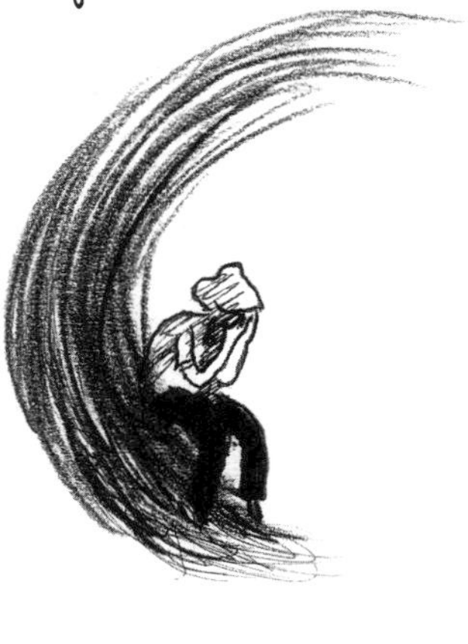

I was ashamed... So ashamed.

I didn't know the alphabet, or trees, or even who was president!

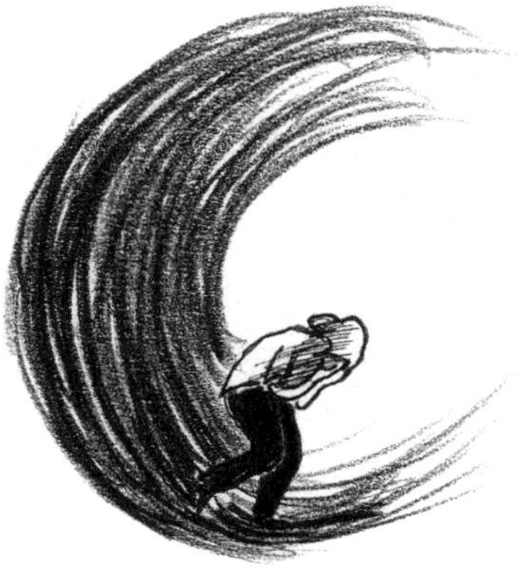

Was this how it was going to be? Me not being able to count?

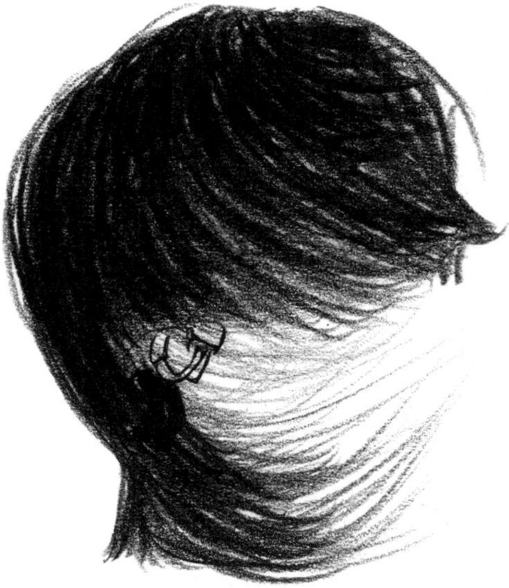

I knew even less than before.

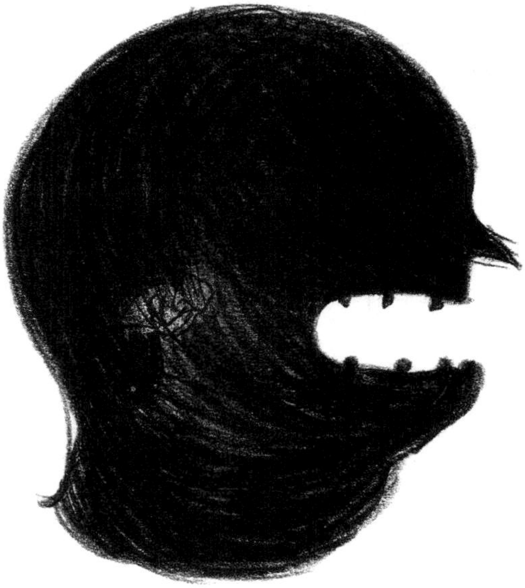

I'd regressed. How was this possible?

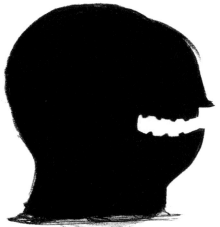

There were simple things I thought I'd know forever once I learned them. But no.

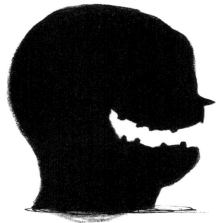

I thought the results should be the same as they would have been before the illness.

Ms. Durand?

We'll pick this up again next week.

The neuropsychiatrist broke off testing early. I was going to have to come back...

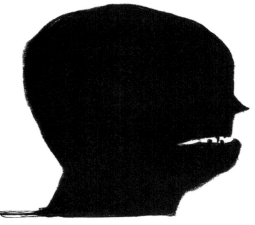

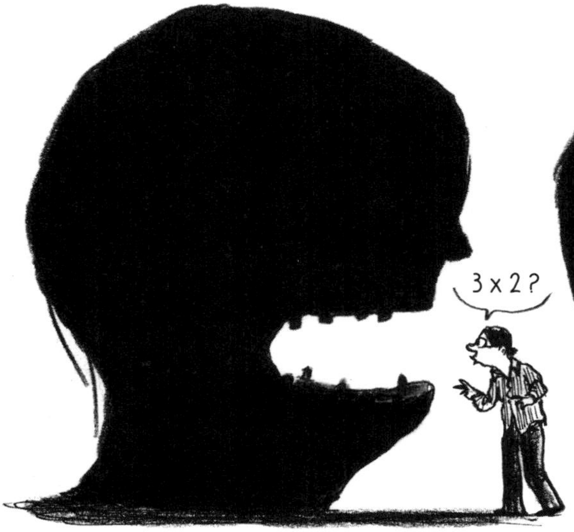
3 x 2?

Back home, we kept slowly torturing ourselves.
I wanted to re-learn everything.

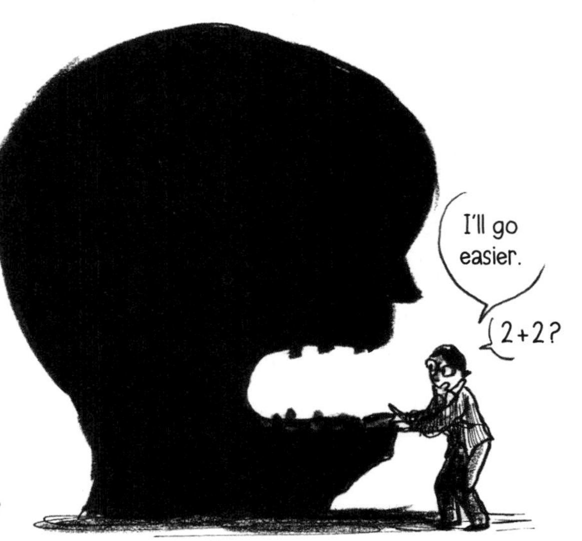
I'll go easier.
2+2?

I asked you to help me. I wanted to be ready for my next appointment.

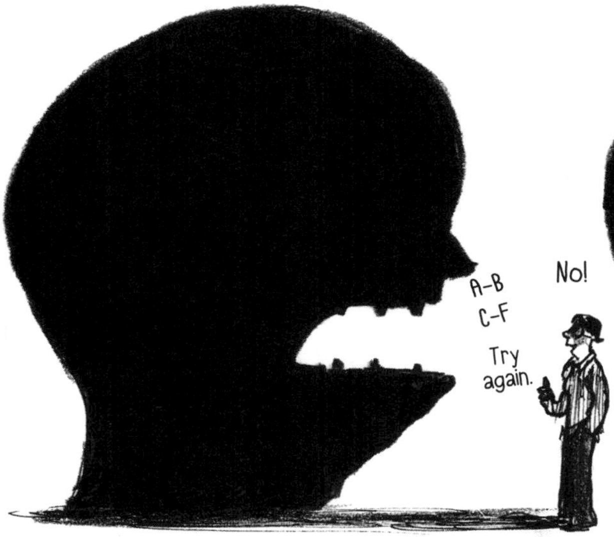
A-B
C-F
No!
Try again.

I couldn't retain anything. I'd managed to learn the president's name.

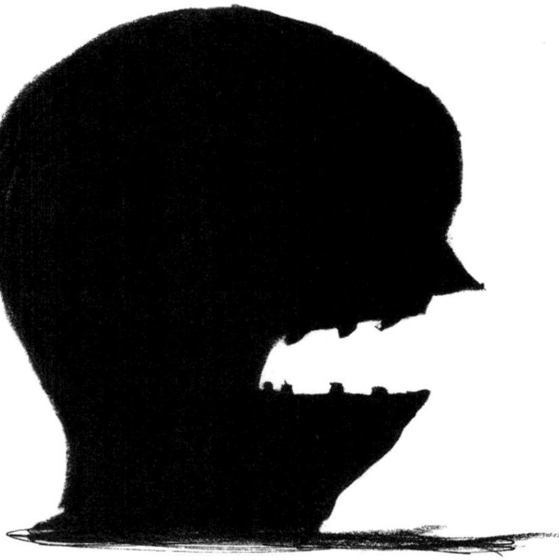

But a few months later, we got a new president. I was out of luck...

On May 17, 1995, François Mitterrand finished his second term as president of the French Republic. Emma was probably an embryo just a few days old in Sandrine's belly... no, wait! I'm getting the year wrong. She was born in 1997.

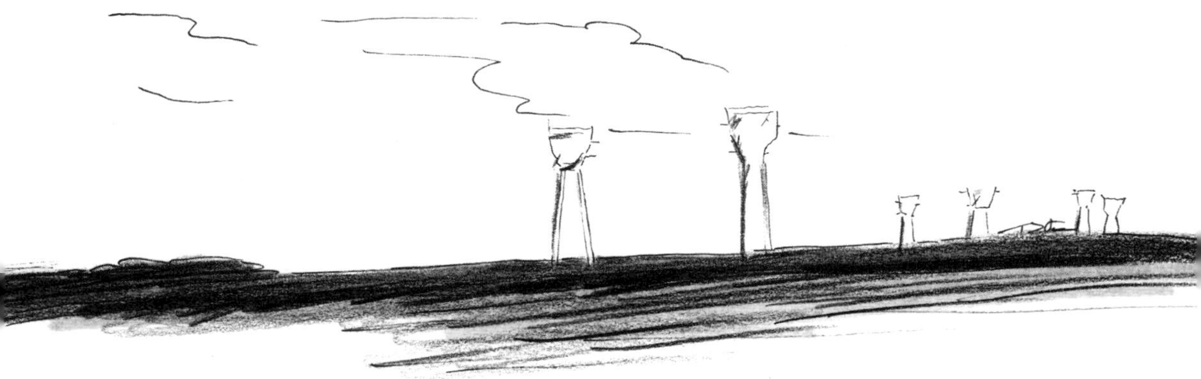

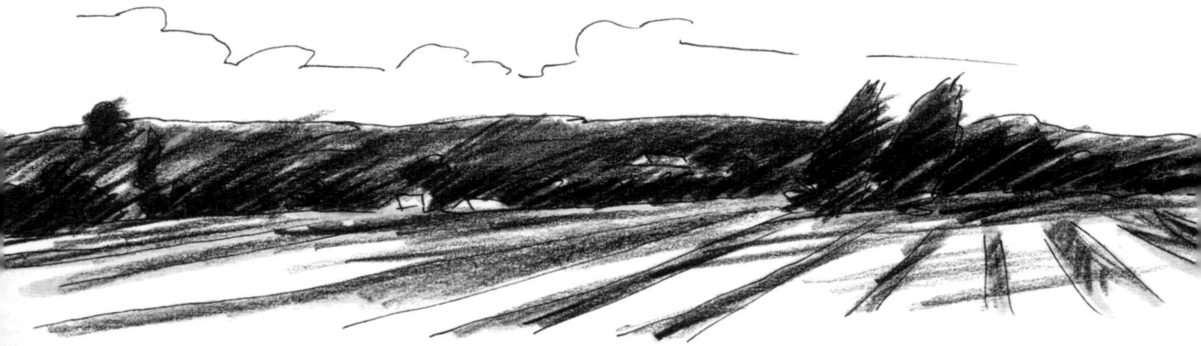

I remember very little of the journey to Marseille.

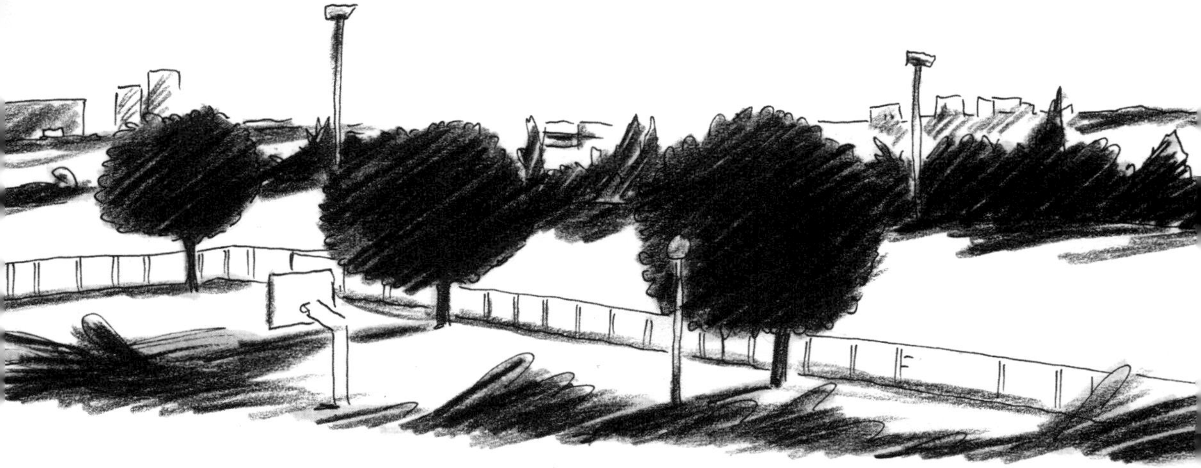

Sometimes, I honestly believe I never even went.

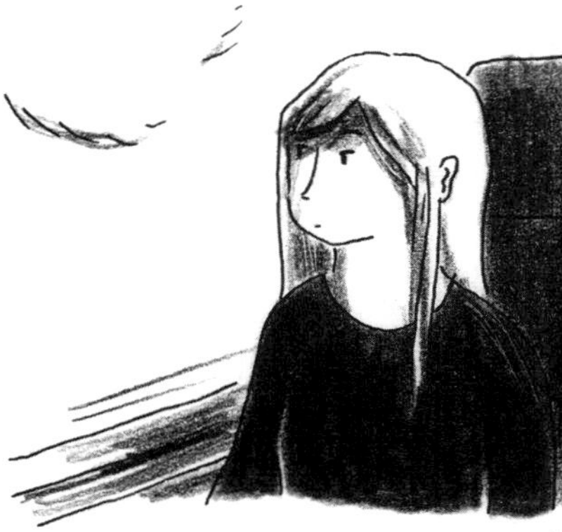

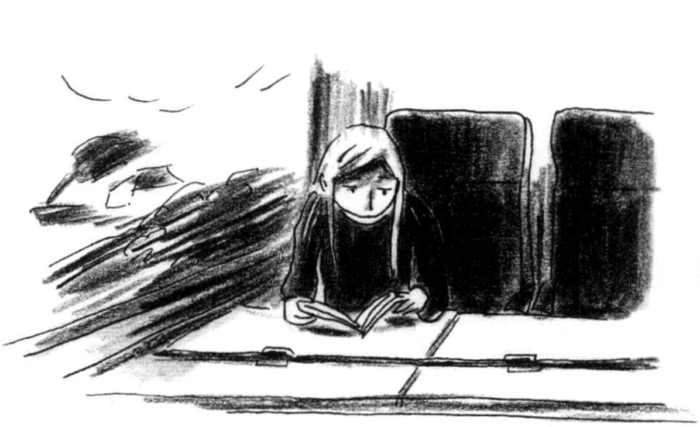

You said we all went together – you, me, and Dad.

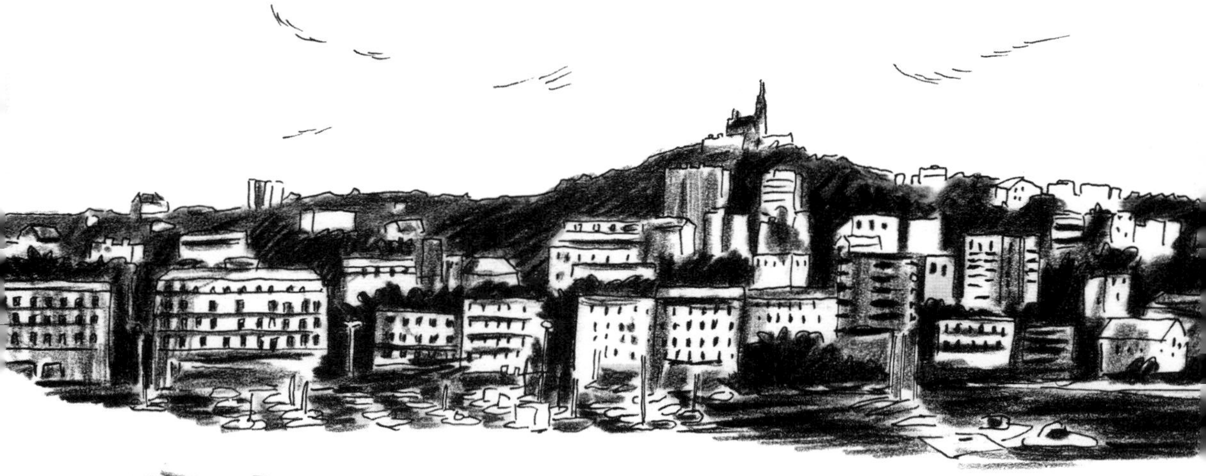

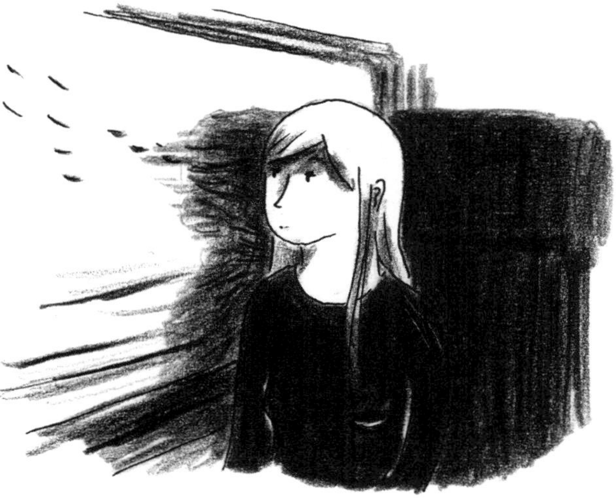

After detailed consideration of your case, you have been selected…

You will be undergoing gamma radiosurgery therapy. This purpose of this document* is to prepare you for…

* Excerpt from the Gamma Unit brochure on this page and the following pages / Department of Stereotactic Neuro-Radiosurgery of La Timone University Hospital Center, Hospitals of Marseille

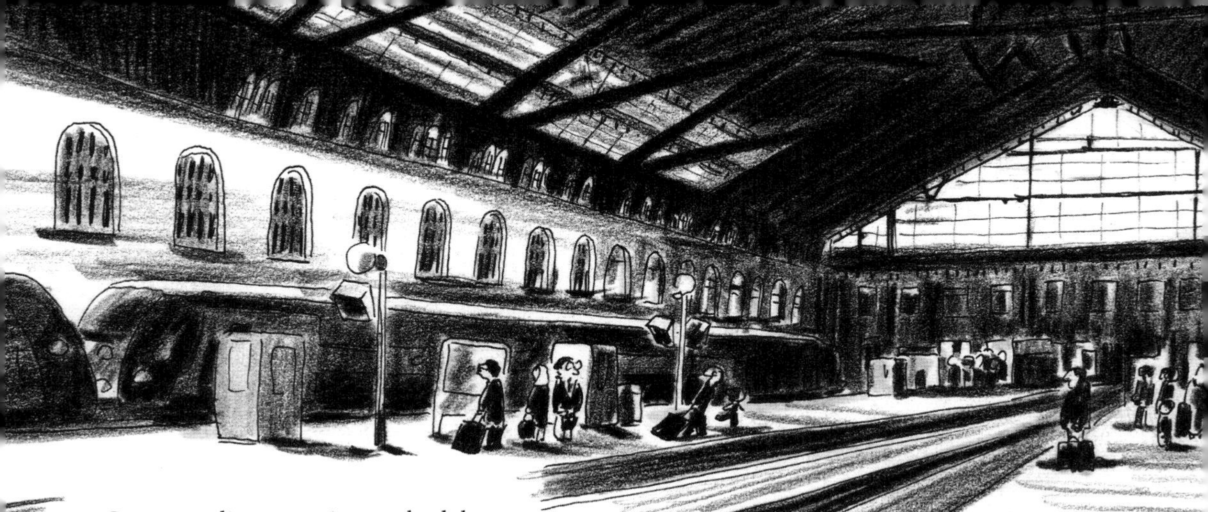

Gamma radiosurgery is a method that allows for the treatment of specific cerebral lesions without opening the skull.

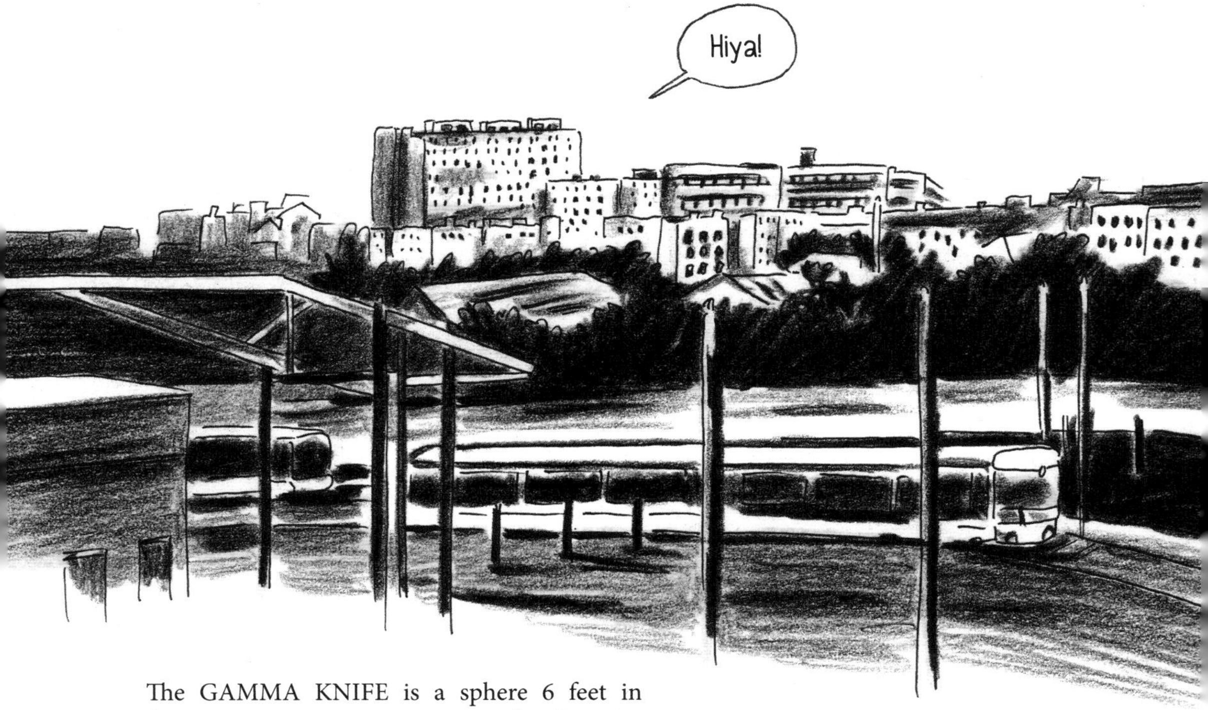
Hiya!

The GAMMA KNIFE is a sphere 6 feet in diameter containing 201 sources of radioactive cobalt. The 201 beams produced converge in the center of the sphere. The patient's head is positioned inside the sphere such that the lesion occupies its exact center.

Taken individually, each beam is of insufficient energy to damage the brain tissue it travels through, but the energy where the 201 beams converge is enough to treat a lesion with precision.

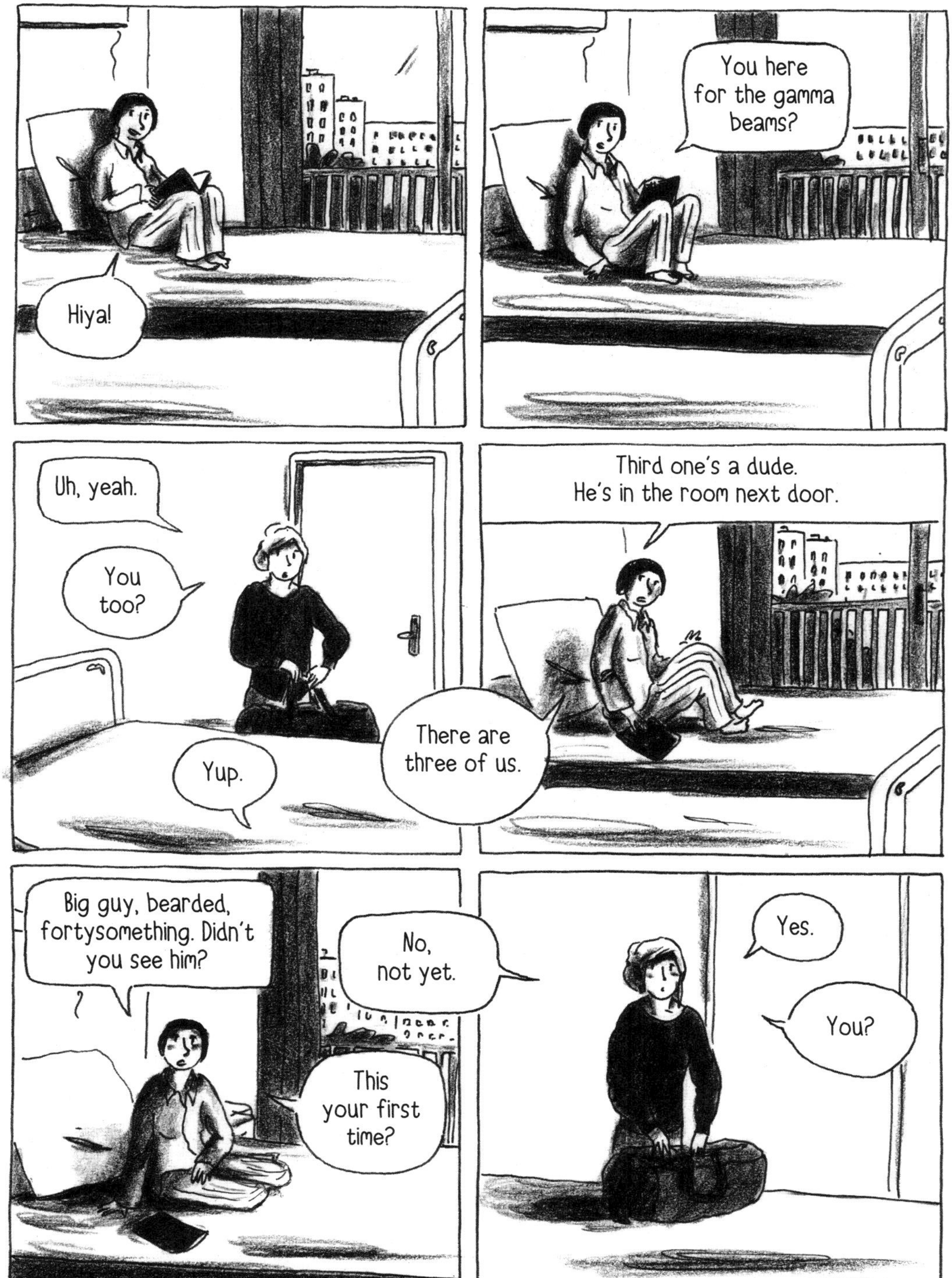
Hiya!
You here for the gamma beams?
Uh, yeah.
You too?
Yup.
There are three of us.
Third one's a dude. He's in the room next door.
Big guy, bearded, fortysomething. Didn't you see him?
No, not yet.
This your first time?
Yes.
You?

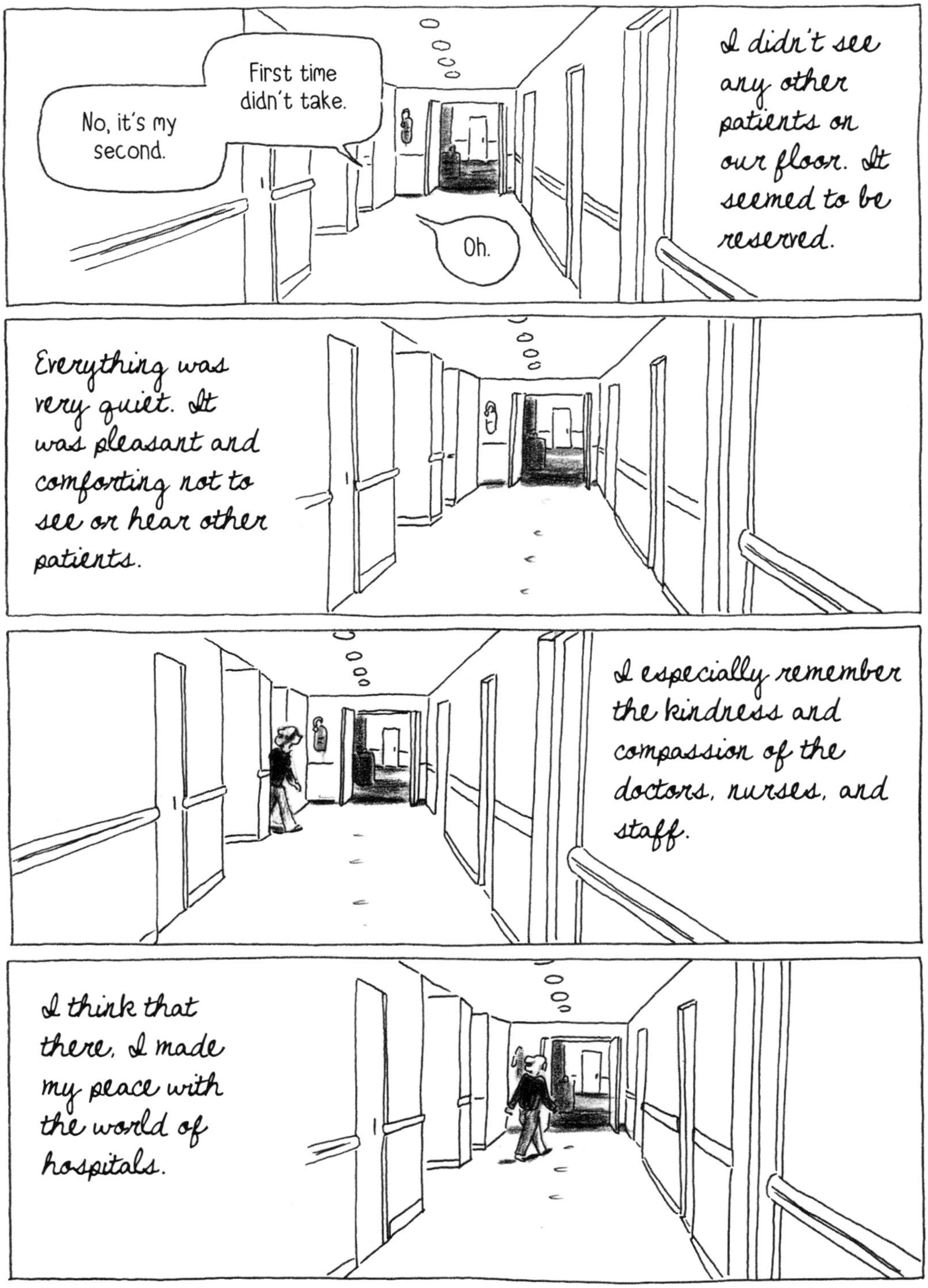
First time didn't take.
No, it's my second.
Oh.
I didn't see any other patients on our floor. It seemed to be reserved.
Everything was very quiet. It was pleasant and comforting not to see or hear other patients.
I especially remember the kindness and compassion of the doctors, nurses, and staff.
I think that there, I made my peace with the world of hospitals.

I wanted to see the sea. So, in secret, a nurse let me out with you into the hospital for a few hours...

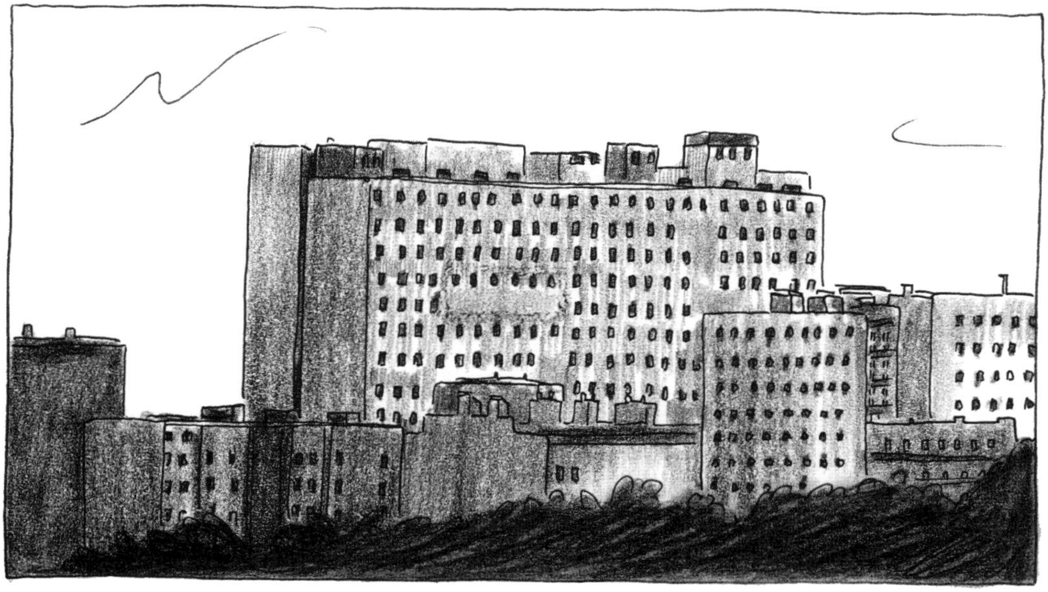

ERE ARE WE? WHERE ARE WE? WHAT TIME IS IT? WHAT TIME IS IT? WHAT TIME

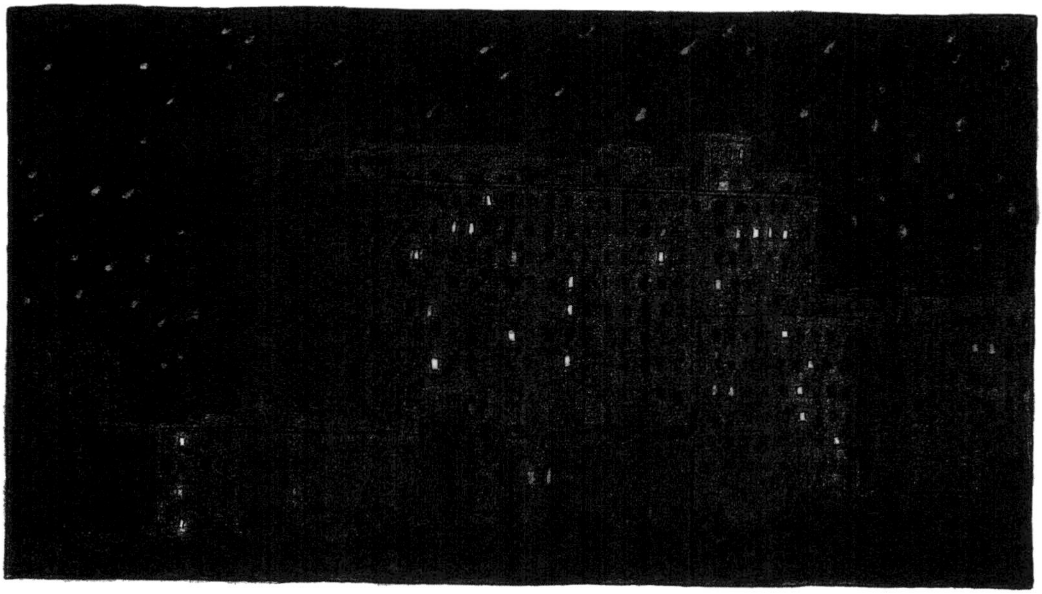

I don't know what we did that day. Did we see the sea?
All I remember is being scared we wouldn't make it back in time.

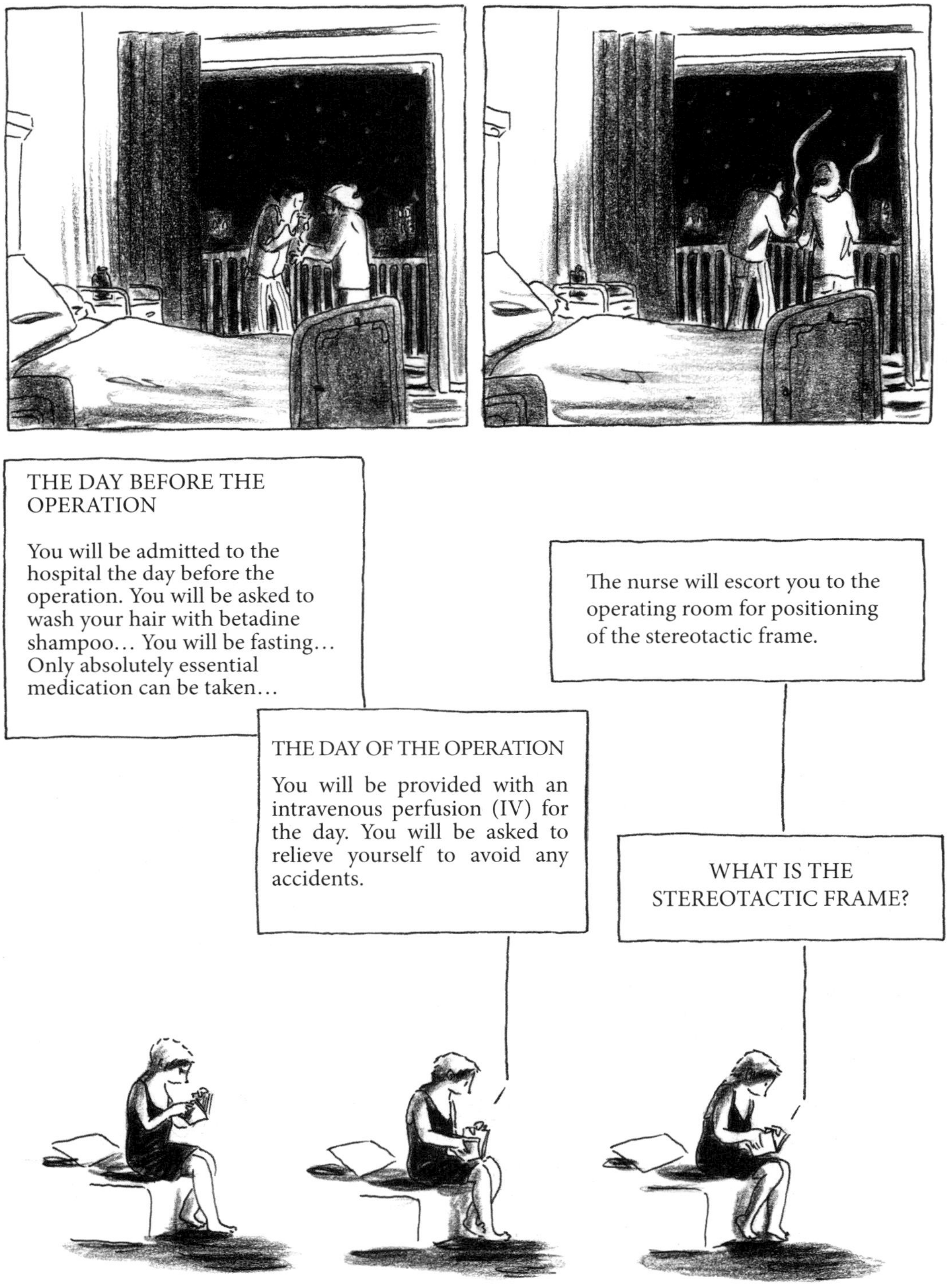
THE DAY BEFORE THE OPERATION
You will be admitted to the hospital the day before the operation. You will be asked to wash your hair with betadine shampoo… You will be fasting… Only absolutely essential medication can be taken…
THE DAY OF THE OPERATION
You will be provided with an intravenous perfusion (IV) for the day. You will be asked to relieve yourself to avoid any accidents.
The nurse will escort you to the operating room for positioning of the stereotactic frame.
WHAT IS THE STEREOTACTIC FRAME?

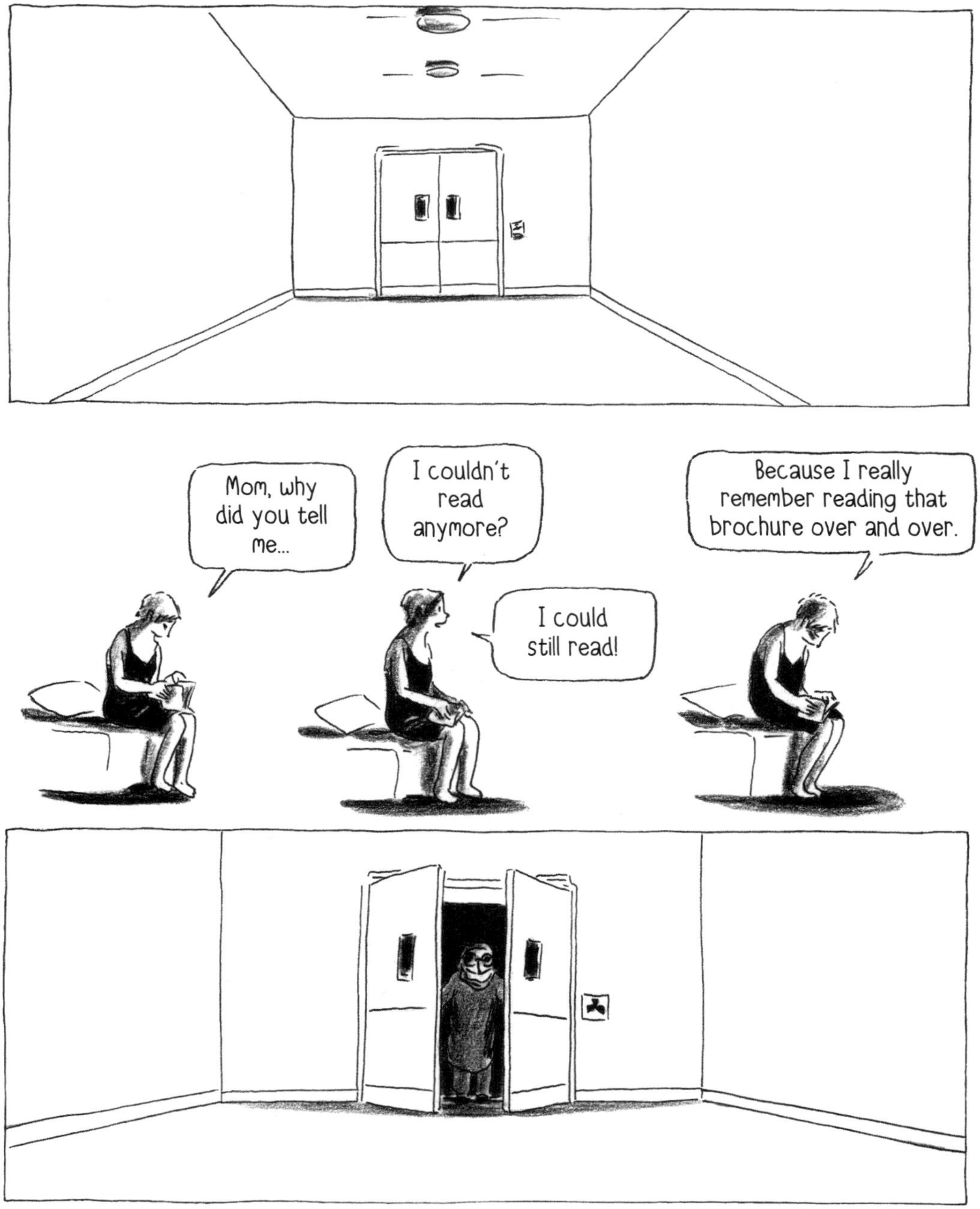
Mom, why did you tell me...
I couldn't read anymore?
I could still read!
Because I really remember reading that brochure over and over.

But you're right, I probably didn't understand much of it. At least I'd understood the operation was painless... So you can imagine how surprised I was when they were positioning the stereotactic frame!

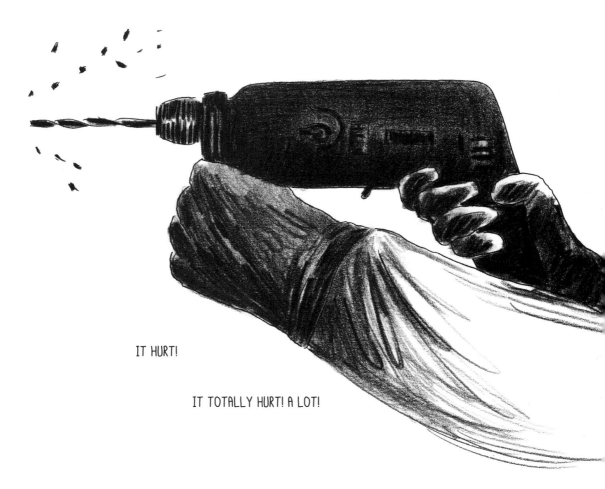

IT HURT!

IT TOTALLY HURT! A LOT!

I WANTED TO SCREAM!

SHOVE ALL THE DOCTORS ASIDE!

AND RUN AWAY!

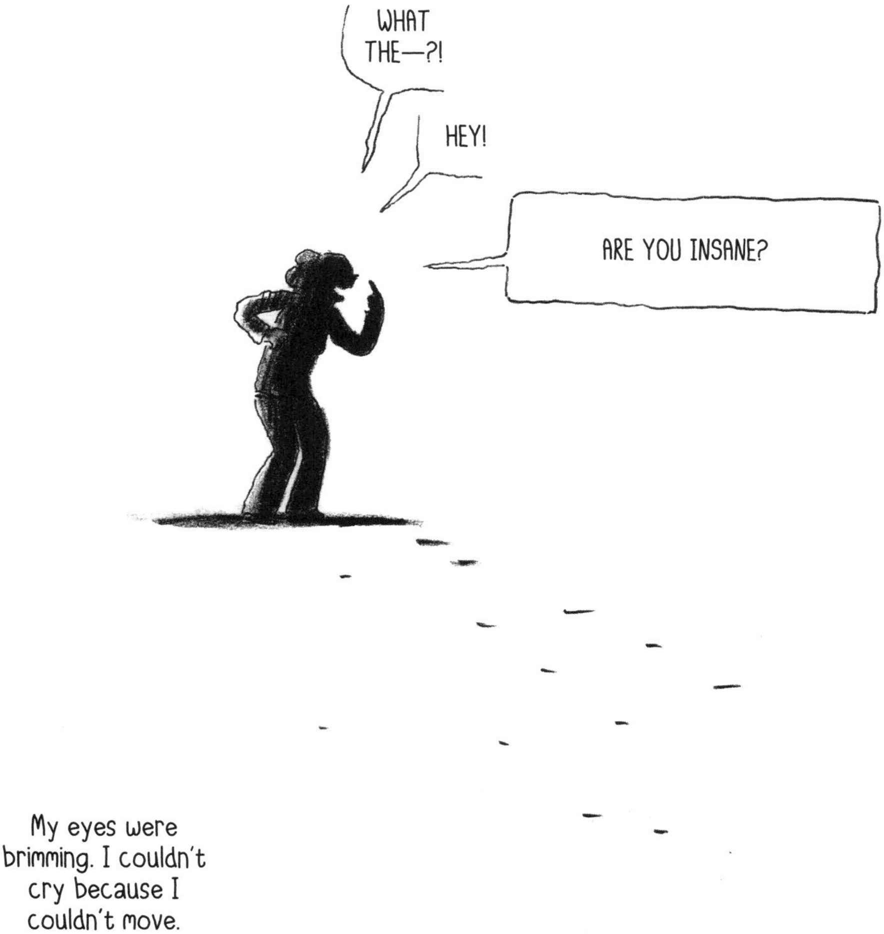
WHAT THE—?!
HEY!
ARE YOU INSANE?
My eyes were brimming. I couldn't cry because I couldn't move.

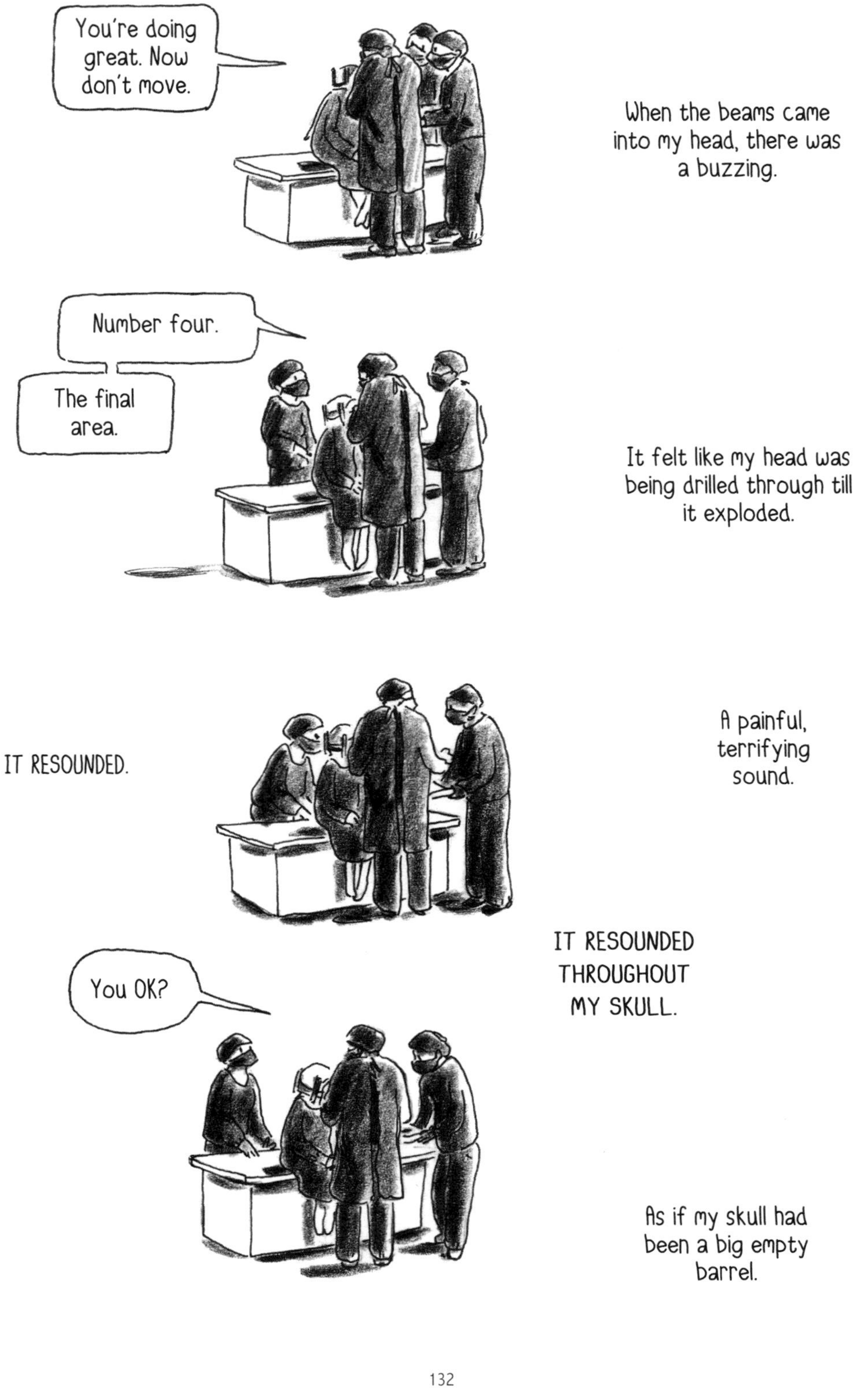

You're doing great. Now don't move.
When the beams came into my head, there was a buzzing.
Number four.
The final area.
It felt like my head was being drilled through till it exploded.
IT RESOUNDED.
A painful, terrifying sound.
IT RESOUNDED THROUGHOUT MY SKULL.
You OK?
As if my skull had been a big empty barrel.

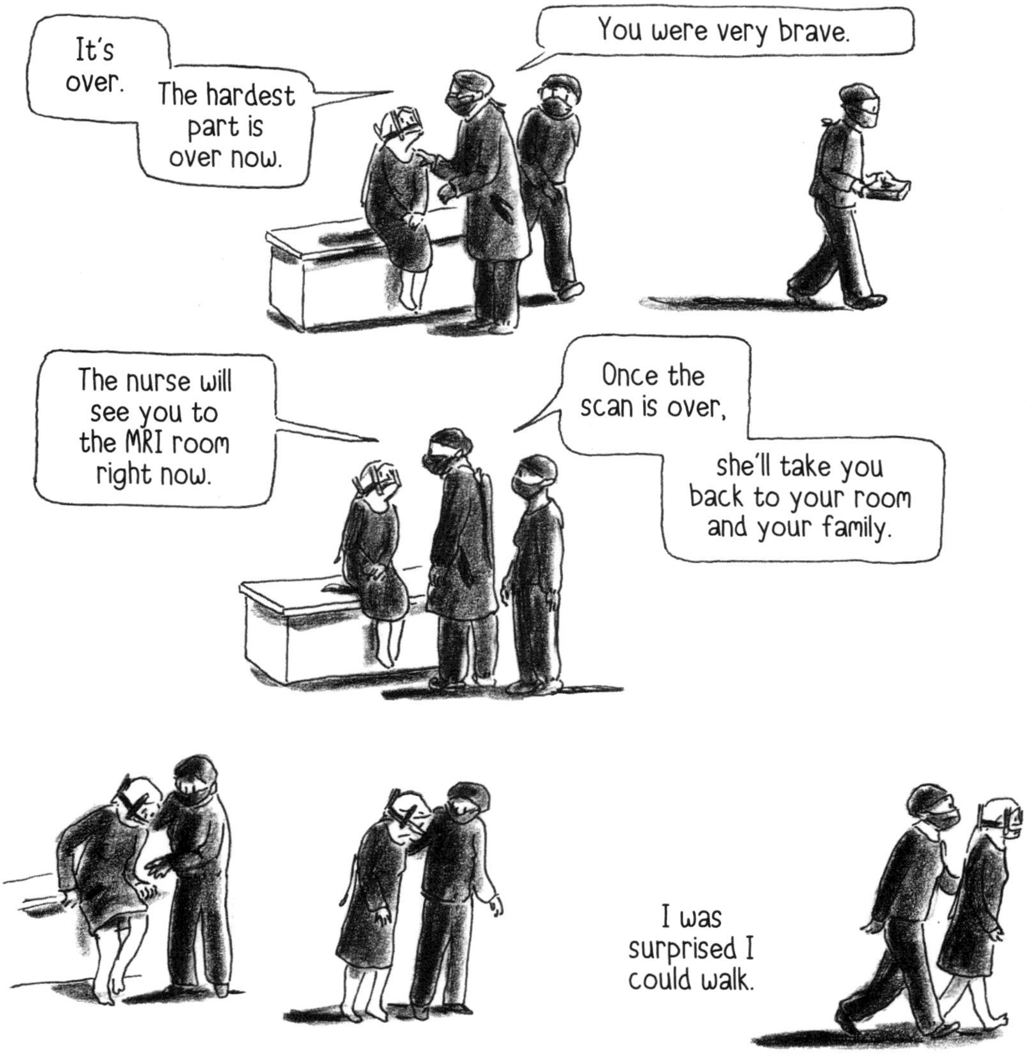
It's over.
The hardest part is over now.
You were very brave.
The nurse will see you to the MRI room right now.
Once the scan is over,
she'll take you back to your room and your family.
I was surprised I could walk.

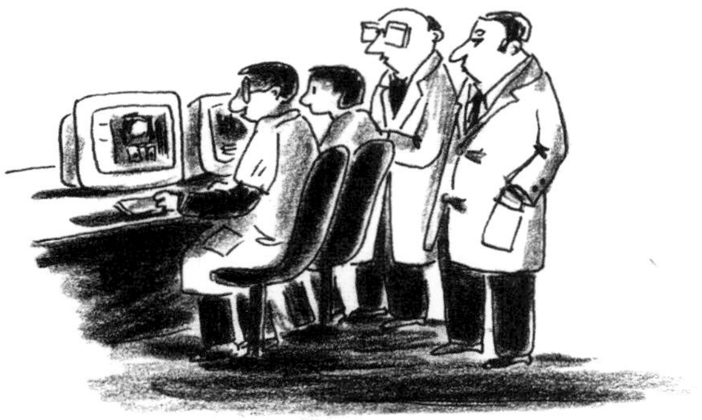

For an unspecified amount of time that may last up to several hours, your team of doctors will confer to pinpoint which areas of the lesion are to be irradiated and for how long.

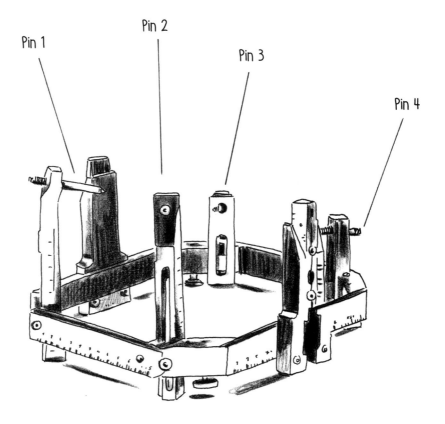

Pin 1

Pin 2

Pin 3

Pin 4

HOW IS A STEREOTACTIC FRAME APPLIED?

Application of the stereotactic frame is ensured by the fixing of four symmetrically placed pins that maintain pressure on the bone through the cranial skin, which has been injected with a local anesthetic. Once in place, the frame is painless. Its light weight makes it entirely bearable. The purpose of this frame is to provide a spatial reference for intracranial lesions. The frame itself will be affixed to the GAMMA KNIFE.

TIME FOR THE TREATMENT

Here you are, in the GAMMA KNIFE at last. You are lying on a table and your head has been anchored with precision thanks to the stereotactic frame.

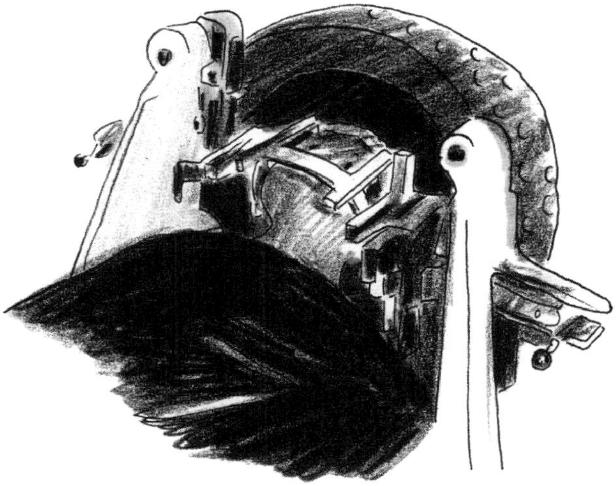

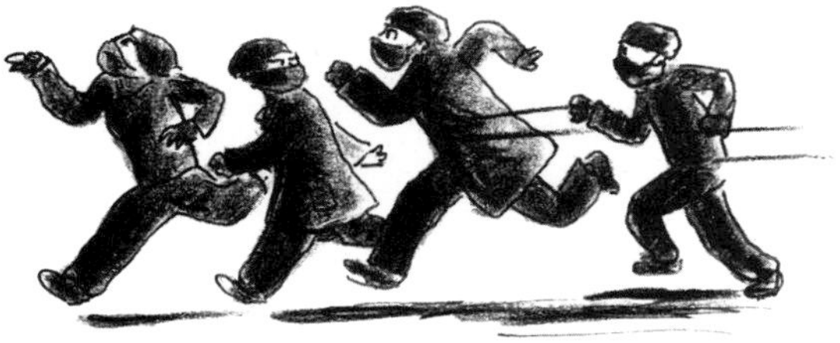

Your team of doctors will leave the room but remain in constant contact with you via intercom and closed-circuit video surveillance. You will be able to talk to the surgical team.

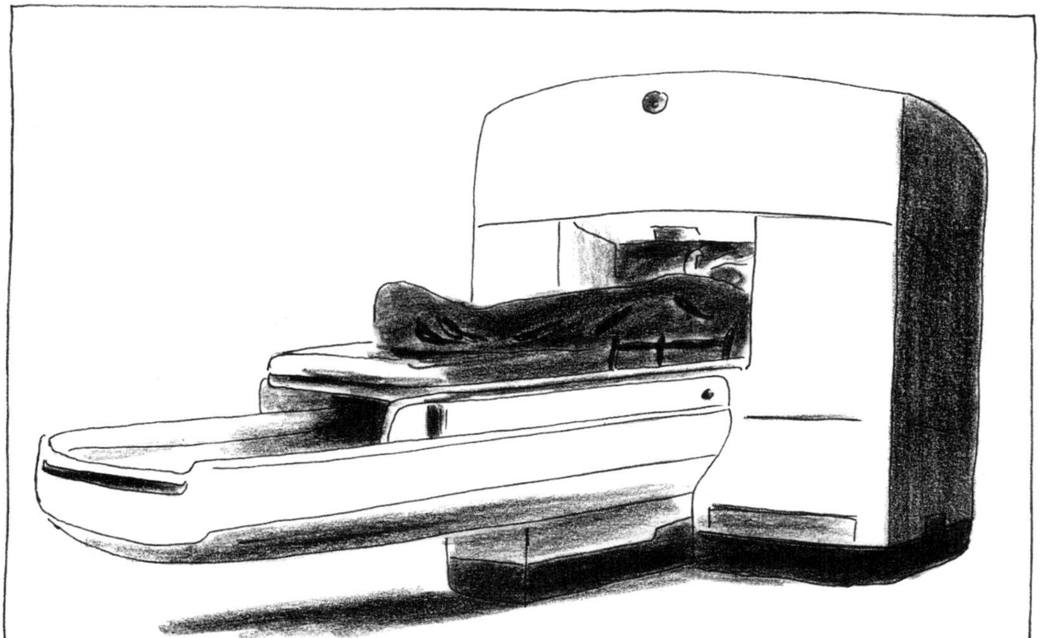

Meanwhile, the sphere is opening, and the Gamma Knife table will enter the sphere. Your lesion is now exactly at the convergence point for the beams. You will not hear or feel a thing.

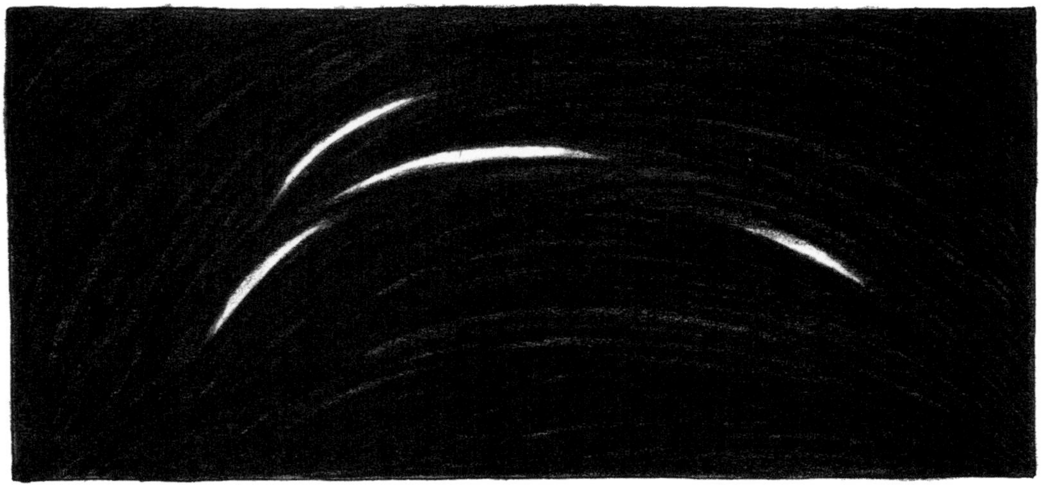

After an unspecified amount of time (from 10 to 30 minutes), the table will come out again. The sphere will close. If a single session proves enough, then you'll be all done!

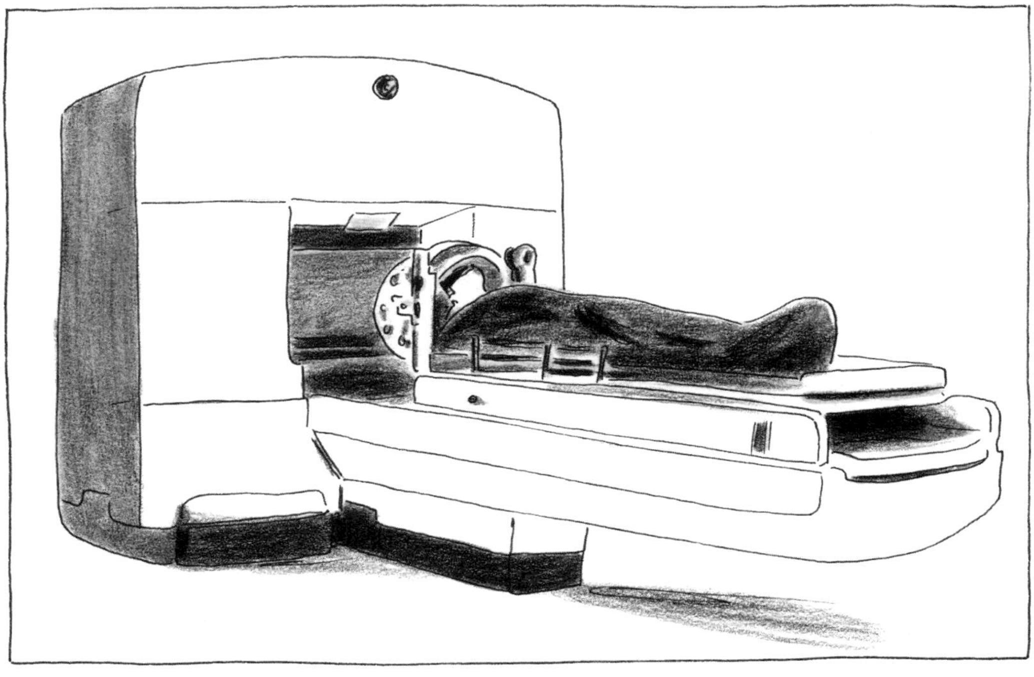

The stereotactic frame will be removed and a light dressing applied. Only in rare cases do sutures prove necessary at the pin entry sites.

We learned that the third patient had struggled when the frame was applied. I don't know if he was even able to undergo the procedure. Nowadays, patients are given gas for the same process.

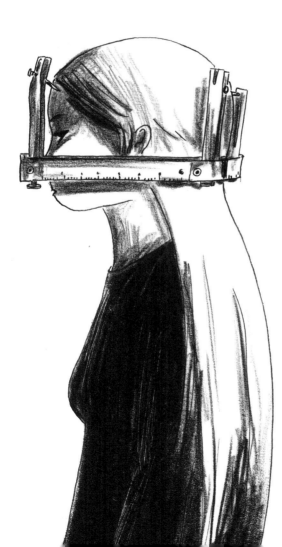

In most cases, you will be able to leave the hospital the next day.

WHAT NEXT?

Since the effects of the Gamma Knife are by definition delayed-action, the next steps will involve close supervision. Any evolution of your treatment will be decided upon in consultation with your doctor.

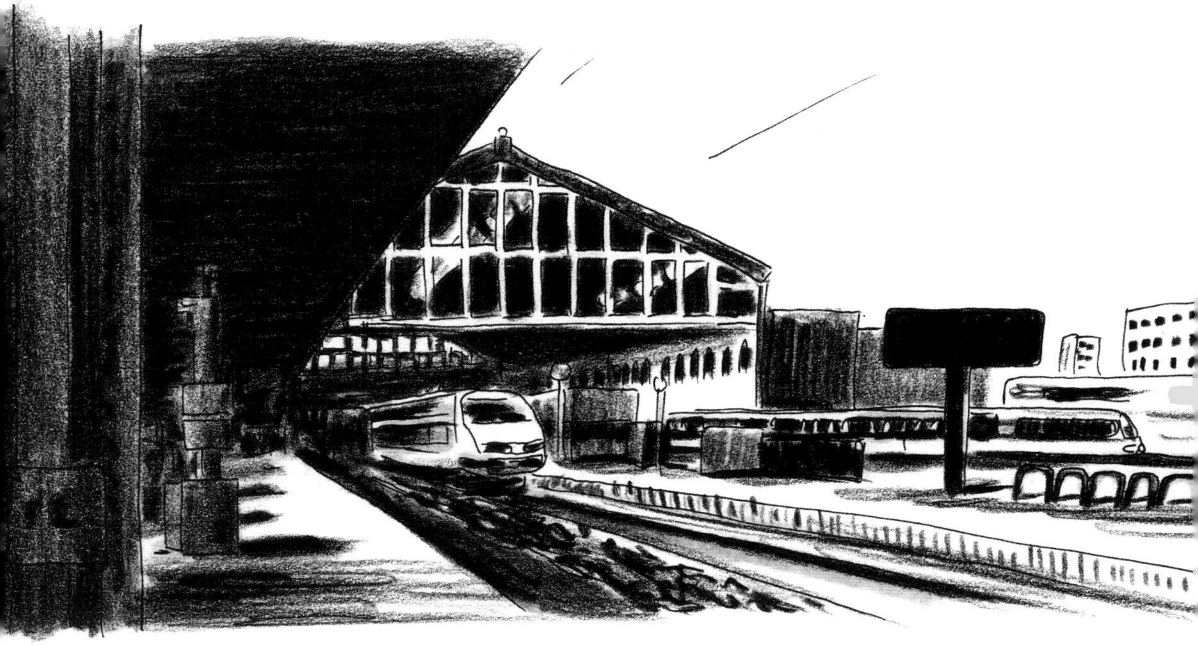

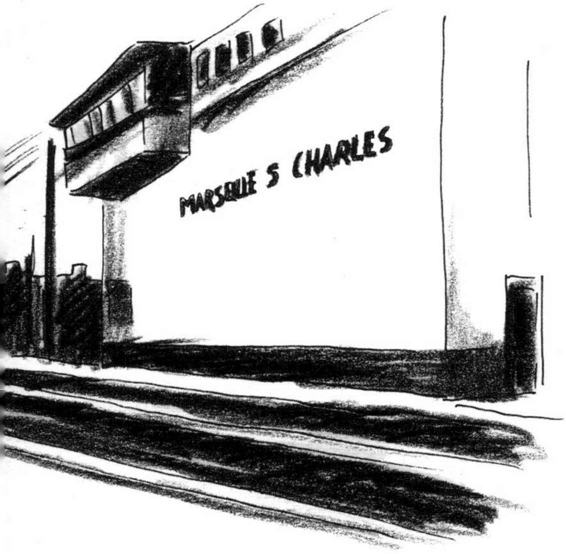
MARSEILLE S CHARLES

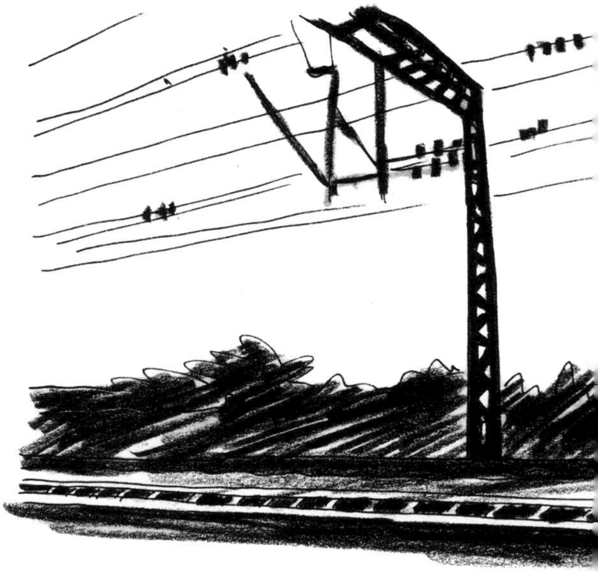

Regular MRI scans will be necessary for the next 18 months, after which they will become less frequent.

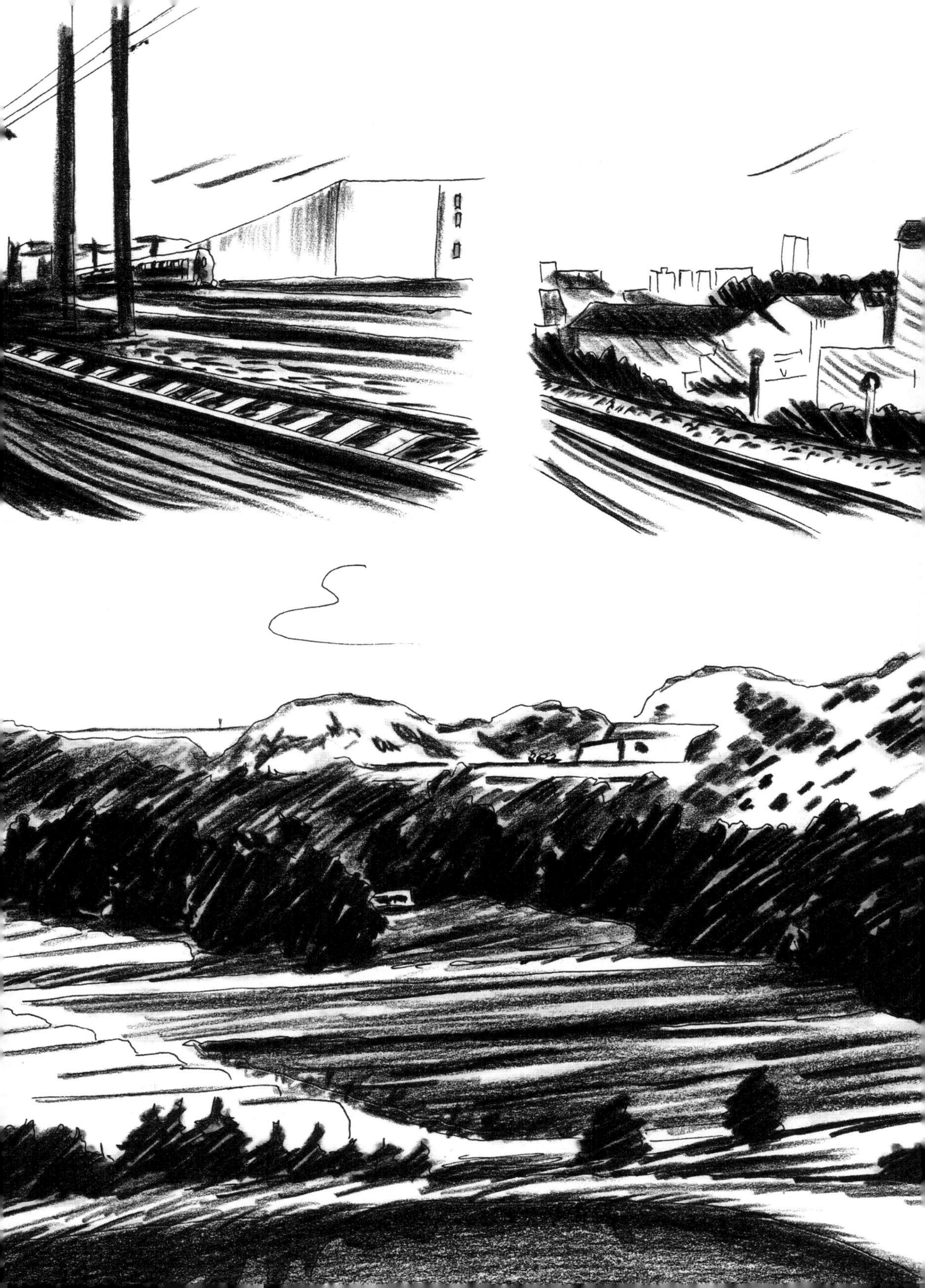

After Marseille, I sank even deeper into illness.

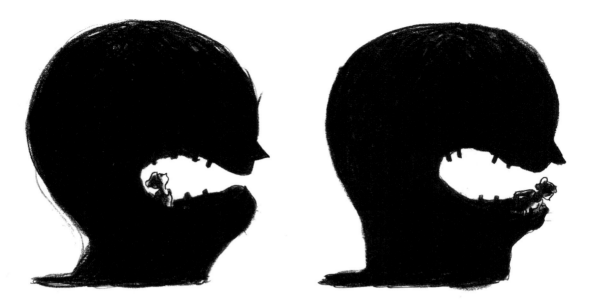

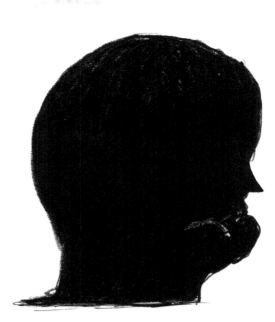

My memory kept getting worse.
I spent even less time awake.

At the time, the neuropsychiatrist
rated my disability at 65%.

It's hard to tell
you this story.
It still makes
me feel lost...

It's hard to explain, to understand a memory that slips through your
fingers. Actually, I don't remember anything at all after Marseille.

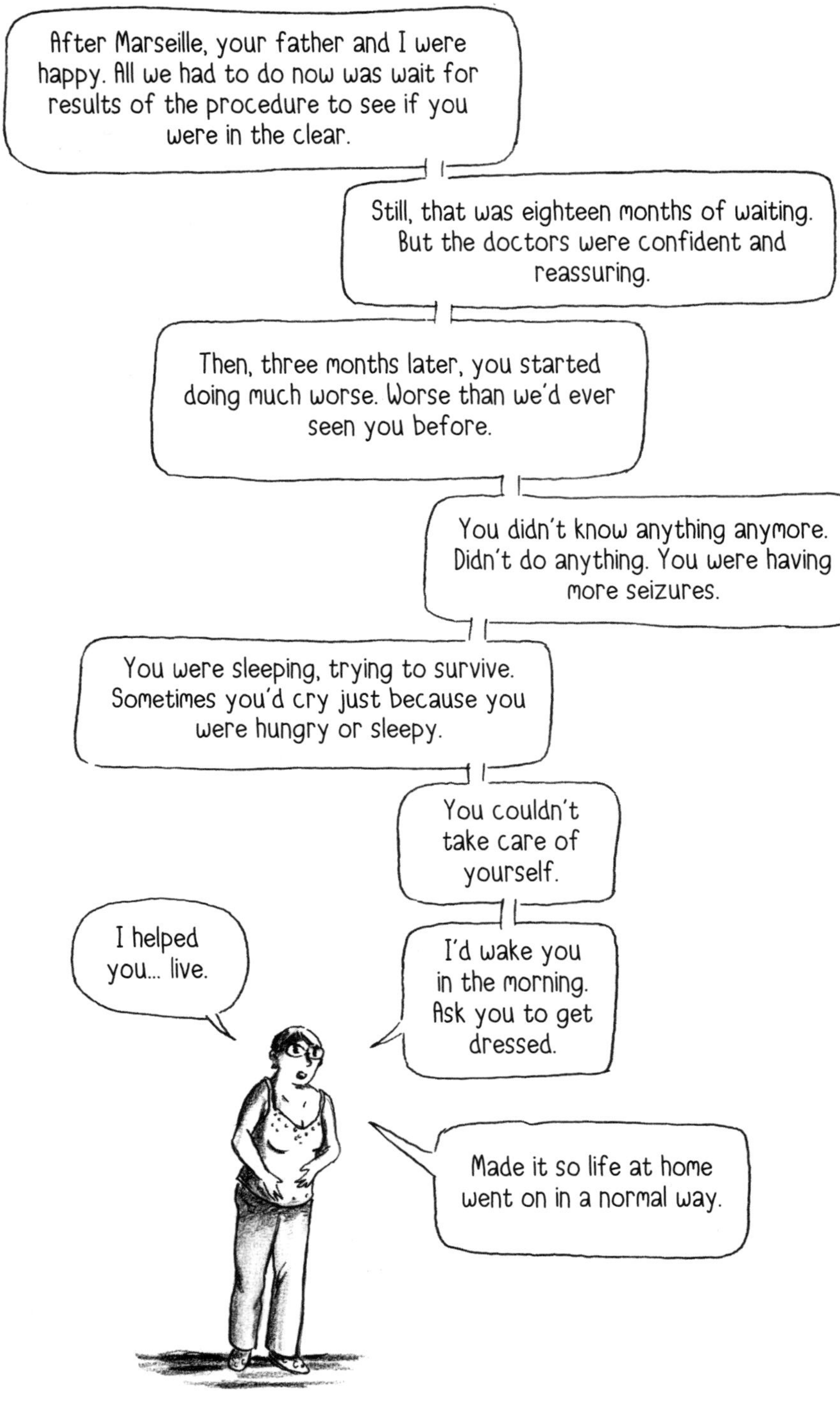
After Marseille, your father and I were happy. All we had to do now was wait for results of the procedure to see if you were in the clear.
Still, that was eighteen months of waiting. But the doctors were confident and reassuring.
Then, three months later, you started doing much worse. Worse than we'd ever seen you before.
You didn't know anything anymore. Didn't do anything. You were having more seizures.
You were sleeping, trying to survive. Sometimes you'd cry just because you were hungry or sleepy.
You couldn't take care of yourself.
I'd wake you in the morning. Ask you to get dressed.
I helped you... live.
Made it so life at home went on in a normal way.

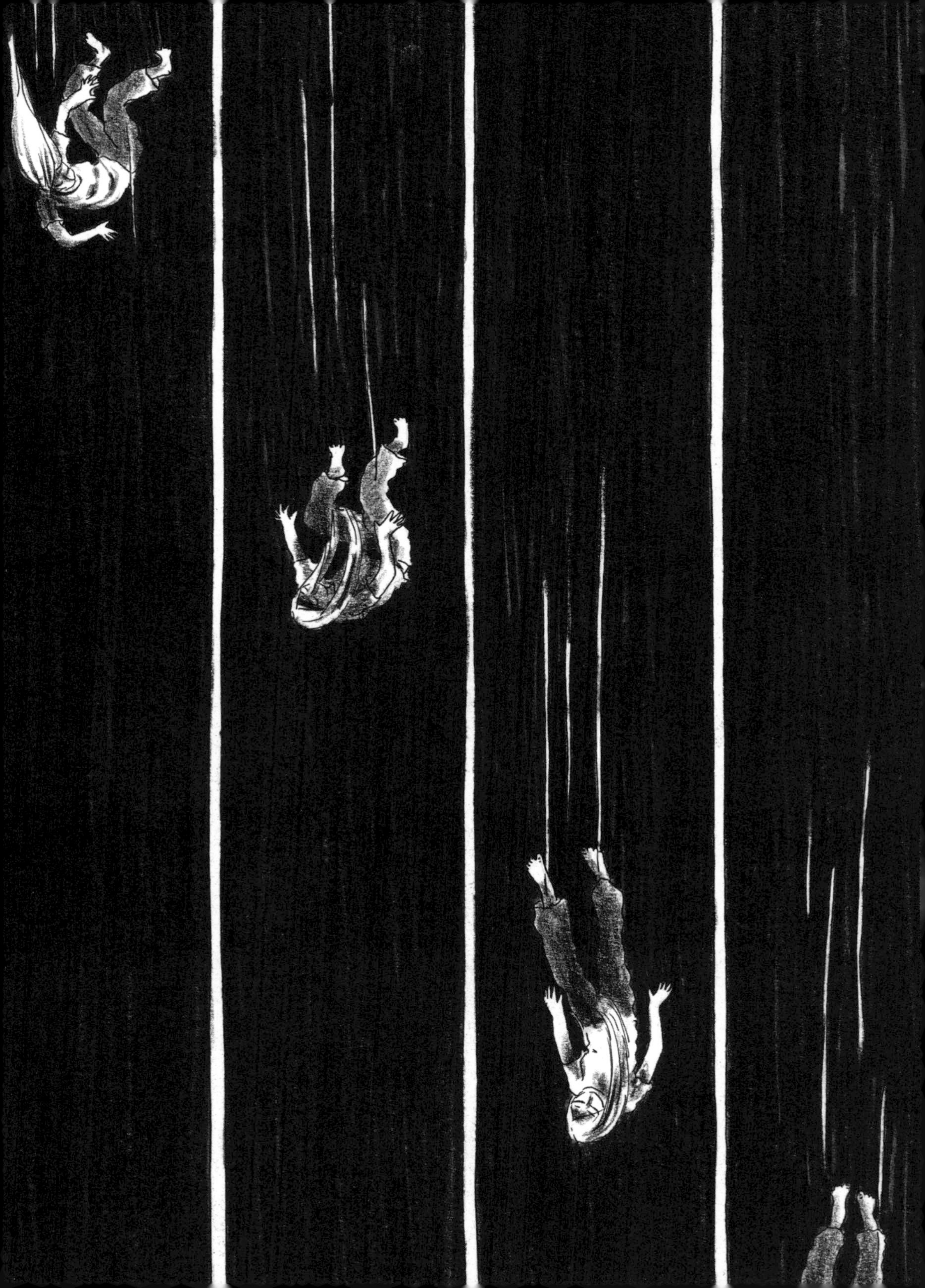

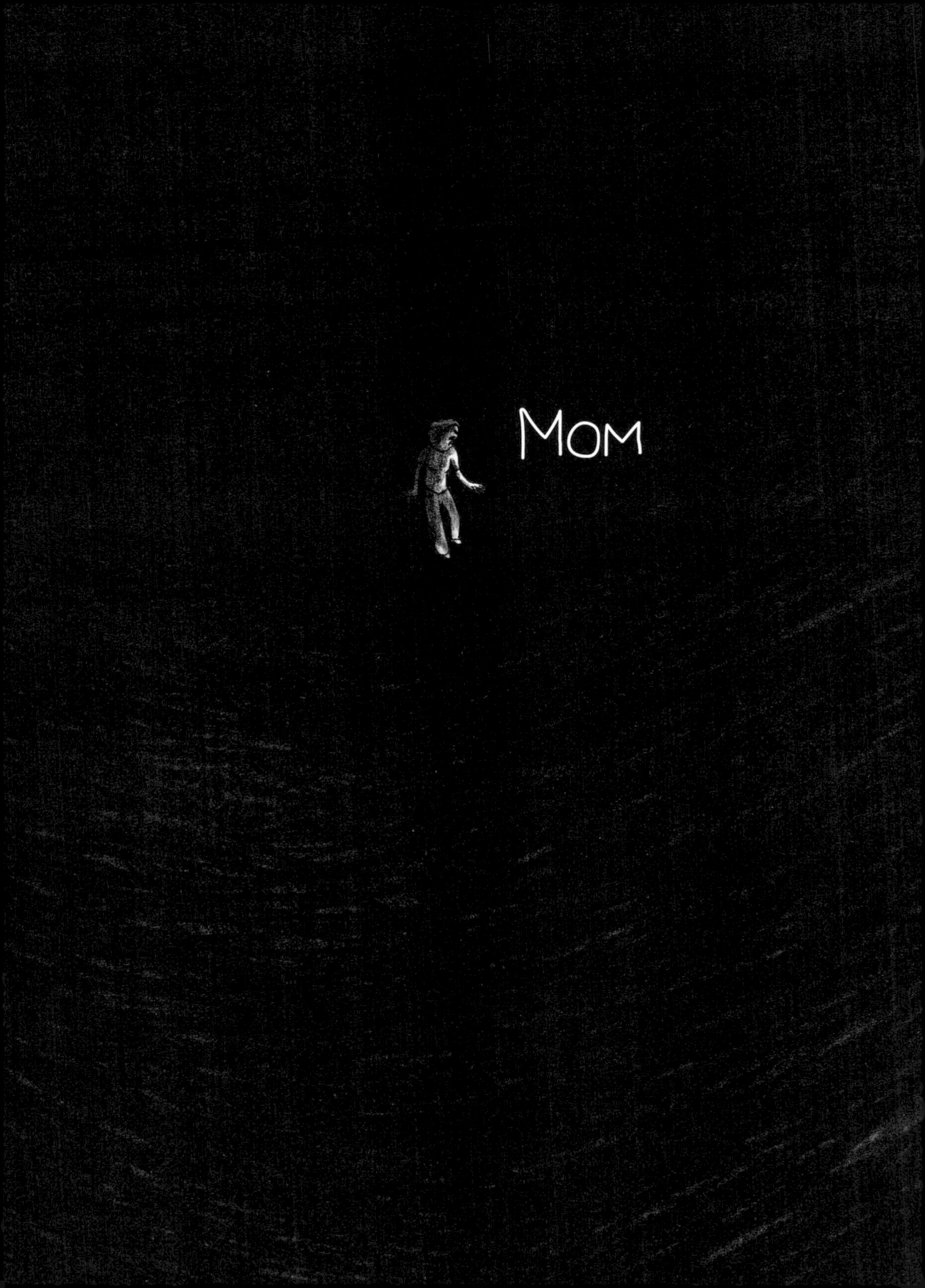
Mom

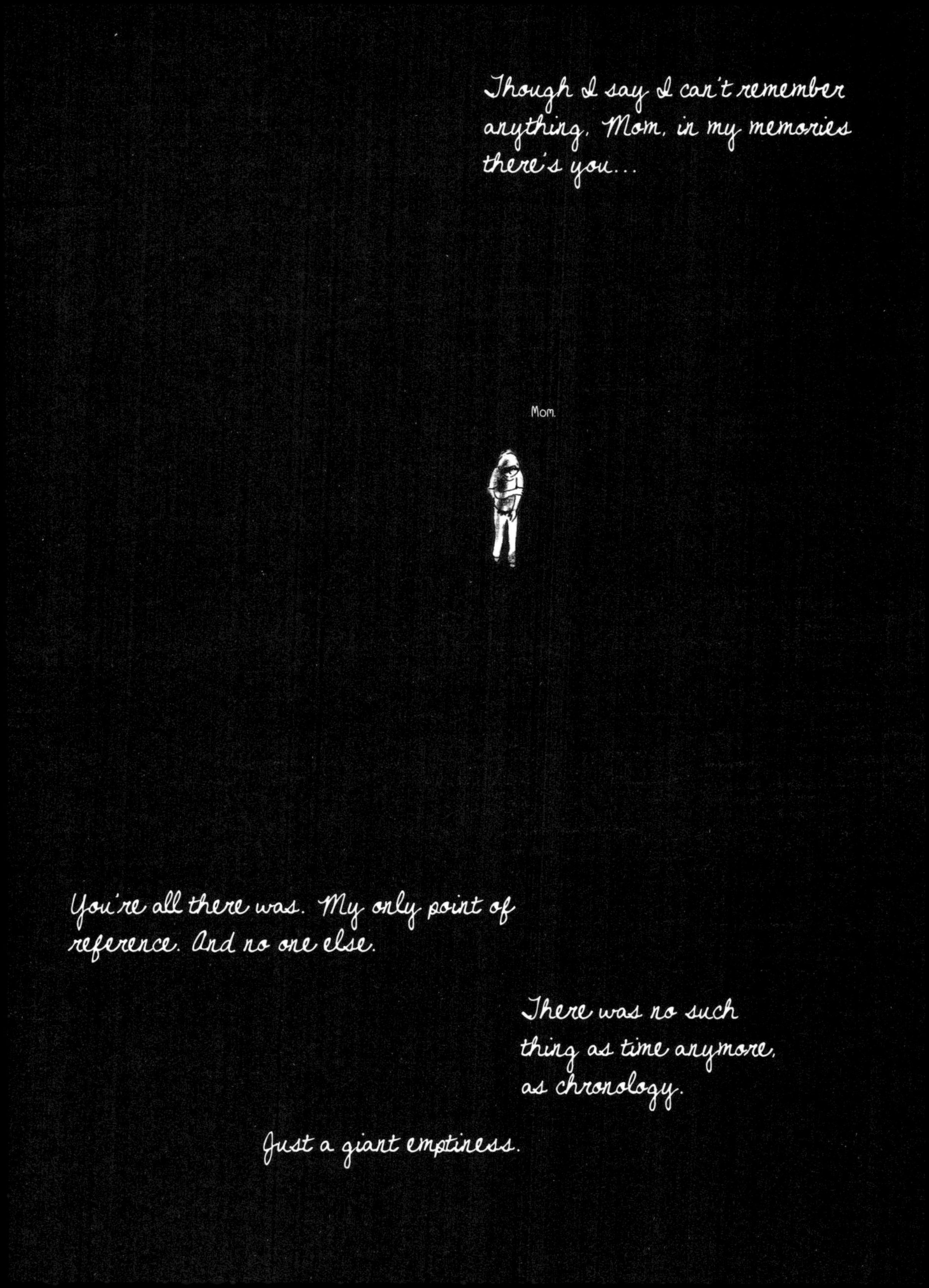
Though I say I can't remember anything, Mom, in my memories there's you...
Mom.
You're all there was. My only point of reference. And no one else.
There was no such thing as time anymore, as chronology.
Just a giant emptiness.

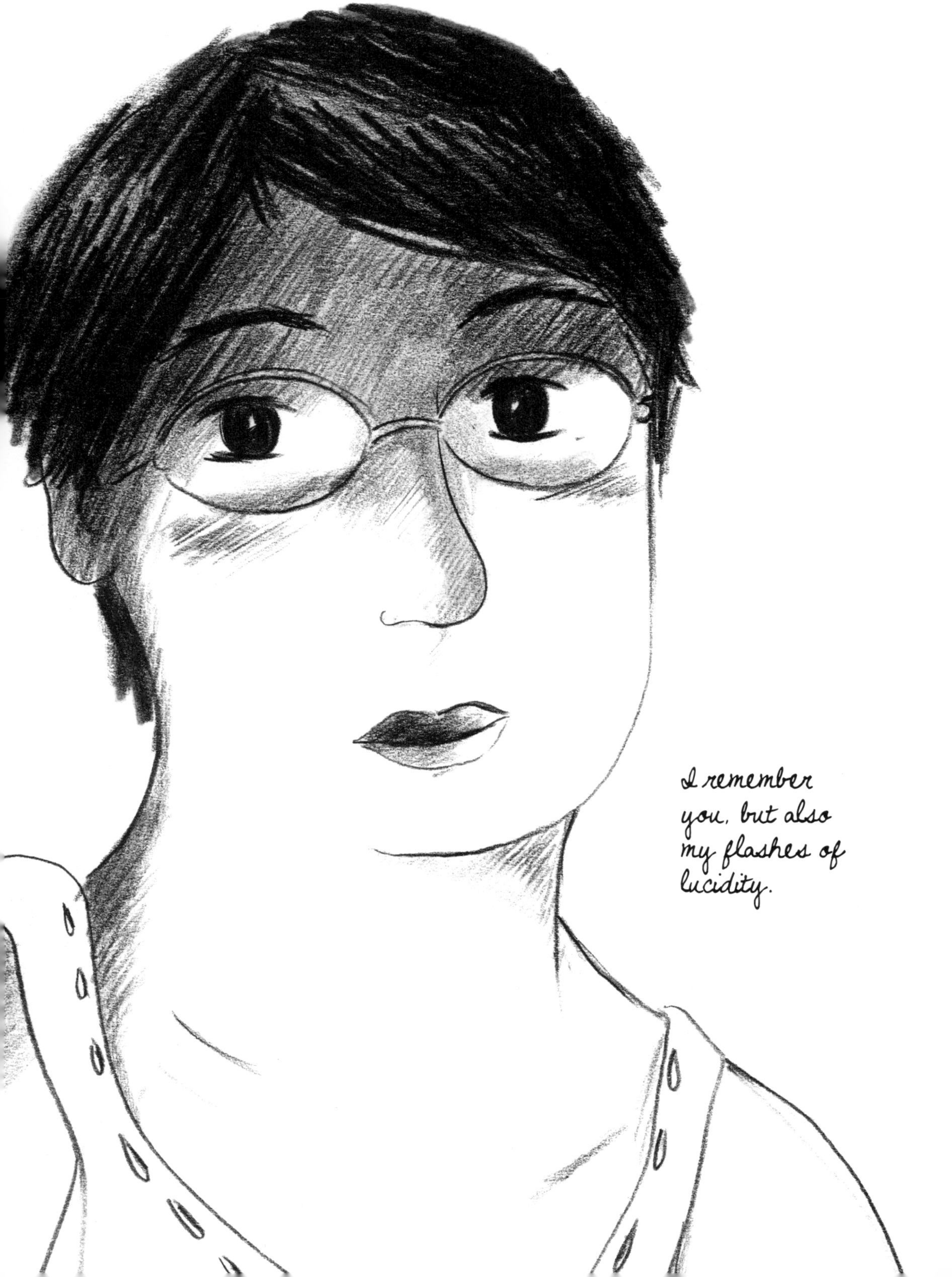
I remember
you, but also
my flashes of
lucidity.

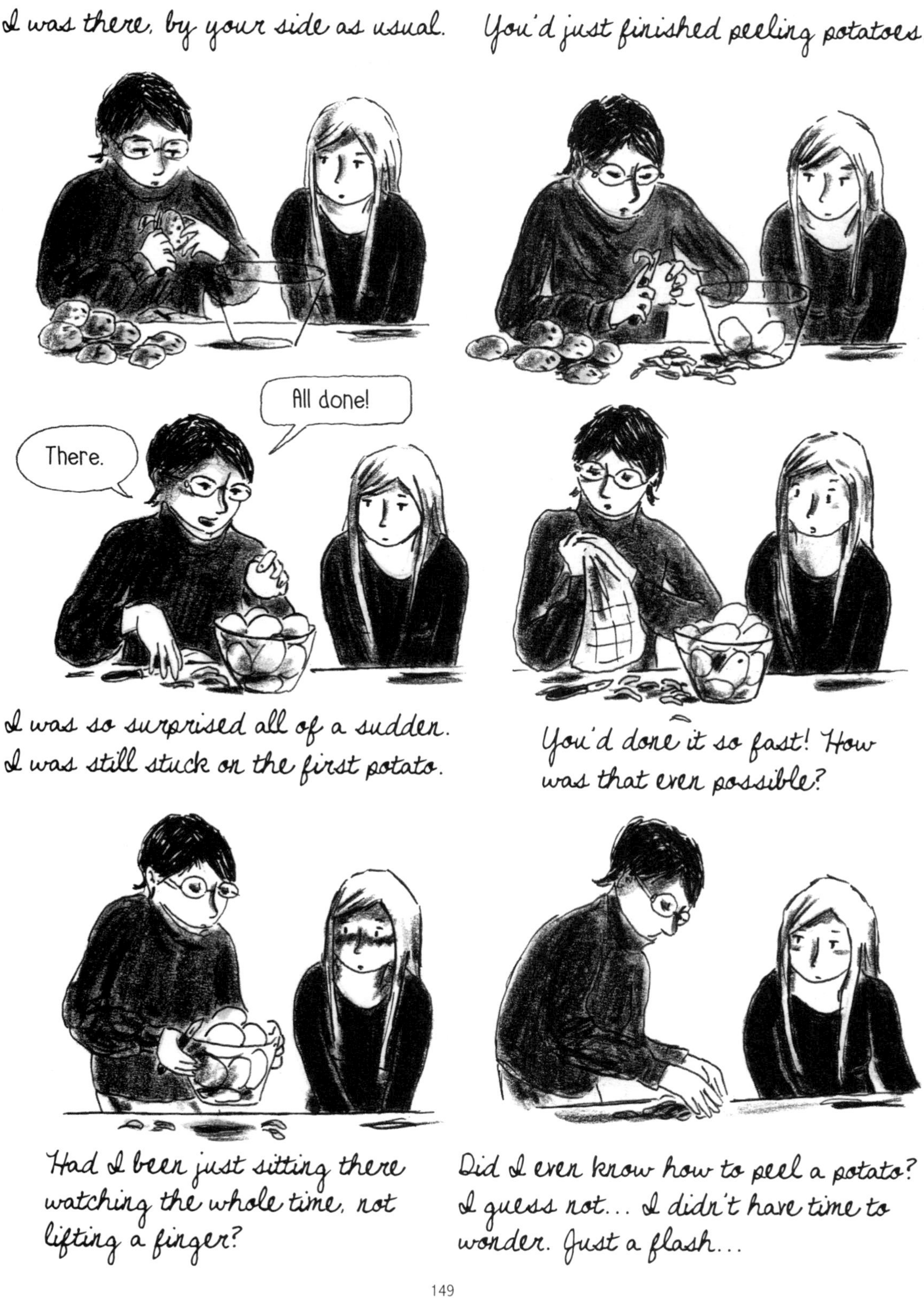
I was there, by your side as usual.
You'd just finished peeling potatoes.
There.
All done!
I was so surprised all of a sudden. I was still stuck on the first potato.
You'd done it so fast! How was that even possible?
Had I been just sitting there watching the whole time, not lifting a finger?
Did I even know how to peel a potato? I guess not... I didn't have time to wonder. Just a flash...

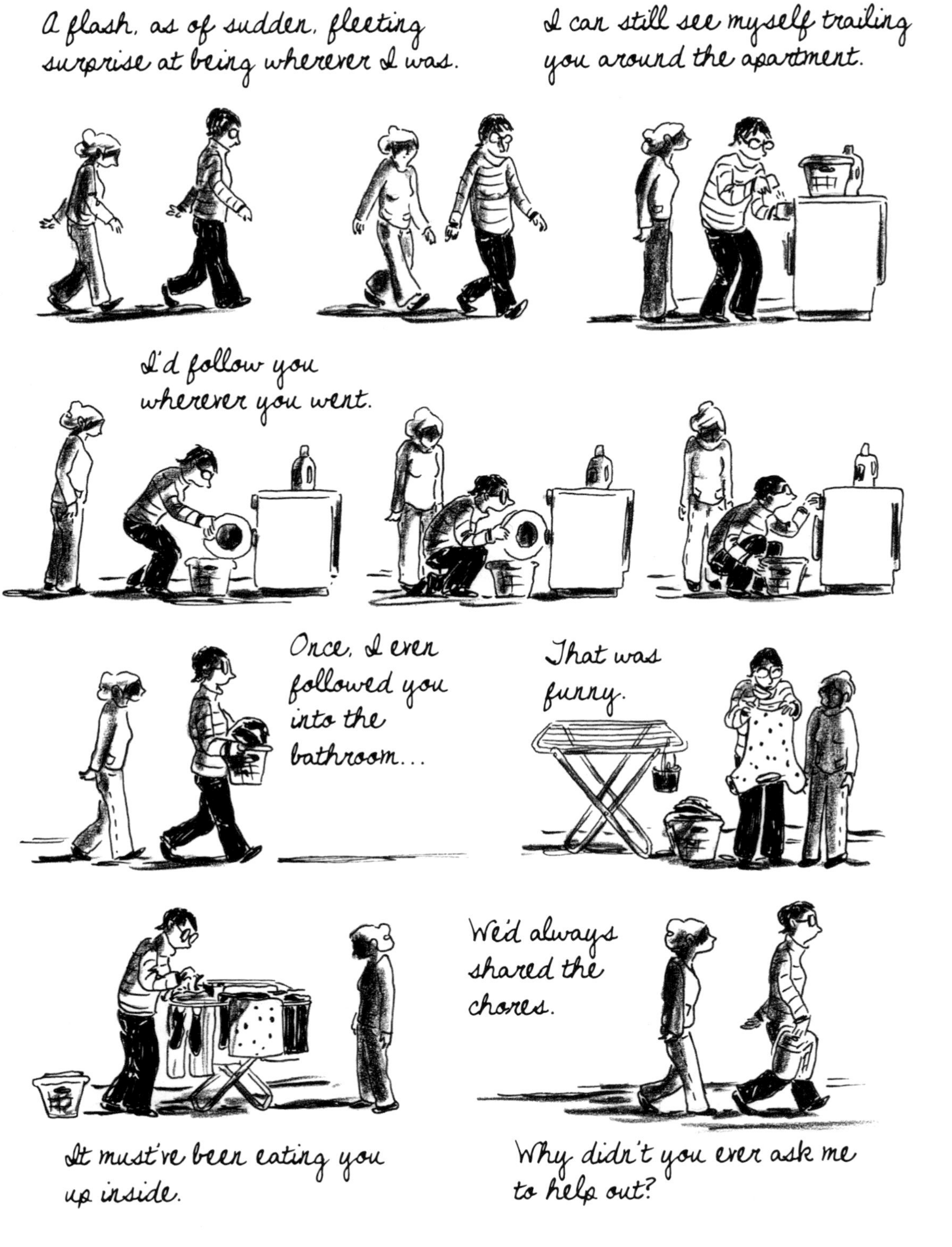
A flash, as of sudden, fleeting surprise at being wherever I was.
I can still see myself trailing you around the apartment.
I'd follow you wherever you went.
Once, I even followed you into the bathroom...
That was funny.
We'd always shared the chores.
It must've been eating you up inside.
Why didn't you ever ask me to help out?

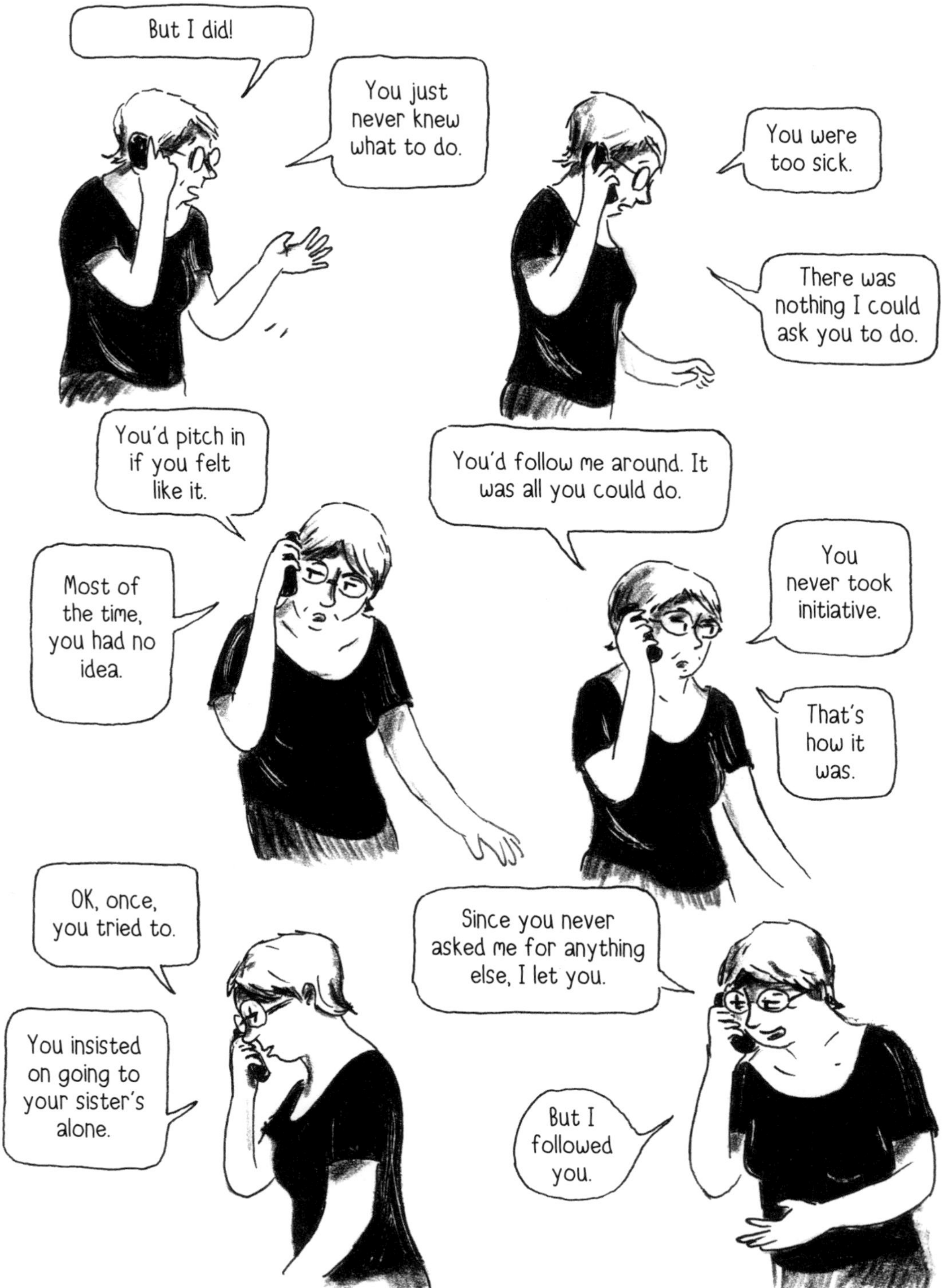
But I did!
You just never knew what to do.
You were too sick.
There was nothing I could ask you to do.
You'd pitch in if you felt like it.
Most of the time, you had no idea.
You'd follow me around. It was all you could do.
You never took initiative.
That's how it was.
OK, once, you tried to.
You insisted on going to your sister's alone.
Since you never asked me for anything else, I let you.
But I followed you.

I found you in the middle of the ped mall at Créteil-l'Église.

Across from your sister's. You weren't moving, so I walked up.

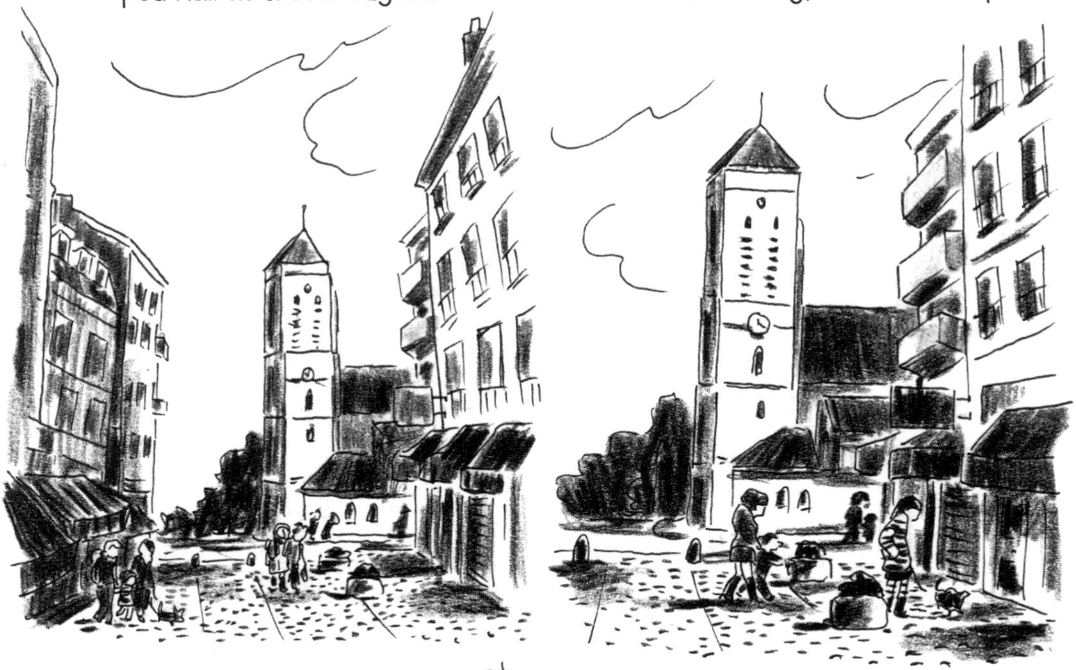

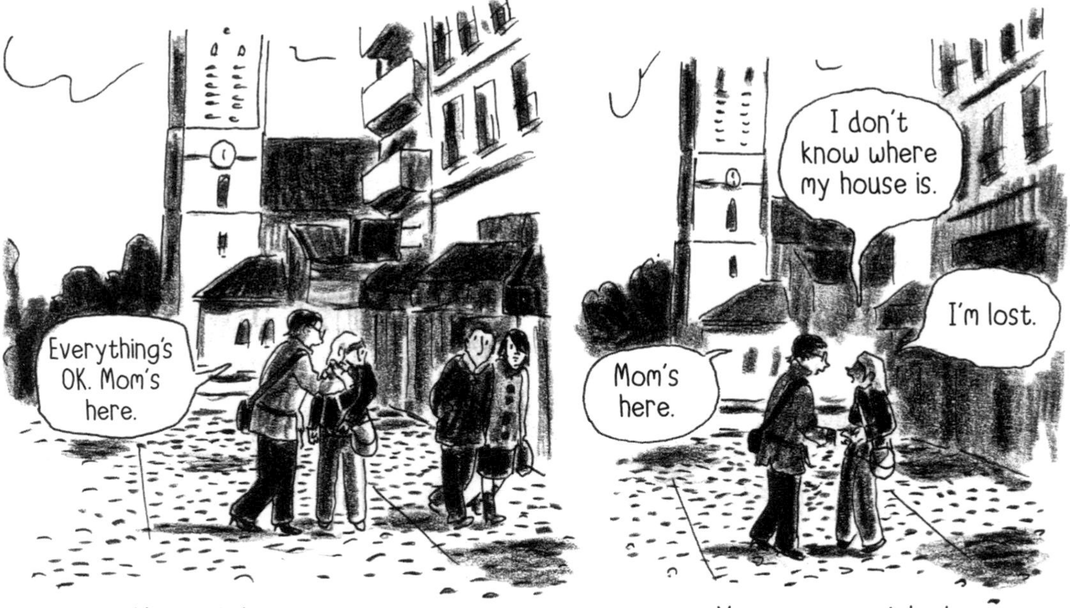
Everything's OK. Mom's here.
Mom's here.
I don't know where my house is.
I'm lost.

You didn't recognize me.

You were panicked.

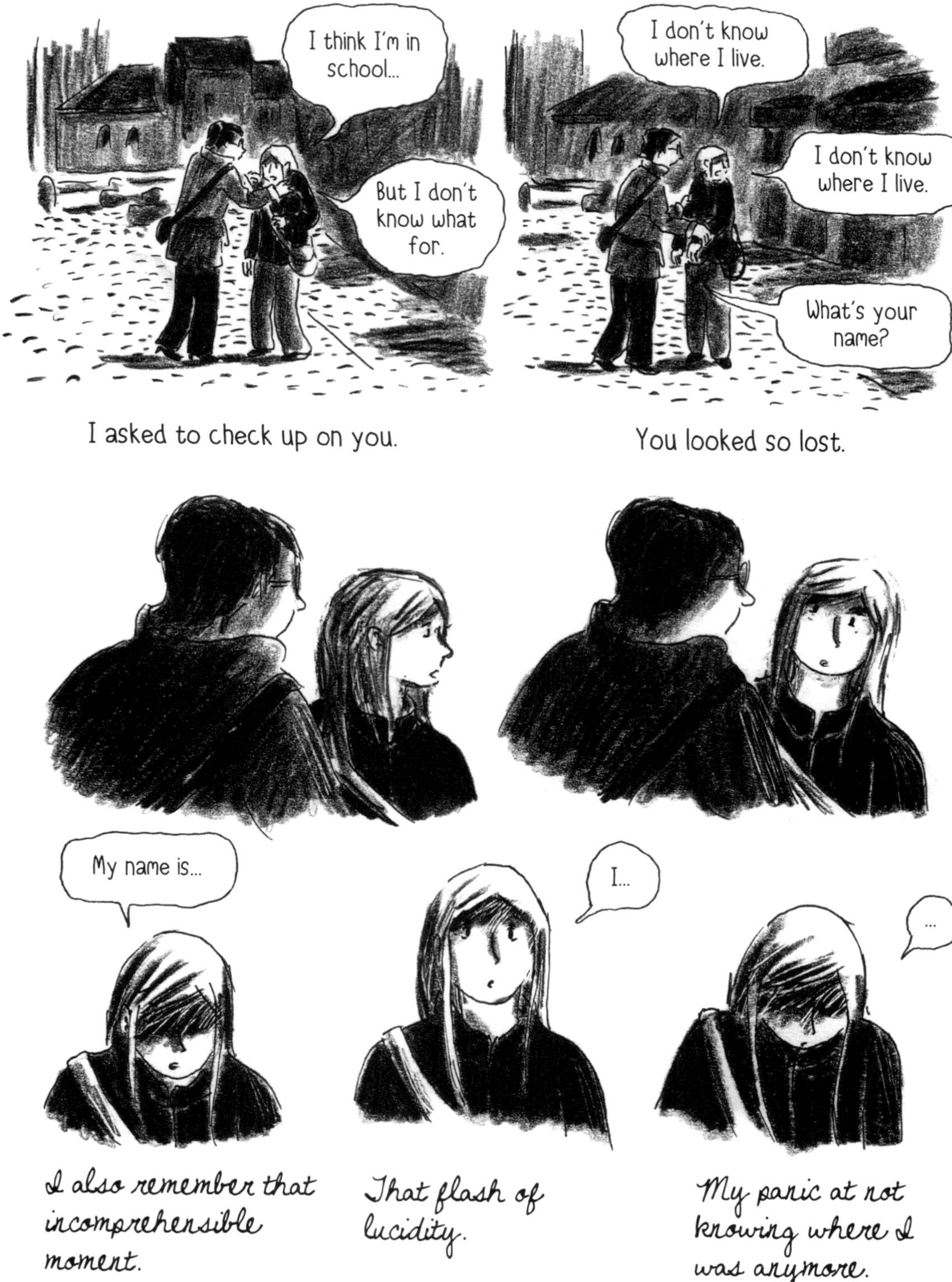
I think I'm in school...
But I don't know what for.
I asked to check up on you.
I don't know where I live.
I don't know where I live.
What's your name?
You looked so lost.
My name is...
I also remember that incomprehensible moment.
I...
That flash of lucidity.
...
My panic at not knowing where I was anymore.

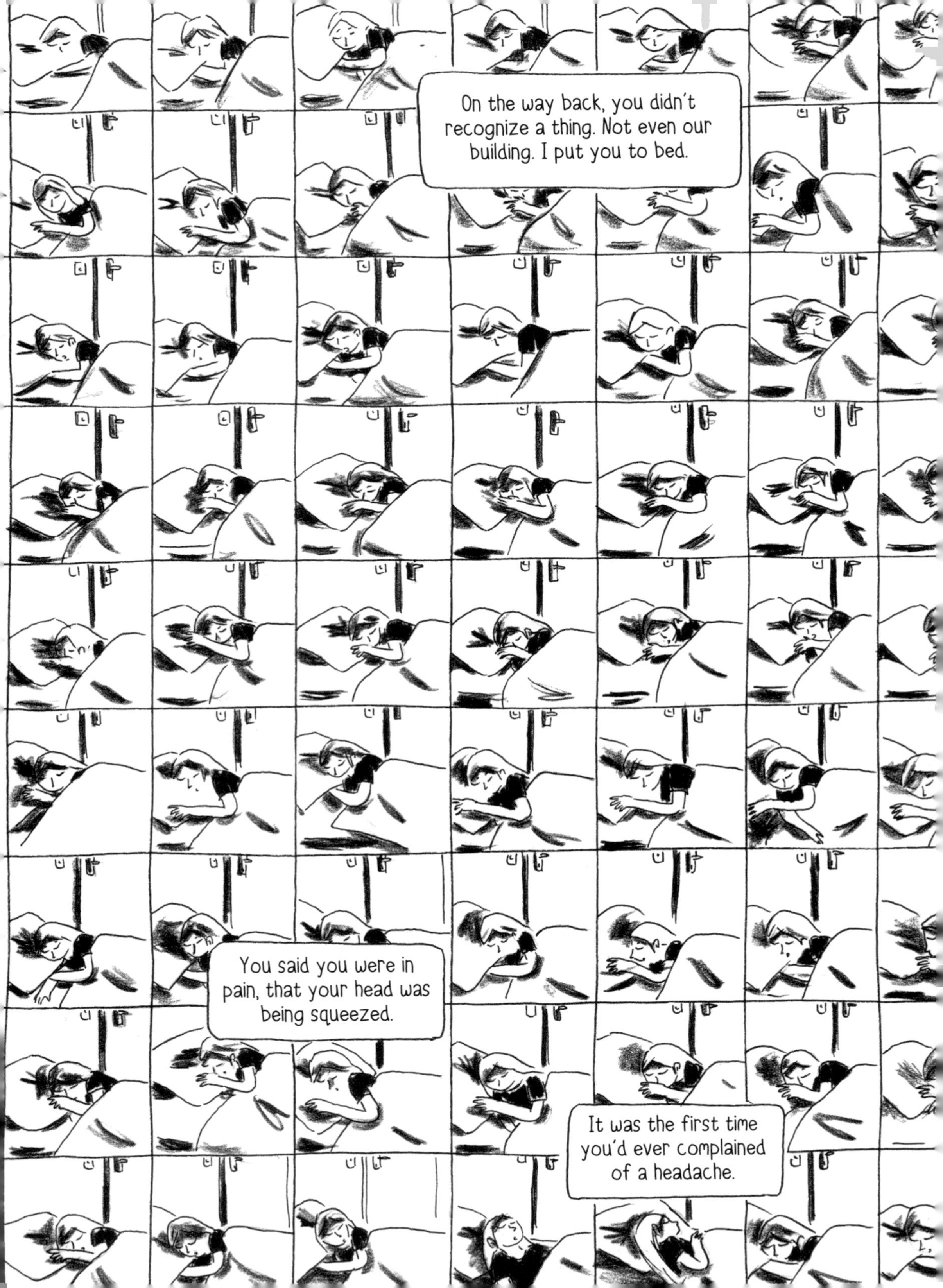
On the way back, you didn't recognize a thing. Not even our building. I put you to bed.
You said you were in pain, that your head was being squeezed.
It was the first time you'd ever complained of a headache.

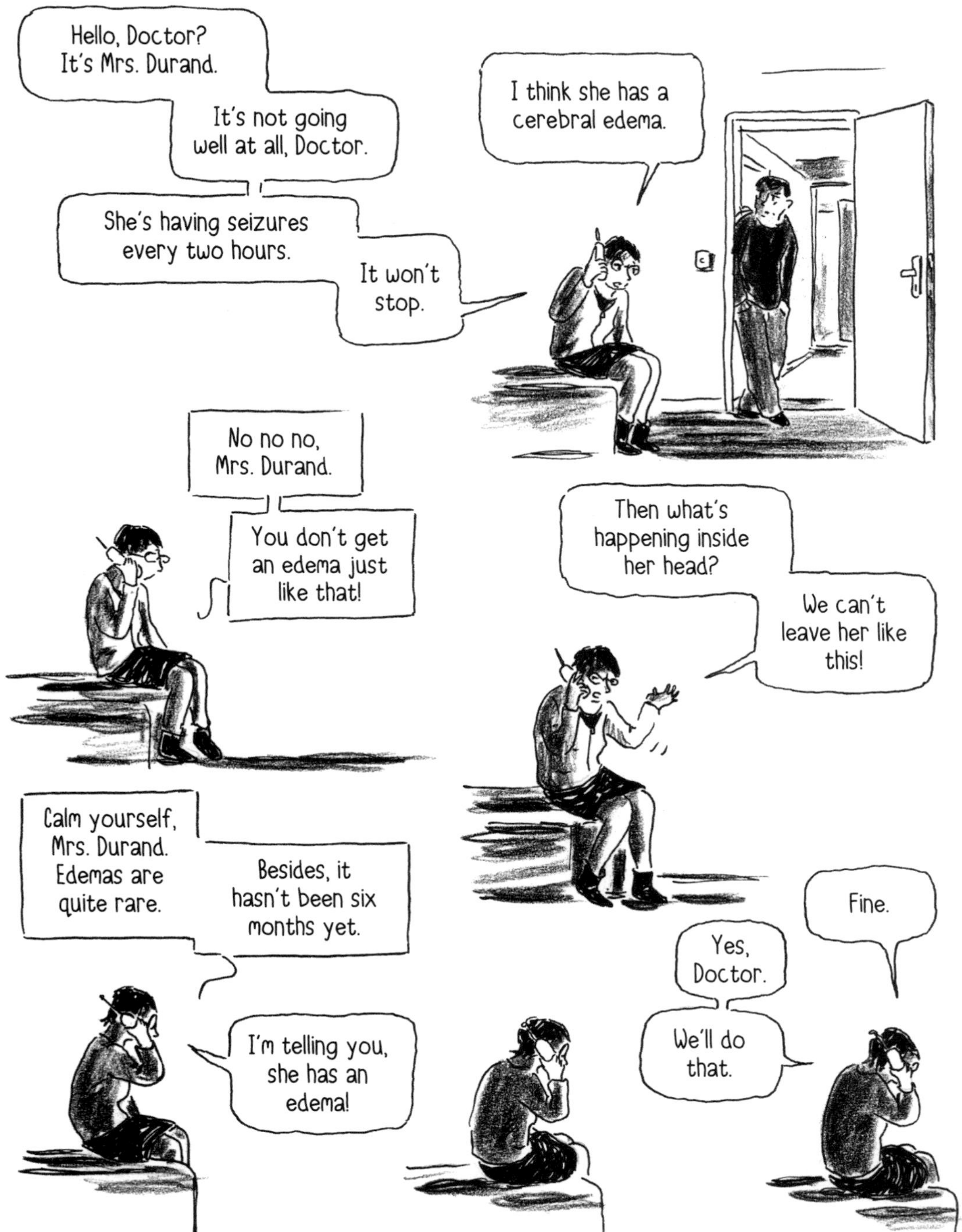
Hello, Doctor? It's Mrs. Durand.
It's not going well at all, Doctor.
She's having seizures every two hours.
It won't stop.
I think she has a cerebral edema.
No no no, Mrs. Durand.
You don't get an edema just like that!
Then what's happening inside her head?
We can't leave her like this!
Calm yourself, Mrs. Durand. Edemas are quite rare.
Besides, it hasn't been six months yet.
I'm telling you, she has an edema!
Yes, Doctor.
We'll do that.
Fine.

It should be noted that the Gamma Knife as a therapy is not entirely without side effects. But these are rare in the extreme.

The potential for a cerebral edema is highest between six and eighteen months after Gamma Knife treatment. It manifests itself in symptoms similar to those caused by the lesion.

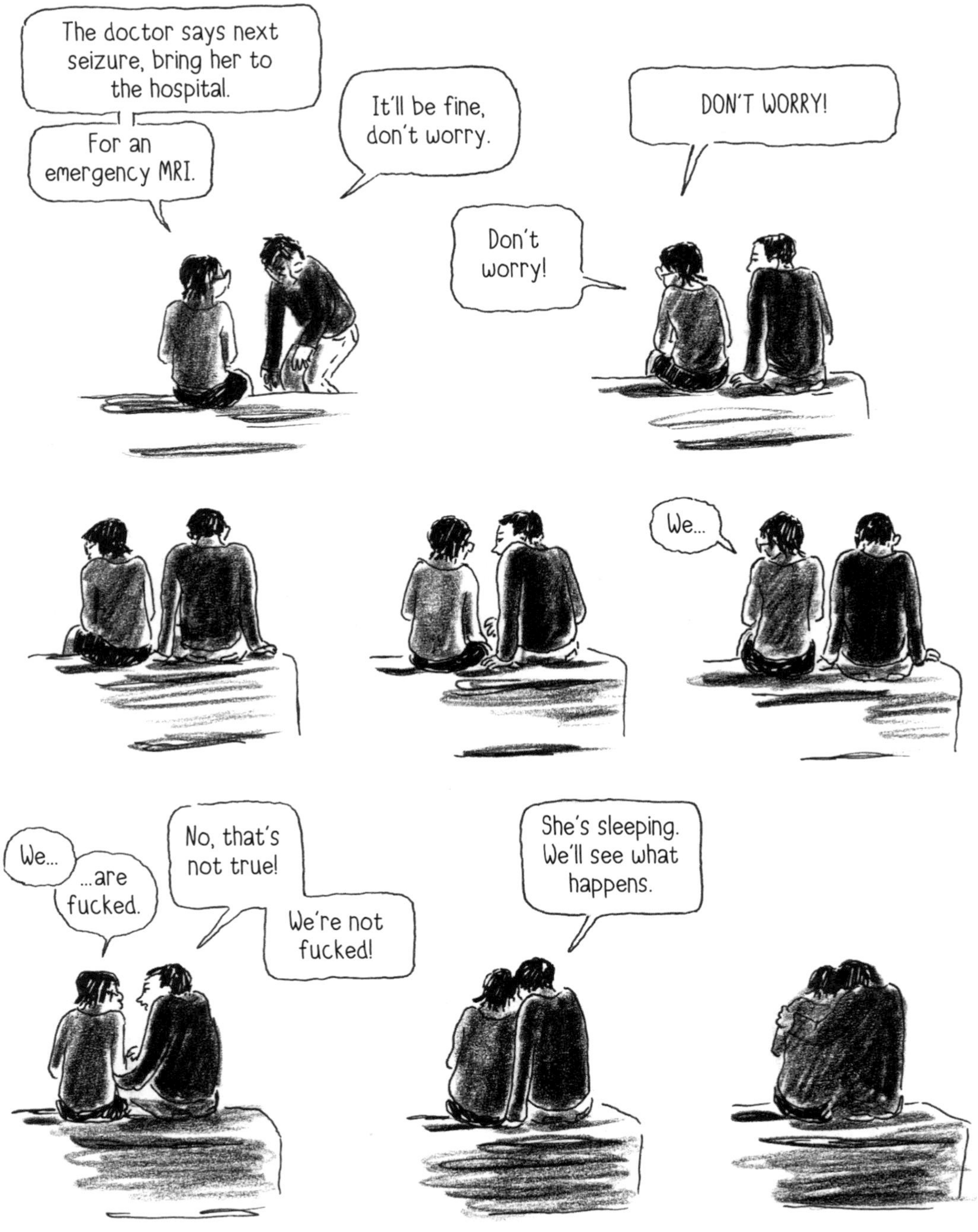
The doctor says next seizure, bring her to the hospital.
For an emergency MRI.
It'll be fine, don't worry.
DON'T WORRY!
Don't worry!
We...
We...
...are fucked.
No, that's not true!
We're not fucked!
She's sleeping. We'll see what happens.

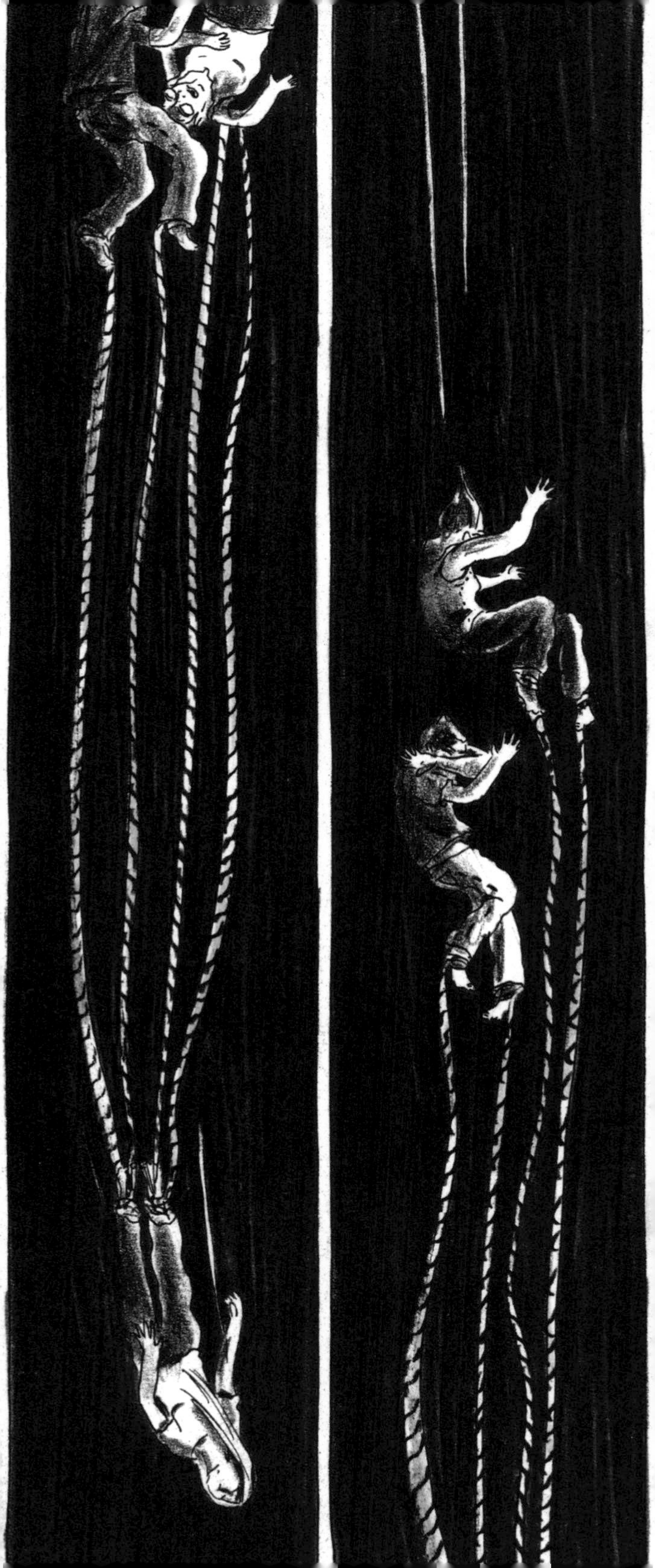

Three months after the beams, you had a cerebral edema. A tumor in your brain had swelled up as big as a fist.

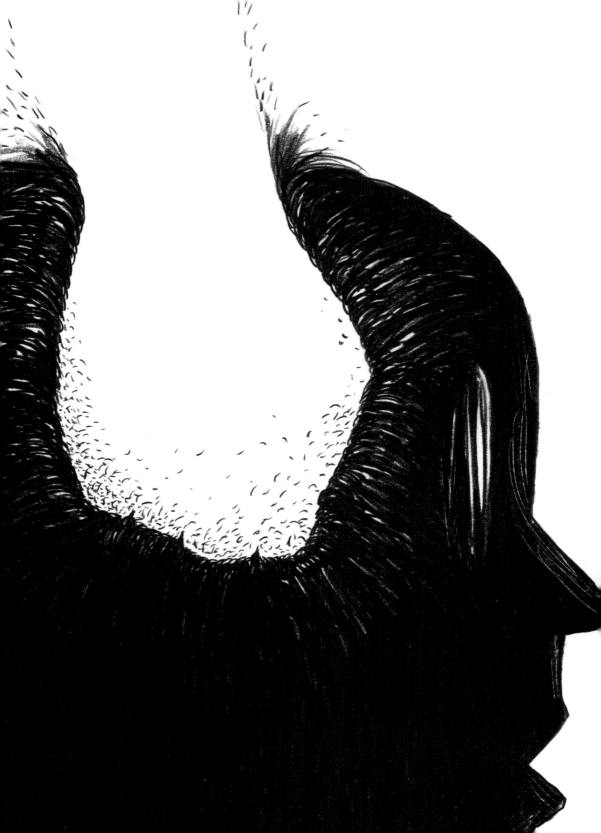

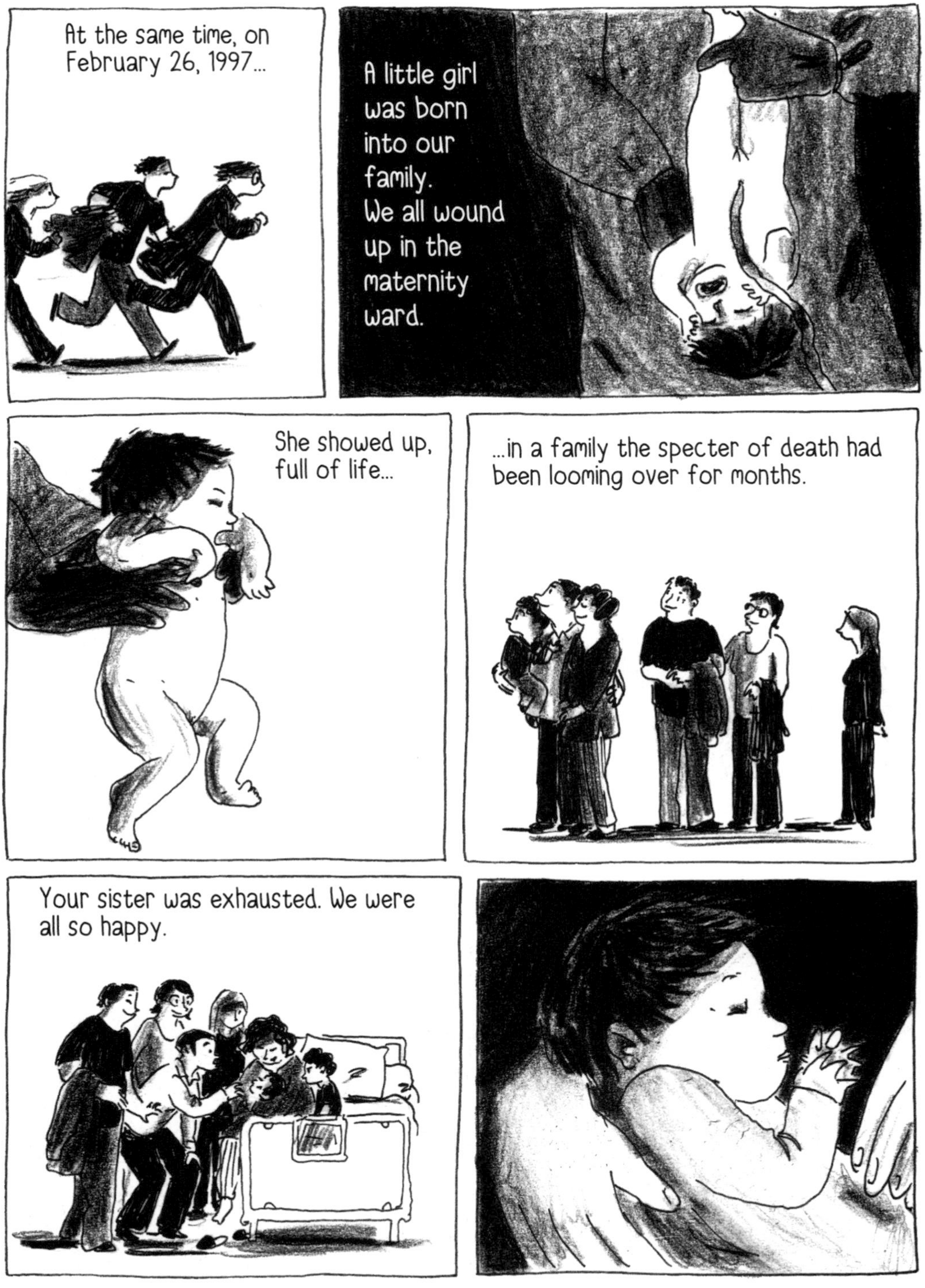
At the same time, on February 26, 1997...
A little girl was born into our family. We all wound up in the maternity ward.
She showed up, full of life...
...in a family the specter of death had been looming over for months.
Your sister was exhausted. We were all so happy.

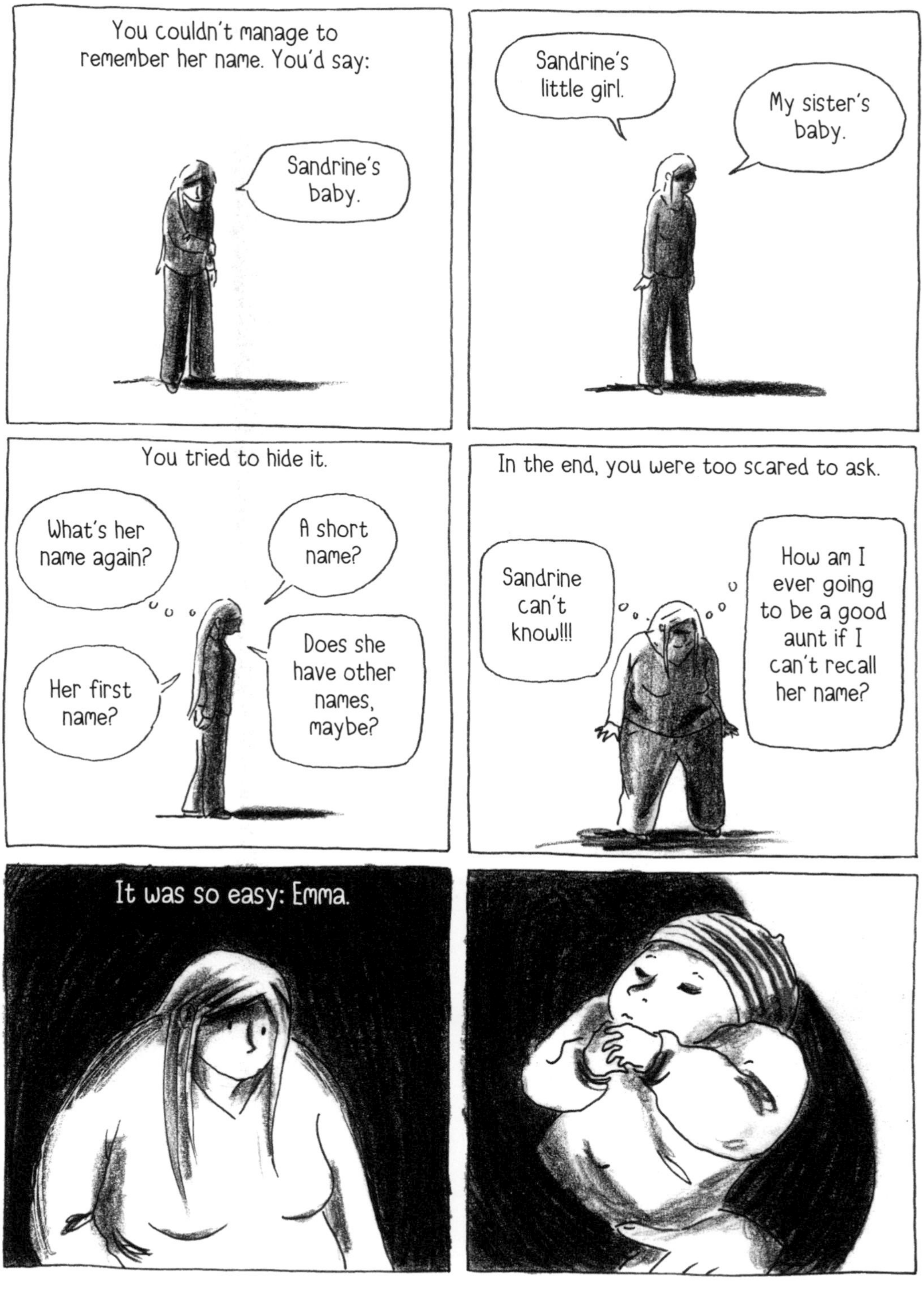
You couldn't manage to remember her name. You'd say:
Sandrine's baby.
Sandrine's little girl.
My sister's baby.
You tried to hide it.
What's her name again?
A short name?
Her first name?
Does she have other names, maybe?
In the end, you were too scared to ask.
Sandrine can't know!!!
How am I ever going to be a good aunt if I can't recall her name?
It was so easy: Emma.

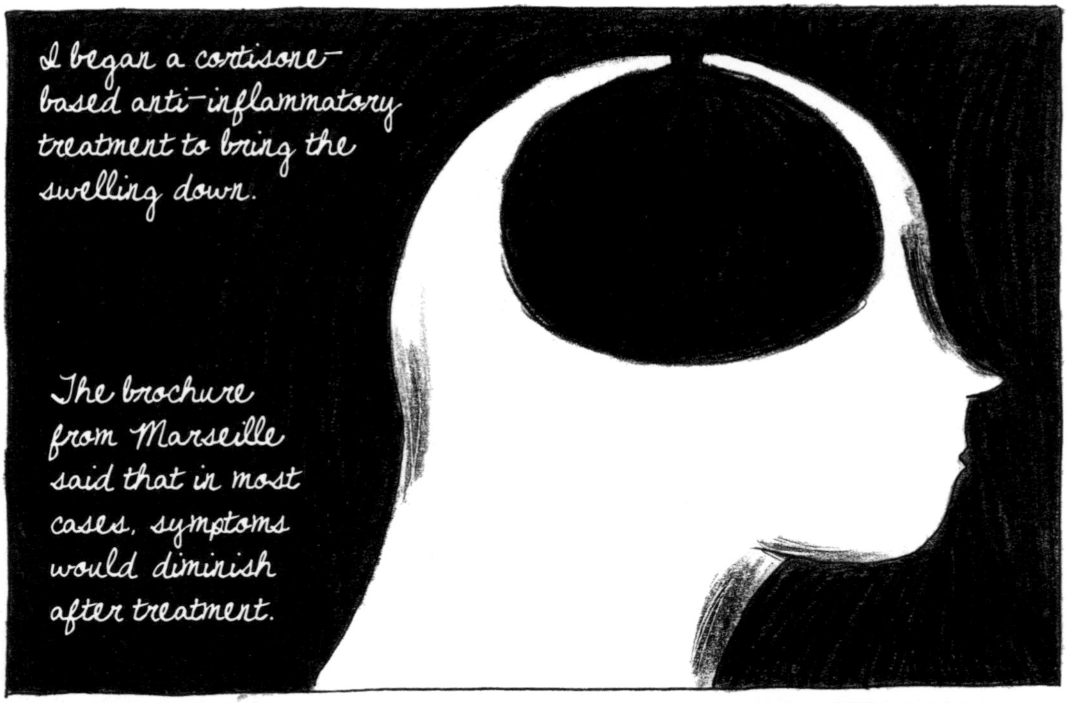
I began a cortisone-based anti-inflammatory treatment to bring the swelling down.
The brochure from Marseille said that in most cases, symptoms would diminish after treatment.

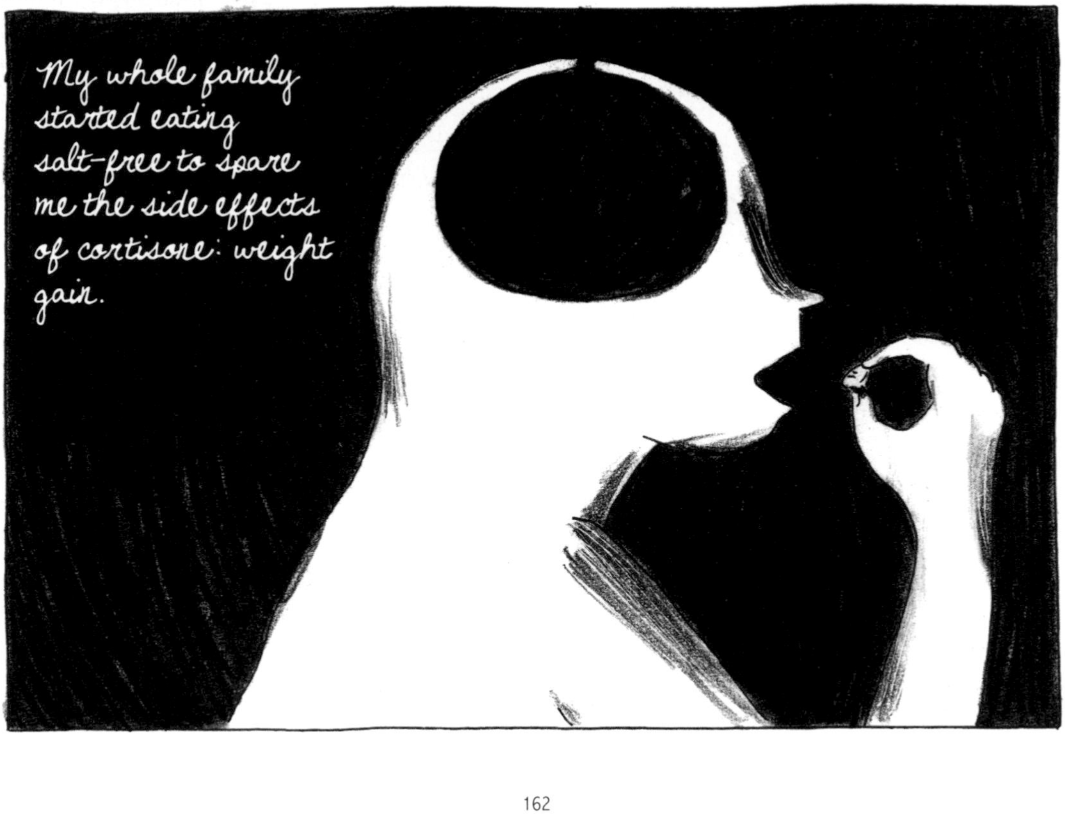
My whole family started eating salt-free to spare me the side effects of cortisone: weight gain.

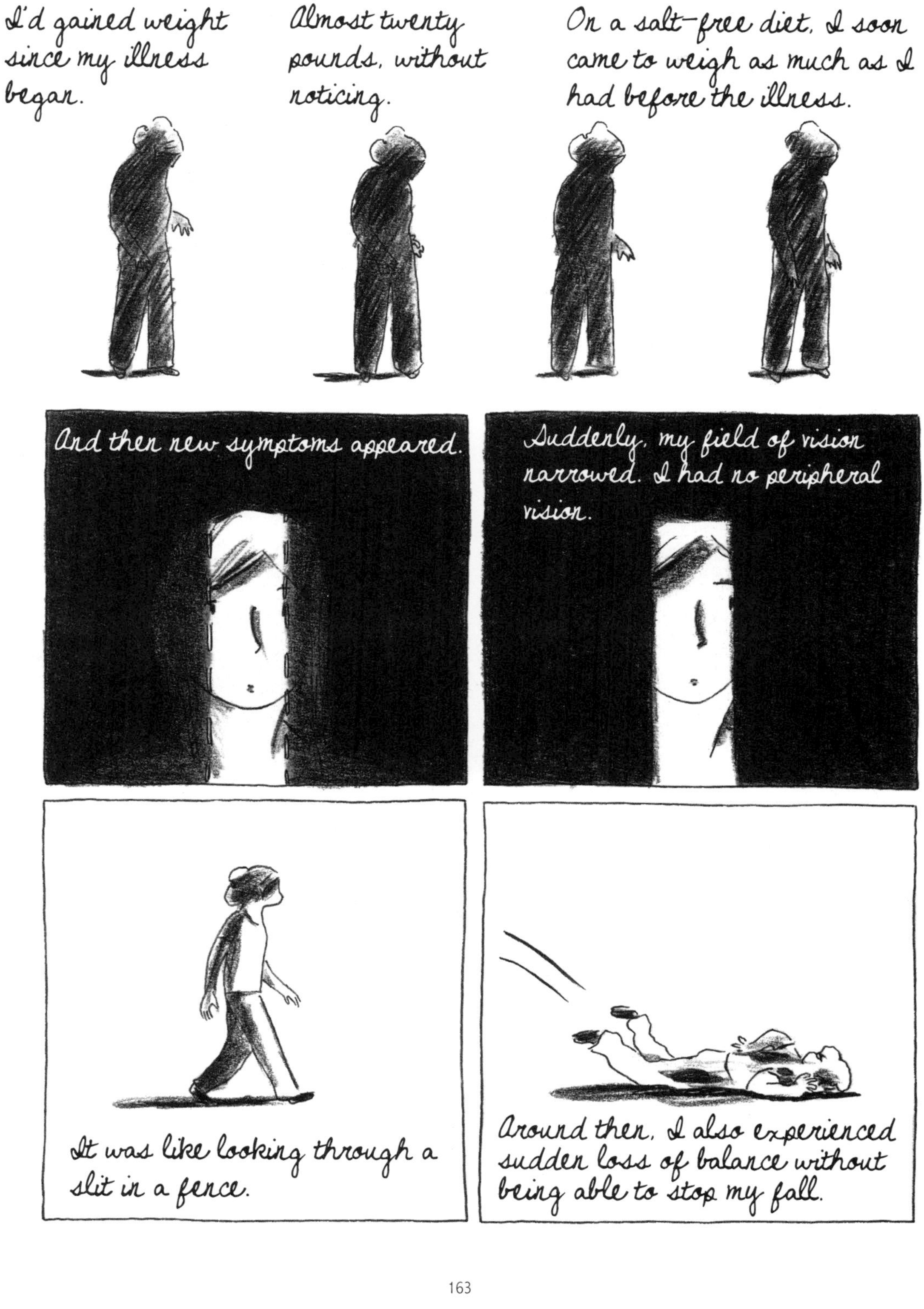
I'd gained weight since my illness began.
Almost twenty pounds, without noticing.
On a salt-free diet, I soon came to weigh as much as I had before the illness.
And then new symptoms appeared.
Suddenly, my field of vision narrowed. I had no peripheral vision.
It was like looking through a slit in a fence.
Around then, I also experienced sudden loss of balance without being able to stop my fall.

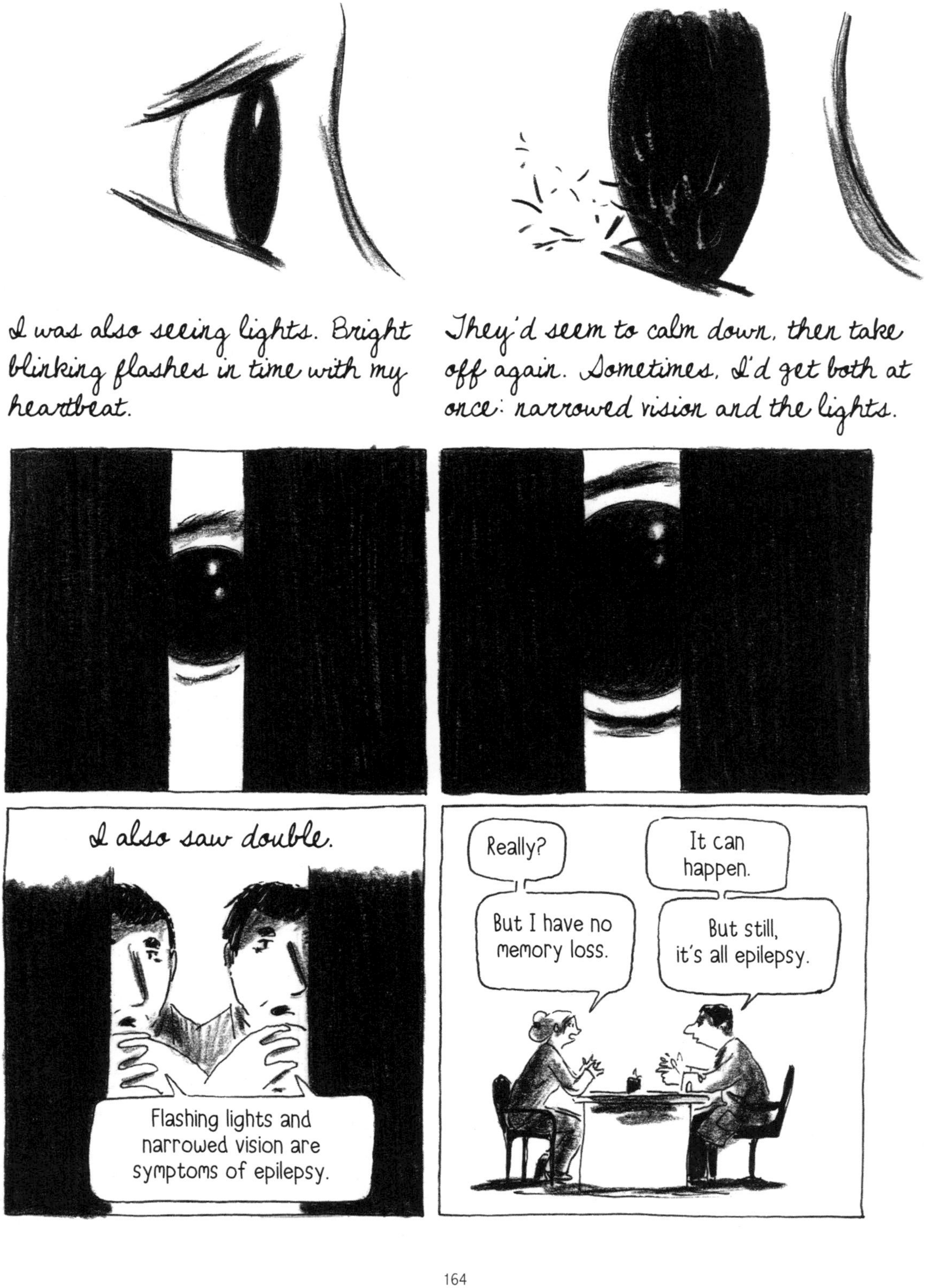
I was also seeing lights. Bright blinking flashes in time with my heartbeat.
They'd seem to calm down, then take off again. Sometimes, I'd get both at once: narrowed vision and the lights.
I also saw double.
Flashing lights and narrowed vision are symptoms of epilepsy.
Really?
But I have no memory loss.
It can happen.
But still, it's all epilepsy.

These new symptoms would last from twenty minutes to over two hours, several times a day.

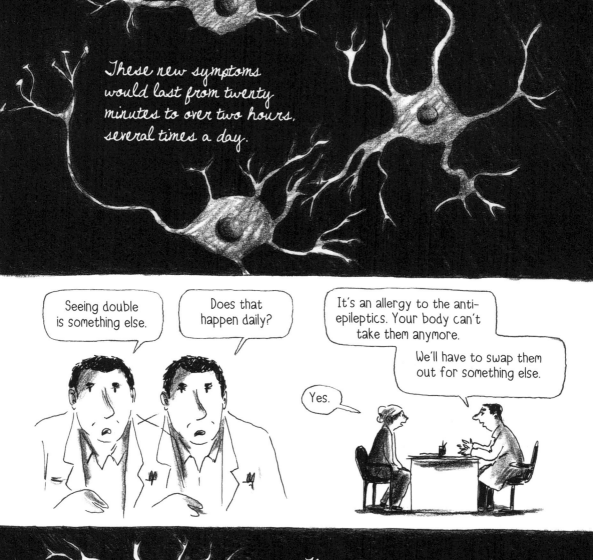

Seeing double is something else.

Does that happen daily?

It's an allergy to the anti-epileptics. Your body can't take them anymore.

We'll have to swap them out for something else.

Yes.

The symptoms persisted, but my edema was beginning to shrink. The actual seizures grew rarer. And it was like I'd gotten back something precious.

Eighteen months after Marseille, the doctors finally gave me the results of the radiosurgery. The operation had been a success! The tumor had necrotized. All that was left of it was a little scar.

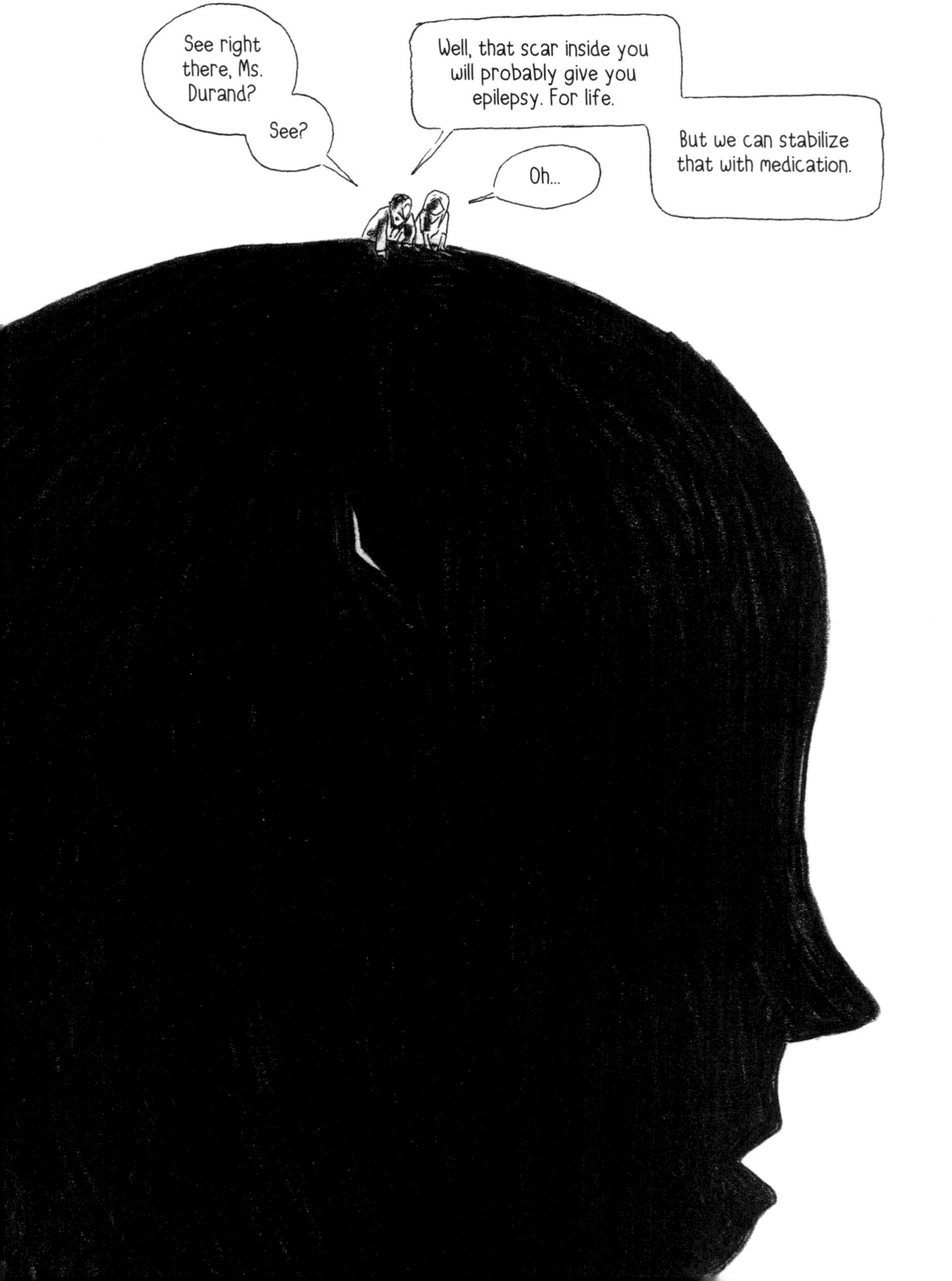
See right there, Ms. Durand?
See?
Well, that scar inside you will probably give you epilepsy. For life.
Oh...
But we can stabilize that with medication.

Créteil, 1998. Bordières and Bleuets neighborhood.

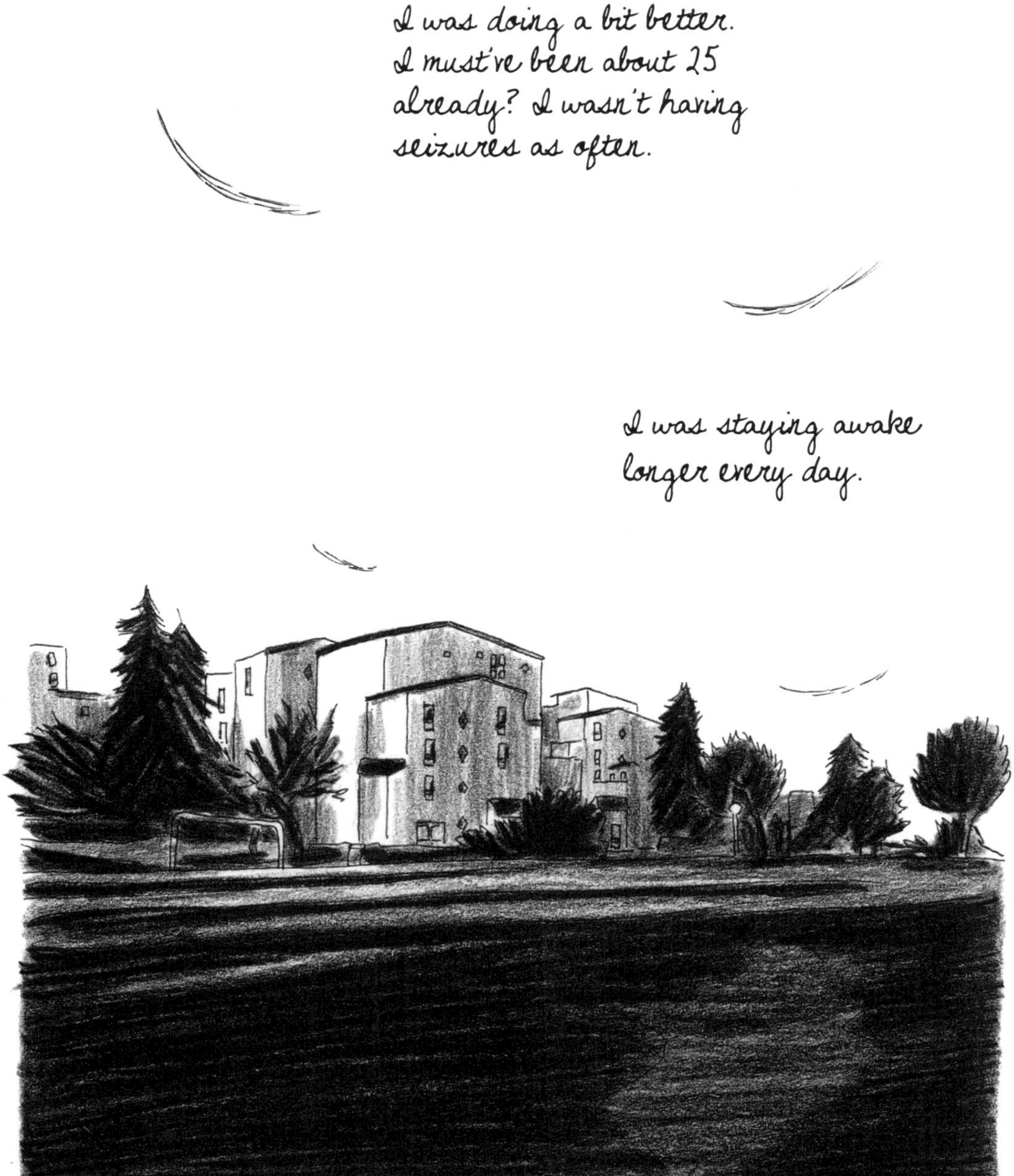
I was doing a bit better. I must've been about 25 already? I wasn't having seizures as often.
I was staying awake longer every day.

I'd started going out a little in the daytime. Never very far. I was staying awake for more than two hours at a time!

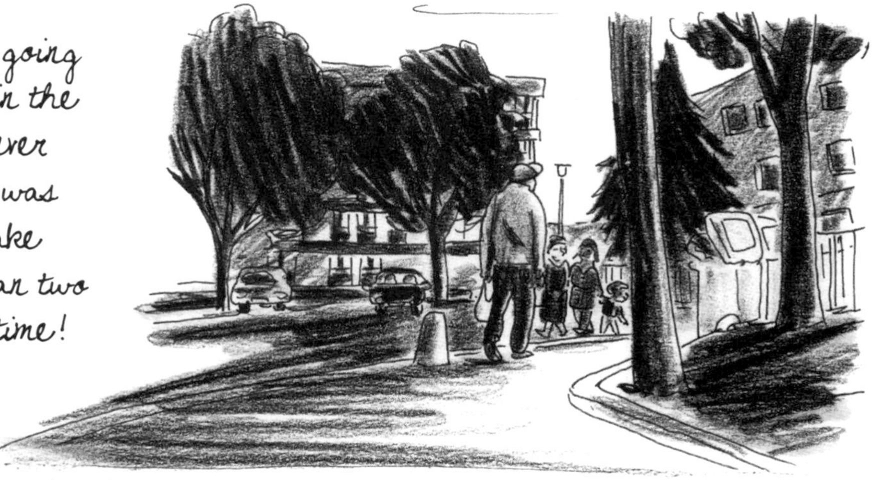

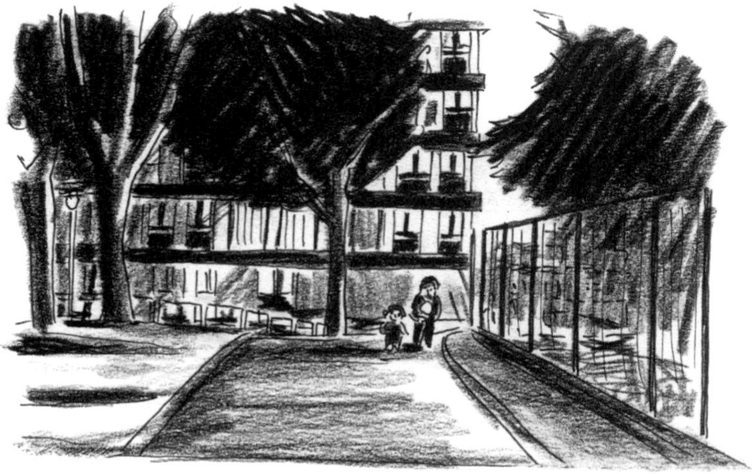

I was still seeing double, and flashing lights, but not every day.

I started hanging out with Sandra again, and met her new friends at her place. I probably wasn't doing a lot of talking.

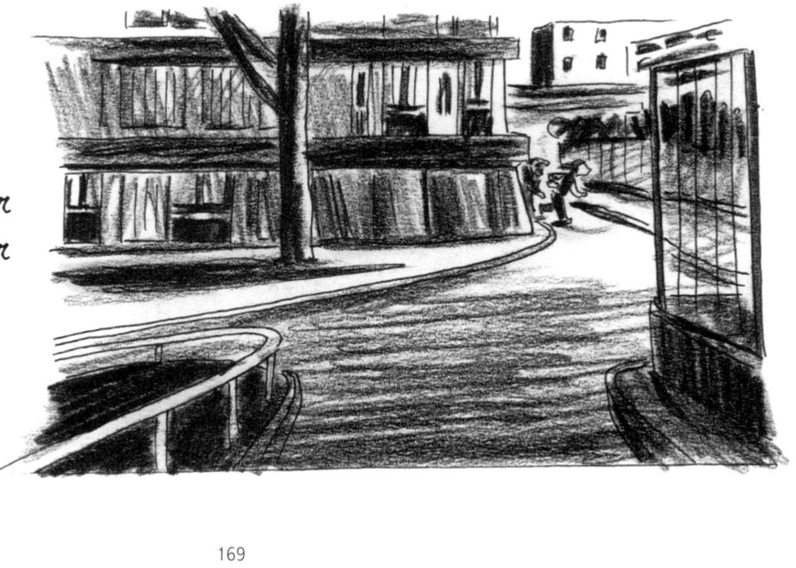

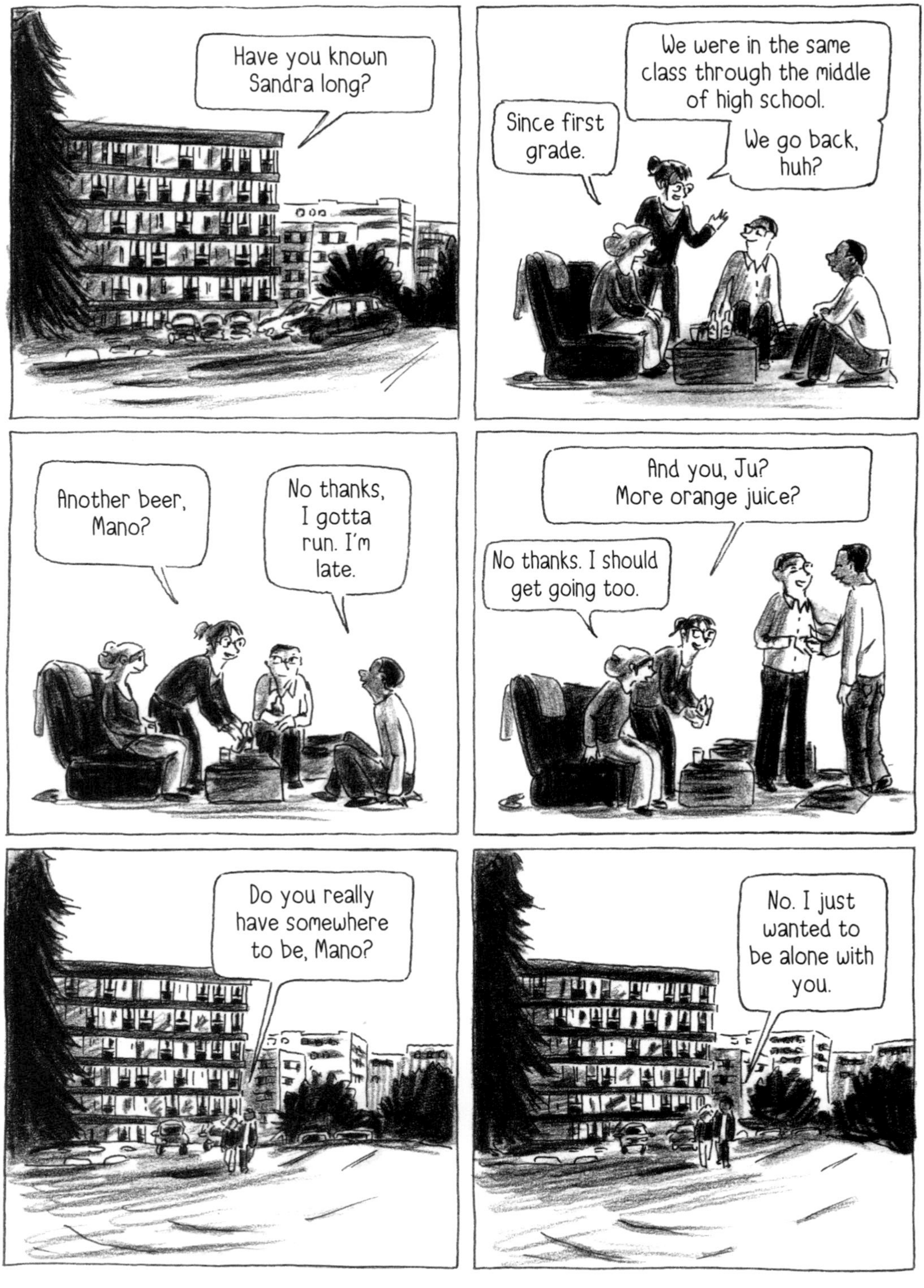
Have you known Sandra long?
Since first grade.
We were in the same class through the middle of high school.
We go back, huh?
Another beer, Mano?
No thanks, I gotta run. I'm late.
And you, Ju? More orange juice?
No thanks. I should get going too.
Do you really have somewhere to be, Mano?
No. I just wanted to be alone with you.

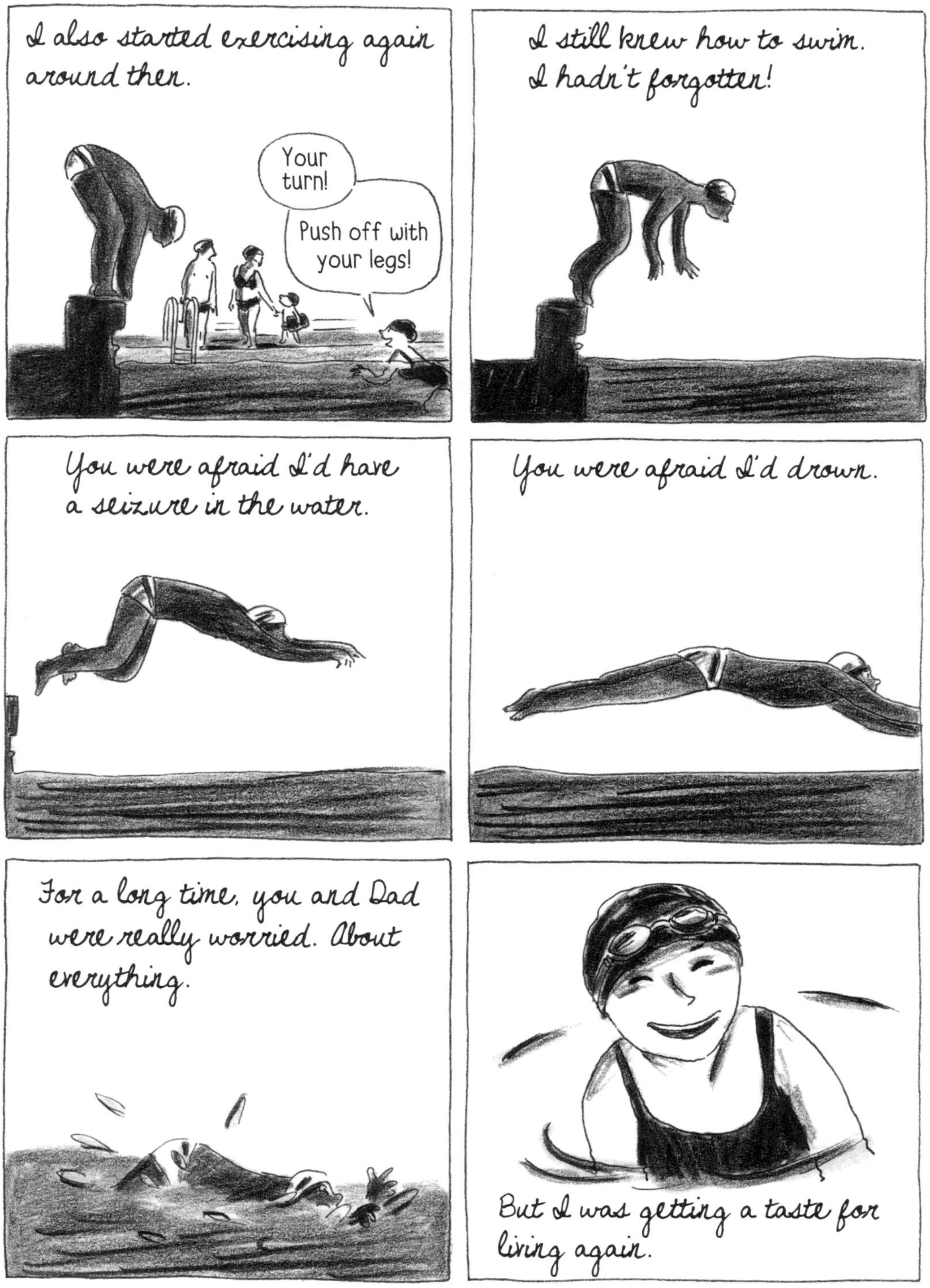
I also started exercising again around then.
Your turn!
Push off with your legs!
I still knew how to swim. I hadn't forgotten!
You were afraid I'd have a seizure in the water.
You were afraid I'd drown.
For a long time, you and Dad were really worried. About everything.
But I was getting a taste for living again.

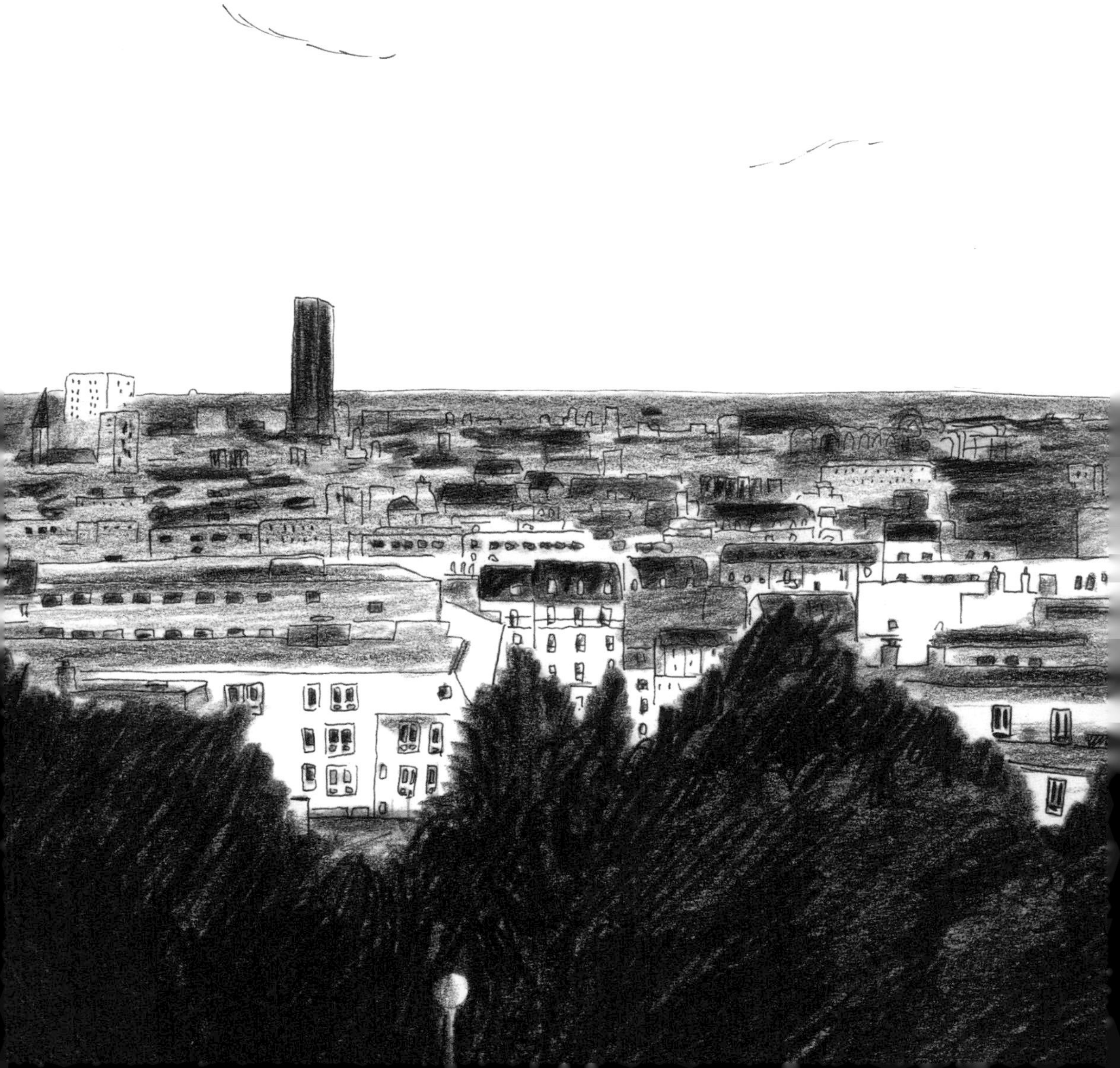

That same year—still 1998, I moved to Belleville. One of your friends, Catherine, found me a small apartment.

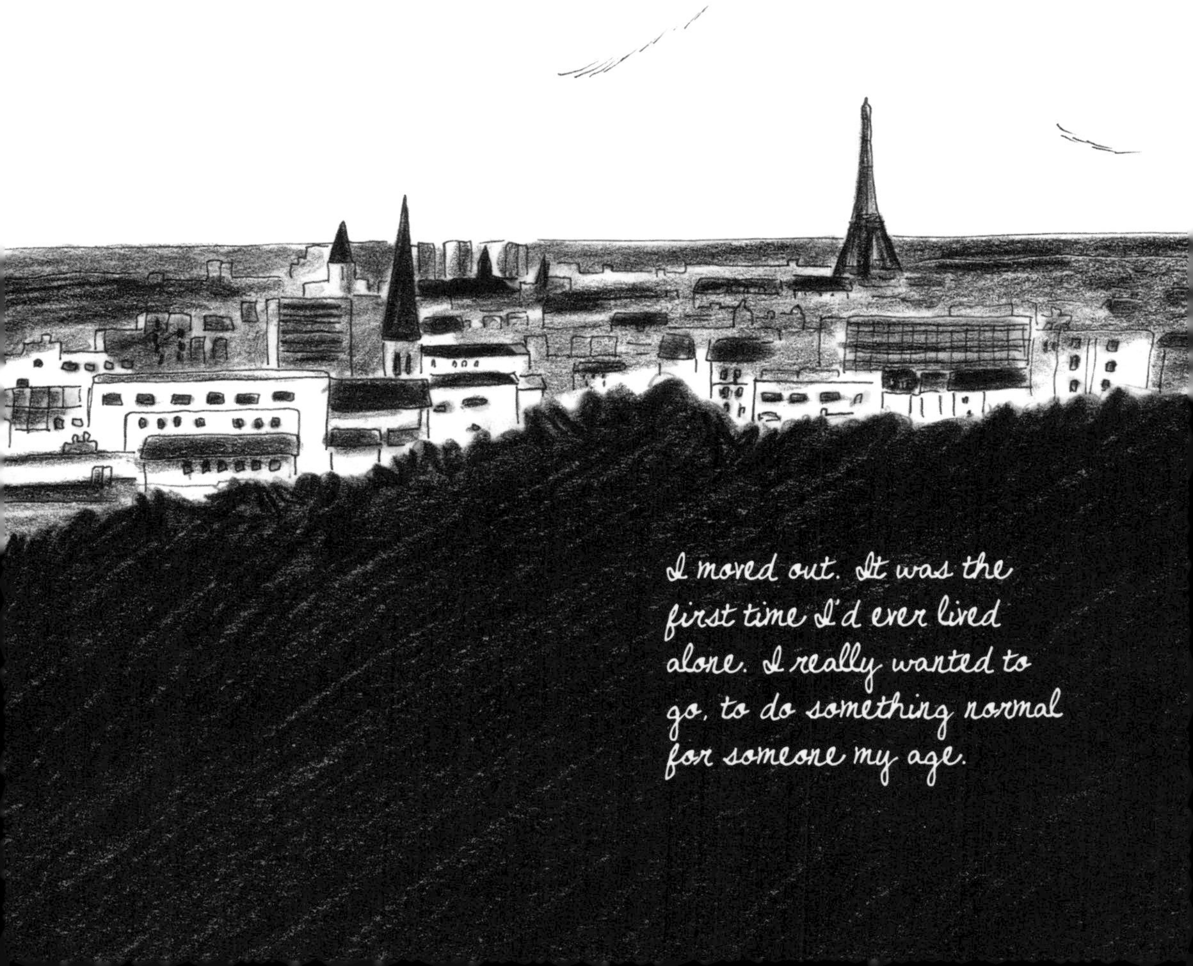
I moved out. It was the first time I'd ever lived alone. I really wanted to go, to do something normal for someone my age.

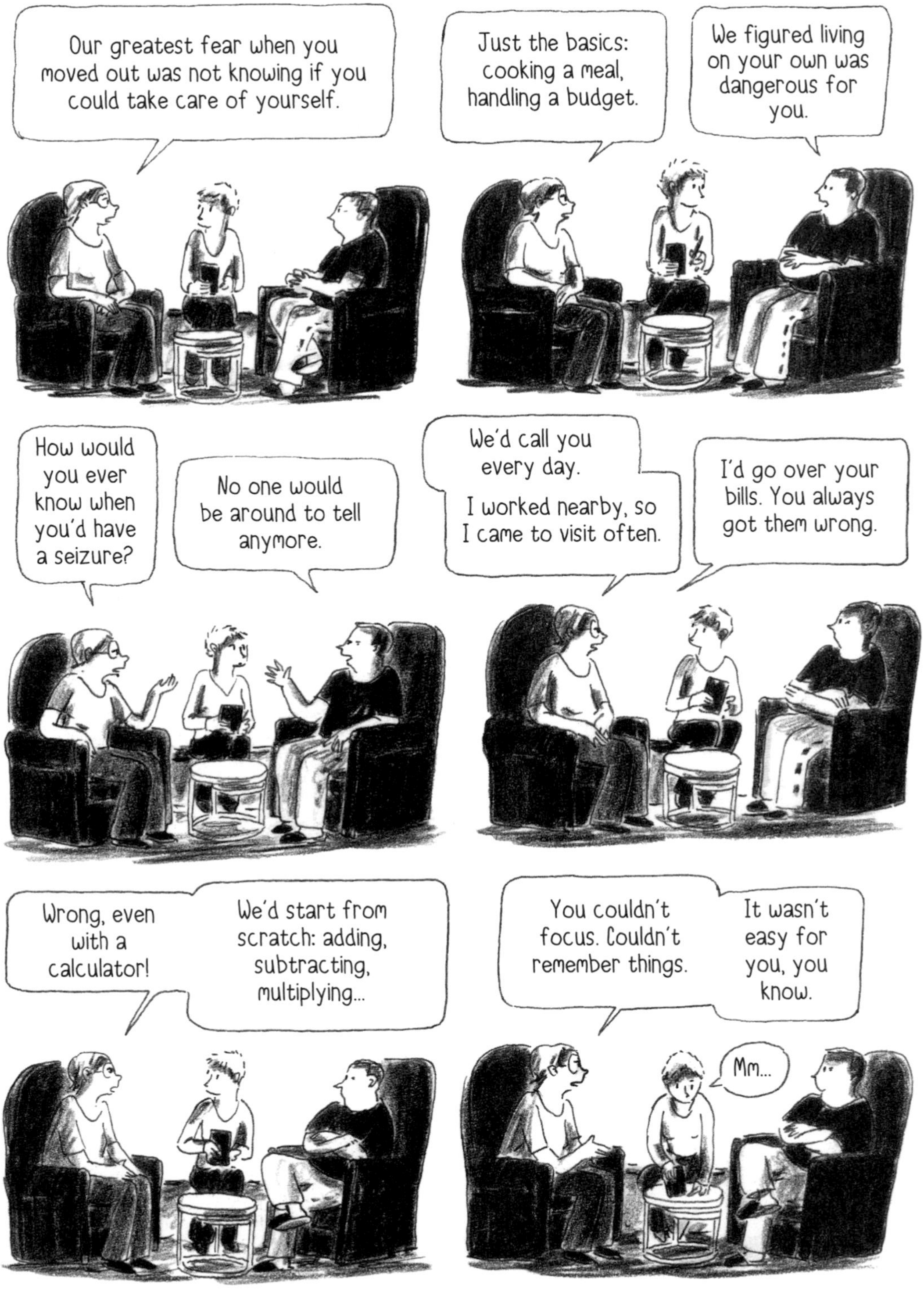

Our greatest fear when you moved out was not knowing if you could take care of yourself.
Just the basics: cooking a meal, handling a budget.
We figured living on your own was dangerous for you.
How would you ever know when you'd have a seizure?
No one would be around to tell anymore.
We'd call you every day.
I worked nearby, so I came to visit often.
I'd go over your bills. You always got them wrong.
Wrong, even with a calculator!
We'd start from scratch: adding, subtracting, multiplying...
You couldn't focus. Couldn't remember things.
It wasn't easy for you, you know.
Mm...

I was still sleeping a lot back then. I took heavy medication. Still had vision problems. But none of that mattered. So much was better for me already. I wasn't following you around everywhere anymore... I'd rediscovered my freedom.

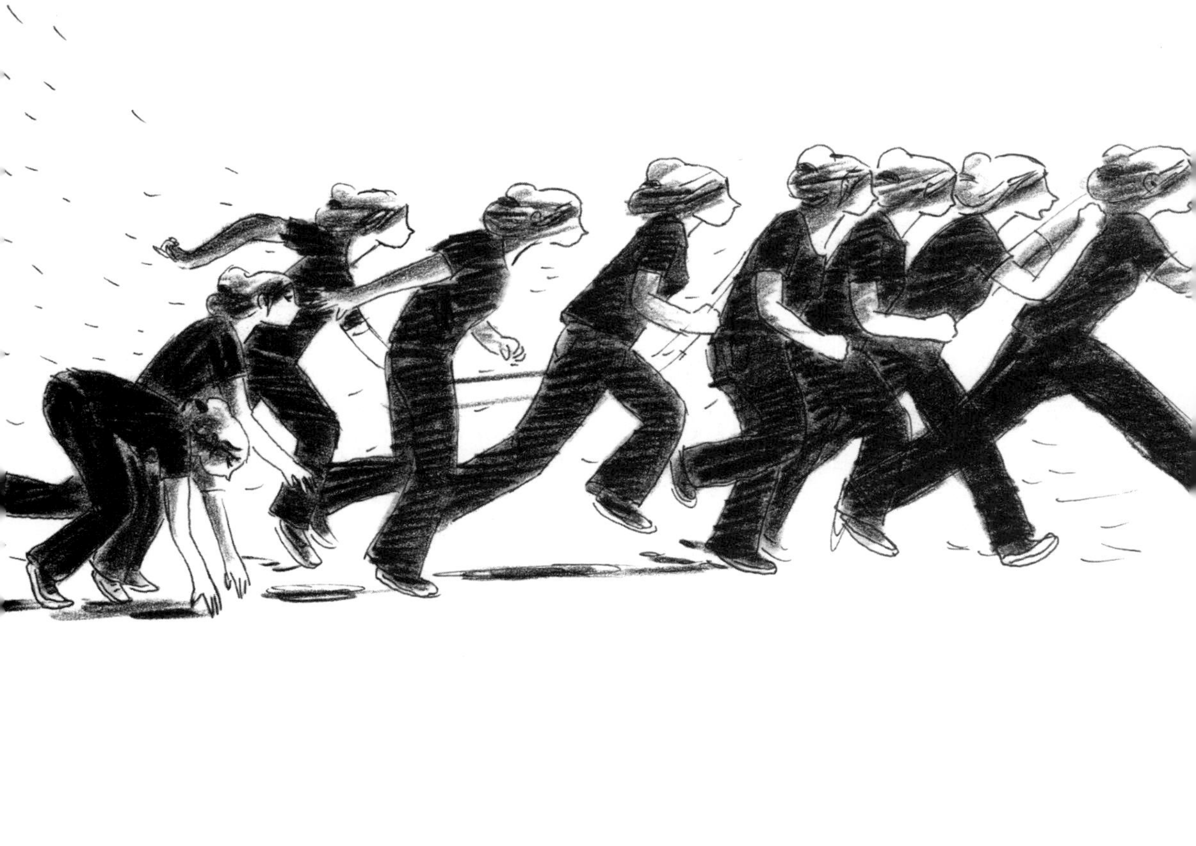

I'd caught my breath again.
It was invigorating!

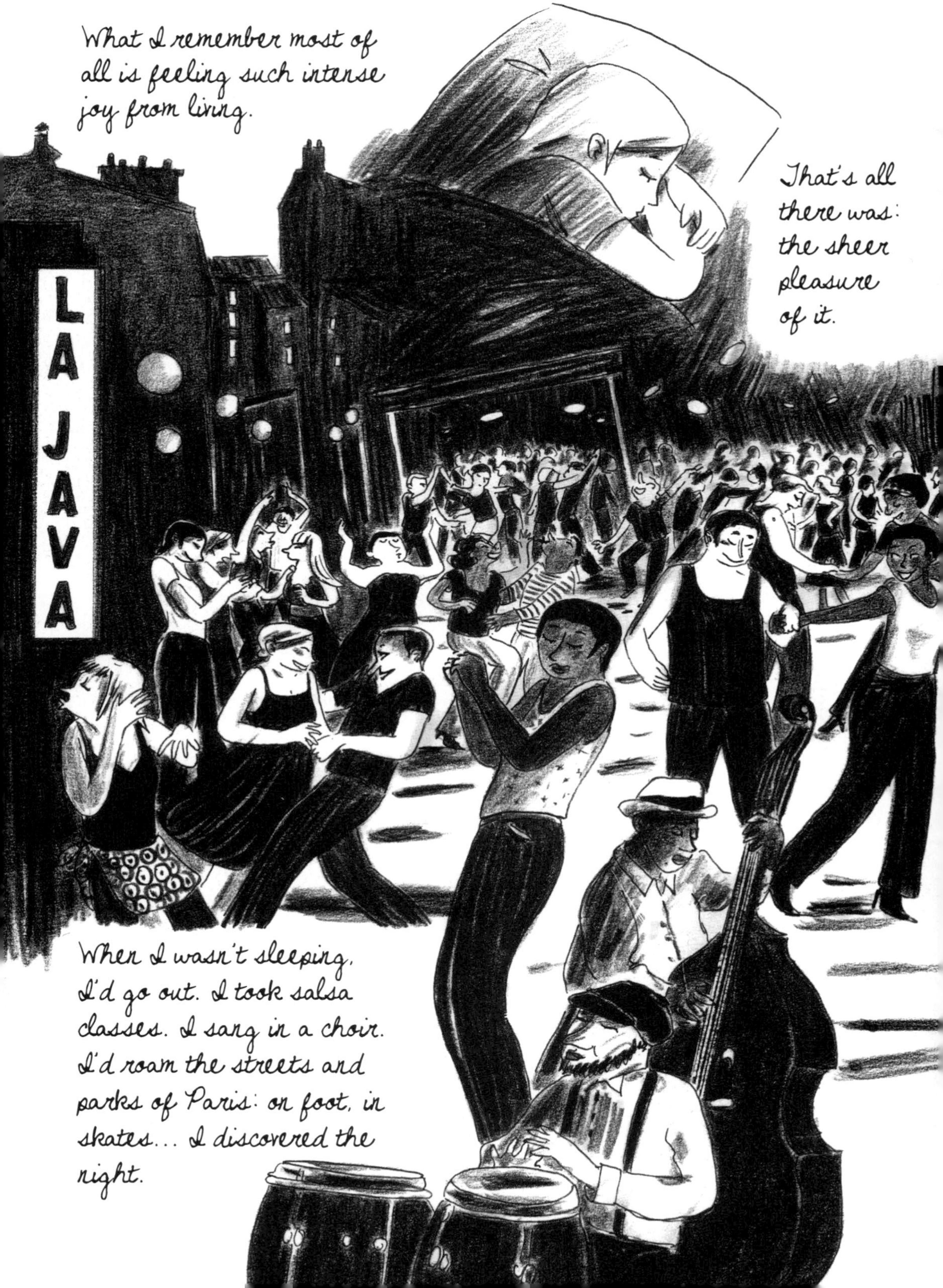
What I remember most of all is feeling such intense joy from living.
That's all there was: the sheer pleasure of it.
LA JAVA
When I wasn't sleeping, I'd go out. I took salsa classes. I sang in a choir. I'd roam the streets and parks of Paris: on foot, in skates... I discovered the night.

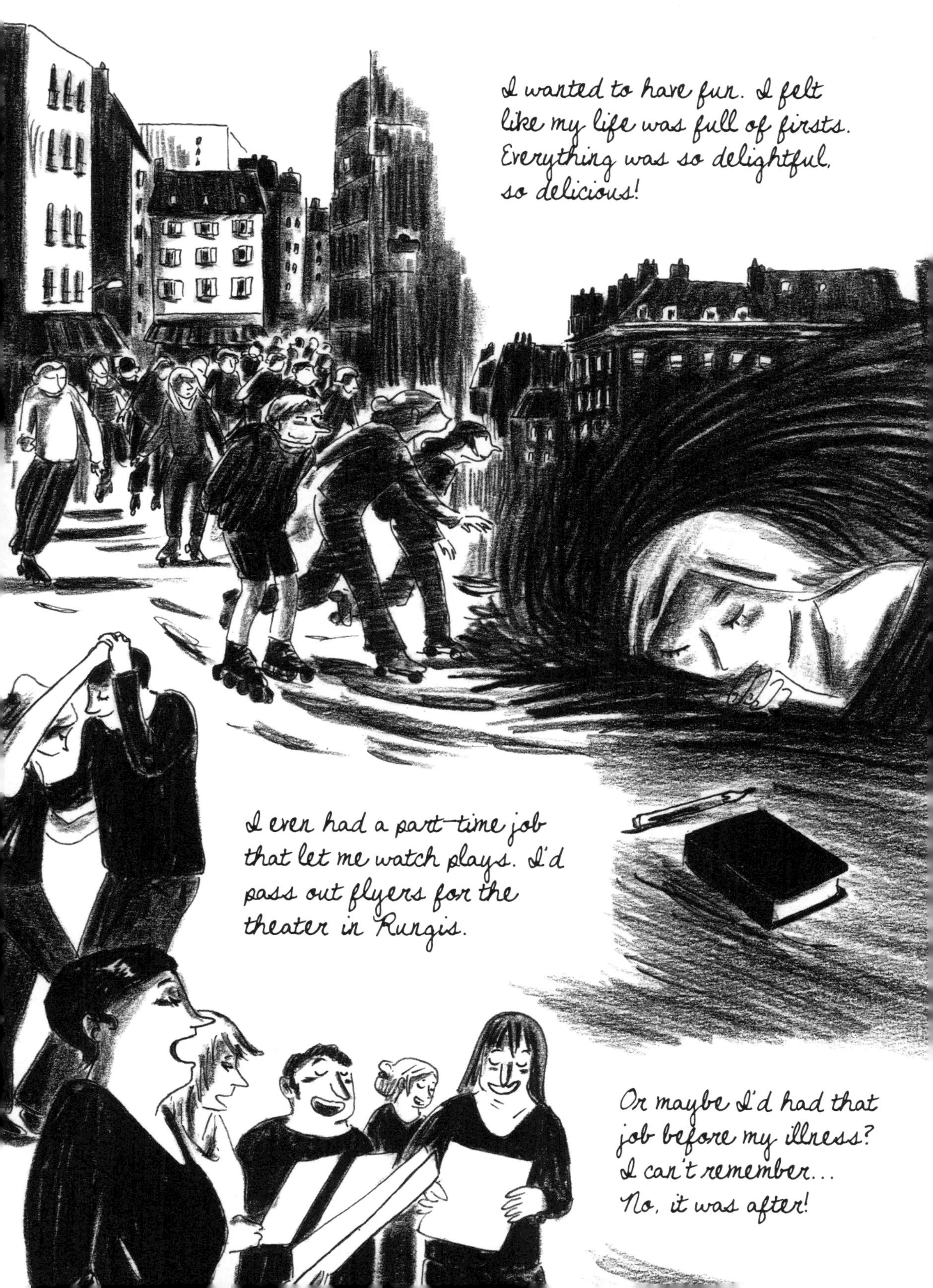
I wanted to have fun. I felt like my life was full of firsts. Everything was so delightful, so delicious!
I even had a part-time job that let me watch plays. I'd pass out flyers for the theater in Rungis.
Or maybe I'd had that job before my illness? I can't remember... No, it was after!

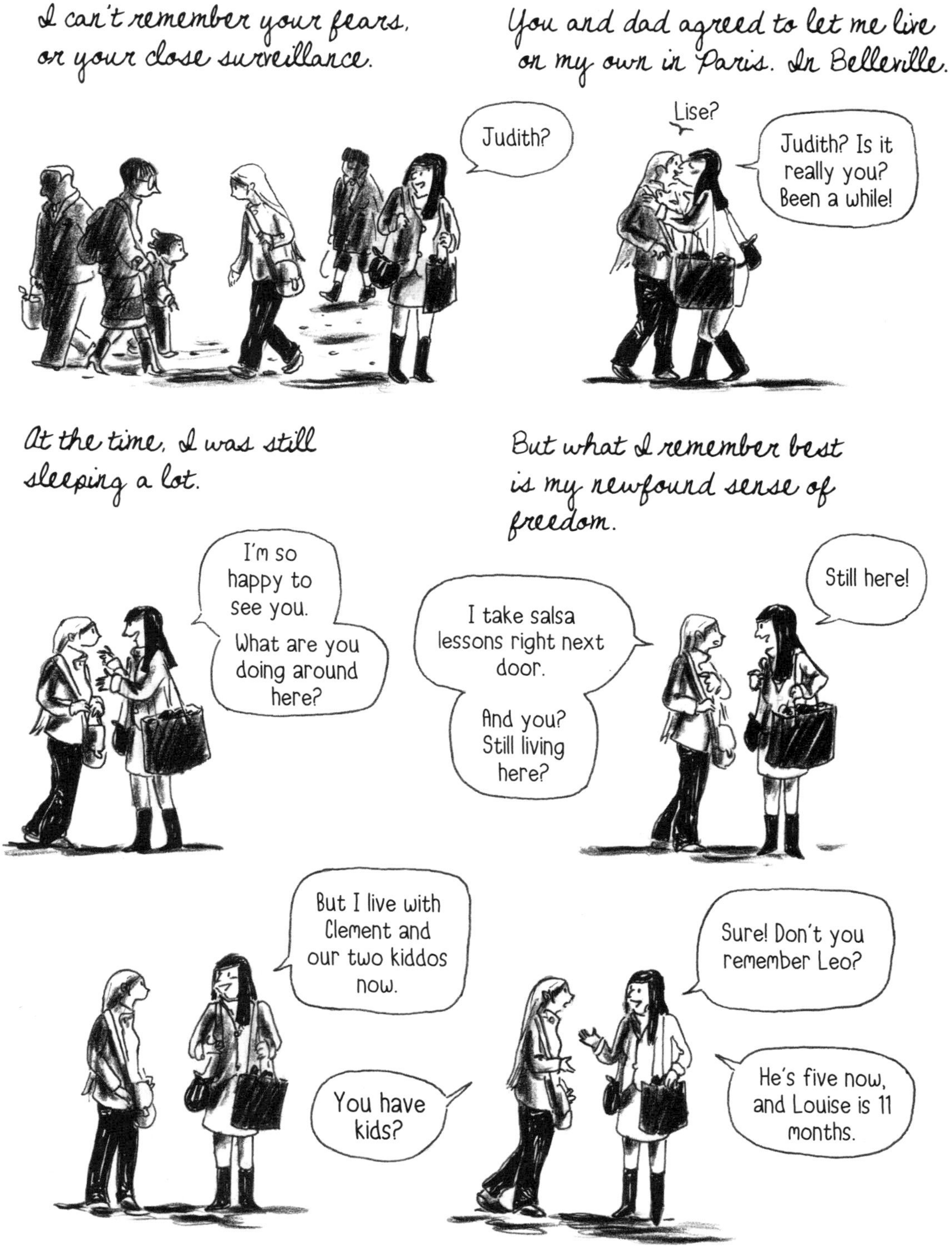
I can't remember your fears, or your close surveillance.
Judith?
You and dad agreed to let me live on my own in Paris. In Belleville.
Lise?
Judith? Is it really you? Been a while!
At the time, I was still sleeping a lot.
I'm so happy to see you.
What are you doing around here?
But what I remember best is my newfound sense of freedom.
I take salsa lessons right next door.
And you? Still living here?
Still here!
But I live with Clement and our two kiddos now.
You have kids?
Sure! Don't you remember Leo?
He's five now, and Louise is 11 months.

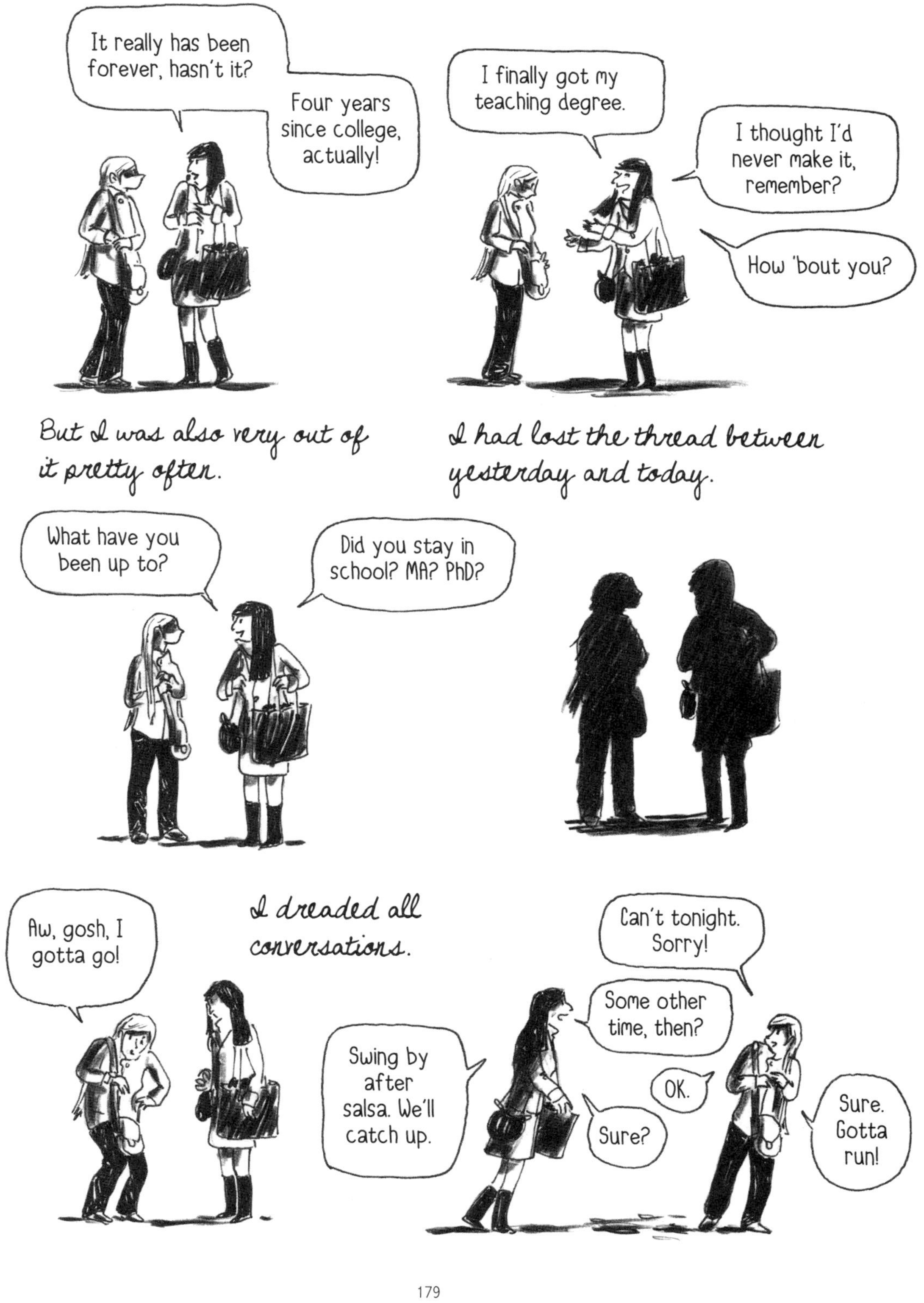
It really has been forever, hasn't it?
Four years since college, actually!
I finally got my teaching degree.
I thought I'd never make it, remember?
How 'bout you?
But I was also very out of it pretty often.
I had lost the thread between yesterday and today.
What have you been up to?
Did you stay in school? MA? PhD?
Aw, gosh, I gotta go!
I dreaded all conversations.
Can't tonight. Sorry!
Some other time, then?
Swing by after salsa. We'll catch up.
OK.
Sure?
Sure. Gotta run!

How 'bout you? What have you been up to? What have you been up to?

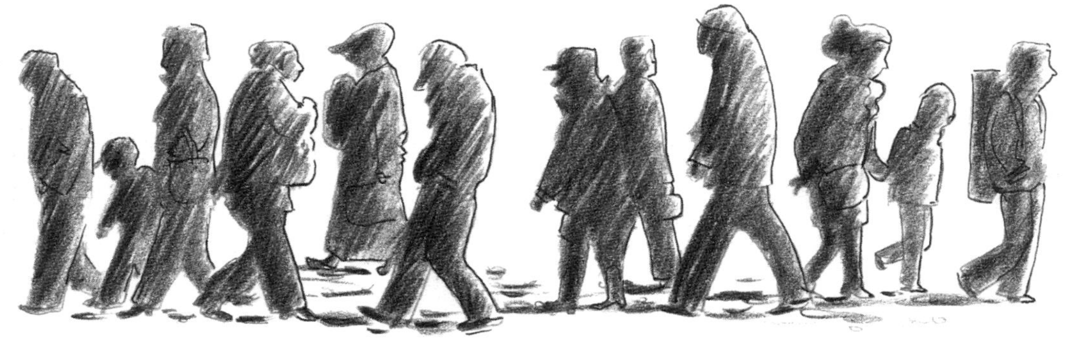

My head felt so empty.

What have you be

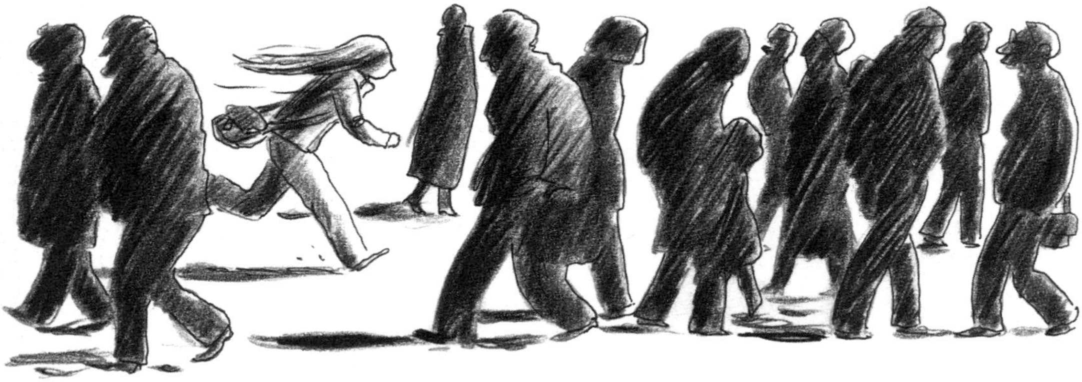

o all this time?

I didn't know what to say.

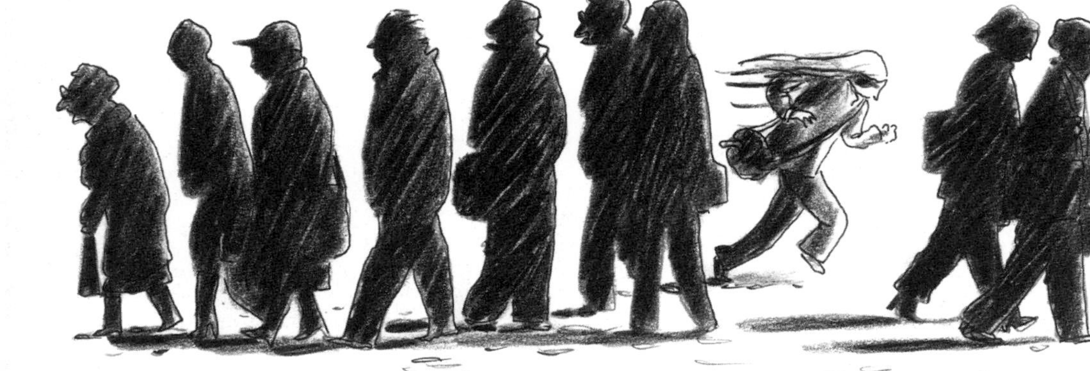

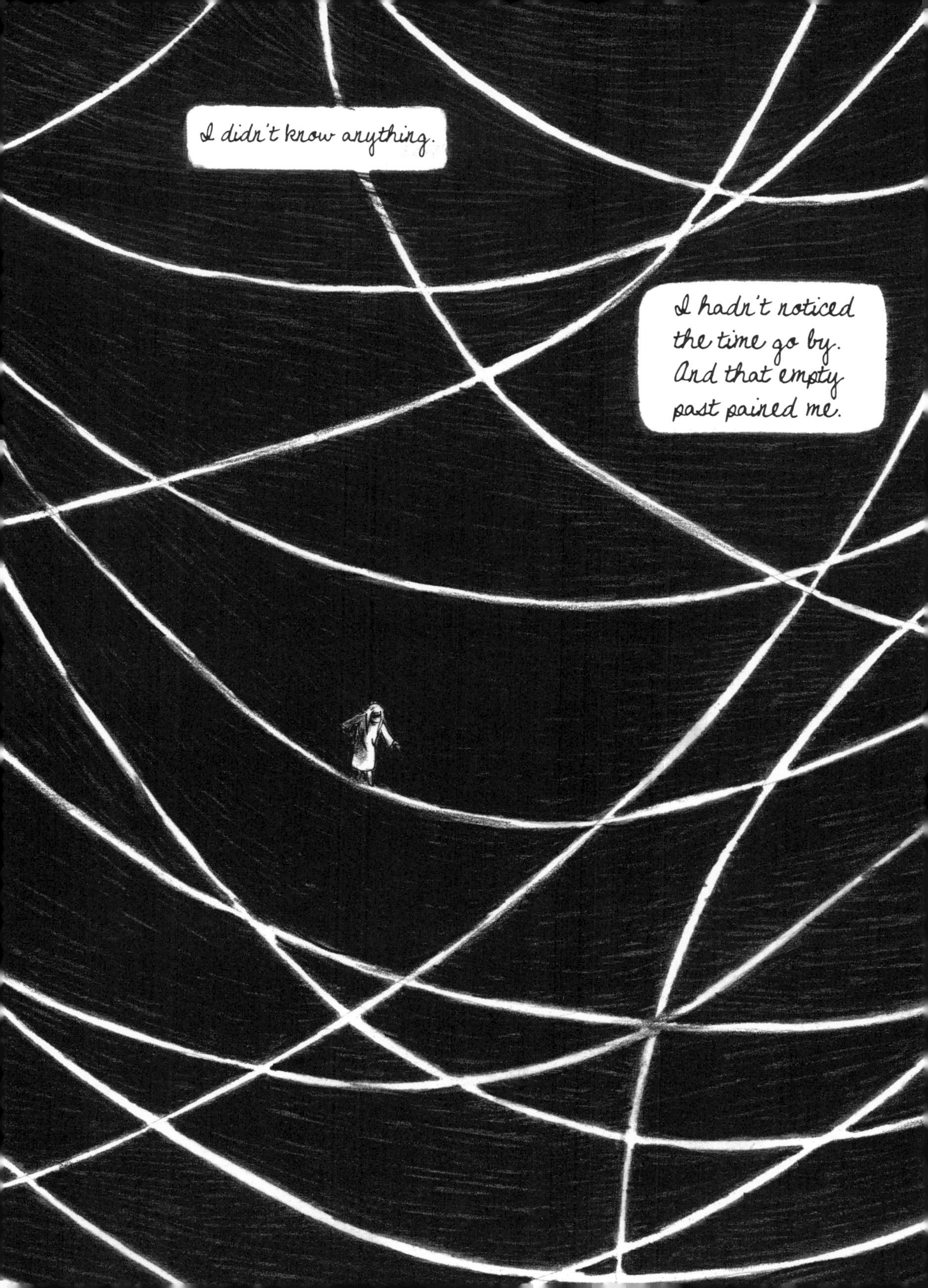
I didn't know anything.
I hadn't noticed the time go by. And that empty past pained me.

At home, I started drawing whatever went through my head... quickly, without thinking. Those drawings helped me a lot. They helped me think, and little by little, recover my ability to concentrate.

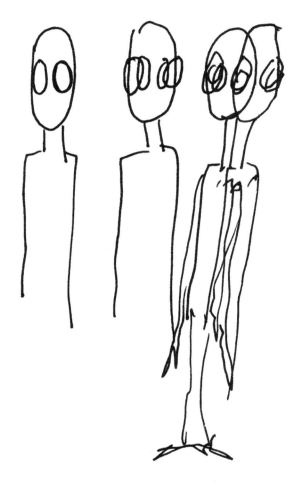

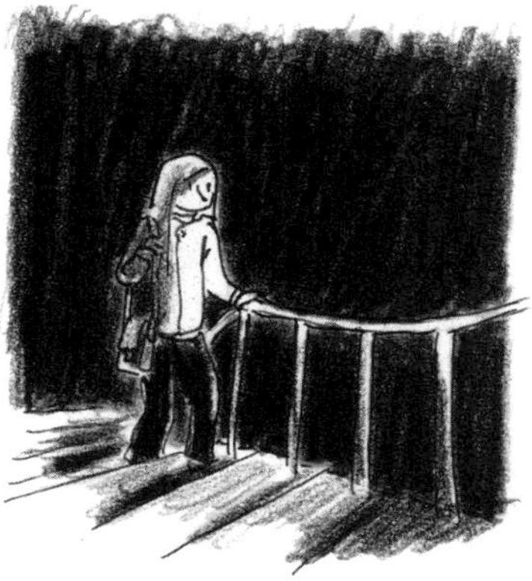
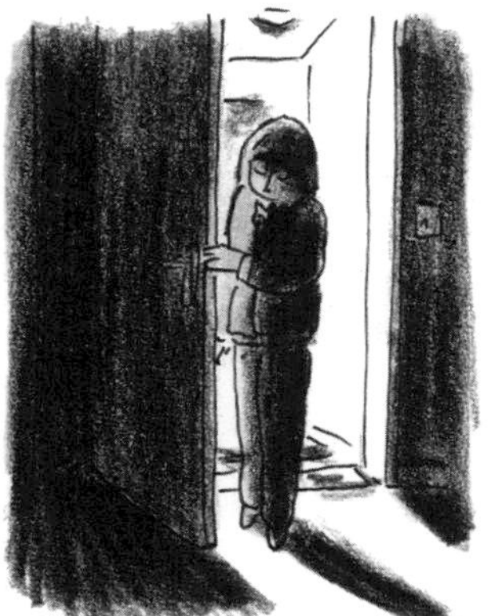
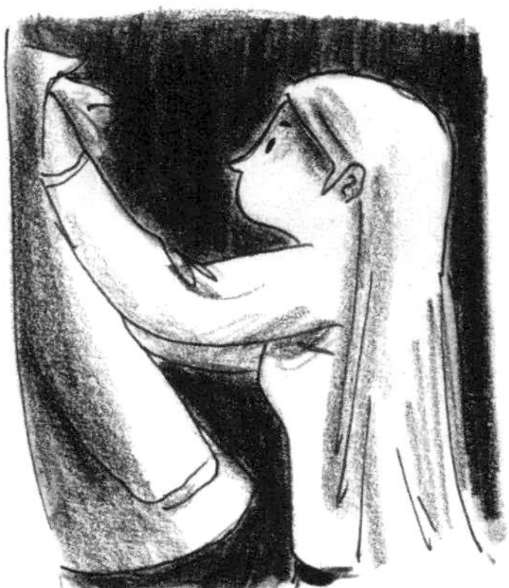

Later on, so I wouldn't have to fumble for words so much, I started reading more and more, systematically checking the dictionary.

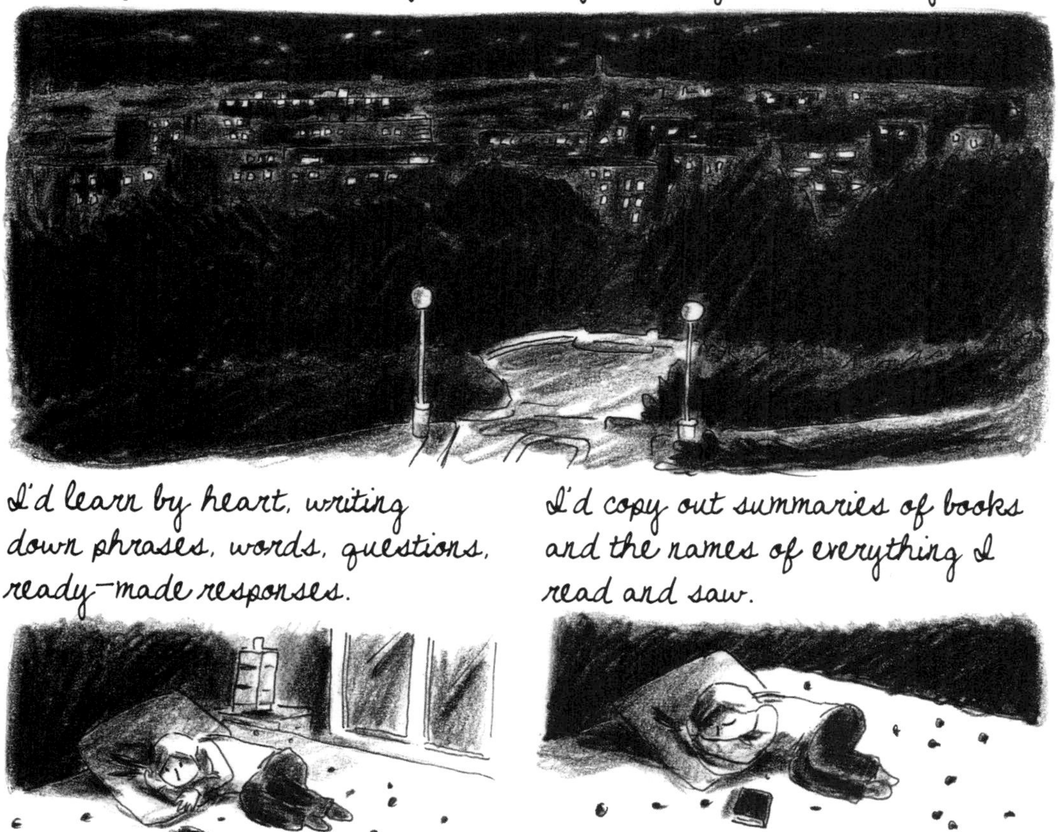

I'd learn by heart, writing down phrases, words, questions, ready-made responses.

I'd copy out summaries of books and the names of everything I read and saw.

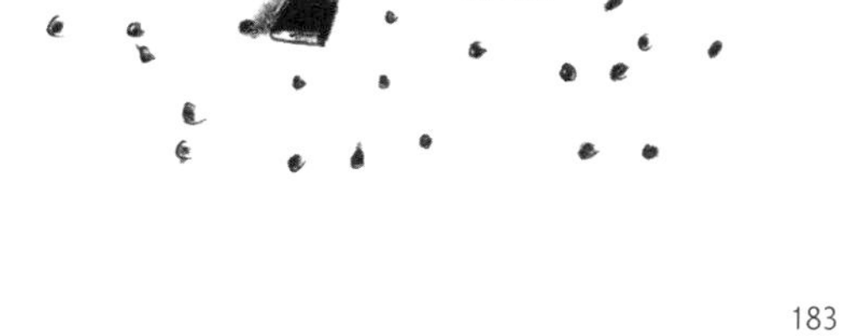
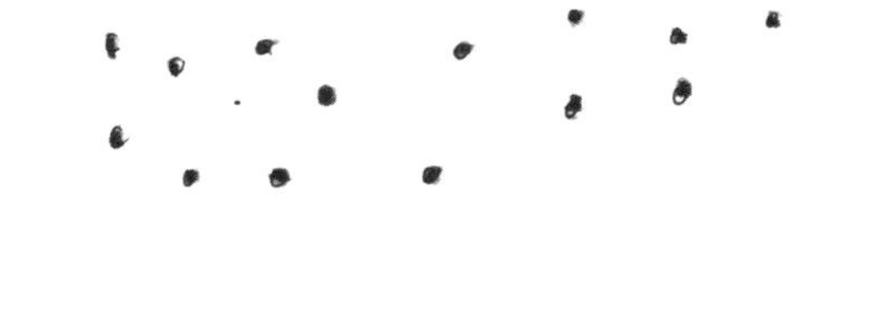

Often
I can't see well...

at night too
all those flashing lights

I go home

seeing double
in the subway

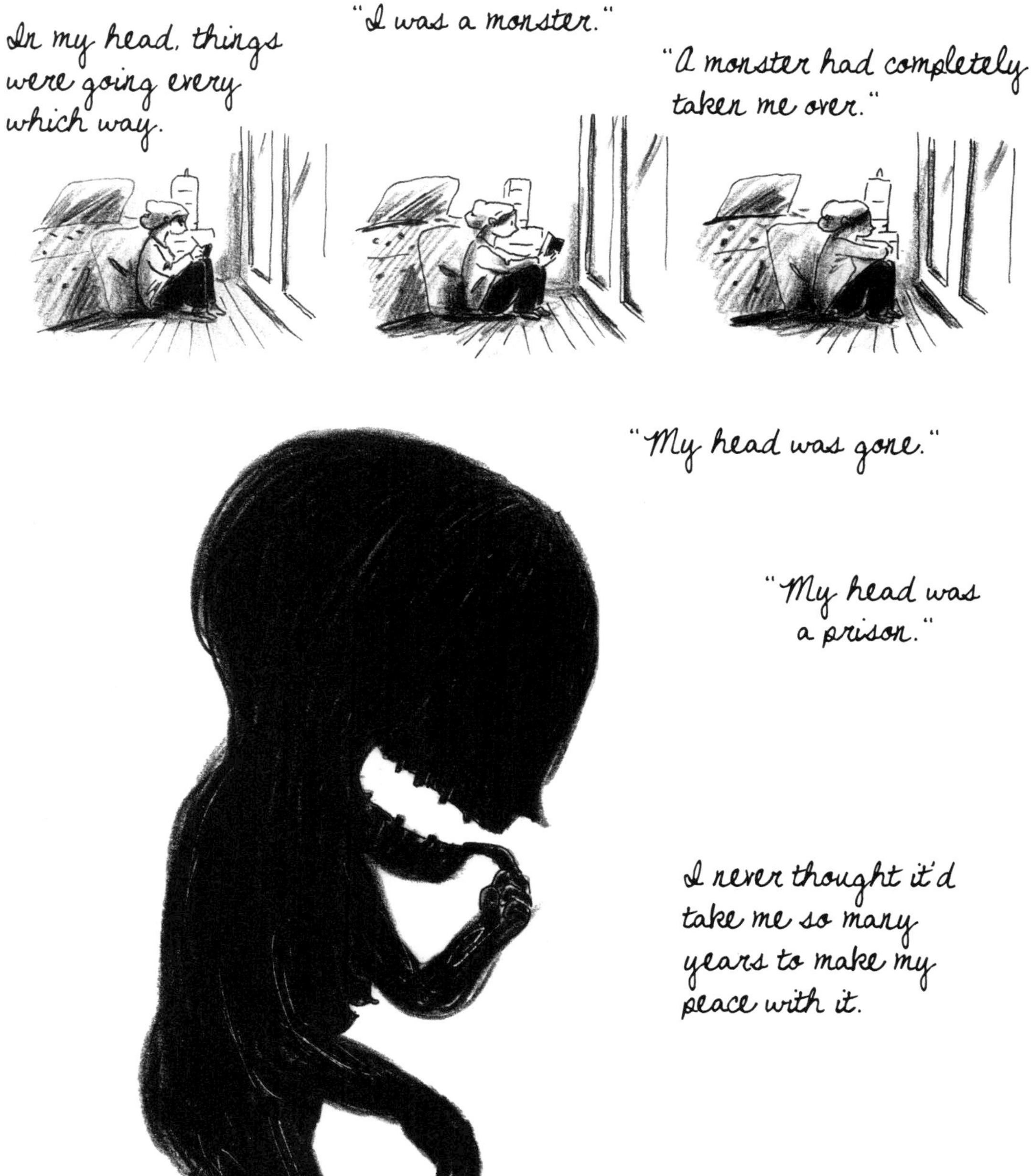
In my head, things were going every which way.
"I was a monster."
"A monster had completely taken me over."
"My head was gone."
"My head was a prison."
I never thought it'd take me so many years to make my peace with it.

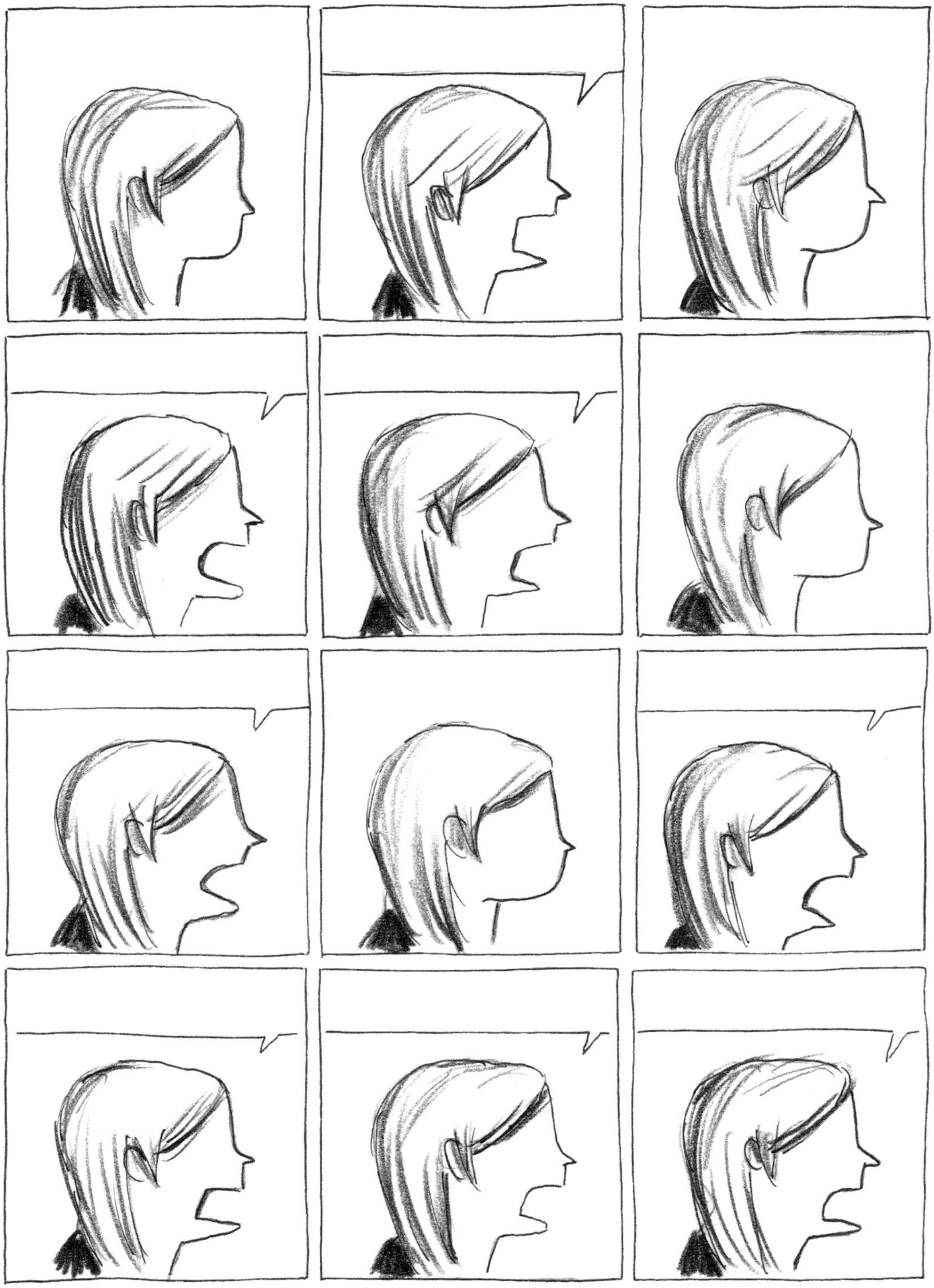

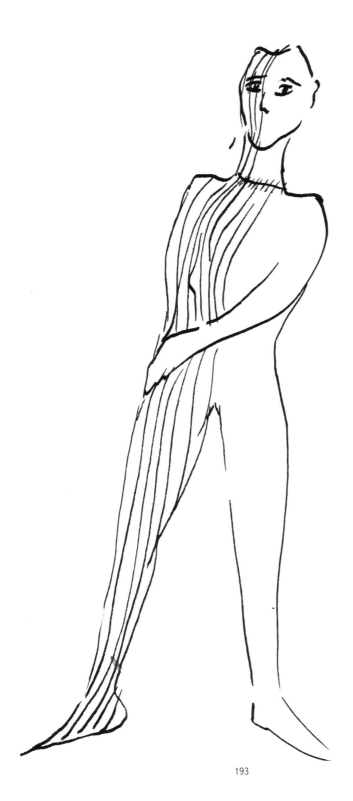

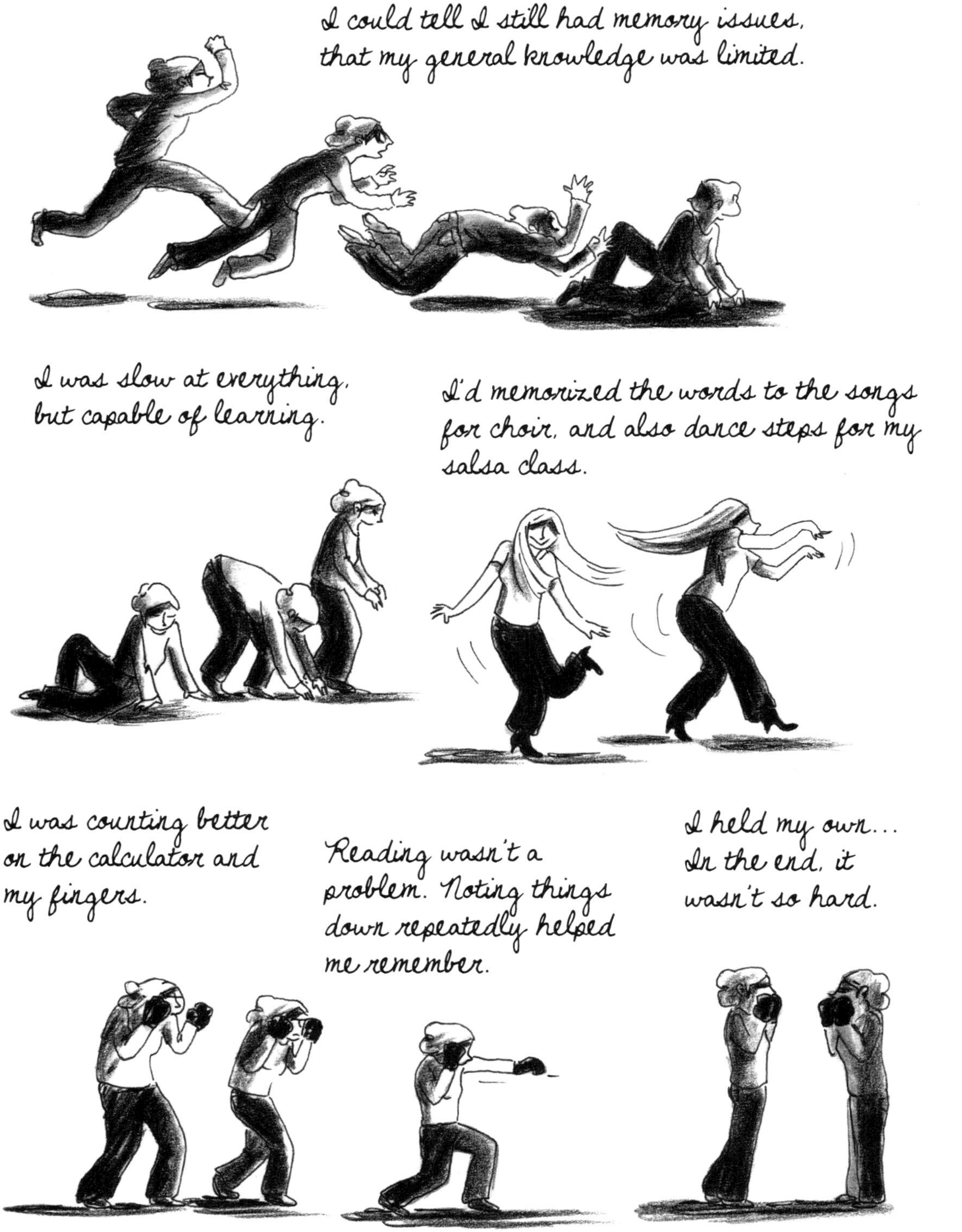
I could tell I still had memory issues, that my general knowledge was limited.
I was slow at everything, but capable of learning.
I'd memorized the words to the songs for choir, and also dance steps for my salsa class.
I was counting better on the calculator and my fingers.
Reading wasn't a problem. Noting things down repeatedly helped me remember.
I held my own... In the end, it wasn't so hard.

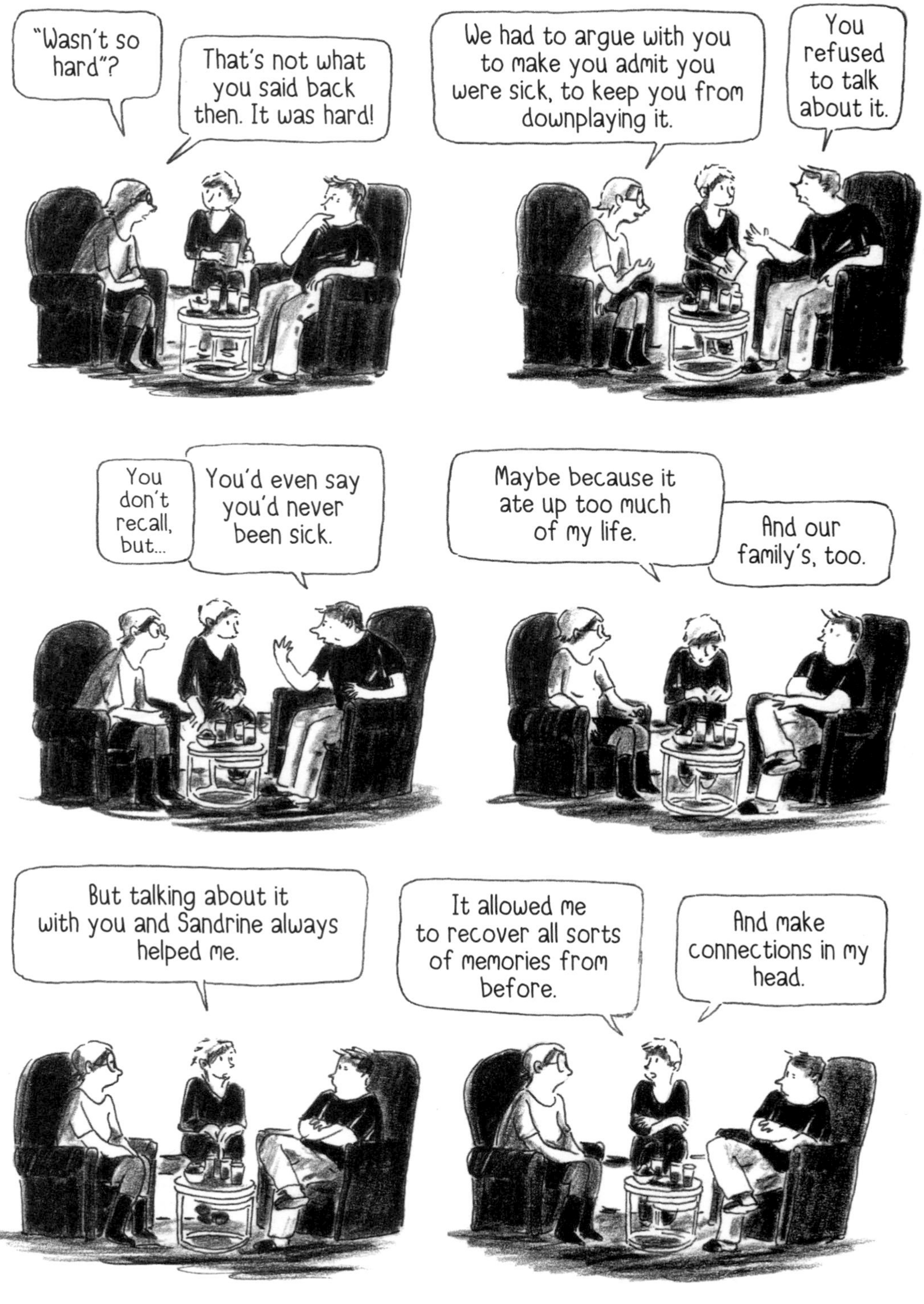
"Wasn't so hard"?
That's not what you said back then. It was hard!
We had to argue with you to make you admit you were sick, to keep you from downplaying it.
You refused to talk about it.
You don't recall, but...
You'd even say you'd never been sick.
Maybe because it ate up too much of my life.
And our family's, too.
But talking about it with you and Sandrine always helped me.
It allowed me to recover all sorts of memories from before.
And make connections in my head.

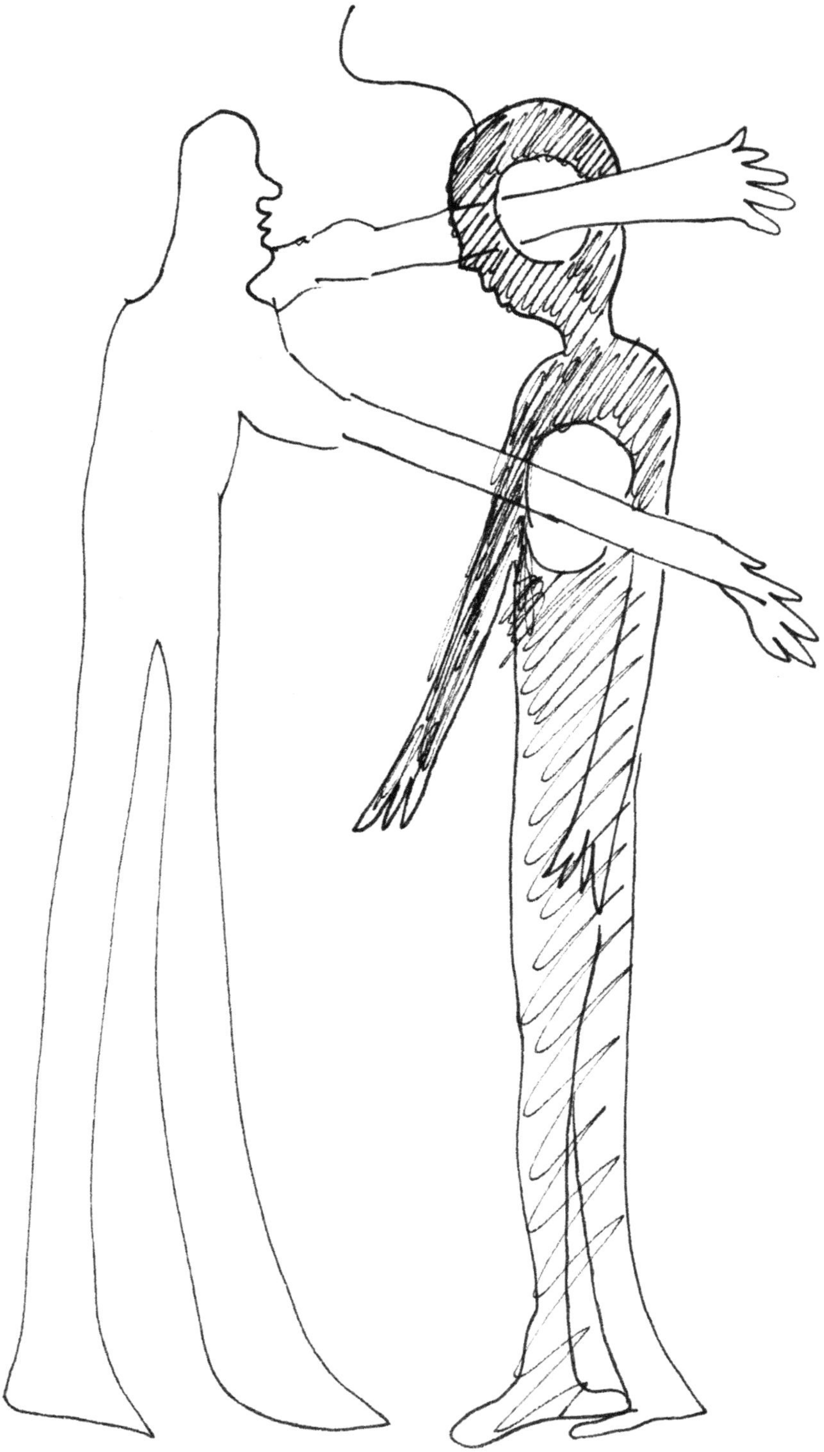

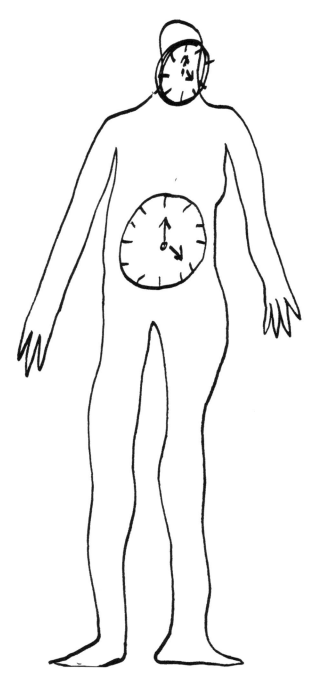

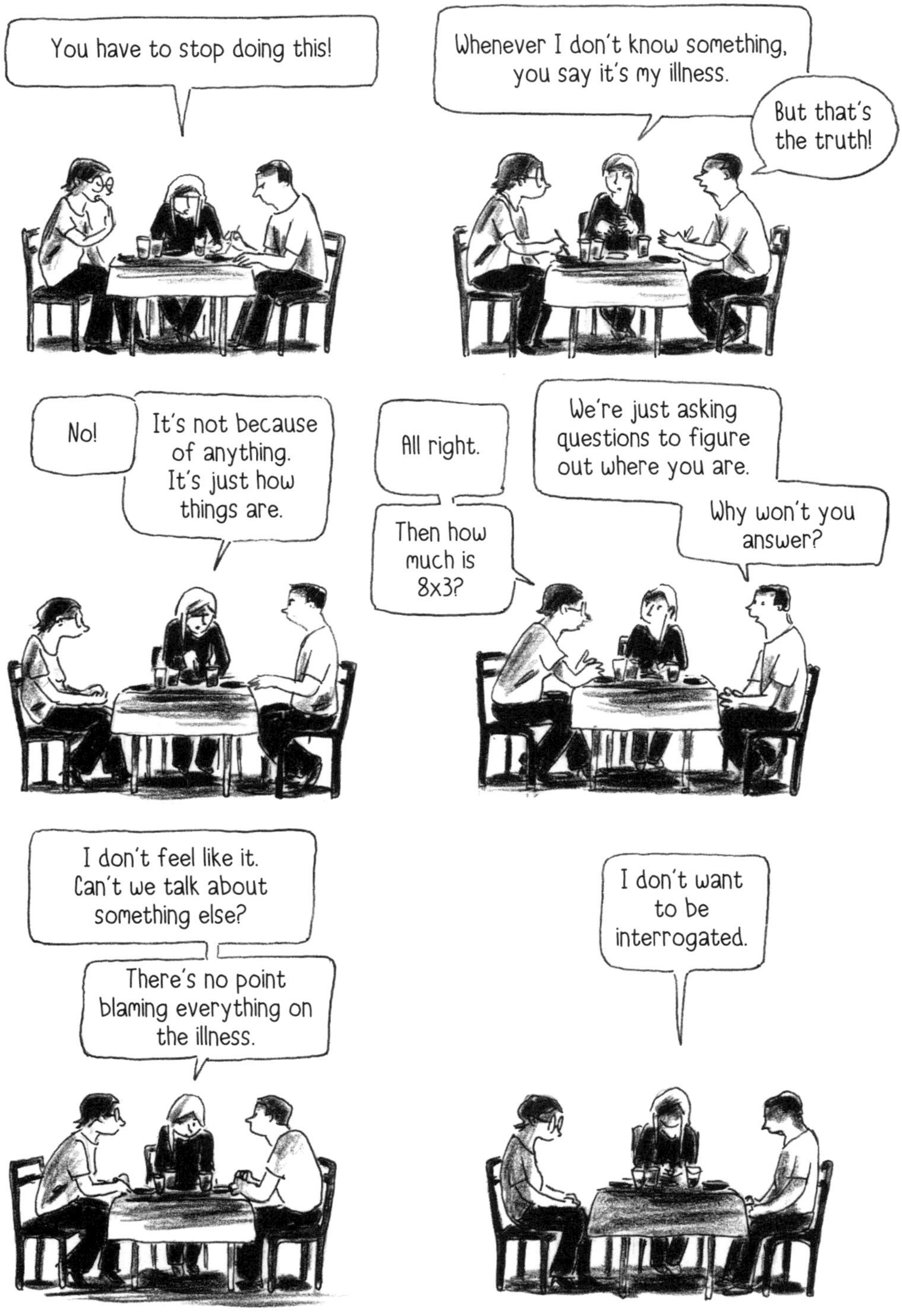
You have to stop doing this!
Whenever I don't know something, you say it's my illness.
But that's the truth!
No!
It's not because of anything. It's just how things are.
All right.
Then how much is 8x3?
We're just asking questions to figure out where you are.
Why won't you answer?
I don't feel like it. Can't we talk about something else?
There's no point blaming everything on the illness.
I don't want to be interrogated.

In October 1998 — still my first year in Belleville — I enrolled in a public school in Rueil, thanks to your friend Catherine again. It was a remedial course for after high school.

For me, that year was an experiment, to see what I was capable of, to find out if I had mental limitations.

At first, I was scared of having seizures at school. Scared of not being able to keep up.

But a little voice inside me said I no longer had anything to lose. I had to try, and to love life.

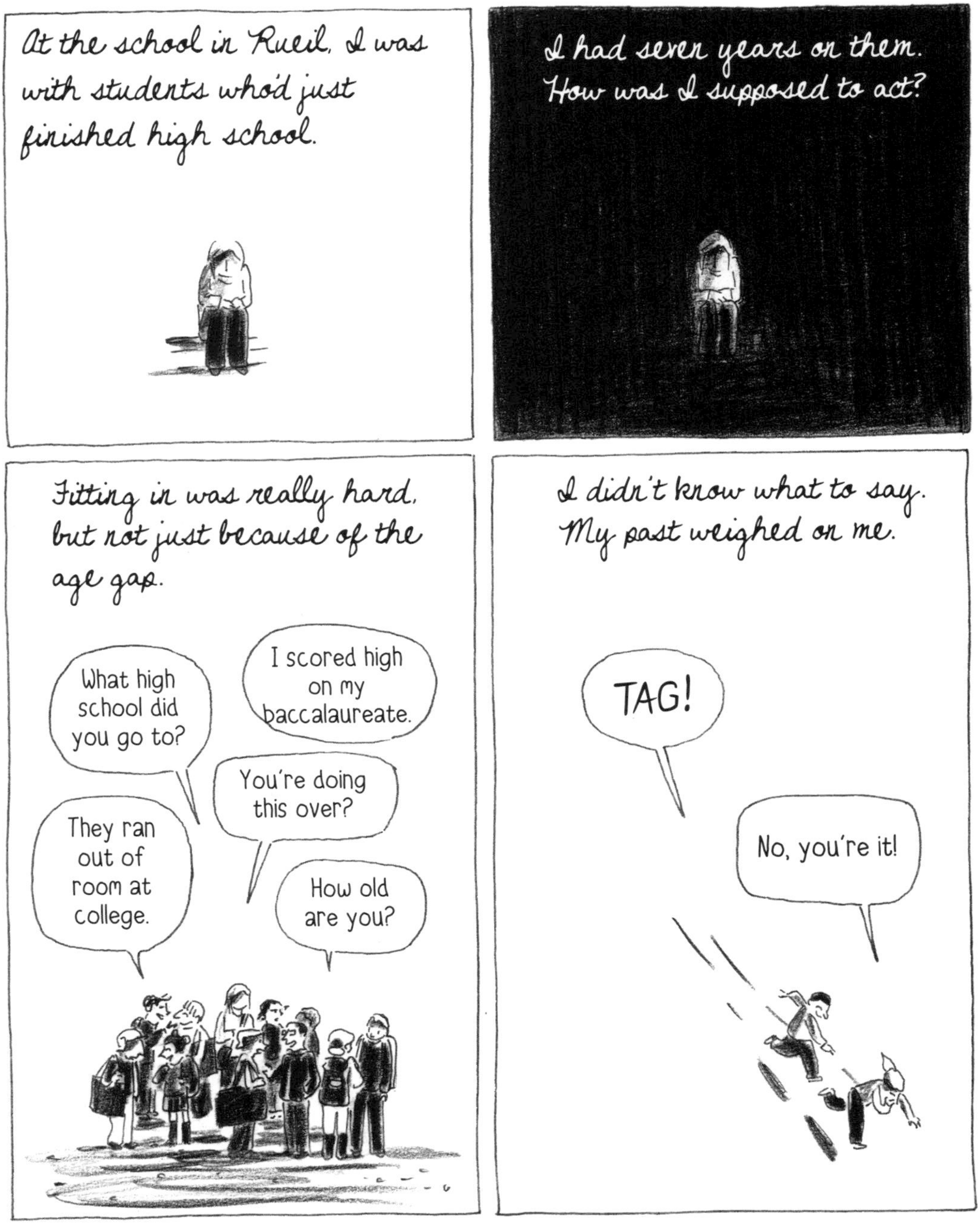
At the school in Rueil, I was with students who'd just finished high school.
I had seven years on them. How was I supposed to act?
Fitting in was really hard, but not just because of the age gap.
What high school did you go to?
I scored high on my baccalaureate.
You're doing this over?
They ran out of room at college.
How old are you?
I didn't know what to say. My past weighed on me.
TAG!
No, you're it!

Now I know it was the best thing I could've done: recover a sense of social life, resume my studies to rehabilitate my brain and re-forge connections.

I was slow, but I could keep up, just like the other kids.

I'd changed. I dared to ask questions and speak up if I didn't understand.

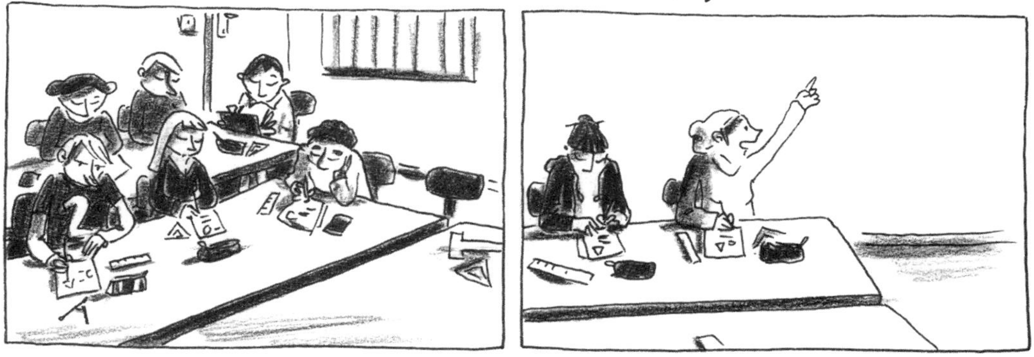

I gave myself permission to ask for the same explanation three times in a row.

I felt like I was starting from scratch. But there were lots of things that came back on their own, too.

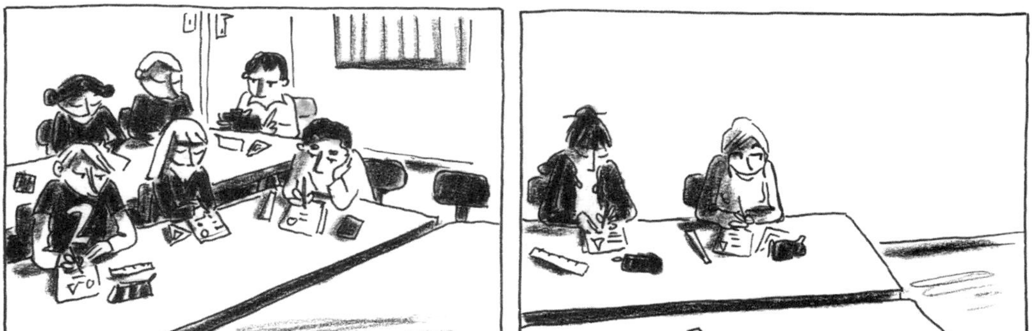

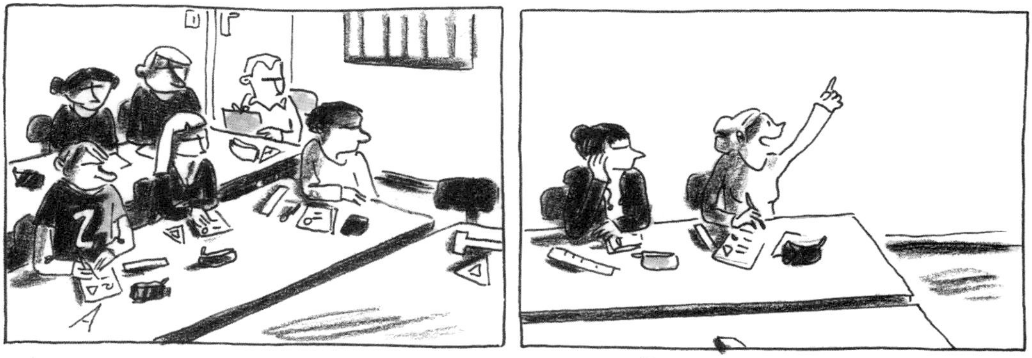

I knew things, had memories from before the illness, and they were still there, just hard to get to. That's why we had such a hard time evaluating my abilities. You wanted to quantify the long-term effects, but I was slowly making progress.

After my experimental year, I went back to college. In 1999, three years after the operation in Marseille, my epilepsy stabilized for the first time. With the help of drugs, I wasn't having seizures anymore! That changed everything for me. I wasn't as tired.

Créteil. Les Choux projects.

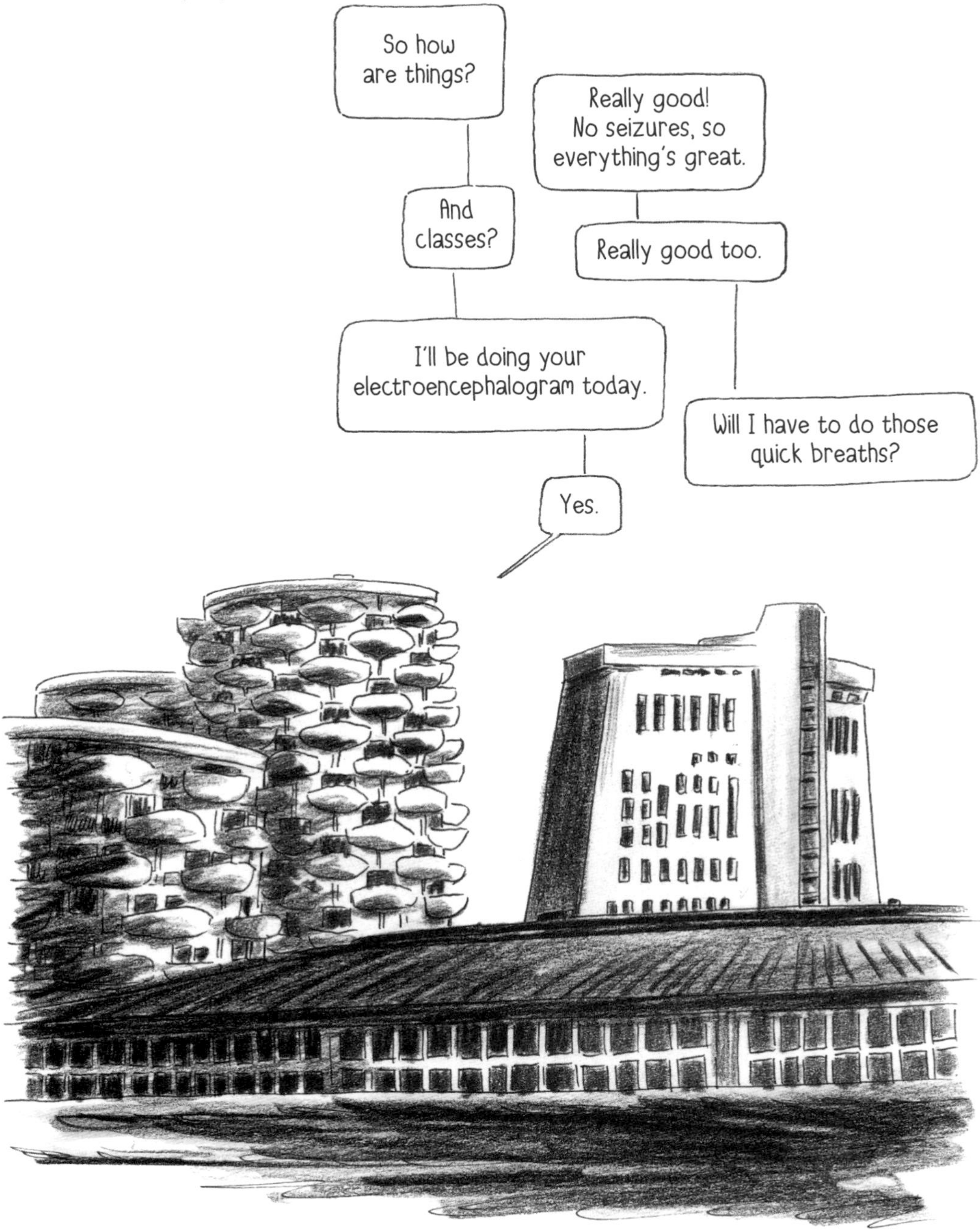
So how are things?
Really good! No seizures, so everything's great.
And classes?
Really good too.
I'll be doing your electroencephalogram today.
Will I have to do those quick breaths?
Yes.

In the years that followed, I kept going to see Dr. Pramalé every three months. In the end, I came to like my neurologist's smile.

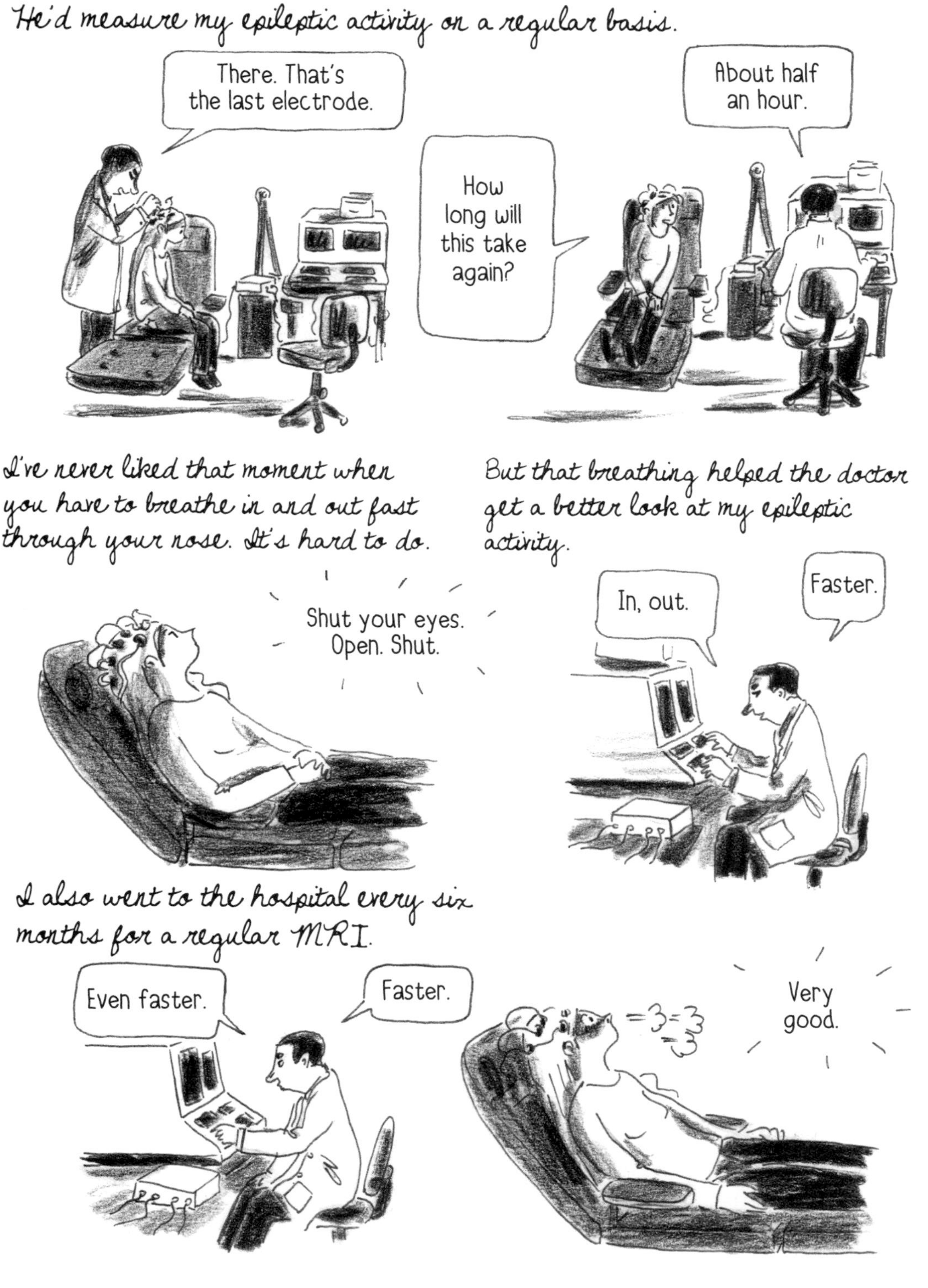
He'd measure my epileptic activity on a regular basis.
There. That's the last electrode.
How long will this take again?
About half an hour.
I've never liked that moment when you have to breathe in and out fast through your nose. It's hard to do.
But that breathing helped the doctor get a better look at my epileptic activity.
Shut your eyes. Open. Shut.
In, out.
Faster.
I also went to the hospital every six months for a regular MRI.
Even faster.
Faster.
Very good.

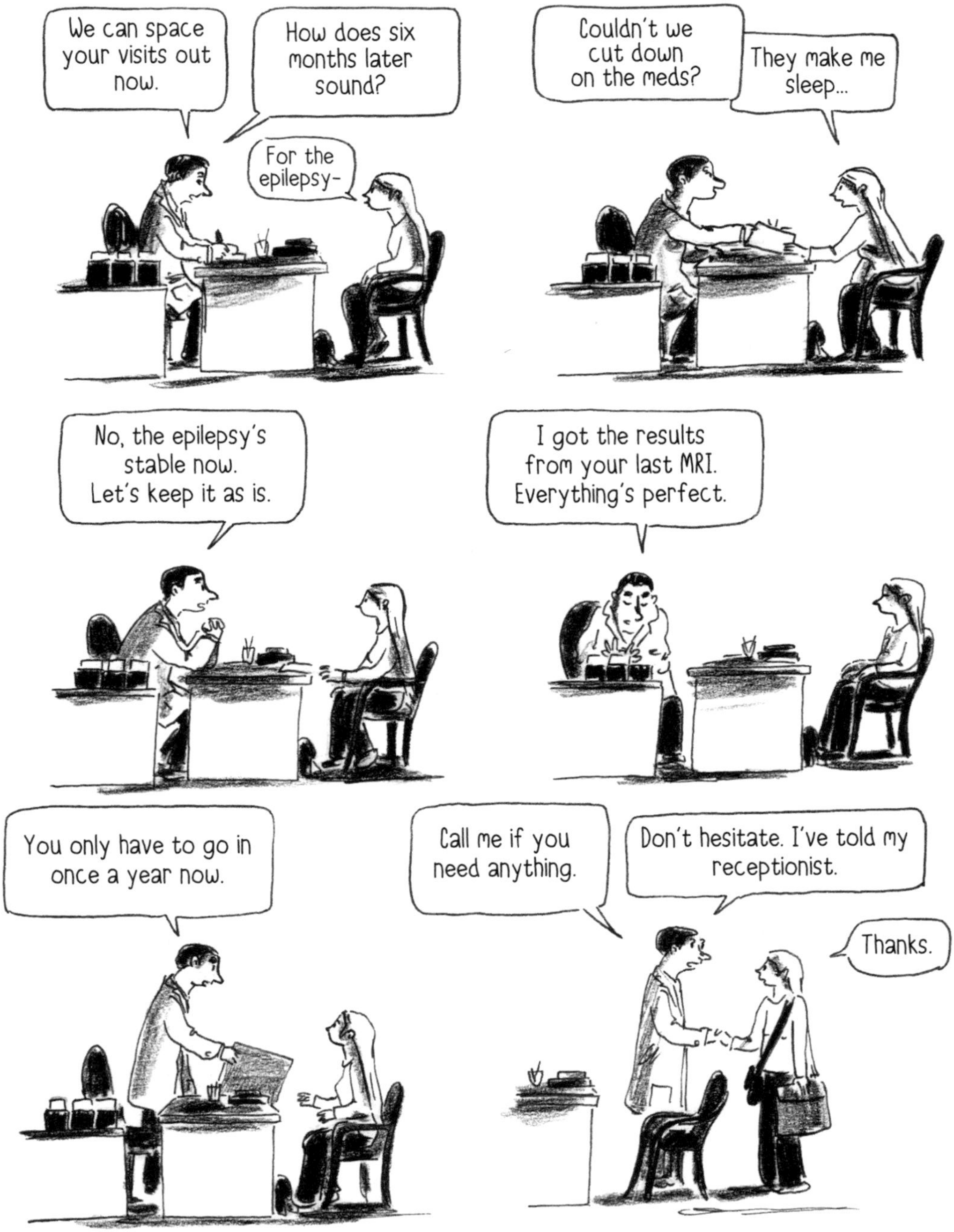
We can space your visits out now.
How does six months later sound?
For the epilepsy-
Couldn't we cut down on the meds?
They make me sleep...
No, the epilepsy's stable now. Let's keep it as is.
I got the results from your last MRI. Everything's perfect.
You only have to go in once a year now.
Call me if you need anything.
Don't hesitate. I've told my receptionist.
Thanks.

I don't know exactly when I decided all by myself to cut back on my meds. I went half a pill every six months, between visits. Since I wasn't having seizures, the doctor didn't say a word.

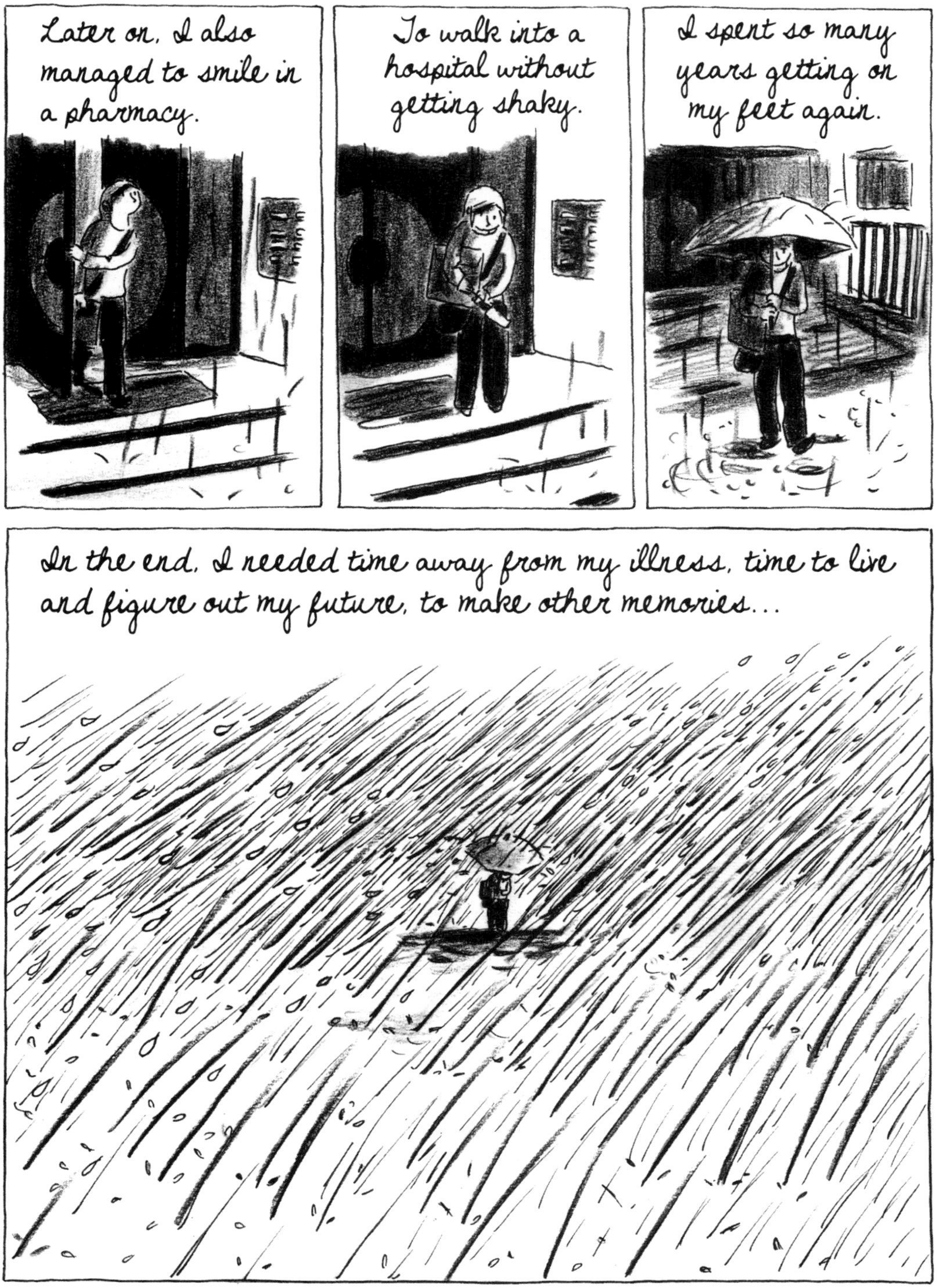
Later on, I also managed to smile in a pharmacy.
To walk into a hospital without getting shaky.
I spent so many years getting on my feet again.
In the end, I needed time away from my illness, time to live and figure out my future, to make other memories...

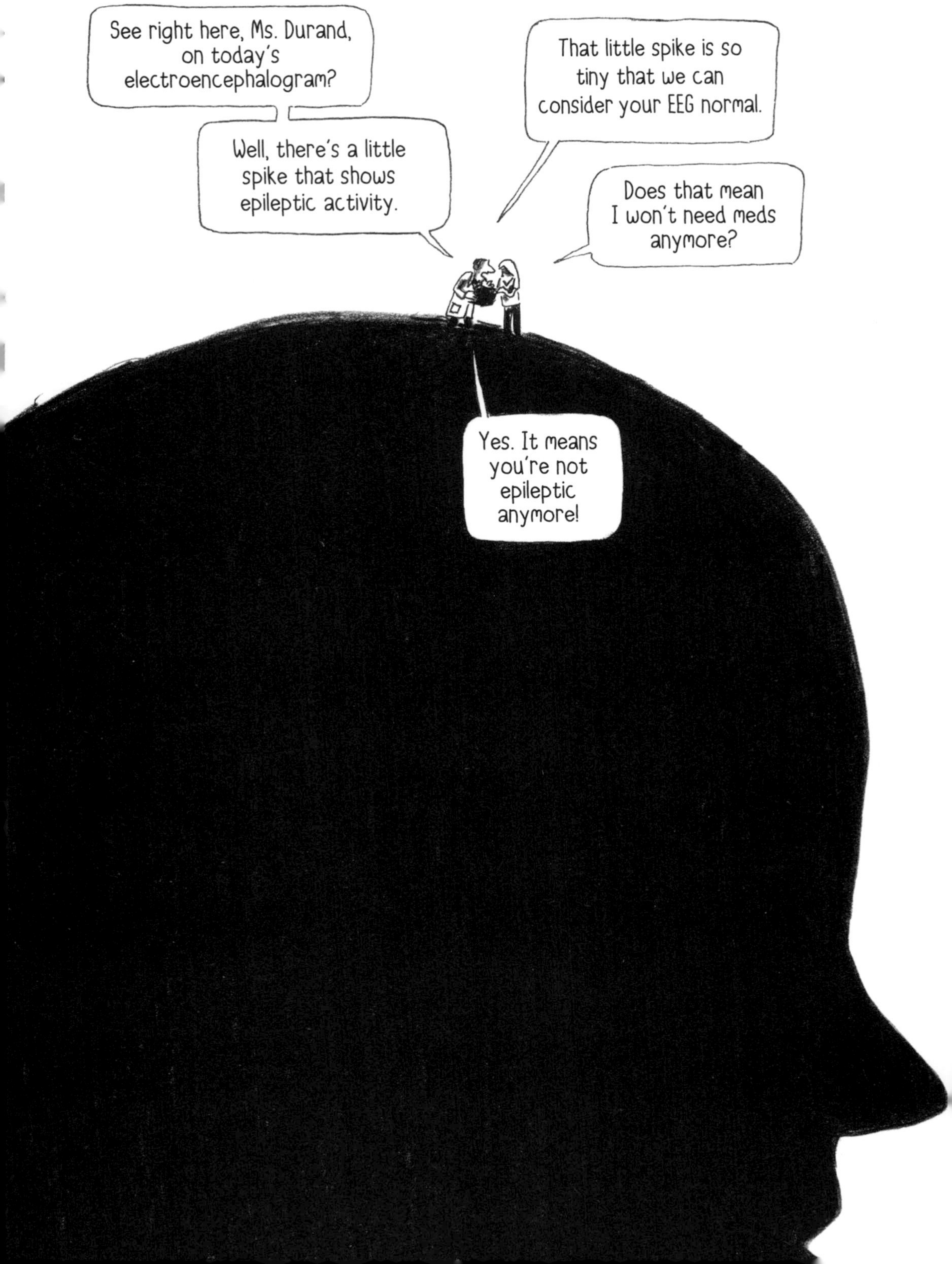
See right here, Ms. Durand, on today's electroencephalogram?
Well, there's a little spike that shows epileptic activity.
That little spike is so tiny that we can consider your EEG normal.
Does that mean I won't need meds anymore?
Yes. It means you're not epileptic anymore!

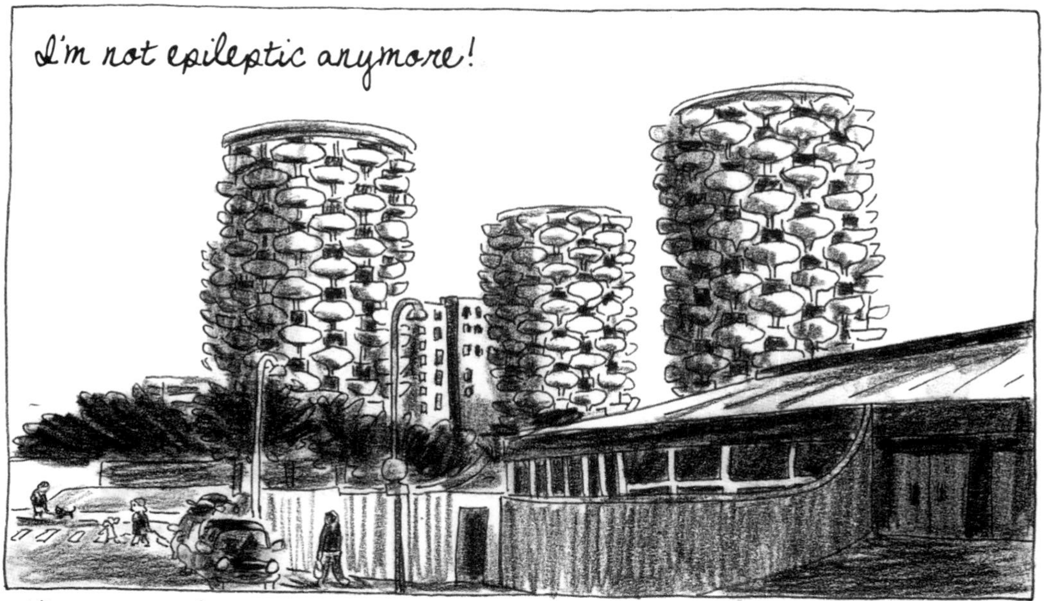
I'm not epileptic anymore!

That day, I laughed and cried.
I could have kids, or take the pill!
I could drink beer, or wine! I had tons of first times ahead of me in my drug-free life! I also thought that maybe I could bury the past...

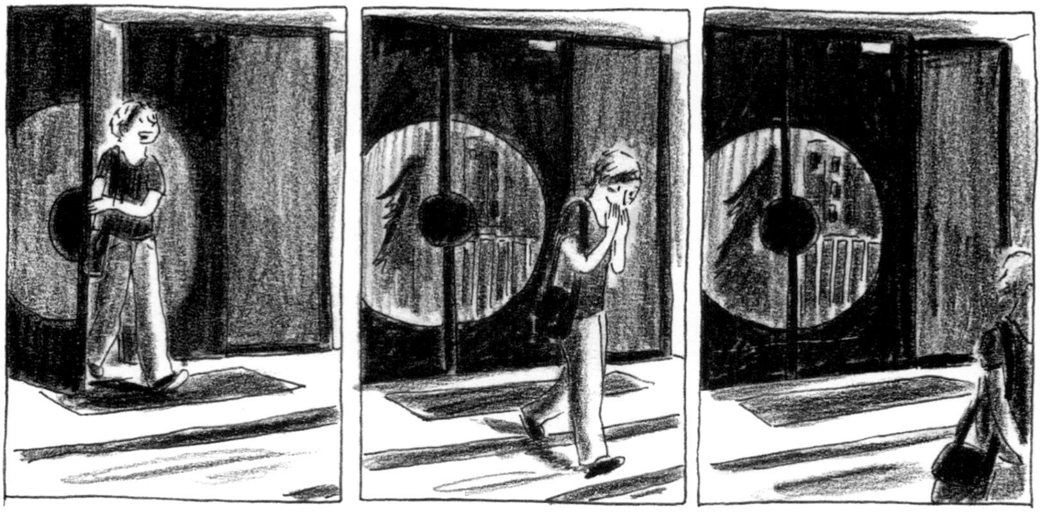

I remember raising a toast with friends to celebrate the incredible news, but back then, no one knew my story. I still had a long way to go.

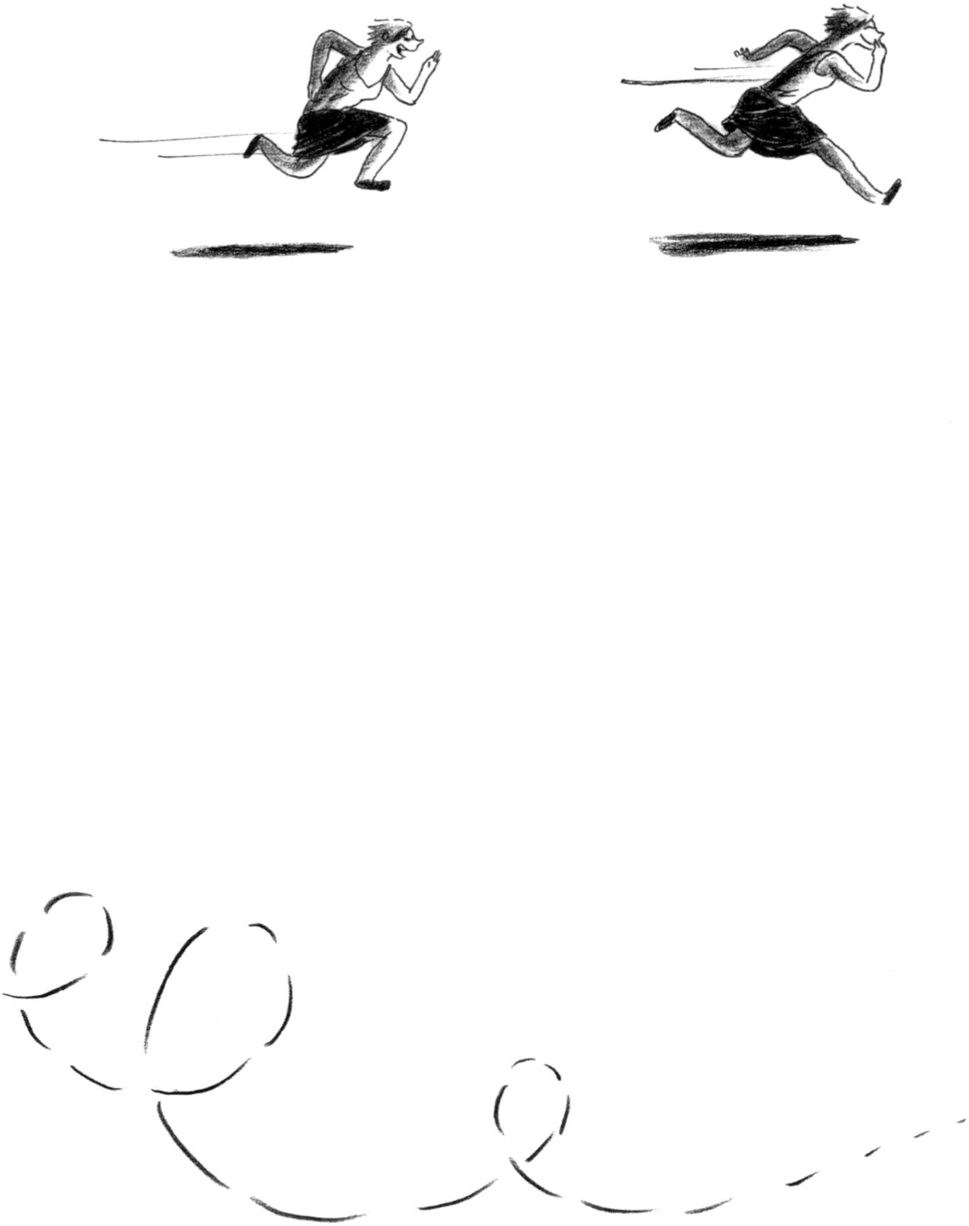

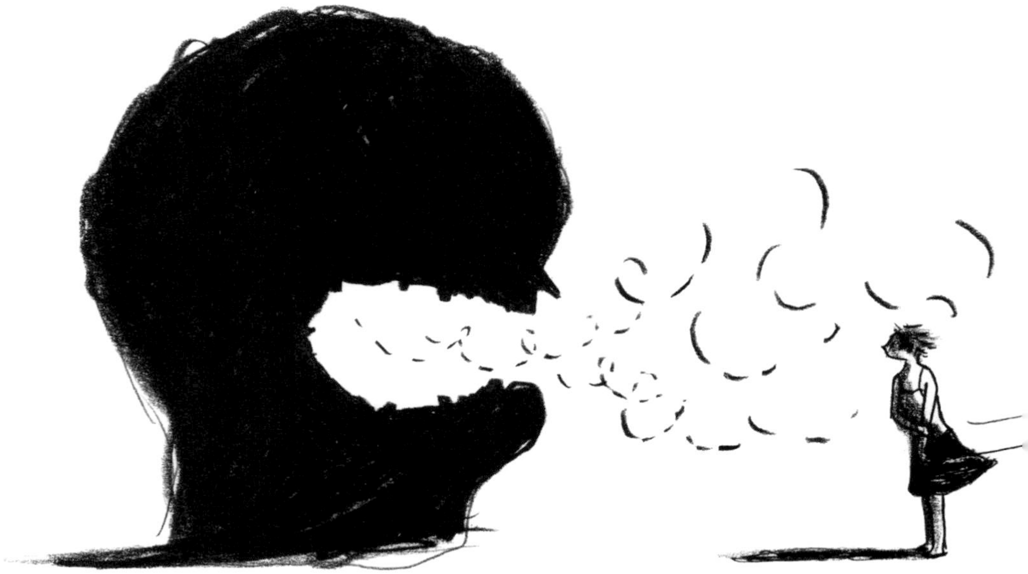

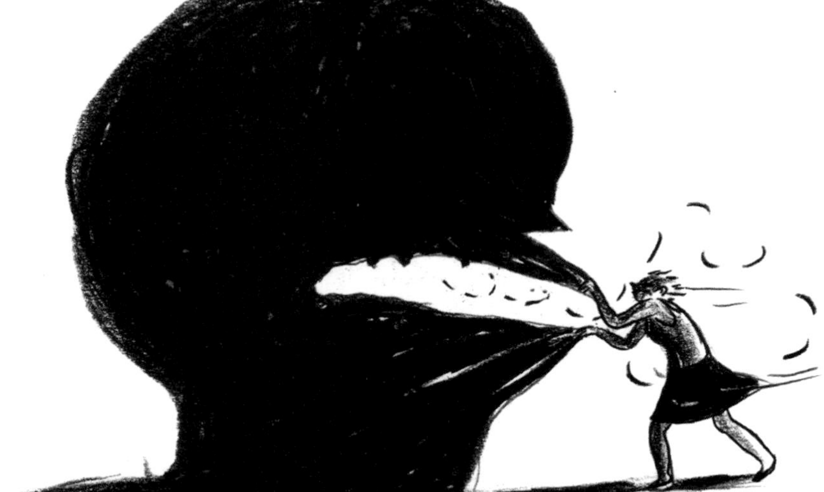

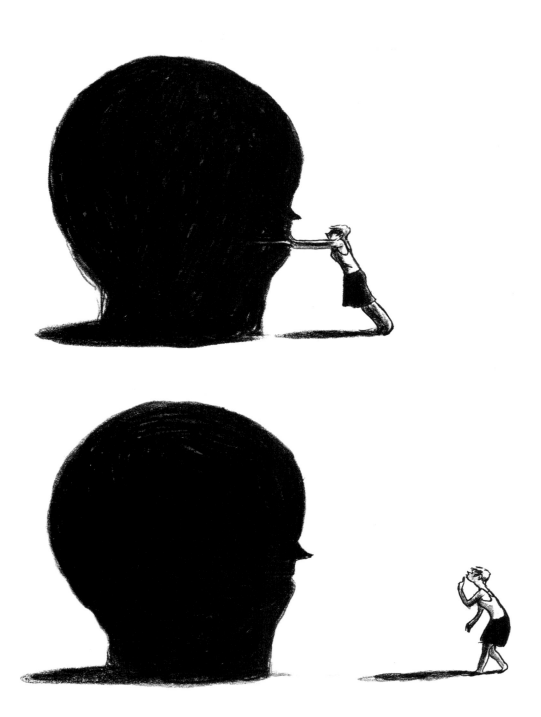

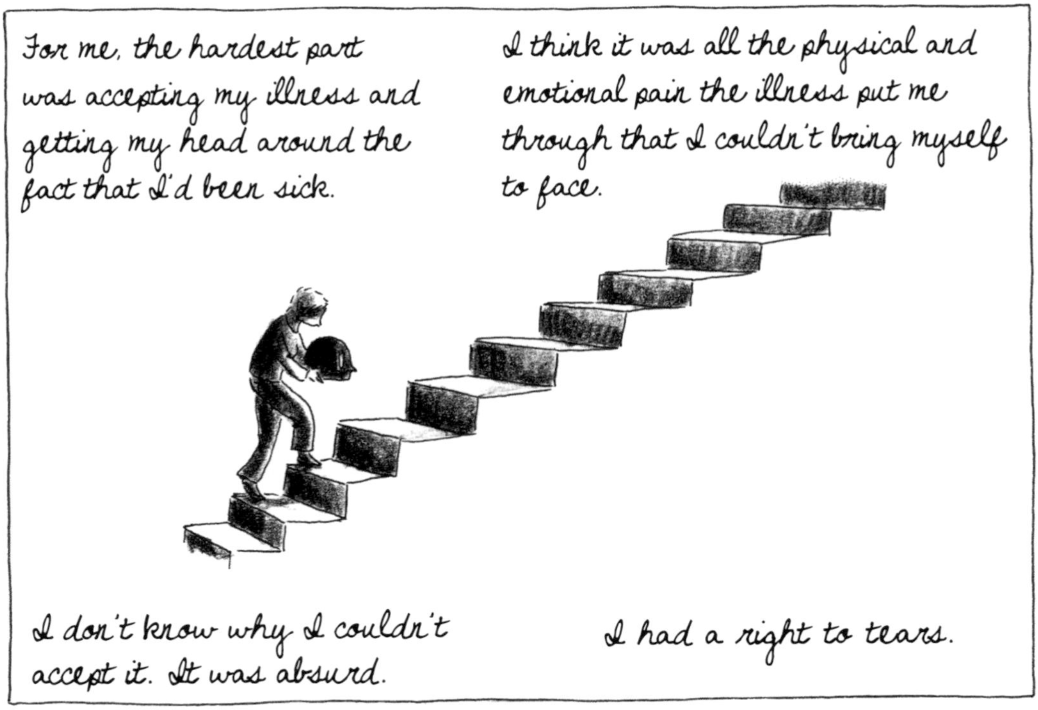
For me, the hardest part was accepting my illness and getting my head around the fact that I'd been sick.
I think it was all the physical and emotional pain the illness put me through that I couldn't bring myself to face.
I don't know why I couldn't accept it. It was absurd.
I had a right to tears.

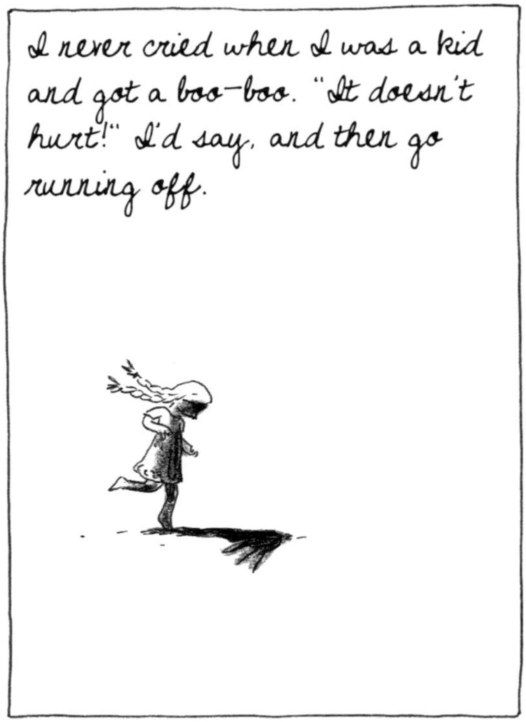
I never cried when I was a kid and got a boo-boo. "It doesn't hurt!" I'd say, and then go running off.

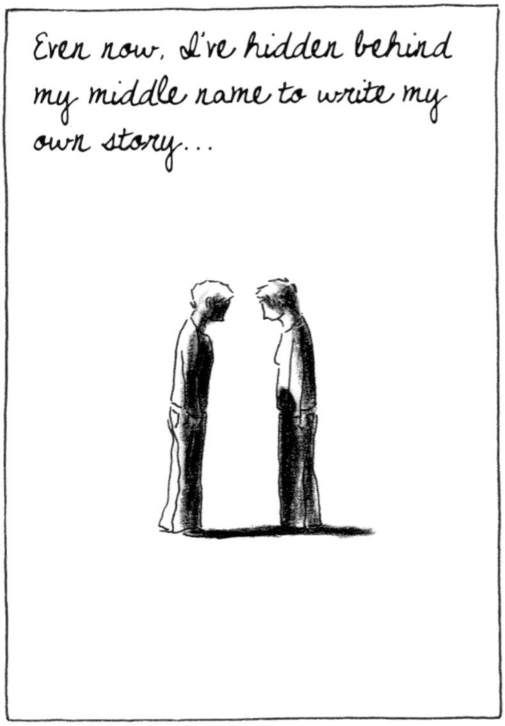
Even now, I've hidden behind my middle name to write my own story...

You're right. I was in denial. And it took a long time for me to come out of it.

Today, I can say I survived this serious illness with no lasting disability. I've recovered my full capacities. I know that you, Dad, and Sandrine keep seeing traces of my illness lingering in me, but... you're the only ones who ever still talk about it anymore, maybe because you knew me before.

One day, you said to me:

If you told your story, maybe it would help us turn the page, too.

Thanks, Mom.

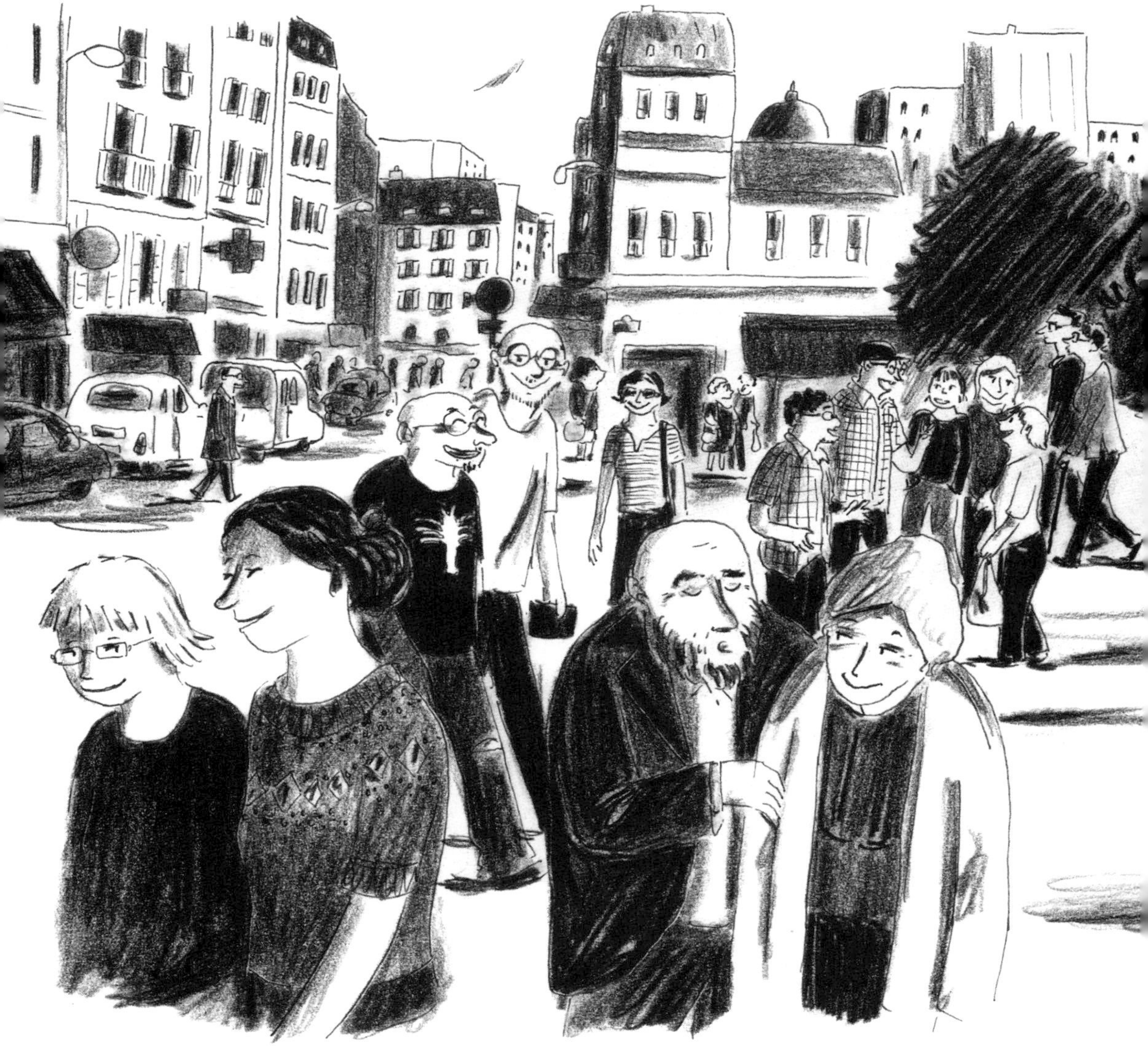

Recently, I learned from Dr. Pramalé that the astrocytoma wasn't malignant. But as a tumor, its potential for growth was to be feared, he said. It had to be watched carefully, like milk on the boil, and if possible, rooted out.

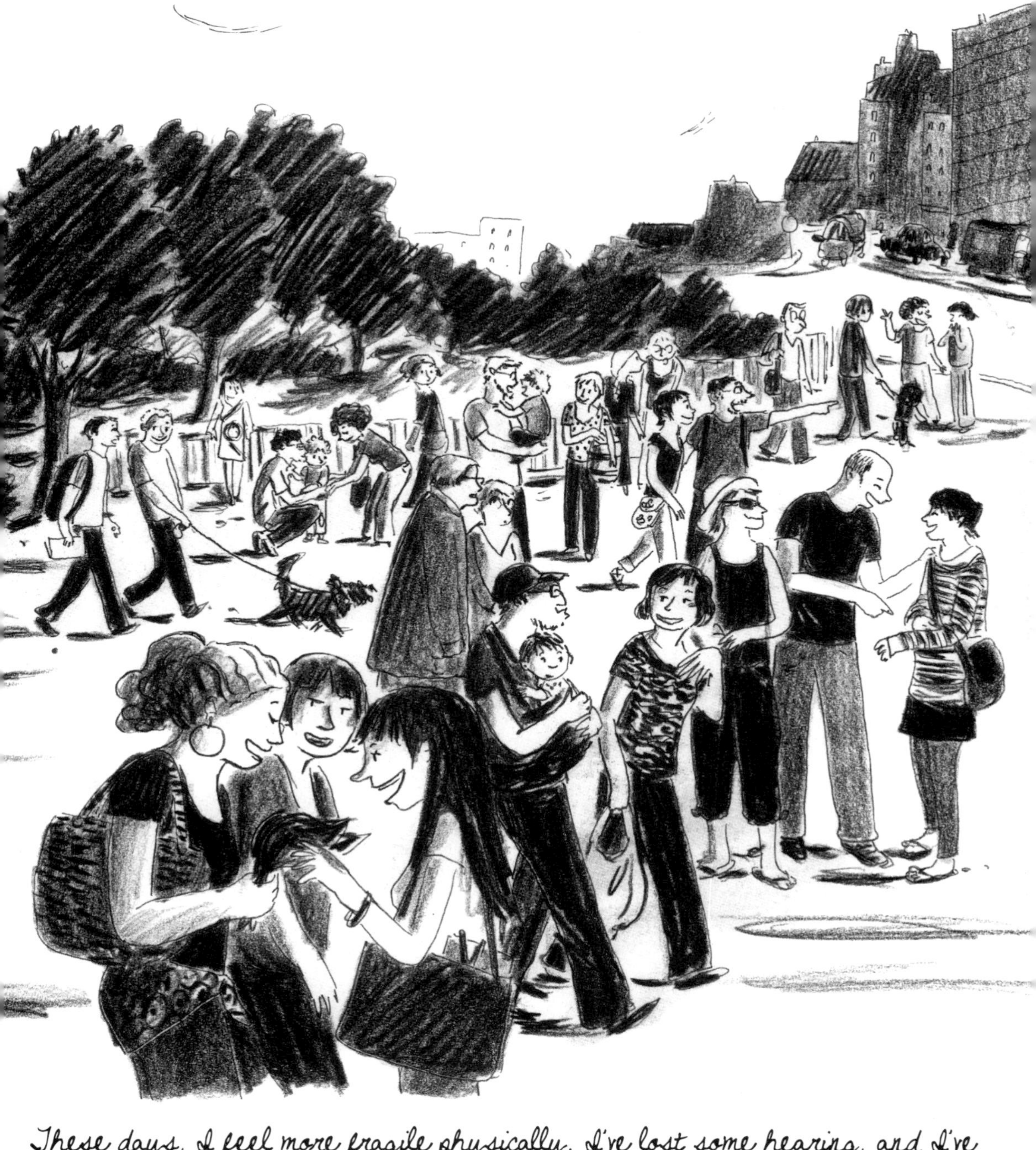

These days, I feel more fragile physically. I've lost some hearing, and I've never recovered the energy I once had, but then again, I used to have enough energy for four people. Whenever I'm tired or emotional, my words still get mixed up a bit. I'm not good with first names, last names, titles.

I tend to forget things easily, but we all know what it's like to forget things or have them go fuzzy. These traces of my own past have become a part of me now.

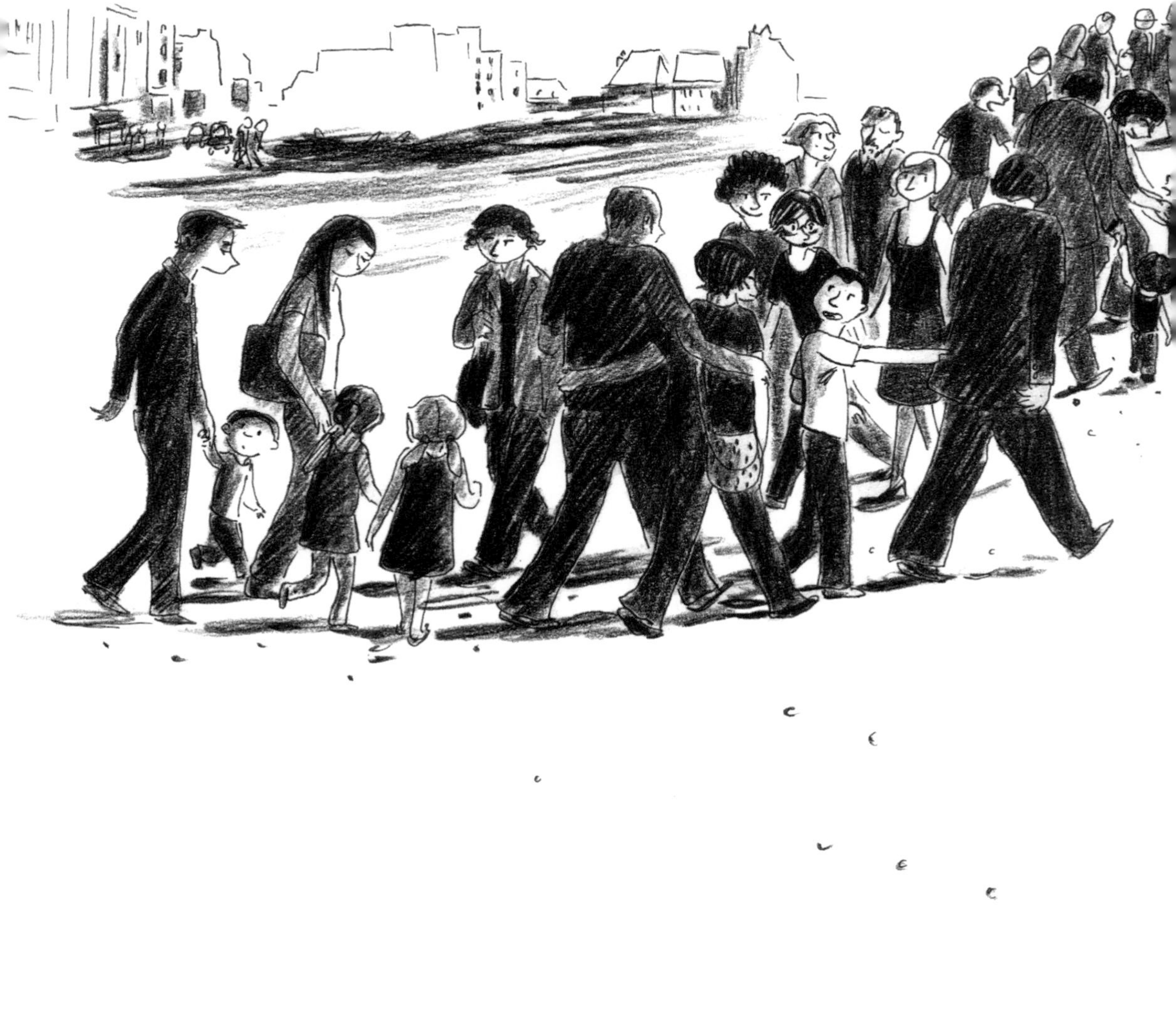

Elo. 2010.